Next Year in Marienbad

JEWISH CULTURE AND CONTEXTS

Published in association with the Herbert D. Katz Center for
Advanced Judaic Studies of the University of Pennsylvania

David B. Ruderman, Series Editor

A complete list of books in the series
is available from the publisher.

Next Year in Marienbad

The Lost Worlds of Jewish Spa Culture

Mirjam Zadoff

Translated by William Templer

PENN

UNIVERSITY OF PENNSYLVANIA PRESS

PHILADELPHIA

The translation of this work was funded by Geisteswissenschaften International—
Translation Funding for Humanities and Social Sciences from Germany, a joint
initiative of the Fritz Thyssen Foundation, the German Federal Foreign Office, the
collecting society VG WORT, and the German Publishers & Booksellers Association.

Originally published as *Nächstes Jahr in Marienbad* by Vandenhoeck & Ruprecht.
Copyright © 2007 Vandenhoeck & Ruprecht GmbH & Co. KG

English translation copyright © 2012 University of Pennsylvania Press

Published by
University of Pennsylvania Press
Philadelphia, Pennsylvania 19104-4112
www.upenn.edu/pennpress

Printed in the United States of America on acid-free paper

10 9 8 7 6 5 4 3 2 1

A Cataloging-in-Publication record is available from the Library of Congress
ISBN 978-0-8122-4466-3

For Noam and Amos

Renault: And what in heaven's name brought you to Casablanca?

Rick: My health. I came to Casablanca for the waters.

Renault: Waters? What waters? We're in the desert.

Rick: I was misinformed.

> —*Casablanca*, Michael Curtiz (director), Julius J. and Philip G. Epstein, Howard Koch (screenplay), 1942

Culture is a book with a red cover. Astonished and opening it up, you ask what kind of book this is. Do you believe it is the Bible that everyone travels with? No, my friend, culture is Baedeker.

> —Gershom Scholem, *Diaries*, 17 August 1914

Contents

The (Mirrored) Playroom

Departing for Paradise

> But oh, Kitty! Now we come to the passage. You can just see
> a little *peep* of the passage in Looking-glass House, if you
> leave the door of our drawing-room open: and it's very like
> our passage as far as you can see, only you know it may be
> quite different on beyond.
> —Lewis Carroll, *Through the Looking-Glass, and What
> Alice Found There* (1872)[1]

"So Isaac lay and looked at the firmament. And since the stars that illuminate the sea are the same stars that illuminate the land, he looked at
them, and thought of his hometown, for it is the way of the stars to lead
the thoughts of a person as they are wont."[2] After setting out for *Eretz Israel*, Isaac Kummer had spent many days and nights in crowded trains that
had carried him westward from his town in Galicia: through Lemberg, Tar-
now, Cracow, and Vienna to Trieste.[3] Now he was lying alone on the deck
of the ship readied to depart the next morning for Jaffa. He thought of his
family and friends back in Galicia. A sense of bitterness entered his mind
as he thought of the Zionists back in his hometown. Of course, many liked
to talk about Palestine, but they never journeyed any further than their
regular summer trip to a European spa: "They'll give you prooftexts from
the Talmud that the air of the Land of Israel is healing, but when they travel
for their health, they go to Karlsbad and other places outside the Land of
Israel."[4] In his novel *Only Yesterday*, the classic Israeli writer Shmuel Yosef
Agnon narrates the life of a young Zionist from Galicia who leaves Europe
at the beginning of the twentieth century as part of the Second Aliyah to
Palestine.[5] About the same time elsewhere in Eastern Europe, in the world

that Yitzchak Kummer had left behind, there was another fictional departure. In his Yiddish novel *The Brothers Ashkenazi*, Israel J. Singer vividly describes a lively scene at the train station in the Russian industrial town of
Lodz. As Chassidim, farmers, and emigrants crowd together in front of the
third-class coaches of a train about to leave for the West, beside other, better
coaches, the wealthier bestow flowers and sweets on their departing friends
and family:

> Before first-class and second-class wagons, well-dressed, self-assured
> passengers were gathered.... Porters struggled under mounds of
> trunks, valises, hatboxes, traveling cases, and portmanteaux filled
> with enough dresses and accessories for two weeks at a fashionable
> resort. Dressed in their long gowns and huge plumed hats, the ladies
> minced along, conversing in German, even though they were still
> miles from the German border.[6]

Fleeing the oppressive summer heat in Lodz, the prosperous Jewish middle
class was, as every year, leaving for a stay at a spa in the West. In but two
short generations, Singer's protagonists had climbed the social and economic
ladder into the middle and upper classes of the city, although they still lived
a largely Orthodox observant Jewish life. And so they traveled to a health
resort that could offer a Jewish ambient and the necessary Jewish infrastructure. People gathered in the Austrian *Kurort* of Carlsbad.

In these two very different tales of departure, the western Bohemian watering place of Carlsbad embodied the image of a place of powerful attraction
for European Jewry around 1900. Carlsbad and its nearby sister towns Marienbad and Franzensbad were a veritable mineral springs magnet, attracting the
Jewish middle classes as well as Zionists and Chassidim; this even while others, as Singer commented with a touch of irony, "had previously avoided the
resort because it had become too Jewish."[7] According to an anecdote from
the 1920s, Carlsbad was an iconic image of the spa as such among Eastern
European Jews: if you asked a fellow passenger on the train, "Are you going
to Carlsbad?" he would answer in the affirmative even if his destination was
another spa.[8]

In actual fact, during the summer season, an unusually large number of
trains from Europe both East and West regularly stopped at Carlsbad Central Station. In the 1870s, the spa was connected up with the continental rail
network, thus eliminating the need for the difficult journey by postal coach.

Figure 1. Carlsbad, *Alte und Neue Wiese,* 1900.

As a result, the popularity of the spa soared, and with it the rapidly mounting number of visitors.[9] The railroad train, as a democratic and affordable means of transport, transformed the structure of the spa public. Now, aside from the old elites, it also brought the broader middle classes and the petty bourgeoisie, blue-collar workers as well as penniless patients, to Carlsbad to "take the cure." Its popularity soon made Carlsbad Central Station an attractive destination for the luxury trains of the *Compagnie Internationale de Wagon-Lits et des Grands Express Européens*: after the number of spa guests had almost doubled in the period from 1880 to 1895, the South Eastern Railway decided to launch a direct line from London to Carlsbad.[10] During the summer, there was a daily through-carriage of the *Orient-Express* (Oostende-Vienna/Istanbul) to Carlsbad, and due to great demand it soon became a luxury train of its own. In the summer of 1900, the *Karlsbad-Paris Express* was launched, and passengers from Russia arriving with the *Nordexpress* in Berlin had a direct connection from there to the spa. After World War I, the *Paris-Prague-Warsaw Express* was also routed through Carlsbad as a central East-West railway line.[11]

Once disembarked at the Carlsbad station, travelers had a short journey to the spa area, either by horse-drawn cab, sulky, omnibus, or on foot. Situated in a long, narrow valley on the Tepl River, surrounded by heavily wooded hills, the town greeted guests on arrival with a memorable cityscape: a dense assortment of historical promenades, lobbies, and monumental buildings—an exuberantly eclectic clutter, a multi-story, gaily colored "rendezvous of the cream gâteaux."[12] In the last third of the nineteenth century, far removed from the everyday hustle and bustle of the metropolis, distant from poorhouses and factories, a tourist and medical center had developed here. Once an exclusive space of retreat for the nobility, it had become a magnet for all those who could afford its amenities.[13]

If the geographical space that was Carlsbad, situated snug in its narrow valley, presented one and the same vista of entry for all who arrived, extending from the station through the commercial center to the district of the spa, the historical place is multifaceted. It offers numerous channels of access. These lead into a literary space, an imagined place, a locality of nostalgic memory, a place of encounter, a site of illness and health, a habitat of pleasure and amusement, a feminine space, a Jewish place, a German place, a Czech one.

Of the possible channels of access, the present study focuses on the above-mentioned and widespread imagination of Carlsbad as a *Jewish place*, with different sides and protagonists, infused with connotations both positive and negative.[14] There were other spas popular with a Jewish clientele, such as Bad Kissingen, Bad Ems, Wiesbaden, or Oostende, and there were summer resorts, such as the small Styrian alpine village of Altaussee in Austria or the Catskills in New York frequented in particular by a large number of Jewish tourists.[15] But if we wish to sketch a Jewish topography of spas in Central and Eastern Europe at the *fin de siècle*, then doubtless the "spa triangle" of Carlsbad, Marienbad, and Franzensbad lies at its center.[16]

Summertime Topography

> It's hard to write about Carlsbad. Not because there's
> nothing to talk about, but because there's just too much
> there.
> —Zevi Hirsch Wachsman, *In land fun maharal un masarik*[17]

Every summer, a network of destinations promising recreation and recuperation were offered anew to an international middle-class spa public. An "imaginary archipelago"[18] of spas extended across the breadth of summertime Europe, which aligned Oostende, Carlsbad, the Semmering, and the Riviera; in a fanciful geography, they were aligned one almost next to the other. This impression of proximity was intentionally generated by the creation of direct rail links between the large spas, and by international spa newspapers and spa directories as social platforms that were readily available not only locally but likewise in the library rooms and entertainment halls of the competing spas.[19] The fact that the daily programs in all spas were virtually identical in structure awakened a sense among spa guests of an encounter with familiarity. This was heightened by the similar architecture everywhere and the kindred aesthetics of the gardens and spa hotels in most localities. Quite a few guests spent the entire summer traveling from one spa to the next—some for their amusement, others in search of a healing therapy for an incurable affliction.[20]

Ever since the middle classes began in the last third of the nineteenth century to create a new form of mass spas, Jewish spa patrons had played a central role in the summertime experience as a key middle-class group.[21] On the one hand, trips to the spa were considered a representative element in the process of bourgeois socialization for both Jews and non-Jews; on the other, spas as modern medical and tourist centers attracted innovative physicians and entrepreneurs, as well as representatives of urban everyday cultures. International spas, which held out the promise of urban anonymity and diversity, were quite naturally more popular among Jewish spa travelers and patients than intimate spas and mineral springs in the countryside, where they frequently could encounter expressions of anti-Semitism. Their extraordinary attachment to the spas in western Bohemia derived from the interplay of various favorable circumstances, among which the central location *between* Western and Eastern Europe was a key factor. Not only were Carlsbad, Marienbad, and Franzensbad easy to reach from all points of the compass. Another important element was that their geographical location provided travelers with a sense at the same time that they had not even left Europe's East or West. In geographical imagination, the western Bohemian spas were in fact not situated either in Western or Eastern Europe: they were in Central Europe, that construction of a uniform area that connected the two sides of Europe with each other, following the borders of the Austro-Hungarian Empire.[22]

A related, powerful factor also served to draw Jewish spa guests from different cultural and national backgrounds to these three spas: a dynamic interplay of local Jewish Communities (*Gemeinden*),[23] spa patrons and physicians, businessmen, and office workers who were resident there for the season. Over the years, this interaction generated functioning multifaceted Jewish networks and infrastructures.

The upshot was that during the summer season, Jews constituted a dominant population group in the spas in the western reaches of Bohemia. Their presence left its stamp on the thriving watering places, serving to shape and constitute their nature. But that presence was not conspicuous in official census figures and registers. Rather, as a loose association, their number, the diverse protagonists and their articulation, were constantly changing. Another factor was that this transient community turned out in practice to be largely heterogeneous and disconnected, because spa guests, doctors, and entrepreneurs from all across Europe differed from the local Jewish Communities and from one another, not only by dint of their nationality but also their differing cultural, social, and religious backgrounds. Yet in the easy-going atmosphere of their spa experience, circumscribed and compacted in space and time, they developed a communicative space for observation and encounter. It imbued the spas not only with the image but the reality of being Jewish places, and indeed concrete counter-worlds of Jewish modernity. Situative repertories for behavior, which found expression in practices such as consumption, folklore, and nostalgia, created temporary connecting links and levels of contact bound up with the special modes of sociability in the spa ambient and the nature of a visit to such a health resort.

An important prerequisite for this perspective is to conceptualize the individual Jewish groups as "cultures" and not as static units. It is necessary to examine the supposed homogeneity of these cultures, pinpoint their differences, and interrogate their discourses of self-assertion and their strategies of self-demarcation and distanciation.[24] Thus, the basis for this study is the ensemble of all types of cultural production surrounding the spa stay as an annual recurrent experience: along with the small extant corpus of documents from the local Jewish *Gemeinden*, there are the regional and trans-regional print media from Germany, Austria, Czechoslovakia, and Palestine, plus an array of travel guides, city maps, address books, and books and articles on popular medicine. Other materials encompass novels, picture postcards, the lyrics of popular songs of the day, entertainment magazines, couplets, jokes, satirical magazines and papers, as well as personal reflections, including correspondence, diaries, and memoirs. In order to combine the kaleidoscopic insights these source materials provide, the best methodological approach needs to be in a space where micro-history and discourse analysis are combined. Such a vantage on the data makes it possible to comprehend the quite different images and texts as evidence of the same history. They gain special relevance from their literary, anecdotal, satirical, or subjective nature; but at the same time this makes it necessary to focus thematically on these special properties of the material.

More recent research on everyday Jewish life and inquiry on the middle classes have also contributed to new core understandings of this complex, along with research in recent years on the history of medicine and tourism. These latter studies go beyond a micro-historical perspective and examine the cultural-scientific relevance of spas, balneology, and spaces for recreation and recuperation.

The time frame for this study covers a long period of some seventy years. My intention is to look in depth at the genesis, transformation, and dissolution of the Jewish places: it extends from the beginning of mass middle-class spa tourism in the last third of the nineteenth century, ending with the events in the late summer of 1938. Since Jewish places existed in the three spa centers Carlsbad, Marienbad, and Franzensbad largely in parallel, both in terms of time and content, lines of development in one locality can exemplify similar patterns in another. If there were significant differences in the local realities, I make explicit reference to them.

Congruent with the spatiality of the topic, the text is structured in circles; as a result, particular content is not just discussed in one place but may be touched on again in other contexts. At the same time, the individual sections, and sometimes whole chapters, are narrated chronologically in order to remain cognizant of the temporal sequences in the spatial structures examined, and indeed to emphasize their relevance. Accordingly, the architectonics of the study is structured with the intention to arrange the dialectic between the spatial and temporal narrative strands in such a way as to facilitate multidimensional insights into the topic.

Part I of the study describes the local factors that formed the background for the realm of possibility of Jewish places: the modernized spa as a place for medical promises of healing and innovation on the one hand, and a space of bourgeois, middle-class conceptions of representation, aesthetics, consumption, health, and sickness on the other.

Part II describes the relations between the different Jewish cultures that constituted the image and reality of the Jewish places Carlsbad, Marienbad, and Franzensbad. This world existed in timeless repetitions, changing only in respect to some details. In its basic contours, it appears as virtually static, until the rupture of World War I triggered the demise of cosmopolitan illusions, thus also significantly changing the associated Jewish places.

Part III deals with the local Jewish Communities as constants in Jewish life and their increasingly insecure position against the background of the German-Czech conflict over nationalities.

The final part of the study explores the changed Jewish places as they presented themselves under the impress of disillusionment and nationalization in the wake of World War I, when the spatial sanctuary of the prewar era was unexpectedly transformed into a meeting point of self-confident Jewish cultures.

Elements of Transition

> We know full well that the insertion of new habits or the
> changing of old ones is the only way to preserve life, to
> renew our sense of time, to rejuvenate, intensify, and retard
> our experience of time—and thereby renew our sense of
> life itself. That is the reason for every change of scenery
> and air, for a trip to the shore: the experience of a variety of
> refreshing episodes.
> —Thomas Mann, *The Magic Mountain*[25]

Spaces stand at the heart of this study. This is why the key questions explore cultural practices bound to spaces, the utopian potential of spaces and strategies of emplacement within their framework.[26] One of my assumptions is that spas had a specific function and meaning in their positioning vis-à-vis everyday life. In part, I orient my thinking along the lines of the fragmentarily developed Foucaultian concept of "other spaces" (*des espaces autres*).[27] In two lectures Foucault gave in 1966 and 1967, he formulated his first thoughts on a theory of *heterotopias*, but he never developed further his call for a "heterotopology" as a science of these "other spaces."[28] Nonetheless, these fundamental structures sketched by Foucault provide a basis for introductory exploratory thoughts on the character and function of spas as heterotopias of modern Jewish cultures.

At the beginning is the supposition that spas around the turn of the century, as destinations of temporary mass flight, had a special value for the society of the time then in flux. As social groups that tended to be in an exposed position in society, Jewish cultures were intensively engaged in seeking out these protective spaces and idealized *counter-worlds* of everyday life. In Foucault's perspective, this cultural strategy was not unusual, since he hypothesizes

> that in all societies, there are utopias that have a precisely determinable, real space that can be located on the map, and a time that is precisely determinable, which can be established and measured according to the daily calendar. Probably every human group excises from the space that it occupies, in which it concretely lives and works, utopian places. And from the time in which it develops its activities, uchronian moments.[29]

These worlds were significantly constituted and shaped by their binding to temporal ruptures and temporary limited experiences that were repeated every summer in a ritualized form. A system of openings and closures did not make entry and participation in these experiences impossible, but clearly demarcated and isolated them from the rest of the world.[30] Within the system of different heterotopias that Foucault ascribes to social groups and necessities, the spa could be described as a "compensatory heterotopia." That is because it constitutes "another real space, as perfect, as meticulous, as well arranged as ours is messy, ill constructed, and jumbled."[31] The spa as an ordered and idyllic space—in which everything would seem to have its place, structure and form—functioned in these terms as a kind of mirror, which serves to make the modern everyday world and everything that constitutes it seem out of place, destructured and deformed. Foucault's heterotopias, as counter-sites of the real world, "ritualize and localize gaps, thresholds and deviations."[32] At the same time, they also reflect the multifarious close-knit ties between secularization and sacralization as characteristics of modern spaces, if we assume that modernity has brought with it a "certain theoretical desanctification of space," but we

> may still not have reached the point of a practical desanctification of space. And perhaps our life is still governed by a certain number of oppositions that remain inviolable, that our institutions and practices

have not yet dared to break down. These are oppositions that we regard as simple givens: for example between private space and public space, between family space and social space, between cultural space and useful space, between the space of leisure and that of work. All these are still nurtured by the hidden presence of the sacred.[33]

Thus, the ritual character of a trip to a spa may have reminded people of the religious connotation of pilgrimages, of spas as mystical places for healing, even though they long since had been transformed into secular medical centers and health resorts. Applied to the Jewish places Carlsbad, Marienbad and Franzensbad, this cognitive paradigm allows us to situate there multifaceted, intertwined, sacred, desanctified, and resanctified levels of modern Jewish life. In this sense they represent liminoid threshold spaces imbued with a potential to ritualize aspects of transition and to offer Jewish cultures in the process of change a temporary space.[34]

The summertime idyll of the trip to a spa, outside everyday horizons of space and time, appears against the backdrop of these reflections as a sensitive and sometimes distorting mirror of societal changes. Accordingly, such reflections address as many aspects of modern Jewish experience as those arriving there left behind in their daily lives back home.

Part I

Be'era shel Miryam

Chapter 1

A Letter

Only water, water, and no *divrei Torah* which were compared
to the water . . .

—Judah Leib Gordon, Marienbad, 18 July 1883[1]

It was still early on a Friday afternoon in August 1883, before the beginning of
the Sabbath, when Judah Leib Gordon wrote in a letter to his friend Shlomo
Rubin:[2]

> It's been already 20 days since I arrived in your country, am drinking
> well water and bathing in baths of manure. In this mudhole,[3] I am
> searching for the Holy Spirit,[4] which abandoned me four years ago
> when I sank deep down into this hole of mud. Since then my spirit
> has been overstrained and I have lost vitality. My sleep has been stolen
> from me, my veins refuse to relax and rest. The doctors sent me back
> here again to regain my health and renew my spirit. Whether I will
> really be completely healed, and the presence of God[5] will return unto
> me and stay, I just don't know. But at the moment I see my pocket as a
> kind of sieve. And I know, this is Miriam's well.[6]

The letter, signed *Yalag* (יל״ג), Gordon's acronym, ends without giving the ad-
dressee any further explanation about the whereabouts of the writer, except
for the note at the very end: "Friday, 17 August 1883, 14 Av, Marienbad."[7]

"Leon Gordon, writer from Petersburg" is the entry in the official list of
spa guests in Marienbad. An exponent of the Russian *Haskalah*[8] and one of its
leading literary figures, Gordon was known for having an exceptional flair for
biblical idioms.[9] He made playful use of a biblical parallel world and language
when writing about social evils or anti-Jewish pogroms, in this way slipping
past the czar's censors.[10] A few years earlier he had already had the idea to

rename Marienbad anew in this way, when, accompanied by his wife, he had traveled for the first time the long distance from St. Petersburg to the western territories of the Habsburg monarchy.[11] With the almost literal translation of the place-name—*be'era shel Miryam,* Miriam's well—which since that time he had customarily employed, Yalag circumvented its Christian connotation, as well as the visible presence of the nearby Teplá Abbey, whose abbots were the owners of the Marienbad springs.[12] In addition, the concept *be'era shel Miryam* likewise opened up a space of biblical association by recalling the mystical well of the prophetess Miriam: according to the *Aggadah,*[13] this well had accompanied the people of Israel during their forty years in the desert and had protected them from dying of thirst. After the death of Moses' sister, the well, which was believed to have curative properties, disappeared in the Sea of Galilee and only appeared later on the surface from time to time.[14] Through his play on words, Yalag, a *maskil,*[15] shaped the well into a kind of distant precursor of the mineral springs at Marienbad, thus establishing a direct link between biblical and modern procedures of healing. If the Marienbad waters actually were still imbued with some final magical touch of the mystical, they owed their success in the meantime to chemical analyses, balneological research, and their reputation for healing diseases of the digestive tract and nervous system.[16]

The belief in the restorative powers of these springs was also what brought the chronically ill writer Gordon repeatedly back to Marienbad. During his stays there, he devoted himself with great seriousness of purpose (at least that is how he described it to friends) to his curative baths and imbibing of the waters. The profane daily routine of the then-modernizing spa, the local power of the spa physicians, and the substantial expenses of a stay in these environs inspired him to jocular wordplay and ironical translations. In writing to Rubin, not only did he call the highly concentrated iron mud baths "manure baths," he also described them as *tit ha-yaven,* that "miry clay," from which, the Psalms promise, tormented humans receive a hopeful exit, metaphysical healing, and recovery: "He brought me up also out of the tumultuous pit, out of the miry clay; and He set my feet upon a rock, He established my goings. And He hath put a new song in my mouth, even praise unto our God; many shall see, and fear, and shall trust in the Lord."[17] The Marienbad springs, from which Yalag drank cup after brimming cup as part of his cure, moved him to draw a comparison with the *mayim ha-me'arerim,* "the waters of bitterness that causeth the curse," which were part of a biblical ritual in the Temple: excruciating stomach pains would prove the guilt of a woman accused of adultery.[18] Thus, in another letter that same summer, Yalag wrote:

> All these past days were rainy and windy, and I suffered so much pain from the waters of bitterness that entered me to torment my stomach. And once when I was leaving the bath, I caught a cold and fell ill. But now the skies have cleared and the rain has stopped. The well water has also started to show its beneficial effects, and now this place is for me like the heavens above, and I hope that my health will soon return. I am to remain here another ten days and then will go where the doctor sends me to empty the remainder from my pockets.[19]

Cold, highly concentrated, and in part with a strong laxative effect, the Marienbad mineral springs suggested to him an association with the "waters of bitterness." Especially the most famous springs there, the *Kreuzbrunnen* and *Ferdinandsbrunnen,* contain such a high amount of sulfur that they have an unpleasant bitter taste and can cause strong stomach pains.[20] Yet it remains speculation to assume that with his reference to the *mayim ha-me'arerim,* the author was also alluding to an identification of spas with zones of more free social intercourse between women and men.

In his invention of *be'era shel Miryam,* Yalag had not only given Marienbad another name. With a touch of literary irony, he had also integrated the place into a biblical and thus Jewish and maskilic space of experience.[21] Precisely at the time of his visit, the small spa was in the midst of a great boom and beginning to enjoy increasing popularity not only among Austrian and Prussian spa guests but among patrons from Russia as well. This was stated in a brochure the city council published in 1882 on the occasion of the Hygiene Exhibition in Berlin.[22] Most of the spa guests from Russia were either from the nobility or Jews.[23] On the one hand, the latter came to Marienbad because of the widespread anti-Semitism in Russia, where they were barred from entry to many spas; on the other, they journeyed there to take advantage of the already well-developed Jewish infrastructure Marienbad offered its clientele.[24] In the summer of 1883, a new synagogue was in construction, now deemed necessary due to the large number of Jews frequenting the spa. Already shortly after the spa's founding in 1818, several Jewish families had settled in Marienbad, set up a prayer hall, and operated a restaurant for Jewish spa guests. Since the 1860s, there had also been an infirmary for the indigent; its attached prayer hall became a gathering place for patients, spa guests, and locals. Ever more Jews from the immediate area and other countries, in particular the southeastern provinces of the Danube monarchy, Germany and Russia, relocated to Marienbad for commercial purposes, to establish restaurants, businesses, and hotels, and in 1875 a formal Jewish Community (*Gemeinde*) was established in the town.[25]

These facts point up the setting that formed the backdrop to Gordon's playful association and are best described that way. Not only did the new development that had also led to the writer's coming to Marienbad bring the growing Jewish middle class to the spas on a regular basis; it also sparked the genesis of spas that were specifically associated with the presence of a substantial number of Jews. This was based on a shift from the *Kurort* laden with a religious connotation to a space infused with relational properties of bourgeoisification and secularization.[26] Around the springs with their formerly mystically powerful curing waters, modern localities now sprang up; in these facilities, an experience of the health spa, here rendered scientific, redefined the relation between physicians and patients, as well as the perception of one's own physical body. The specifically Jewish experience was largely similar to what members of the general middle class experienced there, yet differed from it to the same extent that it influenced that general experience. In order to describe the constitutive aspects of the process of modernization in these places, the following chapters present both general and specifically Jewish levels of representation of Carlsbad, Marienbad, and Franzensbad.

Yalag's magic art with words, which in its way reflected the inner world of the *maskil* and writer, stands here as point of departure.[27] It not only allows conclusions about a new connotation of Marienbad, but at the same time also points to the desacralizing of Jewish religious tales. After all, Yalag's secular *be'era shel Miryam* was no longer a mystical, biblical well, but rather a modern health spa in the western lands of the Austro-Hungarian Empire. His *mayim ha-me'arerim* were highly concentrated mineral springs water, his *tit ha-yaven* was a daily bath in moor mud. It was carefully prepared by attendants so as to have just the right quantity, consistency, and temperature; it was finished with protective rubber pads covering the fingernails, topped off by a final cleansing rinse.[28]

Chapter 2

Consuming Places

A Kind of Stage

> Here in Marienbad it is more comfortable, and the people
> who stay are not so proud of the fact they're here, unlike
> those in Carlsbad.—A large friendly park, where tall and
> beautiful houses stand, all of them hotels; surrounding this
> are modest hills, happy because broad pathways have been
> laid out to reach them. And forests that are happy because
> such well-behaved portly souls go there for a stroll. The
> innkeepers, waiters and porters also sport a smile here;
> while in C., they're all so very serious, and can never forget
> their dignity.
>
> —Arthur Schnitzler to Hugo von Hofmannsthal,
> 10 July 1895[1]

Marienbad wished to be a "spacious garden," not just another conventional spa; it thus sought to formulate a conception of success that offset the disadvantage of its relatively late establishment.[2] Located very near the fashionable Carlsbad, the established health resort of Teplitz and the quiet spa Franzensbad, popularly known as *Frauenbad* (Women's spa), Marienbad presented itself as a charming small town that threatened to disappear into the landscape, dwarfed between the huge spa park and the surrounding forests: "Open only to the south," wrote a travel guide, "otherwise surrounded on all sides by dark green wooded mountains, the spa, with charming paths for strolls throughout, along with magnificent park area, offers the visitor an extremely pleasant and interesting picture. It makes a refreshing impression even on the most gloomy of dispositions."[3] The location, in the midst of wooded hills, promised not only a protected climate but also an ideal spa landscape. Unlike Carlsbad, Marienbad gave an impression of openness; everywhere in the town there were open vistas to a spa forest that seemed endless and a huge park in its midst. The extensive landscaped garden stretched from the promenades and pump rooms at its center to the more distant springs, merging on gentle winding paths into the forest.[4] Paths for patrons on a stroll structured the seemingly virgin character of the thick deciduous forest, culminating in cafés and forest restaurants, bordered by lookout towers, pavilions, and monuments. The numerous pathways at different gradients traversed parks and wooded areas and were an integral part of the medicinal system of the Marienbad terrain cure, which recommended five levels of difficulty for the most varied illnesses and constitutions.[5] From the eighteenth century on, medical science, with a firm belief in the regenerative power of walking, specifically introduced the slow stroll in fresh air as a form of therapy.[6] Spacious landscape gardens, soft hills, and a gentle climate were considered to be key curative factors in a therapeutic landscape. Landscaped gardens, as protective spaces—sanctuaries shielding from feudal and rural constriction, industrial and agricultural landscapes—were attributed the power of exercising a wholesome harmonizing effect on the bourgeois soul.[7] Aesthetic observation of a nature deftly arranged with artful restraint was the romantic pleasure that Marienbad offered to urbanites who had become estranged from the natural world.[8]

The spa city gradually expanded into the extensive park and the margins of the surrounding forest. When the physician Enoch Heinrich Kisch moved to Marienbad from Prague in 1863, he found the landscaped garden fascinating, but the spa itself struck him as a kind of backward village: the hygienic conditions were as poor as the meager architectonic and cultural niveau of the town, which left much to be desired.[9] When Marienbad a short time later was connected to the *Kaiser Franz Josef* railway line, and the number of visitors continued to rise, the abbey and town began to invest substantial sums in the expansion and development of the locality.[10] In the 1880s, there was construction work and renovation everywhere outside the summer season. The upshot was that Marienbad began in the early years of the new century to acquire the image of an urban island in the midst of the Bohemian countryside, with a modern culture of service industries, where metropolitan standards were pursued. Between the palatial edifices of the baths and colonnades, for whose construction architects, building companies, and small-scale artisan firms from Vienna had been contracted, rose townhouses of two and three stories, covered with stucco and painted in traditional Baroque Schönbrunn yellow. Reflecting the stylistic plural-

Figure 2. Marienbad, *Kreuzbrunnen Colonnade*, 1908. Postcard published by Orell Fuessli. Courtesy of Richard Svandrlik, Nuremberg.

ism and construction boom of the large urban centers, the whole architectural palette was present, from Neoclassicism to Art Nouveau (*Jugendstil*) to neo-Baroque.[11] Architects who were experts in theater construction invented grandiose buildings, hidden behind whose palatial facades there were functional pavilions and luxury baths.[12] Colonnades were designed following the model of metropolitan arcades, train stations, and department stores.[13] And mingled in this unmistakable aesthetics of the Austrian capital were elements of the thriving health resort industry, shaping a style typical of the spas of western Bohemia.

Now as before, at the center of this ensemble stood the classicistic Cross Spring Temple, which had been built as a bathhouse around the central mineral spring when the spa was founded at the beginning of the nineteenth century.[14] All around the promenades, a number of pump rooms and colonnades had now been built. These made it possible to promenade in a protected space during inclement weather. The Cross Spring Colonnade, the dominant building, which despite its filigree architecture was also called the Promenade Hall, was a neo-Baroque structure of cast iron, its interior lavishly outfitted with Tyrolean stained glass and intarsia.[15] In the hotels and spa houses that stretched

across the hill behind the colonnades, "for the most part large beautiful buildings, with airy, high-ceilinged, well-appointed rooms," it was possible to rent
apartments and rooms in a range of price classes, with diverse amenities and
comforts.[16] Opposite the colonnades stood the bathhouses, aligned in a row
extending around the spa park: the New Moor Bathhouse, the Central Bathhouse, and the New Bathhouse, concealing behind their neo-renaissance facades modern balneological centers.[17] The diverse fittings of the baths, ranging
from the Baroque luxury of the Princely and Salon Baths to the modern func-
tionality of the general bathhouses, reflected on the one hand the increasing
tendency of the spas to open their doors to the penniless sick and patients on
state health insurance; on the other, it bespoke the growing importance of social distinction.[18] Between the bathhouses was the social and entertainment
center in the spa, the New Spa Hall; concerts, social evenings, and dance reunions were held in the restaurants and dance halls. In the upper stories was
a large reading room, with a selection of 200 newspapers and magazines in
twelve languages, along with a "ladies' reading lounge, a writing lounge, conversation rooms and playrooms."[19] In the town center, spa guests could find for
their further diversion a dramatic theater, later also a movie theater, a lending
library, and bookstores, art shops, stationery stores and music shops.[20] Along
with these amenities, a short distance from the center was an array of sports
facilities for all the popular sports of the day: lawn tennis courts, bicycle courts,
shooting ranges, a golf course, a trotting course, a riding institute, an outdoor
swimming pool, a sports stadium, and a large gymnasium, run by the German
Gymnastics Association on Jahnstraße.[21]

   Within a short period, a diversely structured public space and a rigorously
planned design had come into being. On the one hand, this comprised spaces
for social communication; on the other, places of retreat for individual, physical
experience. The spa area situated various forms of the public sphere in immediate proximity one to the other, in a small-scale and clearly arranged ensemble,
a kind of extended stage. Within the protected space of the parks, promenades,
arcades, and paths for walks, further protected zones opened their doors in
the form of semi-public buildings that distinctively regulated the spa public:
thus, for example, the exclusivity of the luxury and grand hotels, with their "interiorized rules of behavior" of proper hotel etiquette, merged their residents
into a kind of intimate circle, despite the ambience of anonymity.[22] A binding
feature contrasted with this: a corresponding highly structured time went hand
in hand with this structured space. The spa patients of all social strata moved
through the locality during the course of the day in accord with its meticu-

lously choreographed sequencing. Since all guests at all times were occupied with similar procedures and sequences, and were simultaneously observed by a crowd of transient tourists exceeding by far the number of spa guests, there was a constant throng and hustle everywhere in the place.[23] To keep noise levels nonetheless at an intensity deemed "appropriate for the spa," all traffic was prohibited, with the exception of a small number of coaches equipped with rubber tires on their wheels.[24] And the tempo on the promenades was determined by the pace of a comfortable stroll.

The artificial naturalness of the locality sought to conceal the fact that Marienbad was no less modern than any urban center. Hidden behind its historicist facades was a complex machinery that was kept operating with great technical effort and commitment by its large staff. The same amount of investment that had been made in the representative visible areas of the spa was also required in order to modernize the facilities behind the facades. As a place of health and the presence of science, where many congregated in a small space, it was considered absolutely necessary to preserve an especially high level of comfort and public hygiene. Along with citywide gas and electricity supplies— already by 1890 Marienbad had electric lighting everywhere in the town—the main focus of health resort hygiene was on meeting the needs of the sick and the exacting standards of hygiene for tourists.[25] Along with sewerage for the town, two separate water cycles for drinking water and water for everyday use were installed. These were under the constant supervision and monitoring of the Municipal Hygienic and Balneological Institute, along with the mineral springs; it also monitored all foodstuffs and possible infectious diseases.[26] Although general industrial and artisan factories and workshops were not permitted in the spa district, facilities were set up on the periphery of the spa park and near the mineral springs, which were regarded as part of the spa industry. Travel guides presented the specially designed buildings of the Salt Works and the Mineral Water Shipping House as local sights. Their uncovered pumps, similar to those at the bathhouses, imbued the buildings with an exotic charm.[27]

Modernization gave the space of the spa, which strove to exude an air of being natural, a certain charm. That was present likewise at far more visible spots in the terrain. In the middle of the Cross Spring Promenade was the Meteorological Pillar; such a contraption was de rigueur in the townscape of every spa. A weather house was mounted on a cast-iron base. It was equipped with a barometer, thermometer (with degree scales in Reaumur, Celsius, and Fahrenheit), a hygrometer, a table for height above sea level, a daily weather report, and a map of the town.[28] In the form of information boards that gave the respective mineral content of the various springs, scales for people to check their weight, and countless clocks on the promenades and in the bathhouses, the ubiquitous predilection among spa guests for measuring, controlling, and predicting was satisfied.[29] A nuisance that had been much lamented in earlier times, namely the outhouse toilet facilities on the promenades, had now vanished behind the scenes in the colonnades:[30] to the right and left of the niche for the spa orchestra in the Cross Spring Colonnade were the "entrances to the restrooms where the English water closets, urinals and toilets" were located.[31]

The different areas of recreation, amusement, medicine, consumption, service provision, and industry in Marienbad and other spa towns changed in a strikingly coincidental yet controlled manner within a narrow space one into the other. The "spa towns springing up like mushrooms" thus played a central role in conservative urban criticism in the nineteenth century as scenes of processes of urbanization and industrialization.[32] In the eyes of the historian Wilhelm Heinrich Riehl they had been created, like factory towns and tourist destinations, as "artificial towns, shaped by the moods and fashion of our overly refined and demanding lives, and they live virtually on air." The new spa towns were just as "dissolute" as they were "unsafe," and were "oscillating, unsteady like the artificial individuals . . . who now in their thousands attach themselves to the artificial towns." In Riehl's view, nothing was left of the old spas as constants of the traditional social order of estates, whose hermetic boundaries and social differences were dissolving and disappearing in the urbanized forms of the spas.[33] But that is precisely where the great fascination of the new spas lay for a society now caught up in the throes of movement and change.[34]

At a Familiar Place

> Look here, kids. It's not that Marienbad is a beaut—
> beautiful is a dime a dozen. But it has *very* good
> coffeehouses where you can get all the newspapers; in a
> few restaurants, they serve quite decent meals; the theater
> isn't half bad, especially with guest performances during
> summer; you run into people—and the little bit of fresh air,
> you'll just have to put up with it.
>
> —Friedrich Torberg, *Tante Jolesch*[35]

On its paths, moving from one point to the next, in tune with the rhythm of the spa day and its routines, people luxuriated here in one of the most upscale worlds in existence in Europe at the time—everything was available, and everything was extreme. Between the palatial buildings and the broad promenades and in the spacious parks, a quiet prevailed, undisturbed by the din of traffic, punctured only by muffled conversation and the concerts of the Kur orchestra. In the arcades and colonnades, there were tiny shops one after the next, "whose tasteful choice displays could even seduce a frugal person to part with some cash."[36] *Knize, Meinl, Wiener Werkstätte,* and other elegant firms from Vienna had their branches here, scattered among them photography and fashion studios, stores for haberdashery, accessories and dry goods, luggage, furs, cloth from England, Carlsbad porcelain, and crystal.[37] In the coffeehouses and delicatessens, *kurgemäß* Prague ham was sold, as were choice wafers, goose liver, smoked eel, and local specialties such as "unripe hen's eggs," "Carlsbad plums," "Radetzkys," a pastry popular in Marienbad, and "spring cake" or *Brunnenkuchen,* a honey cake unspiced and said to facilitate the cure.[38] It was a land of Cockaigne where the sense of vacationing in style gave one the impression that the pretzels were crispier, the coffee was better, and even the dietary dishes were tasty.

Before Elsa and Max Brod traveled to Marienbad in August 1916, Franz Kafka sent them the guidebook *Führer in die Umgebung von Marienbad,* which he and Felice Bauer had used a few weeks earlier. On the inside and outside of the book cover of this *Guide to Marienbad and Its Environs,* he noted the most important information for a stay in Marienbad:

> Of course Marienbad is the only place to go! Breakfast at the Diana-hof (fresh eggs, honey, milk, butter), then quickly to the Maxtal for a snack (sour milk), quickly on to the Neptune where Headwaiter Mül-ler presides over lunch, to the fruit vendor to stock up on fruit, a brief nap, then a bowl of milk at the Dianahof (place your order before-hand), quickly to the Maxtal for sour milk, on to the Neptune for sup-per, then sit awhile on a bench in the public park and count over your money, then to the pastry shop, then write me a few lines, and so to bed, sleeping as many hours in one night as I managed in twenty-one. All this is better done in rainy than in fine weather, for then there is none of the bother of taking walks.

Especially recommended items available at the Neptune in his opinion were "Vegetable omelette, Emmenthaler cheese, Kaiser stew, rag egg with green peas," while fruit, "cheap but not perfectly clean," could be had "at the beginning of the Judengasse."[39] As an aid in the jungle of what was offered in Marienbad, Kafka's advice sounded a bit breathless. Likewise during his own stay there he had reported on his daily menu in letters to Felice Bauer. That menu was similar to his recommendations to the Brods and was repeated, as he wrote, "daily in grotesque forms."[40] Was the abundance of food actually so large, and could it only be consumed in haste? We can assume that dining in Marienbad, compared with the often quite simple everyday dishes back in their bourgeois middle-class home, really seemed more interesting.[41] In addition, however, Kafka's hasty suggestions also describe the abundance of available time and freedom to decide; these distinguished a day on vacation in the small spa from a day at the office back in town, replete with responsibilities.

As counter-worlds of modern urban metropolitan cultures and yet an inseparable part of those cultures, spas propagated more than just an urbane, bourgeois lifestyle; rather, they simultaneously embodied El Dorados full of options for diverse activity and identification. If a person selected a health resort in western Bohemia, it reflected, along with financial and medical reasons, likewise a wish directed to the place of a temporary stay. The staging of the spa town had to anticipate the requirements of its public, offering nerve-wracked, jaded city dwellers a protected island of familiar, urbane aesthetics. A cosmopolitan spa society, far from political and social conflicts, the daily round at the office, and routines of running a household, was provided with an array of bourgeois leisure activities. No matter whether on the North Sea, in Carlsbad, or in Davos, they unfolded according to the same social and aesthetic rules:

> They were now walking on the city pavement, the main street obviously of an international centre. They met the guests of the cure, strolling about; young people for the most part; gallants in "sporting," without their hats; white-skirted ladies, also hatless. One heard Russian and English. Shops with gay show-windows were on either side of the road, and Hans Castorp, his curiosity struggling with intense weariness, forced himself to look into them, and stood for a long time before a shop they purveyed fashionable male wear, to decide whether its display was really up to the mark.[42]

Despite the internationalism that was celebrated in the aesthetic of the western Bohemian cosmopolites, or perhaps precisely as a result of this, many spa guests felt an individual need for familiar, trusted spaces and zones of retreat imbued with a cultural and religious character. The variety of offerings to the spa public reflected the plurality of this temporary society. Thus, Carlsbad had not only two Catholic churches, but also a Protestant church and an Anglican and Russian Orthodox one. The Viennese cabaret artist Armin Berg, who regularly performed during the summer in Carlsbad, caricatured this situation in a sketch that was soon making the rounds among some spa guests as a popular joke: "Like every year, I was also in Carlsbad again this past summer. All I can say is that I find the place enchanting. As you probably know, Carlsbad has a church for the Catholics, a Russian church for the Russians, and a synagogue for all the spa guests."[43] And indeed, the presence of the large group of Jewish spa guests and their heterogeneity were manifest in the western Bohemian spas in an array of the most diverse sorts of institutions, facilities, and events.

Whoever journeyed at the end of the nineteenth century to Carlsbad, Marienbad, or Franzensbad to take the waters had, aside from any personal contacts and recommendations, various options to inform themselves in advance or on the spot about the local Jewish infrastructure. A helpful first start could be a perusal of the *Kalender für Israeliten,* which beginning in 1895/1896 also included a guide for the Jewish Communities in the Austro-Hungarian Empire, listing all official Jewish institutions.[44] But the networks of Jewish newspapers functioned far better. They often dispatched correspondents to the Bohemian spas, and also published advertisements for Jewish hotels and guesthouses. Since its establishment in 1907, the Prague weekly paper *Selbstwehr* (Self-defense) also functioned as a platform for local Zionist associations, while the newspaper of the B'nai B'rith lodge recommended hotels run by B'nai B'rith brothers.[45] The general press, especially papers with a large Jewish readership, published advertisements for Jewish hotels and guesthouses. The local spa press and the Spa Lists also carried notices about upcoming events, prayer times, and religious services presided over by rabbis from elsewhere who were in the town to take the cure.[46] Yet a genuine forum for Jewish spa guests in Carlsbad, Marienbad, and Franzensbad did not come into being until the heyday of the watering places had already passed. The *Jüdische Bäder- und Kurortezeitung,* which was published since the summer of 1929 by the Brünn-based *Jüdische Volksstimme* as a seasonal supplement, was and remained the only one of its kind in Europe.

Run by Armin Wilkowitsch, the cantor in Eger, in the style of a light entertainment paper, the weekly developed into a forum for Jewish spas and local Jews. It carried more than just announcements of events or references to Jewish spa notables who were in town at the moment. Along with social news from the large European watering places, travel reports from Palestine, short stories, and Chassidic tales, it offered readers all kinds of reports and feature articles on the "Jewish towns" of Carlsbad, Marienbad, and Franzensbad. Extensive advertisements praised not only hotels run along Orthodox Jewish lines but also accommodations available for every pocket book, operated by Jewish owners and popular among a large Jewish clientele. Different from two decades earlier, these adverts now appeared with a greater sense of self-confidence and as a matter of course: "Superb service! Strictly Orthodox! כשר Restaurant M. Herzig. כשר, strictly Orthodox, *kurgemäß* and vegetarian cuisine in the spa quarter. Carlsbad, 'Korfu' House, on Gartenzeile (second building from the main post office)."[47] References to synagogues or Jewish ritual baths were no longer an exception in the *Jüdische Bäder- und Kurortezeitung.*

For travelers who came around the turn of the century as strangers to the place and wished to inform themselves about the Jewish infrastructure in town, any guidebook would also have sufficed for starters. Even if the selection of information there was very eclectic, in most cases they also contained all necessary data on religious services, facilities of the Jewish Community, hospitals, and infirmaries, and recommended a selection of kosher or Jewish-owned restaurants and hotels. In a *Rathgeber und Wegweiser für Curgäste* (Guidebook and Directory for Spa Guests), published in 1900 in Marienbad, the authors also described the architecture of the Marienbad synagogue in all its details along with other representative buildings:[48]

> The building is one of the most accomplished structures that has enriched our spa in recent years, and both its interior and exterior make a surprisingly agreeable impression on the viewer. It is built in the Moorish-Byzantine style, with 320 seats for men on the ground floor and 200 seats for women in the balcony. The balconies and the roof of the central aisle rest upon slender, cast-iron pillars, whose capitals are very tastefully embellished. The design and detailed plans of the layout, the interior decoration of the whole, and the impressively beautiful Ark of the Covenant are the work of the engineer and architect Eduard Stern, house owner in Marienbad.[49]

Figure 3. Marienbad, the New Synagogue on the main boulevard, around 1890.
Photo by Studio E. Pflanz. Courtesy of Richard Svandrlik, Nuremberg.

The synagogue had been built on a plot of land in Kaiserstraße, the main street in the spa town, and had been dedicated during the spa summer season of 1884 by Rabbi Bernhard Löwenstein from Lemberg, a spa guest and promoter of the project.[50] As the periodical *Jeschurun* reported on the occasion of the dedication on 14 August 1884, the synagogue and its adjoining *mikveh* (ritual bath) had been built at the wish of the growing Jewish spa public: "The number of Jewish spa guests grew ever larger, and particularly those Jews who find it unpleasant during their stay here to have to do without their customary joint prayer in an appropriate and dignified place."[51] Later on, toward the end of the century, an organ was installed, a mixed choir was organized, and the Reform synagogue was from then on known as the Marienbad Temple.[52]

The Carlsbad synagogue, which had been constructed somewhat earlier, between 1875 and 1877, also functioned soon after its dedication as an organ synagogue with choir.[53] The Oriental-style domed building in Moorish-Romanesque architecture was located on Parkstraße, a small side street directly behind the Kurhaus.[54] Since the Temple was constructed in a niche of the already densely built-up street, and its base area was limited to 800 square meters, the architect chose to build a tall structure. The result was one of the

Figure 4. Carlsbad, the Synagogue on Parkstrasse, 1901. Courtesy of Richard Svandrlik, Nuremberg.

largest synagogue buildings in Bohemia.[55] A local art historian wrote that the best impression of this architectural "masterpiece" was gained only by a glance into its interior: the high hall was supported by gray marble pillars. Behind the gilded *Aron hakodesh,* the ark housing the Torah scrolls, was a huge organ and a place for the choir. The women's galleries above on the first floor were decorated with wooden pillars and arches embellished with intarsia. "In conjunction with the brightly painted ceilings and the colorful effect of the changing ornamentally glazed windows on the front and side walls, an enchanting, foreign-festive atmosphere in the Temple interior is generated through its myriad forms and colors."[56]

A synagogue was also built in Franzensbad at about the same time as in Carlsbad. It was a small and more modest structure, often mistakenly identified with the large, sweeping domed building of the Emperor Franz Joseph Jubilee Hospital for Indigent Jews constructed some twenty years later.[57] The striking size and central location of the Carlsbad, Marienbad, and Franzensbad synagogues allow us to draw certain conclusions: about the summertime seasonal Jewish communities, whose number and composition are difficult to establish and the needs of which were served by these prayer halls; about the winter congregations, which by comparison were infinitesimally small and did not make use of the impressive religious buildings; and about the large number of spa guests and locals who either did not attend any synagogue or who never would enter an organ synagogue, and instead gathered for prayer in small Orthodox and Chassidic prayer rooms in the kosher hotels.

In the second half of the nineteenth century, in all three spas, a large number of hotels were built. These reflected the different currents in Jewish life, from hotels run on a strictly kosher basis to those where the main thing was Jewish social life and interaction. Many kosher hotels were situated on central squares and in the center of town and were correspondingly costly, while the simple Kur houses and humble, shabbier hotels for pious Jews were located in small side streets close to one another—in Carlsbad they were situated around Elisabeth Park, in Franzensbad a short distance outside the town in Schlada.[58]

The institution of the Marienbad Judengasse or Jews' Lane was extraordinary. Franz Kafka described the small street opposite the Temple:

The place has several buildings and annexes, all clustered together on a knoll, that belong to one owner and can only be entered by partly underground stairways and passages. The names of the houses are designed to confuse: Golden Castle, Golden Bowl, Golden Ball, while

Figure 5. Marienbad, view of the so-called Judengasse with the kosher hotel
Leitner's Haus.

some houses have two names, one in front and another in the back.
Then again, the restaurant may have a different name from the house
of which it is a part, so one does not find one's way right off. Later,
however, a certain degree of order becomes apparent: what we have
here is a small community, arranged by social class and framed by
huge, elegant buildings, the National Hotel and Hotel Florida.[59]

Although the densely packed hotels and spa houses that lined Rudolfstraße
(later renamed Poststraße) could not be compared one with the other when
it came to comfort and cost, they were all run by pious Jews for an observant
Orthodox public; they offered prayer rooms, ritual baths, and cuisine that
was *glatt* kosher.[60] The hotels on Judengasse had a clientele composed largely
of Orthodox Jews from Eastern Europe, among them many Chassidim and
Chassidic rebbes. They would rent entire floors and arrive with their own
ritual slaughterers and kitchen personnel, since they did not wish to rely on

the kosher food available in the restaurants. Here one encountered almost exclusively Orthodox Jews, in an area relatively isolated and turned inward; yet the Judengasse was situated right in the middle of town, directly above the magnificent main street of Marienbad.[61] The news, happenings, and organized events of this parallel world hardly reached the eyes and ears of the general public, but rather were passed on in the battery of practices distinctive to the religious culture. Surrounded by an *eruv*,[62] the Judengasse was a protected sanctuary and familiar place for its residents, especially "on Friday evening, when the invisible boundary exercised its effect."[63]

Chapter 3

In a Large Garden of Modernity

The Open and Yet Closed Place

*If we look at Carlsbad from the viewpoint of a spa, we are
convinced that Carlsbad is actually one big hospital.*
—Franz Zatloukal, *Karlsbad und
seine therapeutische Bedeutung*[1]

In 1912, the *Marienbader Ärzteverein* published a medical guidebook for spa
guests. Its purpose was to provide the reader with

> the conviction—based on one's own observation, and impossible to
> undermine by any dodgy maneuvering through advertising to the
> contrary—that Marienbad is not just some sort of fashionable 'in' spa
> but rather a serious, world-class health resort. And to serve the reader
> as a reliable guidebook for the intelligent use of means and measures
> available at the spa.[2]

Along with a popular-scientific introduction to the climatic, geographical,
and hygienic pertinent facts, the slender volume comprised a treatise on the
Marienbad mineral springs, balneological facilities, and their effect on the
human body. The authors attacked the widespread view that persons who
were more seriously ill went to Carlsbad and Franzensbad, while Marienbad, as the Viennese humorist Daniel Spitzer put it in a somewhat malicious
comment, was a magnet for "nominal patients, no really secret sufferers from
liver disease, but rather at the most obese individuals of the first and second class."[3] The foreword of the guidebook sets out to prove the opposite,

an intention that then runs through the entire work as a demonstration of the power of physicians. Countless similar handbooks and guidebooks were published from the middle of the nineteenth century for Carlsbad and Franzensbad as well. They give the impression that balneologists had nothing else to do but propagate popular-scientific self-help books.

Spas in the second half of the nineteenth century developed from stages and showplaces of noble and upper middle-class sociability into places of longing frequented by a middle-class mass public.[4] Within such international attractions, which viewed and advertised themselves as world-class spas, what appeared ostensibly to continue to matter was the social character of the spa stay, affirmation of one's own position, and a few entertaining weeks in the lap of undisturbed luxury. Marion Kaplan explains the preference of middle-class Jewish women to take the cure with the associated desire to enjoy multifarious comforts and amenities without the pangs of a bad conscience: "The *Kur* was a favorite vacation, because it provided those who needed an excuse with a perfect one." This excuse, as Kaplan explained, could be a particularly "bitterly cold" winter, a strenuous childbirth, a disease from which one had recovered, even a broken engagement.[5]

Sociability and amusement, far removed from the narrow confines of the everyday life they had left behind, were actually an important part of the positive experience of the *Kur*. On the other hand, in many cases there were chronic, incurable, or life-threatening illnesses that prompted the prescription of taking the cure in Bohemia—sicknesses such as diabetes, heart trouble, serious neurasthenia, or hysteria that were less mystifying than the common cases of tuberculosis, but that frequently had just as deadly consequences. The lavish architectural framework of the spa sought to offset and control the ambivalence of the immediate juxtaposition of pleasure and illness. If a spa guest fell seriously ill during or as a result of a treatment, or, not an uncommon occurrence, met his or her death, the individual was brought to the furthest peripheries of the spa district where the hospital was located, out of sight of the spa guests—or even further, to the municipal cemetery.

However, the campaigns the doctors waged against the attribution of the "fashionable spa" at the beginning of the heyday of the western Bohemian spas make it seem likely that their power was not unlimited, and that quite often, they may have gone unheard and unheeded as professionals; ultimately it was not clearly one way or the other.[6] "The most important commandment in making proper use of the Marienbad mineral spring- and bath-cure, is actually with any cure, is: moderation! I cannot recommend urgently enough to the spa guest moderation in food and drink, in moving the body and in general in every pleasure."[7] New spa guests were received with such and similar warnings about misusing the cure, whose power was not to be underestimated. They were repeatedly reminded that they were patients rather than vacationers or tourists. Already back at home, the prospective spa guests were instructed about the strict regimen of the health resort, requested immediately after arrival to find a doctor, and exhorted to remain in his care and supervision until their departure.[8] The effort to correct and maintain the image of the place was intended to ensure that spas were understood to be medical spaces in which every move, from the decision about a hotel room to the prohibited afternoon nap to the *kurgemäß* diet, clothing, and leisure time activity, was under the supervision of the physicians and their strict regimen of daily temporal rhythms.

Astonishingly, the medicalization of the spas in western Bohemia in this manner proved to be a great success. That was manifested, for example, in the circumstance that amusement after dark was specifically dished out and consumed only in medicinal dosages: the theater, like all other evening entertainment, shut its doors early, at 9 P.M., and casinos, the special attraction in the German spas, were prohibited in all spas across the Habsburg Empire.[9] The American writer William Dean Howells stressed this in his 1899 novel *Their Silver Wedding Journey*, set in part in Carlsbad: "By nine o'clock everything is hushed; not a wheel is heard at that dead hour; the few feet shuffling stealthily through the Alte Wiese whisper a caution of silence to those issuing with a less guarded tread from the opera; the little bowers that overhang the stream are as dark and mute as the restaurants across the way which serve meals in them by day; the whole place is as forsaken as other cities at midnight."[10]

Another American observer who visited western Bohemia around the turn of the century noted that Carlsbad "is not supposed to be a pleasure resort. The object of all the visitors is at least ostensibly, the restoration of health that has broken down under the stress of society functions, or political life, overwork or study, or the cares and worries inseparable from the existence of the great financiers."[11] The fact that in addition to the spa guests there were always a large number of relatives accompanying them, passers-by and tourists drawn by luxury and curiosity staying in the town, tends to relativize this impression, leading back to the already formulated ambivalence.

In many respects, the idyllic health resort, the carefree locus of sprightly ease and airiness, revealed itself behind the scenes as a place of bio-political control, "comparable to a gigantic doctor's waiting room,"[12] where various and diverse scientific, economic, and political interests flowed together, intermingling and drawing both spa guests and doctors into dynamic processes of mutual influence.

In any case, the medical guidebook of the *Marienbader Ärzteverein,* the Marienbad Association of Physicians and Surgeons, concluded its admonitory requests to the spa guests with a kind of quiet sense of regret: "The fact that the precise application of spa regulations is left over totally to the patient appears to be a certain disadvantage of treatment in an 'open health resort,' as compared with treatment in a sanatorium, where the patient is under constant supervision."[13]

Spaces of Professionalization of Jewish Doctors

> I know, I know; it is all cramped enough here, compared
> with many other places. But there is life here—there is
> promise—there are innumerable things to work for and
> fight for; and that is the main thing.
> —Dr. Stockmann, medical officer of the municipal baths, in
> Ibsen's *An Enemy of the People,* 1882[14]

In his memoirs, the aging balneologist Enoch Heinrich Kisch remembers the circumstances surrounding one of the most important decisions in his life: "Professor Löschner, [. . .] who probably knew it was my desire to have a scientific education, but was at the same time dependent on a material income, advised me to establish myself as a medical doctor in a spa, because in the winter I could work in the clinics and laboratories of the university in Prague."[15] After he got his medical degree, the twenty-one-year-old physician, who came from a Jewish family that was not particularly wealthy, was confronted with the question of finding a lucrative profession that was at the same time scientifically interesting. When shortly later, in 1863, a spa doctor's post was advertised in Marienbad, he accepted the position with hopes that he would have both a secure income and a post that was scientifically attractive. After arrival in Marienbad, the young doctor complained about the decadence and frivolity of practice as a spa doctor and about the prevailing hygiene in the town. According to him the spa was "in total stagnation, indeed in a lamentable state of decline."[16] That same year he began to work scientifically, initially on the basis of experiments on his own body and later from experiences in his practice, and he published his findings as part of regular "Letters from a Spa Physician" (*Badeärztliche Briefe*) in the newly founded *Berliner klinische Wochenschrift.* He propagated a reform of drinking and bathing therapy in the journal, the introduction of consistent diets to accompany the *Kur,* and the need to do away with personal stagings of events by local spa physicians, such as the public "spring practice" at the mineral springs, which in his eyes was ridiculous.[17] During the winter, Kisch continued his studies at various universities. He began to edit the *Allgemeine Balneologische Zeitung,* and after he had completed his habilitation degree he started to teach balneology at the University of Prague.[18]

In the course of over fifty years as a spa physician in Marienbad, Enoch Heinrich Kisch published some 200 scientific and popular-scientific texts on balneology in general and the Bohemian health spas in particular, especially Marienbad.[19] His efforts to ensure the success of the spa were directed to colleagues as well as potential patients, and had a lasting impact on Marienbad's growing prosperity. As elsewhere, the modernization of the spa was only possible on the basis of a broad popularization of medical knowledge, which replaced the mystical belief in the healing power of the springs by trust in an ostensibly transparent science that disclosed everything openly. The authors there never wearied to stress that the "lack of precise knowledge" had been the basis of the cure in the past, melded together from a mix of experience, "vague ideas," and belief in "powers inherent in the healing waters."[20] Now, the representatives of the new science of "modern balneotherapy" would, with the greatest possible transparency, enlighten and instruct laypersons in the knowledge of this science.[21]

The textual corpus of this modern and secularized spa therapy and its fund of experience made successful use of old narratives. It merely substituted new protagonists for old and slightly altered the stories. Every famous spa had its own narrative of origin. In the case of Carlsbad, this was a story about Emperor Charles IV, who while hunting a deer had discovered a hot spring. Such legends, which had been preserved in the everyday life of the spa as folklore, were supplanted by other new scientific legends of origin.[22] The story of a doctor who *discovered* the spa in the late eighteenth century, classified its mineral springs, and analyzed and confirmed their therapeutic powers became the foundation narrative of the modern spa.[23] The new heroes were accorded their place in the cityscape and its spaces, ringing the pathways for strollers instead of the statues of saints, satyrs, and nymphs. In Marienbad, almost all monuments recalled physicians who had contributed to the development of the spa, in particular Johann Josef Nehr, who was considered the scientific father of the place and had his special memorial in the Cross Spring Temple. Next to the statue of the abbot Karl Kaspar Reitenberger, to whom Marienbad owed its economic promotion by the abbey, there was also the bust of a former spa guest: between 1821 and 1823, Goethe had repeatedly come to stay in Marienbad, where he had unhappily fallen in love with the young Ulrike von Levetzow. The men to whom Marienbad erected so many monuments were not only the new heroes of the spa town but also a symbol and expression of the secularization and transformation of the locality.[24]

The introduction of a medically controlled system around the springs was the basis for the success of the Central European spas, while the simultaneous decline of the English health resorts can be attributed to the concomitant failure to modernize them.[25] In the spas in western Bohemia, medicalization was also accelerated by political changes occurring in the Habsburg Empire. On the basis of the Public Health Act of 1870 and a number of later decrees, sanatoriums now had to be under the direction of physicians and had to be operated according to scientific principles.[26] Behind that decision were significant structural and scientific changes at the Medical Faculty of the University of Vienna. At that institution, where a large proportion of the doctors practicing in Carlsbad, Marienbad, and Franzensbad had graduated or were still on the staff, physical medicine had, by the 1890s, distinguished itself as a subject of its own. On the one hand, the new specialty had been developed from peripheral areas of medicine by then considered antiquated, such as hydrotherapy and climatology, and which offered no basis for building an academic career. On the other, it had been developed building on modern and innovative spheres, such as electrotherapy, light therapy, radiotherapy, and X-ray therapy.[27] In the 1870s, individual lecturers had started to establish balneology and other precursor disciplines of physical medicine at the university.[28] They were followed by a new generation of physicians whose scientific work not only developed the field in terms of therapy and theory, but also rendered it institutionally independent.[29]

Yet the actual development of physical medicine was not in the academy, where this specialty for many years was not accorded proper recognition, but rather in private sanatoriums and spas.[30] Numerous physicians from the universities in Prague and Vienna practiced during the summer as spa doctors in Carlsbad, Marienbad, and Franzensbad, and turned the spas in effect into large-scale laboratories for medical fashions of the day while introducing diverse innovations. A fair number of spa physicians in the health resorts of western Bohemia had no position at the university in Prague or Vienna during the winter months, but almost all maintained contact with medical societies or university institutes.[31] The young physicians brought new therapies and applications from the big city, which often had nothing to do with the local mineral springs, and took home at season's end a wealth of data from observation and empirical experience. Since the end of the nineteenth century, the bathhouses behind their historical facades had long since ceased to comprise only the traditional moor baths, sparkling baths, iron baths, and acidulous spring baths. Now there were also steel baths, carbonic acid baths, oxygen sparkling baths, and spruce needle baths, steam and steam box baths, gas baths, electric water, light and four-cell baths, as well as sinusoidal AC baths. Along with hydrotherapeutic applications, there were blue light treatments, treatment by suction, dust, and hot air treatments as well as X-ray therapies. In addition, there were radium inhalatoriums, Dr. Bulling inhalatoriums, and gargling halls. Modernized versions of therapeutic gymnastics were offered in the Medico-Mechanical Zander Institute, the Institute for Physical Therapeutic Methods, and orthopedic facilities. Guests in the western Bohemian spas also had access to vibration and pneumatic massage and could visit dietetic facilities.[32]

The lecturers who participated in the development of physical medicine in the framework of the University of Vienna were, as the medical historian Wolfgang Krauss has shown, about 75 percent from a Jewish background; those who in the summer months worked as spa doctors or the heads of physical institutes were all Jews.[33] Although since 1867 there was no longer any legal discrimination of Jewish scientists, an existing factual discrimination in established spheres led to a situation where Jewish medical experts had to move into smaller medical specialties.[34] Wilhelm Winternitz, one of the founders of modern hydrotherapy, described balneology at the beginning of his career in 1860 as an unscientific and decadent field, which only slowly was gaining scientific attention: "To deal with applications of common water for purposes of therapy was frowned upon by orthodox medicine as unworthy," he explained in an allusion to his Jewish extraction, as if "hydrotherapy were the poorhouse of medicine [. . .] to which only those fled who had no idea how to make a living in any other manner."[35]

The fact that the field was considered new, innovative, and scientifically attractive, and at the same time promised a lucrative income, made it particularly interesting in the eyes of Jewish medical specialists, who in most cases were working as untenured adjunct lecturers (*Privatdozenten*) with little or no pay at the universities.[36] Jewish medical specialists remained in the position of a Privatdozent for a period far longer than the average, and in many cases until they were of advanced age as professionals. They thus were in a "position which was a unique combination of academic subordination and economic insecurity."[37] On the other hand, Shulamit Volkov argues, the position of Privatdozent provided more freedom in choosing a field of research than a professorship and made it possible to specialize to a far greater degree "at a time when specialization in science was becoming indispensable, indeed a precondition for progress."[38] Thus, it appears that Jewish medical specialists had understood how to transform their discrimination into an advantage and ultimately were "not pushed *out* of the system but rather *into* its peripheral areas, which often proved to be a focal point of scientific research."[39] Over and beyond the question of individual career trajectories, this situation possibly also influenced the propensity to specialize at the Viennese Medical School and the development of physical medicine in particular.[40] Wolfgang Krauss concludes by noting that if one

> looks at the working conditions under which the field of physical medicine came into being—outside state-supported institutions, and above all thanks to private initiative—and if you consider the scientific and economic attractiveness, i.e. the possibility to work scientifically while being economically independent, it is possible to contend that one of the explanations for the impetus in the development of physical medicine between 1890 and 1914 lay in the particular situation of the Jewish lecturers.[41]

The reproach of advancing the specialization of medicine and at the same time furthering its commercialization was a frequently formulated anti-Semitic attack directed at Jewish medical scientists.[42] For the opponents of specialization, it was an expression of the fragmented character of modern, urban life and a newly defined relation between doctor and patient.[43] The "German doctors," as the periodical *Mitteilungen aus dem Verein zur Abwehr des Antisemitismus* (News from the Association for Combatting Anti-Semitism) reported, repeatedly emphasized that "both the excessive specialization and the dominant urge to make money" were "totally foreign to them."[44] These physicians appealed to patients not to go to Jewish doctors for treatment, and even if they conceded to their competitors that they had a role in the positive modernization of medicine, they always explained that circumstance by referring to their commercial interests.[45]

On the one hand, a large proportion of doctors practicing around the turn of the century in Carlsbad, Marienbad, and Franzensbad were of Jewish extraction; on the other, there were numerous lecturers for physical medicine among their ranks. Even specialists from other fields made use of the possibilities afforded by a popular health resort for their research. Gustav Gärtner, Samuel von Basch, Marcus Abeles, Julius Schütz, and Rudolf Kolisch were but a few of the many medical specialists who had a role in the development of physical medicine or other specialized fields, and who earned their living in western Bohemia.[46] The career possibilities for young Jewish doctors and medical scientists were fairly good in the western Bohemian spa triangle, where a large proportion of their potential clientele also came from Jewish circles in Berlin, Vienna, or Prague, and many of them soon had an almost exclusively Jewish group of patients in their office.[47]

Despite his many and diverse scientific activities, the neurologist Max Löwy also worked for more than thirty-seven years as a spa doctor in Marienbad. His name can be found in *Fuhrmanns Aerztliches Jahrbuch für Österreich* (Fuhrmann's Medical Annual for Austria) for the year 1916 with the following entry in the section for Marienbad spa physicians:

> Löwy, Max, spa physician and geriatric psychiatrist, grad. 1900 Prague, [. . .] staff doctor, Prague German Psychiatric Clinic, specialist for internal medicine, neurology and psychiatry, examining physician for Anker and Viktoria Health Insurance, member German Association of Psychiatrists, Association of German Neurologists, German Natural Scientific-Medical Association. 'Lotus,' Prague (winters: Helouan near Cairo, Villa Bonavia), Tel. 132 (7–10, 3–6). - 'Neu-Klinger'[48]

Along with numerous memberships in medical societies, Löwy had been an assistant professor at the University of Prague from 1902 to 1909, but he had opted for Marienbad due to the lack of realistic chances for a career in academe, living in the spa town until 1939, spending winters practicing near Cairo in Egypt.[49]

But how many Jewish physicians were actually living and working in the western Bohemian spas? On the basis of the extant sources, it is almost impossible to determine this precisely, especially since a good many of the doctors practicing there had converted to Christianity.[50] However, the fact that only thirty-five of seventy-eight doctors with a practice in Marienbad were still resident there in 1939 may allow us to speculate: six of the forty-three doctors who had left the town were Czechs, and one can assume that the remaining thirty-seven were of Jewish extraction.[51]

The biography of Enoch Heinrich Kisch, a longtime Marienbad physician cited earlier, conforms to the typical pattern of a Jewish career as balneologist. Despite his quite substantial scientific and monetary success—until 1938 his monument stood along one of the hiking paths in Marienbad—and emphatic support by his professors notwithstanding, he worked for thirty-seven years at the University of Prague as an untenured Privatdozent. Not until he was quite advanced in years was he promoted to the rank of associate professor.[52] In his memoirs, he notes how his career was closely intertwined with the development of physical medicine as a field:

> And with a happy heart, I see fulfilled after decades the fond wish of my younger years for balneology to be recognized as a scientific field with progressive development, generally accorded recognition as an instructional subject at the universities, and likewise my desire that a doctor working at the therapeutic springs be given no less professional and scientific respect than his colleague practicing in the city.[53]

By contrast, only marginally does he mention just how central his role was in the development and maintenance of Jewish networks in Marienbad—as one of the most important initiators of the Marienbad Jewish Hospital, which he not only headed until his senior years, but also attended to on a daily basis as a spa physician.[54] Nonetheless, Kisch, whose father Joseph had established the first modern private school in the Prague Jewish quarter, despised Jewish Orthodoxy, and eschewed conversion to Christianity mainly out of a sense of loyalty to his family.[55] His worldview was the humanistic conviction of a dedicated physician; most likely he would have agreed wholeheartedly with what was stated by his colleague in Vienna, Johann Schnitzler, a laryngologist like his son Arthur:

> The religion of the physician is humanity, i.e. the love for humankind, without consideration for wealth or poverty, without regard for nationality or religion. For that reason, he should and must, as an apostle for humanity, espouse and work for peace between nations and human brotherhood, everywhere and always, where the struggle of

the classes and races, national chauvinism and religious fanaticism prevail. A person whose thoughts and feelings are not these is not a true, genuine doctor.[56]

Laboratories of Ethnic Images

> Thirty-five years ago, when I was a boy in Berlin, the
> saying was common among the Jews there that if a Gentile
> is thirsty, he gets drunk and beats up his wife, but if a Jew
> is thirsty, he would diagnose his thirst as a symptom of
> imminent diabetes and would go to Carlsbad to take the
> waters and regain his health.
> —Gerald Meyer, "Strudel, Sprudel & Chassidim"[57]

"A person is thirsty, and drinks a lot but does not slake his thirst, is hungry, eats much without being able to satisfy his hunger, constantly loses weight in the process and perishes."[58] The family doctor Martin Engländer gave that vivid description of the symptoms of *diabetes mellitus* in a lecture he delivered in 1902 to members of the Vienna association Zion. The metabolic disease played a central role in medical debates around the turn of the century, since it was widespread, its etiology was totally unknown, and it often ended in death. "It is considered to be a disease of the wealthier classes, and is more common in cities than in the country," declared the American doctor Maurice Fishberg and his Australian colleague Joseph Jacobs. "Persons of a nervous temperament are very often affected, and it is not uncommon to find a history of insanity, consumption, and gout among the relatives of diabetics."[59] Since the illness was considered incurable, doctors prescribed exercise out in the fresh air and sent their patients to Carlsbad to take the waters—even later on when, in the 1920s, they successfully began to employ insulin preparations.[60]

Both in popular sentiment and in medical opinion, individual spas played an important role in the treatment of diabetes: because of the composition of its various springs, Carlsbad was considered along with Bad Neuenahr to be the best water cure for serious diabetes, while the Marienbad terrain cure (field therapy) tended to be recommended in cases of mild diabetes and obesity.[61] However, the special identification of Carlsbad with metabolic illness was not only based on the quite controversial claims for success of treatment. Around 1850, the scientific recommendation had been sent out from Carlsbad to treat diabetes by means of a drinking cure.[62] The Jewish physician Leo-pold Fleckles had been one of the first to systematically observe the effect of a drinking cure on diabetics. In his view, the illness was often caused by worry, grief, sorrow, or anxiety, but was in no way influenced by national or heredi-tary factors.[63] He believed that the springs brought the sick no healing but lessened the agonizing hunger and thirst. He considered a consistent proper diet to be much more important.[64]

Shortly thereafter, one of Fleckles's Carlsbad colleagues, Josef Seegen, the doyen of Viennese balneology, diagnosed a quite favorable effect on this illness—albeit only of shorter duration—of the hot spring waters of the spa.[65] The fact that as a result of these recommendations, Carlsbad and Maienbad had developed into centers of attraction for diabetics was not convincing proof of the positive effect of the springs, argued Hugo Lüthje in 1914, based on a perusal of more than fifty years of research on diabetes. During a lec-ture series on balneology organized in Carlsbad, the specialist from Kiel rec-ommended a strict diet and the supervisory and educational effect of taking the waters. In his view, the prerequisites were not available in all spas to the degree they were present in Carlsbad, since diabetic cuisine was costly and complicated: "There must be strict supervision of diet and strict monitoring of sugar secretion. In short, the spas should provide patients with the same supervision and education as are available in good sanatoriums and clinics."[66]

Lüthje, looking especially at the nervous disorder as a component of the illness, stressed the importance of "relative peace and quiet, and a life with-out cares and worries in spas," along with an "inner balance, tranquility of the soul and regularity of one's daily schedule for the course and intensity of the diabetic disorder."[67] Under such ideal prerequisites, it was also pos-sible to eliminate the sorry state of affairs where numerous investigations on diabetes continued to fall short of the necessary scientific demands. Places like Carlsbad could then "certainly contribute to significantly increasing the scientific quality of work on diabetes in view of the significant material on diabetes gathered together here, and the large number of doctors familiar with scientific investigations."[68] The inaccurate and unreliable research find-ings Lüthje was referring to originated in a number of cases right in Carlsbad. This was because for the scientists present only during summertime, the spa was a huge laboratory, since they had an almost unlimited number of cases and medical histories at their disposal. That was a situation that for many years kept alive intensive discussion about purportedly innovative research findings.

When Josef Seegen published his book *Der Diabetes Mellitus auf Grund-lage zahlreicher Beobachtungen* (*Diabetes mellitus* on the Basis of Numerous Observations) in 1870, the study was promoted, despite the fact that it was a specialized medical text, in Carlsbad guidebooks and spa newspapers, and it was warmly recommended as reading both for doctors in town and for their patients.[69] After he had completed a second habilitation degree in balneology at the University of Vienna in 1854, Josef Seegen was considered one of the first medical specialist doctors for modern balneology. In keeping with the typical career pattern of a Jewish specialist, he taught the subject *Heilquellenlehre* (balneology) during the winter semester at the University of Vienna, and in the summer, for some thirty years between 1854 and 1884, he had a medical practice in the Carlsbad spa house *Kanone* located at the Alte Wiese.[70] Seegen, whose special field was metabolic disorders, determined in part on the basis of his investigations over many years in Carlsbad that diabetes was especially prevalent among Jewish patients. He noted that although Jews made up only 10 percent of the spa guests in Carlsbad, they were a quarter of the diabetics he treated. They thus suffered far more frequently than Christians from this stubborn metabolic disorder, and possibly also had a predisposition to the ailment. Seegen believed one explanation for this phenomenon was the painful experience of Jewish history, as a result of which Jews had developed an unstable nervous system, which in turn supported the supposition that the cause of the disease was a psychological disorder.[71] With his brief explanations, which only made up a very small section of the entire book, Seegen had brought the Jewish body as a subject into the arena of scientific discourse, and he remained faithful to his viewpoint over the course of long debates about racial, psychological, or social etiologies. Over time, predispositions for diabetes such as that supposedly exhibited by European Jews were also ascribed to African Americans and the upper classes in India and Ceylon. However, the heart of the debate centered on Jewry in Germany and the German-speaking areas, and people now began to refer in everyday parlance to diabetes as a "Jewish disease."[72] Despite the intensity and international context of this discussion, both Jewish and non-Jewish scientists participated in the debate with an exceptional uniformity of views.[73]

From among the many intertwined strands of this debate—the growing current of biologism in medicine, the increasing perception of the Otherness of the Jewish body, which had started by seeing it as being exceptionally healthy,[74] the cultural, social, and psychological difficulties among Jewish doctors to provide explanations—I wish to look here only at those excerpts that throw some light on the local situation. My interest starts in the arena where the discussion had begun and to which it always returned, namely the spas. Attentive patients afflicted with the disease that first became a racial stigma, and later was declared a class stigma and image of an adversary in the eyes of Zionist doctors, were able to follow the open debate in medical journals available in the reading rooms of the spa salons.[75]

The discussion was already at a high pitch of intensity, with many non-Jewish and a minority of Jewish doctors favoring the biologistic explanation,[76] when Arnold Pollatschek, a colleague of Josef Seegen, expressed his views. Pollatschek, spa physician and surgeon in Carlsbad,[77] published an article at the beginning of the new century in the journal *Zeitschrift für klinische Medizin,* which criticized the established view that diabetes "was especially prevalent among the Jews."[78] Despite all respect for the "views represented by such significant authorities," he sought to refute this conception on the basis of his own research over many years, whose divergent findings he did not wish to keep secret: "As in every other science, it often happens in medicine as well that impressions, supported by statistics (even if not impeccable) and many other circumstances, gradually crystallize into established views and continue to exist as such until conflicting studies and assessments, and at times only contingencies, jolt and unsettle these accepted dogmas."

Proceeding from Seegen's research findings for Carlsbad, Pollatschek found inaccuracies in the scientific proof. He stated that as far as he knew, the number of Jewish visitors exceeded by far the figure of 10 percent given by Seegen for 1875 and 1893. He noted that in the 1880s, their proportion had already been one-fourth, and in the meantime probably constituted half of the total number of spa guests. In Pollatschek's view, later studies that confirmed Seegen's findings for other localities were explainable by pointing to psychological tendencies present among Jewish patients, namely their "well-known fearfulness and their readiness to sacrifice themselves for preserving their health" and their "preference [. . .] for consulting with famous professors."[79] While other research findings even spoke of 60 percent of Jewish patients among the diabetics treated,[80] Pollatschek analyzed local circumstances, such as family disposition, heredity, and the possibility of infection—which could not be ruled out—as potential causes. His actual main argument against these studies was the same he had brought up in regard to Seegen: inaccurate or deficient data on the ratio of the Jewish patients to the total group examined. He had put together his own research findings based on ten years of private practice in Carlsbad, where he assigned the given patients independently to a religion. This was in his view the only possible and therefore standard procedure, "since in private practice of course we don't record the religion of the patient."

Pollatschek, who was the first to reveal the many inaccuracies of the investigative methods, therefore divided his patients for that reason into "Christians" and "Jews or persons of Jewish extraction." According to his research, the latter two groups of patients accounted for about half, which reflected the ratio of spa guests in town that he had indicated. In addition, he stated that three out of four mortalities which had occurred among his diabetes patients during the cure were "Christians." This suggested to him the conclusion that Christian patients often did not seek treatment until at an advanced stage of illness, and that there "relatively more Christians were diabetics" than were treated such. Aware that he was challenging the view held by influential physicians and institutions, the spa doctor prefaced his comments by noting that personally he did not think the question relevant, either in theory or practice, as to whether there was a purported Jewish predisposition toward diabetes.

Although it encountered some vehement criticism, Pollatschek's article was well received in broad circles.[81] Joseph Jacobs and Maurice Fishberg also made reference to his objections in their article on *diabetes mellitus* in the *Jewish Encyclopedia* published at the beginning of the century in New York. Jacobs and Fishberg, themselves protagonists in the discussion, commented on all figures that claimed a special distribution of diabetes among European Jews by referring to Pollatschek: "On the other hand, these statistics have been objected to as valueless, because most of them relate to German bathing-resorts and sanitariums, where well-to-do patients from every country are apt to flock for relief. It is further shown that Jews are attracted to these resorts in relatively greater numbers than other races, because they more often seek relief of celebrated physicians and specialists."[82]

In addition, they concluded that on the basis of numerous studies and international investigations, the place of origin of the patients was decisive. The German Jews, who since the beginning of the discussion had been at its center, were thus most affected. Jacobs and Fishberg found explanations for this in a series of social, cultural, and psychological circumstances and conditions, including high economic status, the stress of everyday life in the metropolis, the tradition of marrying close relatives, and likewise another factor: "With the present knowledge of the pathogenesis of diabetes, the only reasonable explanation of the frequency of the disease among Jews is their extreme nervousness, the Jews being known as the most nervous of civilized peoples."[83]

The theory of a causal connection between diabetes and nervous disorder, such as neurasthenia or hysteria, for which the Jews supposedly also were similarly predisposed, was immediately manifest in the popular-scientific conceptions prevalent among Zionist physicians.[84] In well-attended lectures before a Zionist audience, they expanded on the notion of the nervous, degenerated Jewish body, and conveyed to their public all the contemporary theories of Jewish "degeneration" (*Entartung*) as a result of a "struggle for survival" over many centuries.[85] The Viennese doctor Martin Engländer described to his audience the nature of Jewish nerves as a consequence of life in the Diaspora: "When the ghetto walls fell, the Jews immediately rushed from their narrow little rooms out into the great arena of struggle in order to gain a more comfortable life, but at the same time one that made far more demands on them. [. . .] This struggle, this hustle and bustle, this hunt for happiness could not but have its effects on the nerves. Material capital was gained at the expense of neurological capital."

For some relief to offset this, Engländer recommended to his audience that they consider agricultural occupations for "physical regeneration," toughening up the physical body, avoiding any intellectual occupation that was too intensive, and plenty of "land, air and light!"[86]

Many years later, after numerous physicians had made use of and cited these same clichés, the medical specialist Saul Mezan published his *Morbus judaicus* on the occasion of the Dresden Public Hygiene Exhibition. This text included in the collective volume *Hygiene und Judentum* in 1930 makes clear the extent to which the past fifty and more years of supposed scientific ascriptions had been absorbed into the general understanding, and in what continuities they were communicated to others. Mezan writes:

> As long as Jews do without the influx of invigorating, refreshing purer blood of rural residents, people will probably struggle against 'the Jewish distress,' limit it, but never be able to completely get control over it. And it will continue, just as long as the Jewish people continues to live as it has. And this unfortunate race will continue to fill the sanatoriums for the mentally ill, epileptics and neurasthenics, the sanatoriums for those suffering from scrofula and tuberculosis, it will throng to the spas for diabetics and arthritics, because it embodies a community with an abnormal structure. And all the hospitals, all the

welfare for the poor who are sickly, all charitable institutions will only provide but limited remedy.[87]

Thus, the "ailing," nervous Jewish middle class was still constantly flocking to spas in search of treatment for its diseases of affluence. The extent to which the image of supposed scientific research findings was inscribed in individual physical perceptions is not only reflected in witty commentary, such as that cited at the beginning of this chapter. In a virtual community of the "potentially sick," what predominated was a very real and widespread fear of diabetes.[88] Expressing serious concern, a Viennese doctor wrote in 1931 in the Zionist periodical *Die Neue Welt:* "The disposition of the Jews toward diabetes is well known to broad circles of the Jewish population, and has, even among the Jews, especially those a bit more advanced in age, led to a certain fear, largely exaggerated, of falling ill with this ailment."[89] Many of these potential patients believed recovery was possible in Carlsbad, which, as the spa physician Walter Kohner put it, was still considered "in Jewish circles" to be "*the* spa for sugar."[90]

Chapter 4

Bourgeois Experiential Spaces of Worry and Concern

Constant Worries about Oneself

> She also loved to visit spas and to consult foreign specialists
> whose expertise served as a topic of conversation for the
> whole following winter. She went from resort to resort and
> from physician to physician. All her dressers and bureaus
> were filled with phials, ampoules, jars, and boxes of variously
> tinted medicines, tonics, and pills that she never took.
> —Israel J. Singer, *The Brothers Ashkenazi*[1]

Striking were the words of the eloquent preacher Adolf Jellinek, delivered in a sermon on a late July Sabbath in 1852 in the prayer house of the Carlsbad Jewish Hospital for the Poor (*Carlsbader Israelitisches Armenspital*):

> At no time and no place, my devout audience, are we more inclined to cast the observant and discerning eye around and within us, than during our stay in this city, which calls out the word of consolation of today's Sabbath of Comfort, '*Nachamu*,' to a suffering humanity! [. . .] Surrounded by creatures so similar to ourselves, whose lot is suffering and disease, whose glances disclose at times growing hope, at times troubled longing, sometimes growing satisfaction, and sometimes deluded expectations [. . .]; within us, each individual bears the thorn of various diseases, whose sharp tip is but gradually worn blunt, every day paying heed to the condition of our body, observing its movements and changes—is it then not comprehensible and only natural that now more than ever, we grow attentive to what is happening around and within us, emerging there into being?[2]

The future Vienna chief rabbi came often to Carlsbad to take the cure, which is why he knew precisely the perceptions and feelings of a spa guest. The members of his audience belonged to that new type of spa patient that had begun to fill the promenades in the second half of the nineteenth century. It was an educated lay public, full of individuals who observed their own bodies and discussed their physical health at the evening *table d'hôte*. It was a public that placed its fate confidently in the hands of experienced specialists. The spas were caught up in a transformative process: becoming ever more scientific, driven by ambitious doctors, new technologies, and popular medical self-help literature. All that was bound to impact on the spa clientele. John Efron writes that patients were no longer prepared to continue to occupy their passive role in the doctor-patient relationship, and developed instead into demanding medical consumers: " 'Medicalized,' just as doctors were becoming professionalized, patients now sought to place themselves under the care of 'experts.' "[3] Under the influence of middle-class literature on hygiene and self-help, which instructed readers in "the art of living and the art of untiring worry about oneself," experienced lay persons began to be increasingly interested in medical details and interior views of their own bodies.[4] From the wealth of medical handbooks and guidebooks, those interested were able to inform themselves, long before setting out on a journey, about all the details of the cure, become acquainted with daily routines and rituals, and study the characteristics of the mineral springs whose power they would soon experience on their own bodies.

Once arrived, that body was exposed to the medical glance in situations of examination that overstepped boundaries. The available diagnostic facilities in Carlsbad, Marienbad, and Franzensbad were cutting edge and often the patients' ailments were not properly diagnosed until they came for the cure and had access to the better methods of diagnosis there.[5] Experiences like the very first X-ray allowed the patient to gaze deeply within his or her supposedly innermost chambers, and perhaps to experience this inward glance like Hans Castorp as a sudden recognition of one's own illness, where Castorp "saw his own grave."[6] Multifarious new therapies let spa facilities appear to the eye, as Kafka noted, like "another office almost, in the service of the body." He derided this in a postcard sent to Felice Bauer in May 1916: "If you are there, I intend to be with you, but I do not intend to allow myself to be medicated, mudpacked, electrically treated, given therapeutic baths, examined, informed about the nature of my diseases with unusual accuracy owing to an unusually accurate diagnosis."[7] Kafka's critique targeted sanatoria in particular; their closed character and hopeless atmosphere differed from the situation prevailing in the spa. But a docile spa guest who submitted totally to the rhythms and regimen dictated by the doctors would have experienced precisely these various routines that he criticized.

Over against the intimate self-observation and external observation by the doctor, patients were confronted with a daily experience that occurred almost exclusively in the various public spheres of the spa. It not only offered an opportunity for mutual observation but almost demanded that guests engage in it actively. Behind the doors of doctors' offices and bathhouses, mild or severe illnesses were the center of attention; by contrast, out on the promenades and in the parks, there was in a sense a public staging of joy in life, an enactment of vitality. In the manner of an auto-suggestive game of self-deception, which takes on solid contours in the observer's gaze, health was to be conjured up by simulation.[8] Wolfgang Kos comments: "In such a milieu of a finely woven surface game, modern man perfected the ability to lead a double existence between intimate truth and social costuming. Its virtuosity consisted specifically in veiling over in an opulent manner even oppressive individual realities. The spa offered the possibility to sublimate personal fears of suffering and death through ritualized behavior."[9]

The illnesses hid themselves behind the costumes and masks of a cheery bourgeois society that sought not to display pain to others. The clothes, the "long dresses that dragged along behind on the promenades, stirring up the dust, the brightly colored ostrich feathers that swayed in the wind," were more eccentric and costly, the low-cut necklines plunged deeper, the vitality was more striking than back at home.[10] Doctors were untiring in their repeated emphasis that such styles of dress were not conducive to the proper cure, and they called on the women to replace their bodices and corsets with looser-fitting, healthier apparel, and to devote their time more to caring for their physical health than their external appearance.[11] Max Nordau, a frequent guest in Carlsbad, described the "rambling paths of elegant spas" alongside the "ornate squares of European large cities" as stages for the degeneration of the middle classes. In his controversial book critical of decadence, he observed: "The common feature in all these male specimens is that they do not express their real idiosyncrasies, but try to present something that they are not. [. . .] Thus we get heads set on shoulders not belonging to them, costumes the elements of which are as disconnected as if they belonged to a dream, colours that seemed to have been matched in the dark. The impression is that of a masked festival, where all are in disguises, and with heads too in character."[12]

Almost all who promenaded here suffered in some form from the fashionable sickness of modernity, neurasthenia, which designated "an ailment, a timid, tremulous sense of agitation."[13] It was often associated with insomnia and as a nervous component accompanied a whole range of illnesses.[14] The malady of anxiety was widespread especially in the large cities, where the changes and insecurities in individual biographies were greater and occurred more rapidly. Its protagonists were considered to be mainly intellectuals and Jews, the latter in numerous narratives—anti-Semitic, Zionist, and medical— stereotyped as an "urban dweller, a person of the metropolis, a 'resident of the city par excellence.'"[15]

In 1936, an amused Ernst Bloch wrote his wife about what he saw as a typically Jewish feature of Marienbad: an exaggerated fear about one's own health and the well-being of friends and family. He had observed these symptoms in his friend, the German composer and conductor Otto Klemperer, who lived in exile in America and had joined him for this vacation.

> Tuesday I wanted to return from Marienbad. Then after the bath while I was lying in the most beautiful sun with Klemperer I was bitten by an insect. After half an hour my cheek became a hard walnut, beautifully colored. K. (he has that Jewish fear of the body) drove off immediately with me to the hospital, there everything covered with iodine, smeared all over too, and I got a bandage like after a dueling match. That for K. was a pretext to keep me for one more day, under 'observation.' By evening everything was OK, leastwise it seemed that way to me, but K.['s] doctor, who likes to earn double, wished to 'oversee' the matter a bit longer, he spoke about possible fever (which I didn't have at all), in short: it turned into the most beautiful Jewish Marienbad.[16]

"Safety is nowhere," anxious worry is ever present, declared Arthur Schnitzler in 1898 in his play *Paracelsus*.[17] In his memoirs, Stefan Zweig described prewar society as being obsessed with a need for security, a feeling that was absent, seemingly unattainable: "When I attempt to find a simple formula for the period in which I grew up, prior to the First World War, I hope that I convey its fullness by calling it the Golden Age of Security." A regular income promised a certain degree of security, along with creating a nest egg for summer vacation trips, health expenses and visits to the doctor. Insurance policies that were entered into not only for financial reasons but for the well-being of one's own body transformed health into a describable and computable value within a bourgeois capitalist acquisitive society.[18]

Physicians recommended the relaxing effect of stays in fashionable watering places as an antidote to anxiety and nervousness: surrounded by healthful nature and fresh air, it was possible to enjoy luxury and comfort in the carefree ambient of a bourgeois sanctuary of sorts. The ritualized and synchronized daily routine of the cure had a positive effect on nervous diseases, since it conveyed security and structure, emotional scaffolding in a world that perhaps was going through overly rapid change.[19] In this manner, the stay at a health spa provided space for two central projects of modernity—transparency and certainty, geared to bringing back order into the mounting chaos and to restoring a sense of subjective security, while "the spectre of uncertainty is thus exorcised through regimentation."[20]

In his act, the Viennese cabaret artist Armin Berg made fun of this strict daily routine in Carlsbad, following the rhythms of which the spa guests moved through spa space on their appointed trajectories between the springs, the baths, and the lookout points:

> Right after my arrival I went for a stroll on the Old Meadow. The first guy I met there was my old friend Spitzer. "For God's sakes," I say, "what the heck happened to you? Are you sick or something?"—"Well, listen," he says, "like, I mean, you have any idea what taking the Cure entails? Right after rising two glasses of Mühlbrunn and one of Schloßbrunn, then go walking for an hour, for breakfast just a cup of tea and piece of zwieback. Then go walking again for another hour, for lunch just some side dish of vegetables and a glass of mineral water, at 2 in the afternoon a moor mud bath, followed by two glasses of Bernhardsbrunnen and one glass of Sprudel. Then go walking again for an hour, at 6 in the evening three glasses of Parkbrunnen plus one of Felsenquelle. I mean, it's just awful!"—Then I ask him: "So tell me, how long have you been taking the Cure?"—To which he replies: *"I'm supposed to start tomorrow!"* [21]

This comment notwithstanding, the great extent to which the medical rules of behavior were actually internalized by the spa guests is illustrated by non-official patients' reports contained in letters and diaries. On the one hand, what was important was to demonstrate independence from the doctors' control; on the other, patients tried to follow all the regulations on their own. This serious attitude toward the cure was generally associated with the high hopes that patients afflicted with dangerous and chronic diseases pinned on a stay at the spa, even if the description in their letters at times may reflect wishful thinking. It is surprising that the daily routines described by patients in letters hardly differed in any way from one another even in the smallest details; nor did they depart almost at all from the regulations laid down by the doctors.

> Dear Fred, [. . .] We are both living in strict accordance with the rules. We go to our respective springs at 6 every morning, where I have to drink seven glasses. Between each two glasses there has to be a break of 15 minutes during which one marches up and down. After the last glass, an hour's walk, and finally coffee. Another cold glass in the evening before bed. [. . .] The surroundings here are very beautiful, and one cannot have enough of the walks here over the wooded granite mountains. But there are no birds in these forests. Birds are healthy and do not like the mineral vapours. [. . .] Best regards to all from Moor.[22]

It was the beginning of September 1874 when Karl Marx wrote this letter to his friend "Fred" Engels. That was his first stay in Carlsbad, together with his daughter Eleanor. Incognito as "Charles Marx, Privatier, London," so that nobody would think him to be the "notorious Karl Marx," they were staying in the Kurhaus *Germania,* near the Schlossberg.[23]

The main reason for the trip had initially been the serious illness of Marx's daughter, but he himself was so sick that his doctor "re*quired* rather than re*commended*" that he take the Carlsbad waters.[24] His liver was enlarged and he was suffering from nervousness and a grueling insomnia.[25] Marx, who actually could not afford the cure, had traveled there assisted by Engels's financial support and on his advice. Carlsbad was not costly, Engels had told him, and if you keep the spa regulations to the letter, it is impossible to spend much money.[26] The daily routine according to which Marx and his daughter lived, and which he described to Engels in meticulous detail in a later letter, was actually in keeping with the rules laid down by his Carlsbad physician Leopold Fleckles and the general rhythms of the spa.[27]

At the crack of dawn, between 5 and 5:30 A.M., Marx and his daughter Eleanor went off to the springs. There they met the spa public already gathering. Some had been assembling since about 4 A.M., but most came at 6 A.M. to visit the mineral springs. The morning drinking cure was the most important part of the Carlsbad cure for all spa guests. There was such a throng at the central springs, the Sprudel and Mühlbrunnen, at this time of early morning "that standing in single file it took longer than a quarter of an hour until it was your turn again," and young ladies in white caps then poured the hot water into the glasses for this purpose.[28] In the colonnades and on the promenades, crowded together, there was a "throng of very nicely dressed people who, with great earnestness, were sucking the mineral water through glass tubes while moving slowly back and forth. Every hundred steps there was a scale, where friendly old women laboriously took the weight of the spa guests."[29] The glass tubes, like straws, protected the guests' teeth from staining, while people slowly imbibed the prescribed number of cups of the heavily mineralized water. In fifteen-minute breaks between two glasses, spa patrons took a slow walk along the promenades, conversing about the course of their illness and the first therapeutic successes.[30] All the while, the spa orchestra was playing lively light musical fare, having begun the day at 6 A.M. with a choir performance.[31]

After the last glass, the spa guest went to the bakery to buy breakfast in the form of *kurgemäß* pastries.[32] With breakfast in one's pocket, wrote Marx to Engels, there followed "a walk lasting at least one hour. Finally, some of the very excellent coffee available here in one of the coffeehouses outside town." There guests consumed the pastries they had brought along, and then departed once again for a "walking tour through the surrounding hills." About noon, "in a condition of physical and mental restfulness," it was time to visit the baths or other cure applications prescribed by the physicians.[33]

After a light luncheon, Marx and his daughter, strictly adhering to the orders of their doctor not to sleep after meals, went on a long walk. As an alternative, the guidebooks recommended to use the time for "family correspondence" and light reading, or to attend the afternoon concerts on the promenades, where works by Haydn, Mozart, Beethoven, Wagner, Mussorgsky, Lehar, and Strauss were performed.[34] Less in keeping with the doctor's advice but nonetheless an intensive and passionate pastime of many spa guests was the afternoon card game in the coffeehouse.[35]

After a light snack, Marx reported, people either went directly to bed or went out for some evening entertainment, taking in a theater performance or concert, or making their way to a reading room. However, at the stroke of 9 P.M., everything was already closed, and by 10 the entire city was quiet.[36]

A change from the everyday spa routine was provided only by the so-called cure-free Sundays when people had a chance to go on more extended excursions into the environs of Carlsbad—venturing out to "Amerika," the "Siechenhaus," or other Carlsbad excursion inns as popular destinations.[37]

Not only during his first Carlsbad cure but later on as well, Marx adhered fully to this strict daily routine and regimen. In the two years following the summer of 1874, he continued to follow the cure, spending hours hiking through the Carlsbad forests.[38] He joked that local doctors he had befriended would declare him "Karlsbad's model guest."[39] Beginning in the second year, he felt already so familiar with the therapy and its routines that he decided to do without medical consultations. "As was my intention," he wrote to Engels, "I am now my own doctor, and as Dr. Gans confided to me more in sorrow than in anger, the same applies to one third of the older visitors to the spa."[40]

Already in his first summer in Carlsbad, Marx had interiorized what was regarded as the most important prerequisite for a successful therapy: leave aside "worries about business affairs and domestic matters" as well as all "emotional excitement and inward agitation."[41] He repeatedly referred to this rule, explaining that long letters were just as little *kurgemäß* as was the reading of professional literature or the daily newspapers.[42] He ended a letter to Engels: "'Duty' calls me from my desk. So until next time, in so far as I am not prevented by the magically stupefying effect of the hot alkaline tipple from scrawling a line or two."[43] In general, in all his letters to his associate Engels, Marx did not lose a word about their joint work; rather, he described the Carlsbad forests in detail, along with the course and success of his cure.

Together with Eleanor, Marx was on friendly terms with the Jewish historian Heinrich Graetz, to whom he made a present of an edition of *Das Kapital*.[44] Father and daughter regularly met with a whole series of other German and Polish professors, "half the local medical faculty soon assembled round my daughter and me: all very acceptable people for my present purpose when I have to think little and laugh often."[45] To his daughter Jenny, who never accompanied him to Carlsbad, he wrote: "Here we jog along from day to day, as mindlessly as the cure demands if it is to be successful."[46]

The stays in Carlsbad did Marx remarkable good. Already toward the end of his first cure stay, he declared with satisfaction: "Up to now I have lost about 4lbs (imperial weight) and even with my hand I can feel that the fat on my liver is in a *status evanescens*. I believe that I have finally achieved my purpose in Karlsbad, at least for a year."[47] The therapy had such a good effect even on his nervous complaints that after Marx's return to London, Engels wrote to Wilhelm Bracke: "Marx has returned from Karlsbad a completely different man, strong, invigorated, cheerful and healthy, and will soon be able to get down seriously to work again."[48]

Although Karl Marx was cured of his liver troubles in Carlsbad, his physical condition became progressively worse. A number of other ailments began to afflict him, along with insomnia and nervousness. For financial reasons, he traveled in 1877 together with Eleanor and his likewise ill wife Jenny to the more affordable spa of Bad Neuenahr in Germany. When Jenny's condition began to deteriorate, the doctors recommended a stay in Carlsbad. But in the meantime, the danger that she and her husband would be deported from Germany and Austria was now so great that they could not risk the trip. Jenny died shortly thereafter in 1881, and Karl Marx passed on two years later.[49]

Tsedakah, Philanthropy, Social Welfare: Old-New Networks

> Following his two daughters' conversion, he felt the urge to perform some enormous and compensating good deed with which to weigh the scale in his favour. He built a hospital for poor Jews, a Jewish hospital, where the food was kosher, where no crosses or icons were displayed, where an amulet hung on every doorpost, and where the male patients could wear their ritual fringes without fear of rebuke. There was even a little synagogue attached to the hospital where a quorum could pray for the sick.
>
> —Israel J. Singer, *The Brothers Ashkenazi*[50]

When the Carlsbad Jewish Hospital for the Poor was opened on 28 June 1847, it was the first building in the town to be officially owned by Jews.[51] The Benefactors' Collegium, a group of wealthy Jewish spa guests from Prague, had obtained a permit to buy land, although only within the framework of the existing Carlsbad Jews' Privilege Charter (*Judenprivilegium*). On the basis of this ordinance from the fifteenth century, the city until the mid-nineteenth century was still able to regulate and curtail the Jewish presence in the town.[52] It specified that the stay of Jewish spa guests and peddlers was only temporary, permitted during the summer months, while a general ban on settlement remained in force. The restrictive conditions associated with this permit stipulated that the hospital could only be used in the period from 1 April to

Figure 6. *Israelitisches Curhaus*, Carlsbad, 1901. Courtesy of Richard Svandrlik, Nuremberg.

31 October. During the winter months, the Jewish caretaker had to hand over the task of looking after the property to a Christian custodian. Aside from these restrictions, however, the Benefactors' Collegium was granted permission to establish a synagogue, "and only [to operate] during this duration of time and only for the Jewish believers present in Carlsbad."[53]

The hospital survived mainly on the annual subsidies it received from the Jewish Communities, especially in Vienna, Prague, and Berlin, from the Representation of the Jews in Bohemia[54] and the municipal councils in Carlsbad and Prague, and also from private donations given by spa guests at the prayer house. It was directed and run by Jewish doctors and personnel, as well as by a cantor who was employed for the prayer house. During its first years of operation, the hospital was able to accommodate about eighty patients with cost-free room and board, and the number doubled by the turn of the century.[55] Entitled to stay there were persons in possession of a medical certificate and a certificate of proof of poverty; they then applied to the Prague office for a place in the spa.[56] The patients, workers, and petty bourgeois artisans and small tradesmen generally came from Bohemia, but also from Galicia and other parts of the Habsburg Empire. Aside from a small number of exceptions, they were accorded a four-week period of stay for therapy treatment of their illnesses, mainly gallstones, diabetes, and gout. Although the hospital itself had certain therapeutic applications available, the patients took most of their therapeutic baths in the general bathhouses, and were exempted by the municipality from any payment of fees.[57] In this way, the patients at the Hospital for the Poor did not remain isolated in their building but were largely integrated into the everyday routine of the spa and were part of the general crowd of spa patrons on the promenades.

The hospital, situated at the periphery of the spa area and not far from the public hospital, had another meaning over and beyond its humanitarian function. The discriminatory ban on Jewish settlement in Carlsbad had created an absurd situation: not only did Jewish doctors and business people have to leave Carlsbad at the end of the season—even during the summer they had no common place where they and the Jewish spa guests in town could congregate. The prayer house of the hospital, which could seat 120 persons, now provided a possibility to develop a Jewish public sphere, which at least during the summer months could offset the lack of a Jewish Community. As Rabbi Salomon Sachs explained in his address of dedication, the initiators were not primarily interested in creating just a hospital for the indigent, because there was already a general hospital in Carlsbad for needy persons. But, Sachs went on, "a Jewish prayer house was also a profound and pressing need, it was a general fervent and longtime wish of many hearts in Israel, and since the property of the one can only be maintained and furthered by the existence of the other, both had to be brought together."[58] With the creation of the prayer house in this infirmary for the poor, now there was a public space that—at least during the summer season—served to link religious, social, and cultural processes. Indirectly, this laid the foundation for a Jewish place, even if it would take another twenty years until an official Jewish *Gemeinde* came into being.[59]

This new Jewish public sphere set up networks between spa guests and merchants, and these networks continued to operate and maintain a functioning social welfare system even after the official Community was created. In the framework of the rising demands placed on social welfare institutions within a capitalist acquisitive society, the hospital soon was no longer sufficient. All sorts of modern ailments and a growing trust in physical medicine among the working class and petty bourgeoisie brought more and more people to Carlsbad.[60] Private and ever more government social welfare institutions began to include health spas as large-capacity medical centers in their programs. The more costly and exclusive that such fashionable watering places like Carlsbad became, the greater the number of indigent patients who were also accommodated there.[61] When the Jewish Community was established, a large number of charitable organizations were formed, founded in common by local residents, spa guests, seasonal workers, doctors, and business people. Their intention was to assist needy Carlsbad locals as well as spa guests. The first association created immediately after the Jewish Community was established was the Charitable Association of Jewish Women Carlsbad.[62] This was followed by a *chevra kadisha*,[63] and toward the end of the century by the Carlsbad Lodge of B'nai B'rith[64] and the Charitable and Social Association Eintracht.[65]

In the heyday of the health spa, the numerous inquiries directed to the Hospital for the Poor called for a new and broader infrastructure for welfare. The existing building was razed and replaced by a two-story spa house on the same plot of land. Ferdinand Fleckles, the son of Leopold Fleckles, took over as director.[66] But this did not solve the problem. The chair of the Jewish Community, who had been given responsibility by the municipality for dealing with the situation of indigent Jews in the town, stated: "However, since in recent years more than 500 indigent Jews really in need of cure therapy have been coming annually to Carlsbad, they find themselves forced to appeal to the charitable benevolence of the Community, and since the Community does not have enough funds to cover such great demands, they are constrained to appeal likewise as beggars to the generosity of well-to-do Jewish spa guests."[67]

For this reason, the Carlsbad rabbi Ignaz Ziegler began to press for the construction of a hospice, together with the glass factory owner and chair of the Community for many years, Ludwig Moser.[68] With the support of Clara de Hirsch, the widow of Baron Maurice de Hirsch, and the Viennese branch of the Rothschilds, a generous building in a spacious garden was built according to plans drawn up by the Viennese architect Wilhelm Stiassny and opened in 1903. The Emperor Franz Joseph Government Jubilee Hospice for Needy Jews (*Kaiser Franz Josef-Regierungs-Jubliläumshospiz für arme Israeliten*) would, together with the Hospital for the Poor and the Franz Joseph Vacation Home, accommodate several hundred indigent sick Jewish patients every season.[69] The Carlsbad lodge of the B'nai B'rith, which also counted Rabbi Ziegler among its members, assisted with financing these facilities and helped organize construction of a residential home for the aged, opened in 1925.[70] Along with an entire array of private welfare institutions, a dense network of facilities had been created, making it possible for needy Jewish patients to stay in Carlsbad for the cure.[71]

Beyond the framework of the existing networks, there were also individual philanthropists who integrated the spa in the complex of their own foundation activities. In the summer of 1872, Löbel Schottländer, a successful businessman from Breslau, was in Carlsbad for the cure as was his custom every season, and the municipality issued a new tender for the leasing of the Carlsbad mineral springs. Until then, the lease had been in the hands of the Mattoni family, but after Schottländer managed to submit the closest estimate of the amount of the secret sum for the lease, the mineral springs were handed over to him as successful bidder. The *Löbel Schottländer'sche Karlsbader Mineralwasserversendung* held the lease for the Carlsbad springs and sold mineral water, Sprudel salt, and Sprudel lozenges across the globe until the Nazi occupation in October 1938.[72] As one of the wealthiest families in Breslau, the Schottländers had established hospitals and homes for the aged there. Now they began to support the Carlsbad Jewish Community and to send sick women from Breslau to take the waters in Carlsbad. For Julius Schottländer, who like his father (and unlike his children) was an Orthodox Jew, it was part of his own bourgeois sense of identity to also assist non-Jewish welfare facilities, and he was not the only one.[73] By means of honorary memberships and donations, he and wealthy Jewish families from Carlsbad supported the Carlsbad Municipal Commission for the Poor, the First Carlsbad Association for Support of the Sick, and the Society of the Children's Friend Association.[74]

This special focus of concern for the health of less fortunate others sprang to a significant extent from concentration on one's own physical condition, since thinking about health and sickness played a special role in the spa. The supposed solidarity among the sick, in their consciousness of belonging to a community of fate, originated largely due to metaphysical reflections. It sought to allay the possible pangs of conscience about the luxury enjoyed in a spa by good deeds, while at the same time hoping in this way to accelerate one's own recovery.[75] Speaking on the occasion of the opening of the Jewish Hospital in the Styrian spa of Bad Gleichenberg, Adolf Jellinek commented in a sermon: "But there is nowhere else that there is such a powerful and effective sense of shared emotions, sympathy, pity, and commiseration for the suffering of others than in a health spa. There we are all sufferers, and a single wish inspires each and every heart: to recuperate, to recover, and to return, strengthened, rejuvenated and reinvigorated, to one's loved ones back home."[76]

Using such and similar allusions to fulfilling key *mitsvot* of the Jewish faith, modern Jewish social welfare associations sought to stand in the venerable tradition of old religious organizational structures, yet developed at the same time "modern and sustainable concepts for the solution of new social challenges," embodying a key movement of internal Jewish modernization.[77] What had originated in the framework of a bourgeois culture of welfare in the nineteenth century was imbued with a specifically Jewish imprint in the form of references to religious commandments such as *tsedakah,* charity, *gemilut chesed,* acts of loving kindness, *rachmanut,* religiously motivated compassion, and *bikkur cholim,* the commandment to visit and take care of the sick.[78] Attempts to make a distinction with Christian philanthropy described *tsedekah,* contrasted with *caritas,* not as a feeling springing exclusively from pity, but rather as an obligation, a charity given to an equal member of the community in solidarity.[79]

On the other hand, modern Jewish social welfare was solidly situated in the network of an expanding public health care system and was deemed a necessary supplement to this.[80] A public health insurance scheme for blue-collar and while-collar workers had been introduced in the Habsburg Empire in 1888, which then also established itself in the large health spas. But the need still remained for a specifically Jewish welfare infrastructure.[81] The Berlin attorney Georg Baum commented on this question:

> But the most important field of action consists in making it possible for needy Jews to be granted benefits to which they are entitled by public law in such a way that they are not plagued by religious conflicts of conscience as a result. It must be made possible for persons who need to be admitted to a sanatorium or hospital to avoid coming into conflict in this way with religious regulations which they otherwise observe.[82]

In Carlsbad as well, the intended recipients of bourgeois Jewish philanthropy were in many cases observant Jews, who stemmed for the most part from Eastern Europe, hoping to find a traditional Torah-true religious ambient in the city. Consequently, it is not surprising that welfare for the indigent in Carlsbad repeatedly was caught up in the crossfire of the conflict-ridden relation between secular bourgeois and observant Jewry. Although the situation in the western Bohemian health spas was not comparable to the conditions prevalent in Vienna or Berlin, the intrusion of such provision of aid played an ambivalent role.[83]

Exemplary of such a barely disguised effort to promote bourgeoisification were the activities of Löbl Jakobsohn, a longtime regular spa guest in Carlsbad. In 1889, the spa periodical *Der Sprudel*, edited by Ferdinand Fleckles, reported that Jakobsohn, a native of Frankfurt am Main, had decided "to establish an asylum for the needy Polish Jews who are now so numerous in Carlsbad and up to now settled in the most remote and filthy quarters. This home will provide them with room and complete board, all necessary items and medications for spa therapy, medical treatment and—clothing." The *Jakobsohn'sche Kurhaus* was to be ready for occupancy in 1891 and would offer more than 100 beds to needy spa guests. However, Jakobsohn laid down a strict condition: indigent patients who would be accepted in this facility would be required "during their stay at the spa house to exchange their Polish dress for conventional clothing."[84] Unfortunately there is no documentation on whether Jakobsohn's project proved successful, and if so in what form. When years later similar demands external to the internal Jewish dialogue and discourse were raised and the spa executive boards of several German spas decided to totally prohibit the wearing of the caftan in the area of the resort, that triggered an anti-Semitic debate, the so-called "caftan dispute."[85]

While Löbl Jakobsohn was busy building his spa house, Jewish spa guests from Eastern Europe in Carlsbad had long since constructed their own networks on the basis of old religious structures. However, these networks were hardly manifest in commemorative festschrift publications or annual activity reports. At least that was how Samuel Rappaport, rabbi, co-founder of *Mizrachi,* and head of its sections in Eastern Galicia, described the situation.[86] Rappaport was working on the "religious life of Eastern European Jews" in the framework of a never completed book, and published excerpts of this in Buber's periodical *Der Jude* in 1920. In his view, the system of *gabba'ei tsedakah,* which had vanished among West European Jews at the beginning of the nineteenth century, was still going strong among Eastern European Chassidim, and was sometimes also transferred to the West.[87]

Rappaport, joining the choir of numerous Jewish physicians, declared that the sufferings of the *Galut* were what afflicted Eastern European Jews in such great numbers:[88] life in the cities "in cramped, gloomy streets and dwellings devoid of even the basic sanitary conditions, lacking sufficient light and air," the inadequate and false diet, constant concern for mere survival, "reckless and insecure commercial undertakings," and "trading in non-existent goods, so-called '*Luftgeschäfte*.'" He argued that these circumstances made *Ostjuden* easy prey for nervous disorders and were bringing them in large number to seek recuperation in the spas: "In actual fact, it is well known that the Jews in such spas make up a relatively large proportion of spa patients. It is not always the wealthy who visit these health spas. Likewise indigent and ill East European Jews do not hesitate to undertake a journey to a spa deemed necessary for their health, even if they do not have the necessary finances at their disposal."

Rappaport continued, noting that the person involved, once he could find funds to cover the cost of travel, could begin the journey without trepidation. "The 'gabbaim' active everywhere in the spas take responsibility for finding support for the indigent patients frequenting the places. There is a welfare committee for the sick not only in all health spas in the East, but also in world-class international spas visited by East European Jews, such as Carlsbad, Marienbad, Meran and others." Thus, the potential patient could count on not being left in the lurch in a spa visited by Jews from Eastern Europe.[89] As Rappaport described it, prosperous Jewish spa guests from Eastern Europe formed such committees at the beginning of their stay at a spa, and this committee assumed responsibilities in the future for the regular collections of donations. They paid a visit to newly arriving spa guests and presented them with lists of the donations already received and the names of the donors. In this manner, they sought to persuade them to likewise make generous contributions to the cause. In addition, they launched collection drives among those attending synagogues and prayer rooms everywhere in the town. The recipients of this money, needy spa guests, who in this way were afforded the possibility of a stay at the spa outside the welfare facilities, remained anonymous. The list of beneficiaries was secret, known only to the *gabba'im* responsible. Down to the end of the season, those appointed to the committee of *gabba'im* were regularly selected from among the newly arrived spa guests who had in the previous year generally been participants in the committee's work.[90]

In Carlsbad, where it can be assumed that this subculture of private welfare was alive and well, the Jewish Community was not enamored of the practice and repeatedly condemned it. The head of the Community declared: "The news that the impoverished in Carlsbad received monetary handouts in the summer, sometimes more, sometimes less, is luring a large number of Jewish beggars from Galicia to come here every year, and given the impossibility of monitoring this phenomenon, they find they are quite satisfied with the result." He recommended building new welfare facilities, though presumably with little prospect of success in being able to do anything to offset such a well-functioning network.[91]

Welfare associations and networks played an especially active role in the process of socialization within Jewish life in Carlsbad by forging many and diverse links between heterogeneous Jewish groups, temporarily or permanently settled in town, already even before the establishment of a Jewish Community, and later in parallel with that communal Jewish structure.[92] Together with the transformations in the modernized and secularized spas described in earlier chapters, they formed the prerequisite for the development of specifically Jewish spaces of communication in Carlsbad, Marienbad, and Franzensbad.

Part II

Beit Dimyoni

Chapter 5

A Conversation

Young man: You haven't been here very long, have you?
Young woman: But, you know, I was already here before.
Young man: Do you love this place?
Young woman: No, not especially . . . *(The words become progressively fainter, and the end of the sentence is almost not audible.)* . . . It's accidental: you come back here again and again.
— *L'Année dernière á Marienbad*, directed by Alain Resnais, screenplay by Alain Robbe-Grillet, 1961[1]

In *Shop Talk,* a collection of conversations with colleagues about their work as writers, Philip Roth published a conversation he had with Aharon Appelfeld in Jerusalem in the late 1980s. Over the course of several afternoons, during walks in the city and visits to coffeehouses, the two writers spoke about Appelfeld's novels, which were available in English translation, among them *Badenheim.*[2] In this story, Appelfeld describes a fictive health spa in Austria that is mainly frequented by Jews, and as he says to Roth: "a rather real place, and spas like that were scattered all over Europe, shockingly petit bourgeois and idiotic in their formalities."[3] In the timeless locality, historically impossible to unambiguously identify, extreme characters encounter one another: "Every spring they came back like horses in the stable. Here you could find a schoolgirl who had run away from school, a man with a jaunty manner and a haggard face whose mind was worn out with books, and tall women to whose brows vague secrets clung like skin."[4] The summertime life in *Badenheim* turns into a farce, people consume apple strudel and strawberry cream cake with almost desperate delight, take horse-drawn carriages through the town and go on hikes in the nearby woods. They live with the impression that they are cut off from the outside world, long before they actually are.[5] There is "a secret intoxication in the air" that not only leads to affairs and infatuations, but brings hidden longings surging to the surface, such as a sudden home-sickness for Poland.[6] During the annual musical festivals, a child prodigy takes the stage and sings—in what language? "What a question! In Yiddish, of course, in Yiddish!"[7] Quite a few people decide against a visit to idyllic Badenheim, with the reason that this is a place for the sick, not the healthy.[8]

Almost unnoticed by the spa guests, one day inspectors of the "Sanitation Department" appear in town and, without hesitation or ado, erect barriers at the city gates and transform the entire place into a closed area. Meanwhile, everyday spa life follows its usual round of rituals and routines, and sup-pliers continue to bring in the necessary goods from outside.[9] Not only in Badenheim, but in other health spas and vacation spots, Jews are placed un-der quarantine.[10] The "Sanitation Department" announces a trip to Poland, and the small number who are not Jewish or "not fully Jewish" and are still in Badenheim decide to go along to Poland with the others.[11] The seclusion and closed coherent character of the microcosm, initially still perceived as pleasant, atrophies into a pathological space of suffocating constriction. The health spa becomes a closed epidemic area, a waiting hall for the deportation of its residents to Poland.

In its form, the tale is somewhat reminiscent of the popular spa novels at the turn of the century, but it differs in its cool, reduced language. The description of the place reflects the daily choreography of the health spa as indeed an enactment on stage, while the actors appear distorted into grotesque marionettes. By transforming an idyllic summer resort into an isolated ghetto, Appelfeld created an allegory of European Jewry shortly before its destruction. A reading of *Badenheim* evokes multiple confusion, and thus prompted Philip Roth to inquire about the historical context of the story:

> *Badenheim 1939* has been called fablelike, dreamlike, nightmarish, and so on. None of these descriptions make the book less vexing to me. The reader is asked—pointedly, I think—to understand the trans-formation of a pleasant Austrian resort for Jews into a grim staging area for Jewish "relocation" to Poland as being somehow analogous to events preceding Hitler's Holocaust. At the same time your vision of Badenheim and its Jewish inhabitants is almost impulsively antic and indifferent to matters of causality. It isn't that a menacing situation de-velops, as it frequently does in life, without warning or logic, but that

about these events you are laconic, I think, to the point of unreward-ing inscrutability. Do you mind addressing my difficulties as a reader with this highly praised novel, which is perhaps your most famous book in America? What is the relation between the fictional world of *Badenheim* and historical reality?[12]

Appelfeld replied:

Rather clear childhood memories underlie *Badenheim 1939*. Every summer we, like all the other petit-bourgeois families, would set out for a resort. Every summer we tried to find a restful place where people didn't gossip in the corridors, didn't confess to one another in corners, didn't interfere with you, and, of course, didn't speak Yiddish. But every summer, as though we were being spited, we were once again surrounded by Jews, and that left a bad taste in my parents' mouth, and no small amount of anger. Many years after the Holocaust, when I came to retrace my childhood from before the Holocaust, I saw that these resorts occupied a particular place in my memories. Many faces and bodily twitches came back to life. It turned out that the grotesque was etched in, no less than the tragic. Walks in the woods and the elaborate meals brought people together in Badenheim—to speak to one another and to confess to one another. People permitted them-selves not only to dress extravagantly but also to speak freely, some-times picturesquely. Husbands occasionally lost their wives, and from time to time a shot would ring out in the evening, a sharp sign of disappointed love. Of course I could arrange these precious scraps of life to stand on their own artistically. But what was I to do? Every time I tried to reconstruct those forgotten resorts, I had visions of the trains and the camps, and my most hidden childhood memories were spotted with the soot from the trains. Fate was already hidden within those people like a mortal illness. Assimilated Jews built a structure of humanistic values and looked out on the world from it. They were certain that they were no longer Jews and that what applied to 'the Jews' did not apply to them. That strange assurance made them into blind or half-blind creatures. I have always loved assimilated Jews, because that was where the Jewish character, and also perhaps Jew-ish fate, was concentrated with greatest force. In *Badenheim* I tried to combine sights from my childhood with sights of the Holocaust. My

feeling was that I had to remain faithful to both realms. [. . .] That is
a very narrow bridge, without a railing, and it's very easy to fall off.[13]

Appelfeld requires no more than a season, from spring to late summer, in
order to narrate, as if in time lapse, the history of European Jewry in the first
half of the twentieth century. The literary scholar Michael André Bernstein
criticizes the fact that Appelfeld interlocks three temporal levels in *Badenheim,* each of which symbolizes another historical situation of Austrian
Jewry: from the beginning of the First Republic to the *Anschluss* of Austria
in 1938, the subsequent period of discrimination and persecution, and the
third time level, which the protagonists in the tale, unlike the reader, are not
and cannot be aware of: the Shoah. Bernstein uses the term "backshadowing"
to designate the retroactive predestination inscribed in the situation, and he
suspects there lies behind this a Zionist narrative: "It is as though Appelfeld
could only transgress the Israeli taboo against chronicling the unheroic lives
of ordinary, assimilated Austro-German Jews, as well as the larger prohibition against any representation of the Shoah, by treating his characters as
marionettes whose futile gestures on an absurd stage we watch, half in horror,
half in anxiously bemused melancholy at their foolishness."[14]

At first glance, the tight interweaving of time levels before and during the
Shoah and the teleological inscriptions of the protagonists make the novel
a problematic text for an introduction to the history of health spas as Jewish spaces of communication. My decision to precede the following chapters
with a look at the novel lies, over and beyond its poetic density, in the statement that a second glance yields. As an alternative to Bernstein's reading, I
arrive with a reference to the micro-history of the spas at a different conclusion. In my view, the absurd foreshortening of time in *Badenheim* reflects
largely the historical reality of these places, since they did after all conserve a
specific sociability well beyond World War I, a sociability that had emerged
long before: in Germany until the mid-1930s, in Austria and Bohemia until
the end of that decade. In actual fact, this unchanged atmosphere, especially
after 1933, attracted numerous Jewish spa guests to Bohemia, Austria, and
those German spas that always had been popular among Jews and were still
open to them to visit. These protective zones offered German Jews recreation
and a respite from the everyday constrictions of persecution. But when the
changes finally overtook the spas as well, they shattered that idyll, suddenly
and swiftly.

The ex-territorial protective sanctuary of the western Bohemian health spas, their special Jewish sociability, crystallized during the final decades of the Habsburg Empire, when against the backdrop of intensifying national tensions, the health spas likewise were defined culturally, ethnically, or linguistically.[15] Doubtless these places had from the start been inscribed with ambivalences and discord, which a regenerative program sought in part to overlook, concentrating on care and concern for oneself. This protective sphere had a therapeutic and beneficial soothing effect on everyone whose social position was caught up in the vortex of change—the middle classes in general, and the Jewish bourgeois milieu in particular. Although the health spas were not apolitical idylls, and World War I and the collapse of the Austro-Hungarian monarchy was also reflected in their mirror, their "'paradisiacal' construction"[16] was retained. In nostalgic remembrance of the now bygone Austria-Hungary of the Habsburgs, whose reality was staged here, Jewish spa guests continued to arrive from all parts of Europe, especially from the successor states of the former empire.[17]

The following chapters deal with the formation of the Jewish spaces of communication in Carlsbad, Marienbad, and Franzensbad and their history down to World War I, when the Jewish places changed from spaces of communication into spaces of protection and shelter, a kind of summertime sanctuary. In order to take into proper account the social and political changes in the Czechoslovak Republic, their continued existence after the Great War is discussed despite central strands of continuity in other sections of this study.

The basis of the following chapters are subjective glances and vantages, which via memoirs, travelogues, letters, and fictional texts allow us to craft an image of the western Bohemian health spas lying somewhere between an ironic "too Jewish" (Israel J. Singer) and a "center of the Jewish world" (Franz Kafka).[18] All sorts of perspectives reflected and inscribed the conception of a predominance of Jewish spa guests, even though they appeared and were perceptible as members of heterogeneous cultures and not as a uniform group. These levels of image and representation are ultimately also the focus of the central questions that a scientific approach to the topic can raise, especially since majorities and minorities are not readily identifiable in an unstable society like the public at health resorts—and if contours can be identified, then at the most along lines specific to social class.

Within the ambient of internationality and anonymity on the promenades, national identity took on a growing importance, and spa society began to segregate itself into national and religious groups and smaller grouplets.[19] Hotels, spa houses, parks, and entire stretches of certain streets and neighborhoods were likewise divided up into national zones, just like cafés and restaurants.[20] Within the diverse multifaceted publics in the spa, the various different groups generally communicated at the most via glances that were supposed to guarantee a demarcated differentiation and modicum of self-insurance. Among the strategies of distanciation, anti-Semitism was the most aggressive and radical, even if here it was comparatively reserved in its manifestations. During a stay in Carlsbad, Theodor Fontane wrote polemically:

> What's Prussian, as always, what is Prussian recedes completely into the background, and it would be invisible if a few Jewish ladies from Berlin and Breslau didn't assume the duty of representing Prussia. But we don't wish to have anything to do with such sorts of representation, and rightly so. And what else is there and can be considered "genuine" has a grey Cinderella character. I don't want to say this is second nature among us, but it is immediately in evidence if we go out among other nations.[21]

In this nationally charged atmosphere, there was intensification of a consciousness of Jewish ethnicity that was in any case sensitive and alert. The consequence was that processes of perception and communication between heterogeneous Jewish cultures arose that extended beyond the familiar circles. In a dialectical process that was mutually dynamizing, the Other spa public imagined the different and diverse Jewish groups as part of a single unit, thus strengthening internal Jewish processes. Even more than in the ambient of everyday life worlds, in the temporary situation of the spa stay with its permeable social boundaries, diffuse forms of inclusion and exclusion arose, generating in particular mobile experiences of belonging and situative ethnicity.[22]

Under these prerequisites, the common bourgeois experience of the annual return of the summer season in the spa was able to spawn an array of personal experiences and sentiments: experiences of identification, belonging, empathy, or simple folkloristic interest that were not part of everyday life worlds, along with feelings of dislike and alienation vis-à-vis one's own Jewish background and other Jewish cultures. Reflections of one's own personality, with models of identity that were utopian or had been overcome and abandoned, were possible at all times in the public sphere of the spa. In that arena, a substantial proportion of daily life unfolded out in the open, with people observing and being at the same observed by others. The intention of the following chapters is to describe these spaces of communication, involving encounters and what can be termed "miscounters" or "mismeetings."[23]

Aharon Appelfeld described the spa as "*beit dimyoni*," an "imaginary home."[24] In this sense, his novel points not only to the blindness and naivete of the Jewish spa guests in Badenheim (literally "Bathhome") but also to the quality and power of persuasion of a temporary protective sanctuary. With the intention to reconstruct the historical connections and prehistory of his novel narrated in time lapse, the following reflections end where *Badenheim* begins.

Chapter 6

Miscounters

◆

Among Strangers

... going for a stroll as one goes to a theatre, finding
themselves among strangers and being a stranger to
them ..., taking in those strangers as "surfaces"—so that
"what one sees" exhausts "what they are," and above all
seeing and knowing of them episodically.... rehearsing
human reality as a series of episodes ..., rehearsing
meetings as mis-meetings, as encounters without impact ...
—Zygmunt Bauman, "Broken Lives, Broken Strategies"[1]

In May 1916, one weekend during World War I, Franz Kafka traveled on official business to Carlsbad and Marienbad.[2] The trip was not unusual as part of his work as an insurance officer employed at the Workers' Accident Insurance Institute for the Kingdom of Bohemia. Moreover, it was relatively fast and easy enough to reach the western Bohemian spas from Prague. In the perception of the Prague middle class, these spas were in the city's extended radius of comfortable travel.[3] Although his stay on official business was brief, the weather overcast and rainy, and Marienbad at the beginning of the season empty of spa guests, the journey strengthened the writer's longing to have an extended vacation.[4] Shortly after his arrival at the Hotel Neptun he wrote to Felice Bauer:

> There are ghosts that haunt one in company and those that haunt one
> in solitude; now it's the latter's turn, especially when it's raining, chilly,
> and the yard is full of cab-drivers' gossip. Nevertheless, I wouldn't
> mind staying here alone for several months in order to take stock
> of my position. Time passes, and one passes with it, pointlessly. It is

rather gloomy, and one doesn't even need any special aptitude to be constantly reminded of these things.[5]

As he wrote, he had been contemplating for some time the idea of getting away from the office for as long as possible. He reported about a discussion with his director, who a few days earlier, against all expectations, had promised him a vacation of several weeks, in part because of his "nervous condition," a cardiac neurosis recently diagnosed by his doctor.[6] Almost ready to leave again for Prague, Kafka quickly wrote a last postcard to Felice Bauer on 15 May:

> Karlsbad is rather pleasant, but Marienbad is unbelievably beautiful. A long time ago I ought to have followed my instinct which tells me that the fattest are also the wisest. After all, one can diet anywhere, no need to pay homage to mineral springs, but only here can one wander about in woods such as these. Just now in fact the beauty is enhanced by the peace and solitude as well as by the eager receptivity of all things animate and inanimate; while it is hardly affected by the overcast and windy weather. I imagine if I were a Chinese and were about to go home (indeed I am a Chinese and I am going home), I would make sure of returning soon, and at any price. How you would love it!
>
> Affectionately, Franz[7]

A Chinese who returns home from Marienbad evokes the image of a lengthy trip; this was hardly consonant with the comparatively short distance in geographical space between the spa and Prague—but perhaps the emotionally perceived distance between a place of recreation and the everyday routine in the metropolis that sapped one's energies was great. Kafka used here a coded metaphor for foreignness, being a stranger, common at the turn of the century. Reference to the Chinese is suitable for expressing a feeling of alienation, toward an everyday world left behind as much as toward the reality of modern life as such, raised to an exponential power in the experience of the writer and the Jew. Parallels between Chinese as exotic strangers and Jews as paradigmatic strangers played a role not only in Kafka's own writing,[8] but in broader discourses of the day: in Jewish journalistic writing, this comparison was utilized,[9] and also surfaced in pseudo-scientific anti-Semitic discourse, where a "yellow danger" was compared to an analogous "Jewish danger."[10] In

Carlsbad and Marienbad, a humorous reference to Chinese was always a confirmation of the exotic and international character of spa society, although in
contrast with Argentines, Australians, North Americans, or Persians, there
were almost certainly no Chinese to be seen on the promenades.[11] The *Karlsbader 'Kikriki'*, by contrast, a satirical magazine which began publication a
few years after Kafka's stay there, expressed its critique of the ambivalent aspects of the local anti-Semitism by equating Chinese and Jews as prototypical
strangers.[12]

A sense of being a "stranger in the land" was a recurrent contemporary
topos of longing. An unprecedented prosperity and desire to travel, never
before experienced with such intensity, triggered and drove a broad tourism
among the middle classes, which promised temporary respite for a growing
Heimweh nach der Fremde, a homesickness for foreign places.[13] This originally romantic concept was actualized and modernized in the attempt to seek
to rediscover a *Heimat*, a home and place of belonging believed to be lost.
The modern sense of dislocation was felt as a profoundly nostalgic experience, while authenticity and reality were something to be searched for elsewhere, in a kind of counter-world.[14] Sometimes useful was just a short trip to
a nearby unfamiliar place, a large city or internationally known spa, whose
exotic public at the same time facilitated an experience of the foreign right at
home, *Fremde in der Heimat*. "Perhaps I'm not allowed to remain too long in
one place," wrote Franz Kafka to a young friend; "there are people who can
acquire a sense of home only when they are traveling."[15]

When Kafka was in Marienbad in May 1916, the spa was in a period of
transition, the last stages of transformation from a village-like small town to a
summertime cosmopolitan city. Once the image of the fashionable health spa
had been successfully acquired, Marienbad would soon embody and project
once again that miniature edition of the world, one of the most popular local advertising motifs for the spa: "Captivating images of international life, a
dynamic hustle and bustle unfold here before the eye of the enchanted visitor.
All languages of the world reach one's ears: here the stranger breathes the
atmosphere of the great world beyond."[16] Being a stranger was here shifted
to the foreground as a privilege, to be experienced with delight and not as a
threat, especially since everyone was in effect a stranger, breathing the same
air of the unknown.

The staged cosmopolitanism created the reality of an anonymity that was
experienced as positive, which through the limitation of space and time for
one's stay generated another condensation and compression of experience

Figure 7. Carlsbad, crowded promenade near the *Mühlbrunnen Colonnade,*
1905. Courtesy of Richard Svandrlik, Nuremberg.

different from life in the large urban centers. This was because the structures
of the spa conserved a public sphere long past, infused with a romanticiz-
ing nostalgia: in the parks, cafés, and theaters of the eighteenth century, a
communicative diversity had crystallized that was not available solely to the
members of the elites. The term "cosmopolitan" appeared, a "man who moves
comfortably in diversity," a perfect public person who feels happy surrounded
by anonymity and foreignness.[17] In the eyes of Jean-Jacques Rousseau, this
kind of public sociability generated a relation of mutual dependence: people
were transformed into actors and lost themselves for the sake of staging a
"perverse opera."[18] In Richard Sennett's view, this public sphere found paths
into the nineteenth century, forming spaces of refuge within a secularizing,
capitalist acquisitive society, into which persons swamped by the changes of
modernity could retreat.[19]

The great international spas conserved and ritualized these old structures
of the public sphere, but at the same time developed a system of modern,
fragmented public spheres strung together, to which different qualities and
functions were ascribed. In order to regulate questions of nearness and distance, inclusion and exclusion, people engaged in new routines of action
within the shell of the old structures.

The promenades were originally the communicative spaces in the spa, stages for social consolidation and a kind of a distanced mutual attempt to come nearer, a bridging space between the different social classes.[20] In the period of the Enlightenment, the spa had been marked by great social heterogeneity, and in its constricted narrow space had simultaneously emphasized maintaining a distance while making it possible to go beyond boundaries.[21] The process of bourgeois transformation of the spas in the second half of the nineteenth century resulted in a changed and more uncertain spa society, which viewed the promenades as spaces for experiencing and practicing bourgeois middle-class etiquette.[22] In the anonymity of the mass of spa guests and tourists who populated Carlsbad, Marienbad, and Franzensbad in the summer season, sociability began to atrophy and dwindle more and more, as it did in the urban public realm, rendering monologue the basic form of communication.[23] Now the figure of the *flaneur* also made his appearance on the promenades, moving among strangers without pausing to tarry with deeper impressions.[24] Strangers lost or increasingly chose to forgo the right to speak to one another in favor of the right to be left alone. Public life in the spa, which in earlier years had been an intimate space, became a matter of silent voyeuristic observation, a "gastronomy of the eye," as Balzac had described the practice for Paris.[25]

The promenades in the spas differed from representative urban spaces for moving in public and along paths for strolling through the dominance of the mineral springs, to which were attributed a power of social leveling. A Marienbad guidebook described the supposed protective social space of a kind of sanctuary:

> During the high summer, the procession of pilgrims to the Kreuzbrunnen lengthens prodigiously extending all the way to the promenade. There is no difference in rank between the spa guests there, and the principle of equality is "Come earlier, drink earlier." Even the rules of gallantry are set aside, in a pardonable manner, and the ladies, who are used to enjoying the priority of being the first in line, must often acquiesce and let the gentlemen go ahead of them.[26]

The image of a community of solidarity of the spa guests and the equalizing effect of illness corresponded with the efforts by the spas to gain medical recognition. Thus, it was not very surprising when in 1906, a photo supposedly made the rounds through all the papers "in which King Edward of England in Marienbad was drinking his glass of mineral water next to a man dressed in a caftan."[27] In this manner, the predominant intent was not to portray the anti-elitist attitude of the British monarch, friendly toward the Jews. Rather, an image of the spa was to be projected that created a sense of nearness even between the most antipodal figures of the local hierarchy. This staging cited the "exclusive promiscuity" of the spas as places of entertainment for the elite, which was predominant in the recent past.[28] But in the era of the modern mass spas, the individual no longer had a fixed, unchanging place in society, and thus, hidden behind this ostensible egalitarian image, there lay an intensive experience of difference.

The communicative spaces shifted from the promenades as stages of distanced observation to more exclusive locales that selected their public in advance. The doors of the coffeehouses, restaurants, hotels, and spa salons opened only for their particular guests, and the intimate areas and niches hidden behind those doors were also respected by the guidebooks, which otherwise tried to cover the local topography in meticulous detail. These places took over the role of social distinction, which given the anonymity of the masses and the changes in fashion was no longer a ready possibility. Because a neutral and unobtrusive style of clothing had become commonplace since the mid-nineteenth century, a style that rendered differences in appearance more subtle and masked the actual material affairs in the public realm, it had become virtually impossible to determine the social position of the Other with any degree of certainty.[29]

Within the social gathering rooms and nooks of the hotels, the behavioral rules of hotel etiquette bound the spa guests together in an intimate society, despite the prevailing anonymity beyond the walls.[30] In the restaurants and dining halls of the spas, *table d'hôte* was maintained, a practice that brought strangers together for the duration of their stay at a single table. Nonetheless, even in the hotel, the right persisted to be left alone. When Franz Kafka in the summer of 1916 returned for a longer stay in Marienbad, he frequented the lobby of his hotel, the beautiful *Schloß Balmoral*, when he wished to write a letter: "I'm writing in the lobby, a wonderful facility for people to disturb each other and get on one another's nerves, by means of minor irritations."[31]

Figure 8. The Grüngard family from Berlin in Marienbad, 13 July 1922. Feiwel Grüngard ran a popular cultural salon in Berlin. Courtesy of Anat Feinberg, Stuttgart.

At the Springs, on the Promenades, in the Hotels

In Carlsbad the effect of the spa guests as a mass, and how each contributes his own to the impression: world-class spa—but you mustn't look at them one by one if you want to feel the great thing here—'coz then those are just tricksters, diabetics, Polish Jews, dandies . . . a few really elegant persons, a couple of delightfully beautiful American women.—I'll be leaving C. soon—a person can either only spend two days here, or four weeks.
—Arthur Schnitzler to Hugo von Hofmannsthal,
10 July 1895[32]

People moved in circles through Carlsbad, Marienbad, and Franzensbad and spent the time of their cure largely encircled by acquaintances or relatives.

In the heyday of the western Bohemian spas, from the end of the nineteenth century down to the beginning of World War I, members of Jewish cultures from all parts of Europe traveled to take the waters in Bohemia. They came following their everyday networks and relations and continued to nurture these ties rather exclusively once at their destination. Although many perceived them as a coherent group within the spa society, they differed not only in their points of departure but also reflected the entire spectrum of possible identities existing at the time among European Jewry, ranging from conservative to socialist, communist, Zionist, and on to observant in the full array of different religious currents. It was exceptional for Jewish patrons to establish ties to spa guests outside their own circles, though not as rare as contacts with non-Jewish spa guests.[33] People moved unerringly through the great masses on the promenades in order to discover old or new contacts in familiar circles, and to direct the interest of their children toward suitable playmates or potential spouses.[34]

The imagined collective of Jewish spa guests projected a fictive and at times confusingly illogical separation into Western European and Eastern European Jews. This reflected an intensive contemporary debate; however, in the dynamics of the spa society, that debate took on a grotesque dimension.[35] This was because it largely was reduced in the spa to representation and observation as practices of demarcation and self-reassurance via social, linguistic, or aesthetic codes. To present oneself in public and at the same time to observe the Other, to recognize in the mask of the Other's external appearance a mirror of one's own personality, was a part of the special amusement on the promenades, in the coffeehouses and the parks.[36] If one assumes with Deleuze and Lacan that observation of the Other always has the aim of reflecting on and fulfilling one's own image, this observational pastime reveals itself to be largely a narcissistic practice.[37]

By reading through the official Spa Lists, it was possible to establish who (aside from oneself) was in town at the moment and appeared interesting—which in turn highlighted one's own positioning within the temporary society. The middle-class pleasure in taking part in the life of celebrities played a large role in fashionable watering places such as those in western Bohemia. If the general interest was concentrated on European high nobility, Jewish spa guests directed their eyes in addition to the elites within European and American Jewry. Along with noble families, such as the Rothschilds and Hirschs, special interests were stirred in Carlsbad and Marienbad by the numerous rabbis and chief rabbis from all corners of the European continent, about whom the Jewish papers and spa periodicals carried repeated reports. Announcements were made in the press when well-known artists, writers, doctors, or politicians were in the spa to take the cure, no matter whether Theodor Herzl, Richard Beer-Hofmann, Arthur Schnitzler, Sigmund Freud, Yitzchak Leib Peretz, Chaim Nachman Bialik, Sholem Aleichem, Morris Rosenfeld, or Abraham Goldfaden.

From time to time, festive banquets and celebrations were organized, to which a smaller or larger select company was invited, such as in the summer of 1879 when the historian Heinrich Graetz completed taking the cure for the twenty-fifth time in Carlsbad.[38] Celebrities coming to town under a false identity and hoping not to be recognized only contributed to the mythical flair of the cosmopolitan spa. In the summer of 1908, shortly after the attempted assassination of Alfred Dreyfus during the burial of the ashes of Emile Zola, who had died six years earlier, the Prague *Selbstwehr* reported: "Major Alfred Dreyfus has arrived incognito in Carlsbad a few days ago, and only the insiders know under what name he registered in the spa list and where he is staying. He wishes to take the Cure here without being disturbed, which he indeed appears to be in need of. His appearance still betrays the mental torment he feels, while the major probably has survived the physical agonies."[39]

The necessary lure of novelty that the spatial change engendered was part of the attitude of expectation of the spa society, which regarded itself as cosmopolitan. Thus, within this "imagined community" that crystallized here for a limited time on supranational territory, identities were not only affirmed but changed for the duration of the stay and sometimes longer. It began with the fact that guests in the spa dressed differently, strengthening or altering habitual practices, seeking to achieve a persuasive embodiment and self-representation of their own group in contradistinction to others. If the new arrivals went beyond the borders of the spa district, as a rule they did so dressed in elegant attire in keeping with their sojourn at the spa. In most cases, that meant light-colored suits of striking elegance for the men and white summer dresses, more costly and bolder than at home, for the ladies.[40] The children, if they were brought along and not sent off to some summer vacation spot, were likewise dressed in bright summer clothing and traditional sailor suits.[41] The Munich lawyer's son Philipp Loewenfeld, who was allowed as a teenager to come to Marienbad for the first time, recalled that for this purpose he got a whole new set of clothes: "Before we set out, I was outfitted with my first pair of long white pants and white shoes, of which I was tremendously proud."[42]

In most cases, far greater was the symbolic transformation for travelers from Eastern Europe. Yiddish writers often made fun of their obsession with representation and need to adapt to the Western cosmopolitan culture. In his novel *The Brothers Ashkenazi*, Israel J. Singer crafts a caricature of the changes in clothing and habitus that the wealthy Jewish middle class in Lodz subjected itself to on the Carlsbad promenades: "The women trailed trains over the paved sidewalks, displaying gowns that couldn't be worn in Lodz because of the filth and grime. The men, in their short jackets and tight trousers or in light, vented frock coats with high collars and pointed-toed patent leather shoes, bowed and waved their handkerchiefs with disdain."[43] Already when they arrived at the Austro-Hungarian border, the man had unpacked and donned his high silk top hat "so as not to embarrass his wife before the lordly Germans," Singer continues.[44] The reference to "the Germans," a polemical expression often found in Yiddish literature, in this instance is critical less of the "assimilated" Western European Jews and more of the *Ostjuden* trying to orient themselves to them: if they traveled to Carlsbad, they lost their self-consciousness and began to behave like *daytshe*, Germans.[45]

The mockery from the pen of Sholem Aleichem, the famous Yiddish novelist from Russia, went in a similar direction. Since the onset of his tuberculosis in 1907, he and his family had spent most of their time in sanatoria and climatic spas in Italy, Germany, and Switzerland.[46] To Marienbad, which had no treatment for tuberculosis, Sholem Aleichem had come for other reasons. His visits to resorts and health spas were generously facilitated by his patrons; nonetheless, he had to interrupt them periodically to go on reading tours throughout Europe in order to raise money. This is what had first brought him to Marienbad in August 1907, and the continuous visits there stimulated him to write an entertaining spa novel.[47] In the satirical epistolary novel *Marienbad*, he ridicules the transformations of the wealthy Jewish middle class that travels from Warsaw to Marienbad to find a cure for its illnesses of affluence:

And more than anything I would write about our Nalevkis women who, the minute they cross the border, become "ladies," forget our Warsaw language and start speaking German, pidgin German. Many of them, those from Odessa, speak only Russian—but what a Russian it is! Their clothes, their dressing up and showing off to one another! Those hats and the jewelry and the lace. You should see what goes on here! They're everywhere.[48]

It wasn't enough that they tried to hide their origin. No, many of these "pious young women," once in Marienbad, would also cease to wear their traditional wigs, an external emblem of their religious observance and identity.[49] The trips westward were not without consequences for them, because these were in the main women who subordinated themselves, in the polemics of the Yiddish writers, to the changed conditions in the spas. They were not satisfied with only making the trip but also wanted to take the West home with them, keen to go shopping for the large assortment of Western "necessities and luxury goods" they found on sale in the centers of consumption Carlsbad, Marienbad, and Franzensbad, and then to return home to Warsaw or Lodz laden down with "suitcases full of silks, jewelry, lace, crystal, antiques," even though they knew they might have to "smuggle these items past the customs officials."[50]

Such consumerist behavior, if we assume that this literary exaggeration was indeed based on reality, reflected, inter alia, changing conceptions of identity that could be played out in the anonymity and harmlessness of the spa public sphere. "In consumer society, everyday aesthetic practices come not only to *reflect* the new 'identities' of modernity, but also help to *form* people's sense of self, of likeness and difference." Leora Auslander's observation regarding the impacts of consumption on conceptions of the self within the Berlin and Paris Jewish middle classes would appear to be applicable to the temporary spa society, all the more concerned about surface external appearances, just as to large urban societies.[51]

In Yiddish literature, Carlsbad, Marienbad, and Franzensbad are described on the one hand as extensions of Eastern Europe into the West, promising a familiar infrastructure and atmosphere to be encountered in the Bohemian spascape: "You think Marienbad is just Marienbad? Marienbad is Berdichev, Marienbad is Warsaw, Marienbad is the Nalevkis."[52] On the other, the authors draft a negative image of the western Bohemian health spas as temples of consumption, a topography in which the entire decadence, superficiality, and declining morals of the West are concentrated. In this field of tension, strung between familiarity and seduction, the generally naive protagonists react with a show of weakness. In Shmuel Yosef Agnon's tale "Ascent and Descent," written in Hebrew, the very downfall of an entire family begins with the spa trip of a young woman:

> The daughter-in-law of Rabbi Chanan Abba had beheld in Franzensbad a new world. If someone comes to the health spas and isn't really ill, what is more natural, in this idle interim, where a person

has no worries and money is meant to be spent, than to pursue the wishes of one's heart? And if that person is usually stingy on top of it, here he becomes a wasteful spendthrift. Since the person has ostensibly come "in order to regain health," he has to take care of his body. And the body that feels well pampered by food and drink, baths and massages and the other pleasures of life, soon reaches the point of wanting everything. From that point on, he is beset by lusts and desires formerly unbeknownst to him. Now if such a person comes spouseless to the spa, parading proudly on one's heels through a place where he or she is unknown, the evil urge says: that one's mine. Perish the thought that Rabbi Chanan Abba's daughter-in-law would have done anything to transgress, but the delights and pleasures of life led her astray. When she returned home, her small town had become too constricted and narrow a place for her, and everything she had seen in Franzensbad continued to ensnare her here. If she saw beautiful adornments, a beautiful dress, her heart burned immediately to have it.[53]

The sometimes painful incompatibility of tradition and modernity was a recurrent theme in Agnon's tales and novels about Jewish life in Eastern Europe. The Galician writer knew the different worlds of Europe West and East very well, and when he wrote "Ascent and Descent" he had been living for several years in the German spa of Bad Homburg.

In actual fact, middle-class Eastern European Jews within the ambient of the West(ern)-Eastern sociability of the health spas often found themselves in a dynamic force field between two extremes, the self-confident Western European middle class and the anti-bourgeois Chassidim from the East, in their way no less self-assured. They shared with the former middle-class values and aspirations, and with the latter the same language and often also their religious culture and tradition. Although the middle class constituted the largest proportion of the spa public from Eastern Europe, there was far more public attention when a Chassidic rebbe arrived at the station with his whole entourage, sometimes hundreds of followers, or if he promenaded through town in a group of traditionally attired men between the many spa guests out for a stroll in their summery bright colors: "Their black caftans were of silk and flowed like robes, their side-whiskers were decoratively curled down their cheeks, and their beards, which varied from reddish and black to ermine white, were beautifully combed and wavy, like those of the biblical

Figure 9. Chassidim in Marienbad with drinking cups. Photo by Studio Hans Lampalzer, Marienbad, 1920. Courtesy of Richard Svandrlik, Nuremberg.

patriarchs in the churches."[54] In the spa society, the Chassidic rebbes were striking as exotic "itinerant royalty,"[55] and they garnered along with rejection and ridicule much folkloristic interest and religious veneration.

In numerous important Chassidic dynasties, the annual trip to the western Bohemian spas was a longstanding tradition: thus the Gerer Rebbe came just as regularly as the Belzer Rebbe, and after him his son, the Satmarer Rebbe, the Munkatsher, the Vishnitzer, the Aleksander, the Bialer, the Tshortkover, the Husiatiner, and many more.[56] Ruth Shaingarten, whose family had owned a kosher hotel in Marienbad, recalls that the Gerer Rebbe along with his followers used to rent an entire floor in the hotel. In her memories, not only the hotel but the Marienbad streets appear as mainly filled with throngs of Chassidim.[57]

The rebbes utilized the cure not solely for purposes of health but also for aims of self-representation, so that a journey to Carlsbad, Marienbad, or Franzensbad often turned out to be a publicity and fundraising tour to the West.[58] Already while traveling through Eastern Europe, they attracted many followers and after arriving in the spa even more. For them, Bohemia was easier to get to than some remote court of the rebbes in the East. Their presence honored the western Bohemian spas, making them into pilgrimage sites for wealthy or needy Jews. Comparable to the attraction generated by high nobility, the rebbes also were a reason for many potential spa guests to travel to Bohemia, and they gave hope to the indigent sick for special charity to be made available in these temporary centers of the Jewish world. Numerous devotees also gathered around their hotels, who had come to give them presents or donations, or to consult with the rebbe for advice or assistance in legal or family matters.[59]

Their presence triggered a mixture of strangeness, confusion, and fascination among Jewish spa guests from Germany, Austria, or Bohemia. The only contact many of them had had previously with *Ostjuden* was limited to philanthropic expressions of concern toward impoverished, needy refugees from the East. To directly come into contact with Eastern European Jews who not only were self-confident in representing their own Otherness but in addition embodied a visible air of authority was frequently described around the turn of the century as a new experience. "The international character of Marienbad, with its bathing and promenading, was completely amazing and unprecedented for me," recalls Philipp Loewenfeld. "But there for the very first time I also learned the difference between Western Jews and East European Jews, all from different countries." Prior to that time, Loewenfeld had only encountered Eastern European Jews on Munich's streets, individuals barely distinguished from him externally. They had their own synagogues and had no contact with the circles in which his family moved:

> In Marienbad this was different. There, for example, the rich Polish and Galician Jews exhibited a material opulence that was completely new to us. On the other hand, the Orthodox appeared on the scene in their historic garb, with their long coats and beards and sidelocks. One noticed this especially in the case of stately young men with enormous brown and red beards. On this occasion I experienced for the first time the feeling of strangeness that can occur among Jews. Of course, at that time I did not yet suspect that for others such external details could cause feelings of disdain and hostility. For me their whole appearance and in part also their animated gesticulations simply seemed comical, especially when one encountered a procession of such long coats in the middle of the forest or on the promenade.[60]

The Chassidim did not bother much about the rest of spa society during their visit; they stayed exclusively in their own circles and rhythms, in the spatial framework of Orthodox kosher hotels and their own prayer rooms which they set up, in accordance with their laws and customs and in their language. In the polemical jargon of the spas, people thus dubbed them "the Poles" without making any distinction of class or nationality, although they came from all over Eastern Europe. They were a target of ridicule and provided material for rumor. Siegmund Deutsch, a dentist from Slovakia with a practice in Vienna who worked in the years before World War I in Carlsbad, described to his sister the beginning of the season there as a curiosity:

> My dear little Adél, [. . .] everything here has turned into a "Persian fair."[61] Carriages and cars keep arriving one after the next, with many spa guests, most of them Jews—elegant Viennese, quarreling Hungarians and Poles with *peyes*.[62] There's a story that these "Poles" are not prepared to get undressed and that they sit fully dressed in the baths like huge black frogs. But my hope is that their teeth are not in particularly good condition. However, there are so many pastry shops around that I'll probably have a secure income.[63]

The director for many years of the Marienbad Jewish Hospital, Enoch Heinrich Kisch, went so far as to express his irritation in his memories over the fact that in the waiting rooms of many colleagues, "the dirtiest, most disheveled Polish Jews [are allowed to] sit along side the most splendid aristocratic individuals." It was no accident that in the spas, the West-East Jewish conflict was waged more than anywhere else via an array of habitual and external features.

Dislike and insecurity were elements on both sides of the fence in dealing with one another, as Sholem Aleichem polemically formulated it in his novel *Marienbad*. The Warsaw merchant Chaim Soroker complains to his wife who has stayed back at home in Poland: "And Marienbad itself has remained exactly the same as it was a few years ago. [. . .] The same overdressed Germans who consider themselves more pious than anyone in the world only because they wear a hat at mealtimes and don't shave their beards between Passover and Shevuos. The truth is, I hold them in contempt, these half-Jews!"[64]

Lalla Kaden, the daughter of a bourgeois middle class family from Dresden, accompanied her mother as a fifteen-year-old to Franzensbad. In her memoirs, she describes the conflict experienced for the first time in Franzensbad as an impetus to ask questions about what connects and separates people, something that kept the most varied Jewish cultures in a force field charged with tension:

> I certainly don't wish to make myself out as better than I actually was. But I also don't want to appear more superficial than it was in reality in the eyes of the later generations of the family! So I can definitely say in keeping with the truth that aside from the external things, a whole bunch of more serious questions started to become important for me. For example, why did the many Orthodox Jews whom we used to see creeping around in Franzensbad in caftan and *peyes* have to eat in special kosher restaurants? Did they really please their God more if they ate no pork, slaughtered cattle in a special manner and prepared their meals in separate plates? Why did we please this same God just as well, as it seemed to me, we who made no difference between "milk dishes" and "meat dishes," and who after our bath would always relish our bun sandwiches with Prague ham?[65]

The everyday practices that people could observe in each other's behavior in the constricted spatiality of the spa had effects that served both to separate people and to bring them together. When a good bourgeois German family had dinner on Friday evening in a small Chassidic restaurant, they already were overstepping an invisible boundary. In the memoirs of Gerald Meyer, the son of a Berlin lawyer, such an evening becomes for him the central experience of the summer in Carlsbad. Wistfully and nostalgically, many years later, he described the meal in the small family restaurant:

> I do not want to bore you with a detailed recital of the boiled carp in its juice, consisting of a perfect blending of onion and fish flavours, of which every fish I had eaten in the past had given only a slight hint; how the chicken was both tender, yet of firm texture; and finally, how a cherry strudel combined the juiciness and tartness of fresh cherries bounded by an almond flavoured delicacy of its crisp and flaky dough.[66]

If food played a fundamentally important role in the everyday round of life in the spa, this experience also had a symbolic meaning that went even fur-

ther: to dine "ethnically," in a Jewish way, triggered a powerful feeling tinged
with folkloric sentiment among those present, in combination with the atmosphere exuded by a traditional Chassidic Friday evening around the table.
This was not coincidental. In a world caught up in the vortex of transition,
breaking free from religious and social traditions, such an evening was imbued with a power to temporarily provide an impression of community and
belonging. Thus, the great range of eating and everyday practices on offer in
Carlsbad, Marienbad, and Franzensbad to the different Jewish cultures visiting there also had the potential to point up diverse conflicts and differences
between the generations. The Loewenfeld family from Munich usually took
their meals in an elegant and expensive restaurant that was kosher, but far
less strict in its orthodoxy than others:

> Only with difficulty could my grandfather be convinced that he could
> eat in the "New York" without sinning against his religion. He didn't
> really quite trust the rabbinic supervision under which the restaurant
> claimed to run. His suspicion that there was something funny about
> the "New York" was nurtured by the fact that they sometimes served
> roast venison. Since, as is well known, a pious Jew may eat only ritu-
> ally slaughtered meat, he resisted the explanation that these deer were
> in keeping with the religious requirements, since he knew that, as
> a rule, deer were shot. It required skillful persuasion on the part of
> my parents to convince him that the roast venison in the "New York"
> came from captured and ritually slaughtered deer. Again and again
> he asked my father whether we were not duping him in a sinful way.
> I think that this is why the food in the "New York" never tasted quite
> right to him.[67]

Similar generational differences were repeatedly and clearly manifest in the
heterogeneity of Jewish life in the spas. In his memoirs on Carlsbad, Gerald Meyer recalls having experienced his grandfather once in a situation that
seemed exceptional to him as a young adult. By accident, he passed an area
he was unfamiliar with on his path through town, Elisabethpark, a meeting
place for observant Jews:

> Suddenly, I saw on one of the benches a familiar figure. There sat my
> grandfather, tall and erect in his well-tailored suit, with his dignified,
> starched wing collar, pearl gray tie and matching Homburg hat. Next

to him on the same bench sat several bearded Jews in their caftans and round fur hats, while others were standing around the bench. The bearded men were actively talking to each other, obviously deeply engaged in a heated argument, and completely oblivious to my grandfather, the 'yecke' sitting next to them, who, they must have thought, could not understand a word of Yiddish. [. . .] Whatever it was, my grandfather was sitting there, his steel blue eyes gazing forward into the void, and gave no sign that he was following the conversation around him. Yet, looking at his face, which I knew so well, and in which I was able to recognize the reflections of the debate (of which, this time, he was only a listener), I for one knew that he was nevertheless an alert although silent participant.[68]

Given the variety of possible Jewish life that existed at the turn of the century in the narrow spa districts one next to the other, processes of positioning and distancing the self were a part of the everyday experiences of a stay in the spa. Via distanced perceptions and observations, a Jewish space of experience came into being: within it, interactions were rare, but there were by contrast frequent emotional reactions all the more. A growing understanding and recognition of the Others was accorded ever more space in the expanding consciousness of Jewish ethnicity. It sometimes triggered rejection and anxiety, and at times a kind of folkloric empathy. Aline Bernstein, a pioneering costume and stage designer from a New York Jewish background who visited Carlsbad in July 1928, described the place in a letter to the writer Thomas Wolfe, with whom she was romantically involved: "I wish you could see Carlsbad, it is a fantastic place. [. . .] I've never seen women so beautifully dressed anywhere, the finest from all over the world and Jews, Jews, Jews from the richest to the poorest. I hated it at first but now find it interesting."[69]

A common interest that brought together the different cultures was an enthusiasm for regents who, like Emperor Franz Joseph, had a reputation of being "well-disposed" toward Jews. One whose annual presence regularly created a stir among the spa guests and in the Jewish press was the Prince of Wales, later King Edward VII of England.[70] It was said that he had many Jewish friends and stubborn rumors were rife that he supposedly was of Jewish extraction.[71] His political engagement on behalf of the Russian Jews had earned him their special respect. "It was obvious that not only the distinguished, but also the humbler Russian Jews in the Bohemian spas were full of admiration for King Edward, for they expressed it by contributing generously to his philanthropic schemes," wrote Sigmund Münz, who had observed the king in Marienbad for several summers.[72]

Edward's respect for Jewish life in Marienbad contributed significantly to the genesis of an image of Marienbad as a Jewish place. It was not only the photo of him next to a Chassid at the spring that went around the world; information spread that the passionate regal gourmet was dining regularly at the *New York* on Kaiserstraße. That made a strong impression on the Loewenfelds from Munich, who generally took their meals the same hour as the king. Although Edward had come to Marienbad to lose weight, "his appetite for good things [. . .] was almost boundless, which was reflected in his corpulent body," recalled Philipp Loewenfeld. The family was very pleased with his presence and thought it "extraordinarily democratic that when dining, he was only concerned with quality, and did not try to separate himself off among the many Jews with whom he shared the room when dining."[73] Yet Edward's extreme popularity in Marienbad—when people awaited him in front of his hotel and followed him on the promenades—at times annoyed him to the point that he threatened to leave the place at once.[74]

In his novel *Marienbad,* Sholem Aleichem jokingly went to such lengths as to describe Edward VII not only as an honored prince among the Jews present from Western and Eastern Europe, but as a central figure in the Jewish place that was Marienbad. The loss after his passing was distinctly perceptible:

> In my opinion, Jewish Marienbad has gone downhill since the British King Edward died several years ago. When I was last in Marienbad, I remember what a fuss was made over Edward, who ate gefilte fish in the biggest Jewish restaurant. Not just the owner of the restaurant—a fat, well fed German with a nose like a cucumber—was honored to have the English King eat fish at his place, but every guest here for the cure, every Jew, was proud that he was dining in the same place as the British monarch. [. . .] One can easily say that King Edward's death had a greater effect on the Marienbad Jews than it did on the rest of the world.[75]

In the Eyes of the Others

> They were of all nations, but there were so many New
> Yorkers whose names ended in berg, and thal, and stern,
> and baum that she seemed to be gazing upon a cyclorama of
> the signs on Broadway.
>
> —William Dean Howells,
> *Their Silver Wedding Anniversary*[76]

Although it was the intention of those responsible to present the image of the spa district as an island in paradise and an ex-territorial protective space, the spa society reflected social and cultural developments in the world outside, distorted and following entopic dynamics. Here too the growing consciousness of Jewish ethnicity went hand in hand with experiences of rejection and anti-Semitism in the eyes of the Others. The diversely segregated spa society was constantly occupied with creating strategies for demarcation and distance, and also developed along these lines a special manifestation of anti-Semitism. This social variant of animosity toward Jews, termed "spa anti-Semitism," was oriented only in a limited way to political developments and followed its own codes and rhythms.[77] In a spa topography where ultimately all were strangers, it seemed logical to view Jews not only as strangers in the sense of persons unknown but rather at the same time as outsiders.[78] This chapter seeks to answer the question: in what glances, images, and stereotypes was this rejection articulated? A detailed history of spa anti-Semitism is presented elsewhere in the study (Chapter 10).

In the performative public sphere of the spa, the dominant cultural practices were observation and representation, to see and be seen. Observers on the promenades were avidly engaged in "decoding the body," seeking to deduce from the appearance and habitus of the person confronting them something about his or her character.[79] Vis-à-vis Jewish spa guests, this meant recognizing a familial relation between the members of heterogeneous cultures, so as to draw conclusions based on the rejection of indigent spa guests from Eastern Europe about the Jewish middle class—and the politics of the Habsburg Empire deemed friendly to Jews and declared decadent. In a sketch of the Austro-Hungarian monarchy at the turn of the century, the American travelogue author Francis Palmer described the Carlsbad spa guests as in the main "great financiers from Vienna or Pest, and their less influential but more picturesque *confreres* from Galicia, unmistakable in their long shiny gabardines, as well as from Prague and all parts of Bohemia and Austria."[80]

In the European topography of spas, the western Bohemian health resorts were, like most "large international spas," considered to be places where there was relatively little anti-Semitism and Jews could feel rather safe and secure.[81] Jewish spa guests there were confronted far less often with anti-Semitism than in small spas, especially since the segregated mass public had fewer surfaces of contact and less potential for conflict. Nonetheless, experiences such as those described in the case of petty bourgeois spas in the *Mitteilungen aus dem Verein zur Abwehr des Antisemitismus* (News from the Association for Combatting Anti-Semitism) in July 1912 allow us to conjecture about the situation here:

> Comparatively speaking, the best situation is still that of someone who has a decidedly Jewish facial appearance or a clearly Jewish name. He knows at least how to respond and is prepared for eventualities. Anti-Semitic types will as a rule avoid him, and whoever joins him will probably have already overcome the prejudices of a dark former era. But someone who doesn't look particularly Jewish and cannot be identified may often find himself in an uncomfortable situation.[82]

To identify Jewish spa guests was comparable to the pleasant pastime of correctly guessing the nationalities of others on the promenades. Frequently, however, the supposed unmasking was followed by descriptions replete with racist anti-Semitic comments, formulated in the light style of anecdotal spa life and for that reason confusingly ambivalent. Appearance, habitus, and name were instrumentalized as epistemic aids in decoding one's opposite while one observed people promenading and studied spa lists. In 1893, acclaimed German novelist Theodor Fontane wrote from Carlsbad to his daughter: "If you read through the spa lists, you find that with the exception of Australia, Uruguay, Buenos Aires, and Cape Town, all nations are represented here. On closer scrutiny (fortunately only of the names), you of course find that one and all, they stem from Jerusalem. And they just have 'God Save the Queen' and 'Yankee Doodle' played out in order in this way to feign a foreign nationality."[83]

During the last five years of his life, from 1893 to 1898, Fontane spent four to seven weeks every summer with his sick wife in Carlsbad, where what he encountered was "always things kind and nice."[84] Before he traveled to Carlsbad, Fontane had for over twenty years regularly frequented German spas. No matter whether in Misdroy, Norderney, Bad Kissingen, or elsewhere, he commented on the respective spa societies in his letters with remarks that were often aggressive and anti-Semitic.[85] In his view, Carlsbad exceeded anything he had previously encountered, and during the first summer there he continually complained in letters to his daughter Martha. Shortly after arrival he wrote: "I'd never have believed there were so many Jews in the entire world as there are here assembled in a crowd. I think highly of the Jews and know what we owe them, and I'm not even considering the money here in my calculations. But what is too much is too much. The situation has something quite alarming about it, also when you look at it from the Jews' point of view."[86] But in spite of everything, the couple returned to Carlsbad every summer thereafter until Fontane's death in September 1898.

Despite his susceptibility for engaging in stereotypes, in many realms the writer Fontane was attributed with having a certain passion for things foreign. But if talk in private turned to the Jews, his comments ranged "from diverse forms of everyday 'garden-variety anti-Semitism' on to conservative anti-capitalist cultural criticism, extending all the way to racist ideological statements."[87] As a typical representative of bourgeois anti-Semitism in the Kaiserreich, he was on the whole careful not to make public statements, but in private correspondence Fontane expressed himself all the more vehemently, knowing that his statements would be understood and accepted by his recipients "as a public metaphor of self-understanding."[88]

In his Carlsbad correspondence, Fontane articulated his disgust for the "caftan Jews with their side-locks, displaying defiance and cockiness, who make every path and trail here unsafe," and whom he termed elsewhere a "lower Jewry."[89] Ultimately he had no worries about them, since on the one hand they constituted no competition and on the other it was not difficult to identify them. Things were harder to deal with when it came to the "higher Jewry," not quite so easy to identify. Thus, Fontane stated that he was not only in search of Jewish family names in Carlsbad but also on the lookout for distinctive Jewish facial features that he believed he had discovered, despite much confusion, in the mass of the spa public. After he and his wife had made a whole series of new acquaintances through the agency of Berlin friends, he wrote to a friend: "By the way, the fact that Baron Lauer looks so Jewish can be excused, because his mother was a Fränkel. But what is inexcusable is that he comes here. Where there are already so many Jews (at least two-thirds), the overall situation should not be made even more confused

Figure 10. Picture postcard from Carlsbad, 1903: "Zoological specimens from Carlsbad: bear from Galicia (male, full-grown)." Courtesy of Wolfgang Haney, Berlin.

by barons like him whose Germanic Christian name is proven a falsification every second."[90]

In actual fact, both the old and new acquaintances the Fontanes spent time with in Carlsbad were in most cases Berlin Jews. The not particularly wealthy couple was invited to dinners in elegant hotels and had a quite enjoyable time there, even if Fontane in his subsequent letters always postured as the cynical observer.[91] Envy, utilitarianism, and a touch of fascination lay in this supposed superiority. "As a prototype of the educated middle class," wrote Wolfgang Benz, " 'he had Jewish friends,' shared the reservations against the minority, but only engaged in expressing such views in private. He displayed neither an anti-Semitic fanaticism nor missionary zeal, and remains with his life and work symptomatic for the phenomenon of modern anti-Semitism."[92] According to recent research, Fontane's private anti-Semitism also influenced his poetic works. He included narratives from contemporary anti-Semitic discourse in order to stigmatize Jews as a social group, but in so doing made use of an "indirect formulation, in deference to the ideal of social conversation."[93]

As a matter of course, Fontane disliked visiting petty bourgeois German spas, with a clientele of quite a few anti-Semitic guests and no Jews; he seldom went there. Not only did he prefer the upper-middle-class atmosphere and amenities of the international spas, he also had several positive stereotypes in regard to the Jews there. After his return to Berlin from Carlsbad in 1895, he wrote: "The days in Carlsbad once again were very beautiful, and I made my peace even with the Jews. In the beginning I was beside myself, soon I'd almost reached a point where I got frightened when I saw a Christian, especially the ladies—they all had the look more or less of a bowl of watery gruel. The Jews, even the most ugly, still at least have faces."[94]

Images of stereotypically distorted faces, as Fontane sketched them in his private correspondence, were also present in Carlsbad and Marienbad in the form of iconographic representations: caricatures on display in the shop windows of book and stationery stores, in hotels, cafés, kiosks, and newsstands, at the train station, with hawkers on the street, and from postcard vending machines.[95] Among the picture postcards that provided stereotypical images of the international spa society, there were quite a few anti-Jewish caricatures, in the sheer richness of their anti-Semitic motifs exceeding by far the offerings at other spas.[96]

In collections of what dealers today call in German "*Judenspottkarten*" (cards ridiculing Jews), spa postcards from the turn of the century constitute a significant proportion. Picture postcards from Carlsbad and Marienbad are especially common, while Franzensbad and the German spas are but sparsely represented.[97] As the card collector Wolfgang Haney noted in an interview, these cards were issued and sold in very large numbers: "Very often you can find spa cards from Marienbad and Carlsbad offered for sale. At every market and in every auction catalogue, you can find these motifs. So now they've correspondingly gone down in price."[98] The preponderance of cards are from the heyday of the picture postcard, when around 1890 firms started to produce cards with a huge array of different motifs. Cards from the western Bohemian spas present caricatures of spa society, sights in the town and environs, graphic art from the Wiener Werkstätte, and increasingly photos and photo montages as well. Although anti-Semitic motifs were only a small proportion of the picture postcards generally on the market, in the western Bohemian spas they were frequent.[99]

A large number of cards from Carlsbad and Marienbad contain caricatures of the entire spa society. Apparently in bonds of close friendship, grotesque figures encircle the springs or dance around the colonnades: stiff Prussians, Bavarians in Lederhosen, Africans in a fez, and grinning Chinese. There is no lack here of slender Eastern European Jews in caftans and wealthy, portly Jews in suits, both depicted with a stereotyped physiognomy presented as Jewish. The images on these cards seem comparatively harmless, since the individual types fade into the throng of people on the promenade.[100]

Along with this are numerous motifs embodying caricatures only of Jewish spa guests. On the one hand, they show the parvenu, the image of the assimilated, prosperous Jew, generally a heavyset, satisfied man, sometimes a thin, effeminate figure. He symbolizes the reservations against democratizing the formerly elitist spa.[101] Sometimes he is hand in hand with an overweight, plain-looking matron, who with her many male characteristics is meant to represent an "emancipated" woman.[102] Caricatures of Jews in traditional dress on the promenades are meant to point up their distinctive costumed character, which makes any national dress seem unnatural should they wear it and consequently denies them a place in the national groups of the spa society. It is no accident that the motifs as presented make little distinction between the Jewish middle classes from the West and East of Europe, but rather subsume one and all as nouveaux riches, whose mask of assimilation needs to be torn off and behind which another truth is suspected.

An especially large number of cards make fun of observant Eastern European Jews in caftans, since they embody a distinctively foreign element that had vanished among Western European Jewry. They are uniformly portrayed as unkempt, dirty, and gesticulating groups of men. Their uncommon appearance, for many a "decidedly foreign look," made them a popular butt for jokes, ridicule, and contempt.[103] Almost none of these cards are humorous and devoid of bias: they go beyond limits of propriety, especially in portrayals where the "stock market Jew," for example, is seen sitting on the toilet, engaging in "dirty" deals, a Chassid waiting in line in front of an outhouse has already had to answer nature's call, or naked, deformed Jewish bodies rise up from the moor mud baths.[104]

In the beginning, these cards were printed by large commercial presses, such as the Munich Verlag Ottmar Zieher. From the turn of the century, local producers also sought to get a piece of the lucrative trade. Among them was the Carlsbad book dealer Hermann Jakob, later mayor of the town, whose Kurhaus already at the turn of the century was regularly in the special lists that warned Jewish guests every summer what specific anti-Semitic hotels to avoid.[105] The fact that the Jewish book dealer Leopold Weil also was one of the producers and distributors of anti-Semitic postcards reflected an entopic ambivalence. It was not until the mid-1920s, when sensibilities for anti-Semitic discourse became more finely tuned, that a spa guest noticed this paradoxical situation and informed the Central Association of German Citizens of the Jewish Faith (*Centralverein deutscher Staatsbürger jüdischen Glaubens,* CV), an organization founded in 1893 in Berlin whose aims were to unify German citizens of Jewish faith and to combat rising anti-Semitism. The CV then contacted the Carlsbad chief rabbi Ignaz Ziegler, requesting that he take action:

> This card, if distributed by a Christian shop, would give rise to anti-Semitic sentiments. All the more so quite naturally when such postcards are offered for sale even by a Jewish merchant. Consequently, we wish to ask you to use your influence to ensure that similar cases do not occur in the future. This card, which doubtless stems from the prewar period, only contributes to damaging the good name of the spa, and to fuel anew the rumor of prevalent anti-Semitism there.[106]

As Iris Hax was able to determine on the basis of the Haney collection, anti-Semitic cards were generally sent by men to men, while other types of picture postcards were in the main sent by females. Frequently the senders were in localities with many Jewish guests, especially observant Jews from Eastern Europe.[107] Only rarely did the writers comment on the anti-Semitic motifs on

Figure 11. Anti-Semitic picture postcard printed by Leopold Weil, handwritten date 25 May 1910, and the remark, "It stinks terribly of garlic!" Courtesy of Wolfgang Haney, Berlin.

the card's front. Sometimes they sought to amuse the addressees with harmless sayings, though on occasion they turned more aggressive, with statements such as "it stinks of garlic."[108] Likewise, on cards sent from Carlsbad and Marienbad, commentaries could be found such as "Polish Jews in huge numbers!"[109]

In 1898, a discussion developed in Germany on anti-Semitic picture postcards, since postal employees had returned cards to their senders with the note that the content was insulting. The CV was delighted that the German postal service had defended the actions of its employees in this matter.[110] Despite the huge wave of such postcards mailed, there was just this one discussion, and one can assume that anti-Semitic cards were normally handled by the postal services without problems or comment.

The fact that postcards with anti-Semitic motifs were sent out across the planet in large numbers from Carlsbad and Marienbad, also in significant measure as advertisements for these spas, suggests underlying utilitarian reasons. On the one hand, it reflects a local anti-Semitism, offered to the spa guests and in part also accepted. On the other, the anti-Semitic content of the cards is not comparable with the radicalism of petty bourgeois spas in Germany, which already at the turn of the century sought to profile themselves as being "Jew-free localities."[111] It is possible that spas such as Carlsbad and Marienbad, which in anti-Semitic circles were disparagingly termed "*Judenschwemmen*" (Jewish watering places), sought in this way to correct their image in these circles.[112] The supposedly harmless humorous content of the caricatures provided them with legitimacy in the spa district without scaring away their loyal clientele of Jewish guests.

The animosity toward Jews in the Carlsbad and Marienbad postcards extends along a spectrum from humorous mocking to outright defamation. None of these representations is simply poking a bit of fun devoid of bias; it is always infused with a negative connotation that promotes prejudices and defamation.[113] On the basis of a process of the formation of norms and identity that was already rather far advanced by the turn of the century, the iconography of these postcards propagates "a racist image by emphasis on what is essentially 'Other', it provokes feelings of resentment, popularizing in an entertaining manner, under the guise of humor, anti-Semitic clichés. As low-cost means of propaganda that reaches all social classes, these cards, with the aid of catchy visual patterning, are able to condition one's sight, thus leading to a distorted and prejudiced perception."[114] Via their popular and entertaining character, caricatures can formulate ideological ascriptions "in a culturally normed packaging, i.e. one that can be generally decoded." Moreover, ridiculing Others provides cheap insurance for one's own identity, possibly even a feeling of superiority.[115]

In spaces of social consolidation like the health spas, reference to Jewish spa guests diverted attention from the circumstance that the middle class here as a whole was a new development. To unmask Jewish spa guests as parvenus who had no idea of how to behave only concealed one's own insecurity regarding this social phenomenon.

Juxtaposed to the two variants of anti-Semitism described—statements in private correspondence on the one hand, and the broad public sphere of the picture postcards on the other—there are neutral and favorable perceptions of the spa as a *Jewish place* in the eyes of the Others. For example, the caricatures that the Munich painter Fritz August von Kaulbach painted in the years 1909 to 1913 in Carlsbad portray the spa public and pious observant Jews in particular without a pejorative connotation like that in the picture postcards.[116] On the other hand, written reports express a sense of curiosity and interest in marked contrast with Fontane's one-sided commentaries. When the American writer Mark Twain visited Marienbad in 1891 he described the phenomenon of the Chassidic presence in town with sympathy and respect: "Uniforms are so scarce that we seem to be in a republic. Almost the only striking figure is the Polish Jew. He is very frequent. He is tall and of grave countenance and wears a coat that reaches to his ankle bones, and he has a little wee curl or two in front of each ear. He has a prosperous look, and seems to be as much respected as anybody."[117]

Georges Clemenceau, later the French prime minister, published a book entitled *Au pied du Sinaï* in 1898 while he was engaged in defending Alfred Dreyfus. Along with individual Jewish biographies, he describes travel impressions from Galicia and Carlsbad. The original deluxe limited edition was embellished with lithograph drawings by Henri Toulouse-Lautrec, who had completed these sketches working in the Jewish Tournelle quarter in Paris. With his nicely differentiated descriptions of Eastern European Jews, Clemenceau criticizes the anti-Semitism Jews were confronted with throughout much of Central and Western Europe: "Next to the Sprudel, the Polish Jew is undoubtedly the greatest curiosity in Carlsbad. The Occidental who comes here unprepared is startled by these strange figures."[118] Clemenceau appears largely to have dedicated his stay in Carlsbad to the Chassidim. He visited their restaurants and prayer rooms, observed their religious services, and described their festivals and dances. Although he also presented his readers with a stereotypical image, he nonetheless noticed that the Chassidic Jews in Carlsbad could not be classified in terms of a single type in respect to their appearance and social status.[119] Irrespective of that, he jokingly admitted that he did not share their taste in general, and particularly when it came to their sidelocks—though he recognized their usefulness: "As the curls have the quality of curling up in dry and straightening in damp weather, they present infallible means of anticipating atmospherical disturbances. As soon as I see them straighten, I take my umbrella and have never cause to regret it."[120]

Chapter 7

Encounters

In the Shadows and Hiding Places

And you, my most distinguished visitor to Marienbad,
how are you? No news as yet, content myself with what the
familiar walks tell me—today, for instance, the promenade
of sulks and secrets.
                        —Franz Kafka to Felice Bauer, 18 July 1916[1]

When Franz Kafka arrived at the beginning of July 1916 in Marienbad, Felice Bauer, who had just got there from Berlin, was already waiting for him at the station.[2] After he had decided in May to come for three weeks to Marienbad, he and Felice Bauer chose to spend part of that vacation time together. Two years earlier, with the outbreak of the Great War, they had broken off their engagement but since then had come closer again, primarily through their correspondence.

Though their time together began with many initial difficulties and ambivalences, these largely disappeared after a few days; that was quite different from their meeting in Carlsbad a year before.[3] Almost in euphoria, Kafka wrote to Max Brod that he was spending "such lovely and easy days, such as I never thought I would experience again. There were of course some darker intervals, but the loveliness and ease predominated."[4] The woman he knew almost exclusively from just a great distance by correspondence was now near to him: "I was only familiar with F. in letters, and as two human beings only for two days. It is certainly not so clear, doubts remain. But the look of her calmed eyes is beautiful, the opening up of womanly depth."[5] After a few days spent together, the two became so close once again that they unofficially renewed their engagement and planned to marry after the war's end.[6] Kafka wrote to his sister that he was feeling much better "than I could imagine, and maybe also better than F. thought."[7]

After some ten days, Felice Bauer left, and Kafka stayed on another eleven days alone in Marienbad, during which time his elated and happy mood continued. In his letters to Felice, who was back in Berlin, he wrote about quiet days he spent going on long walks, reading in the coffeehouse, meeting occasionally with acquaintances, and enjoying some good food. Even if his headaches and insomnia never disappeared completely, both improved. These letters, full of tender intimacy and humor, played with the romantic atmosphere that infused the locale after their time together there: "At the Dianahof I struck up a conversation with Liselotte, the tiny round-cheeked one, and yesterday, while fastening a rose to her breast, I gave her a lot of advice,"[8] he wrote to Felice shortly after her departure. About a week later he reacted to her response, which is not known but was probably tinged with a bit of jealousy: "And Liselotte? I have read that passage many times, and am still afraid of making a fool of myself if I were to take it seriously. Do you really think me capable of such bad taste as to—I won't say engage in—but boast about—that kind of thing? It is the plump little 3-year-old girl, who once made us laugh at the Dianahof. She was given a rose, and that's what it was all about. Dearest Felice!"[9]

Back in Prague, his liberated mood continued, and Kafka experienced, as he wrote, "the after-effects of that inner and outer calm which, with your help and that of the great forests, was granted to me in Marienbad."[10] Even years later he remembered the time as a happy moment in the generally complicated relationship with his fiancée: "It only remains to solve the riddle," he noted 1922 in his diary, "of why I had fourteen days of happiness in Marienbad."[11]

It is impossible to know what actually happened between Franz Kafka and Felice Bauer during these days. We can only comprehend the atmosphere surrounding a young, unmarried middle-class couple at the beginning of the last century as they came together again in Marienbad after months of physical separation. Because like other large spas, Marienbad not only offered a relaxed vacation atmosphere, it also constituted a protective sanctuary for young women and men who wanted to escape the narrowness of their bourgeois environment. Here they had the rare opportunity to step beyond the customarily strict social boundaries and to enjoy relatively great freedoms.[12] In the case of Franz and Felice, this freedom meant among other things two hotel rooms with a connecting door that was kept unlocked.[13]

In his memoirs, Stefan Zweig described the everyday experience of young

women and men of the prewar generation that he and Kafka belonged to, seeing the social situation as hypocritical, constricted, and lacking in freedom:

> For often when I converse with younger comrades of the post-war
> generation, I must convince them almost by force that our youth was
> by no means specially favored in comparison with their own. [. . .] We
> lived better and tasted more of the world, but the youth of today lives
> and experiences its own youth more consciously. When today I see
> young people [. . .] akin in all forms of healthy, carefree life without
> any inner or outer burden, then each time it seems as if not forty, but
> a thousand years stand between them and us who, in order to procure
> or to receive love, always had to seek shadows and hiding places.[14]

Youth was supervised with prudery and the permanent demand to preserve
decency; despite that, or perhaps precisely because of that, they were also
"a thousand times more erotically inclined," Zweig wrote.[15] The demands
placed on young adults within the middle class were high: young men were
only allowed to think of marriage after they had acquired "a social position"
for themselves, and then were usually between thirty and thirty-five years
old. And although the young women were younger when they married,
most generally between twenty and twenty-five, bourgeois society in this
way created a prolonged youth and a large number of young singles.[16] That
significantly lengthened the time period in which young men and women
had to seek out love in the shadows and in hiding places, with prostitutes
and paramours, in a "sticky, perfumed, sultry, unhealthy atmosphere. This
dishonest and unpsychological morality of secrecy and hiding hung over us
like a nightmare."[17]

A survey done around 1914 among young middle-class men and women
indicated that a large proportion of the male respondents had had sex with
prostitutes, servant girls, and waitresses before marriage, but also with
middle-class girls. A surprising finding was that also a bit more than half
the female respondents stated that they had had sexual relations before
their marriage, although almost exclusively with significantly older middle-
class men.[18] Even though doubts were mounting about old moral views in
the years before World War I, books on etiquette continued to defend this
existing social arrangement. They predicted the end of any erotic attraction
between the sexes should the customary regime of prudery be abandoned:
"The moment the woman is stripped of her characteristic attraction, when

there is no longer that tensely laden atmosphere and playful tone and heightened nervous tingle on both sides between men and women in the bright halls of houses and on the green lawns of the sports grounds—in that moment, society will have become, completely and totally, nothing more than a professional association."[19]

Hysteria, neurasthenia, and numerous other nervous disorders of the day, which inter alia were a product of these bourgeois conceptions of morality and strategies of repression, made spas into points of magnetic attraction for young people. Unlike today, *youth* in the spas around the turn of the century was not some abstract desire permeating the promenade air with its symbolic meaning: real young women and men constituted the largest group with spa society out on the promenades.[20] If they did not come for medical reasons, social occasions played a role, and often both one and the other. Intent on finding what guidebooks promised, they hoped to improve their social and professional position by a stay at the spa, and in the sensuous atmosphere of the locality to have fleeting encounters with the opposite sex or to meet potential future spouses. This is satirized in a short tale by Sholem Aleichem describing a train ride to Bohemia: "In the next car I found a huge woman from Ekatrineslav traveling with her engaged daughter. That is, a daughter who should have been engaged, who *wanted* to be engaged, for it was high time for her to be hitched. For that reason, she was taking the girl to Marienbad."[21] Days there were free from everyday obligations and could be dedicated to intensive social life in the spa with its large number of possibilities for encounter.[22] In the Carlsbad spa park, during excursions and evening parties, "though all boisterous excitement is tabooed by the medical authorities, who are here supreme, a vast amount of mild flirtation is carried on."[23] This free space for dalliance and undermining the moral codes of society spawned a young adult subculture.[24]

In particular, young middle-class women whose life often unfolded under permanent control enjoyed their relative freedom in the anonymity and simultaneous protectedness of large spas such as Marienbad and Carlsbad. In contrast with the male domain of the cities, the spa was considered a female space where life was more gentle, sensuous, and physical.[25] Franzensbad and other spas attracted so many women on the basis of their medical condition that they soon had the reputation of being spaces where women could be undisturbed and among themselves. And in actual fact, the number of female patients frequently traveling alone in several of such "women's spas" was so large that the protagonist of a popular novel, seeing the public on the promenades, wondered if the German empire had been built with the "blood and iron" of countless young women.[26]

Here self-confident, narcissistic young women, such as the writer Hermine Hanel, found an ideal platform for their own self-staging. The young Prague girl, her mother Jewish and her father a Catholic, found in Carlsbad at the turn of the century her long-desired entry into Bohemian high aristocracy:

> In June grandmama went to Carlsbad. The doctor had stressed that she must not be upset during the cure, but since she could not leave me alone, she took me along, to the detriment of her gallbladder problem. The poor woman was upset about her foolish granddaughter who, instead of choosing a husband among her young admirers, amused herself with older aristocrats. The governor of Bohemia, Count Franz Thun-Hohenstein, associated with me so much that the Polish Jews who stood in their long kaftans in front of the Kreuzbrunnen shook their sidecurls worryingly, and Frau Meier and Herr Vondraček feared for my innocence.[27]

The young woman had met the much older bon vivant fleetingly in Prague, but got to know him better for the first time in Carlsbad. As she writes in her mannered memoirs, they talked during those weeks mainly about a possible conversion to Catholicism, which the Count sought to persuade her to undertake.[28] Although she was not opposed to the idea, she decided after returning to Prague to wait before taking that serious step, since she felt herself to be a "citizen of the world."[29]

The eccentric Hermine Hanel does not exemplify young women of the prewar generation. In actual fact, encounters beyond social, cultural, and religious boundaries were as rare in spas as elsewhere, even if these transgressions were considered especially attractive. The prospect that young adults here had the possibility to ignore social boundaries and to redefine their biographies or parts of their identity was an image that the spa novels had created and cultivated. In these fictions, spas were depicted as sensual spaces of possibility for approaching others and for forging unusual ties and relationships.[30]

The topic of literary examination was often an eroticized atmosphere in the intimacy of the hotels or on the busy promenades.[31] It is no accident that the fateful meeting between Severin, the protagonist of Leopold von Sacher-

Masoch's scandalous novel *Venus in Furs*, and the title heroine Wanda takes place in a Central or Eastern European spa.[32] The literary hyperbole of the topics had its real basis in the numerous men and women who looked for relationships during their spa stay. Such a romantic relationship, Georg Simmel commented, "possesses the nuances of a fleeting dream that not only makes no commitments but is also attractive precisely because its brevity tempts one into the greatest intensity in exploiting and yielding to it."[33]

Middle-class men—spa guests, locals and residents from the surrounding villages—maintained affairs in Carlsbad, Marienbad, and Franzensbad with registered prostitutes, waitresses, domestic servants, or women of their own social class.[34] By contrast, for the many women traveling alone—an unusual and nonexistent social group elsewhere—the hotels engaged young men as *Eintänzer*, male dance escorts. Generally in their late twenties or early thirties, these "dime-a-dance men" looked after the often older women traveling alone, unaccompanied, who attended the afternoon dances and evening reunions. Intermingling among these *Eintänzer* at times were amateurs, teenagers from villages in the environs who needed some money and wanted to have some diversion at a dance, whereas their professional colleagues regarded the dances less romantically as means for their necessary income. Though some of them were gigolos, many did not overstep the realm of light conversation and dancing.[35] In addition, there are indications that spas were also popular rendezvous sites for homosexuals. References to this generally, as in Marienbad, can be found only in rumors and local narratives.[36]

The romantic image of the health spas was also substantially connected with their importance as marriage markets. Associated encounters occurred far less in the shadows and hiding places than in circles of acquaintances, friends, and relatives and left correspondingly numerous traces. The western Bohemian spas enjoyed a special role as a marriage market with the Jewish middle classes from Western and Eastern Europe, since it was a safe assumption that there were many Jewish male and female candidates on hand.[37]

Bourgeois Jewish circles tended to reflect the general attitudes of the middle class in their views of love and marriage: they preferred arranged marriages, which guaranteed financial security and also sustained existing systems of parental control and possibly even economic networks.[38] The premise of the arranged marriage changed in the course of the nineteenth century, and young women and men acquired a certain say in the choice of their future spouse. The turn of the century ultimately ushered in concessions to love as a basis for marriage, although this was often only lip service, and generally just meant that marriages were no longer arranged by newspaper ads or marriage brokers but rather through coincidental acquaintanceship and adroitly engineered encounters.[39] "If one refused to marry for money or good family, it became proverbial that one might be persuaded to go where money or good family could be predicted," comments Peter Gay.[40]

One of the most popular places to introduce people to one another was the carefully selected spa where there were not only many Jewish spa guests but also enough romantic spots suitable as the background for public yet intimate meetings.[41] Thus, many young Jewish men ventured off to the spas in order to go in search of suitable young ladies, along with a promising dowry, who were waiting there for them to arrive.[42] In order to control the market, there were marriage brokers who specialized in spas and their clientele. In return for a fraction of the dowry, they arranged, as clients desired, official meetings or clandestine accidental encounters. The *shadchan* or matchmaker took over the negotiations on the dowry, whose amount decided whether the lady in question could "afford" a merchant, doctor, lawyer, or an academic professional, the latter going with a high premium in the market.[43]

All these many and diverse romantic (or perhaps less romantic) encounters that played out or were staged in the eroticized ambient of the spa were brought together under a masterful literary lens in Sholem Aleichem's satirical novel *Marienbad*. He provides caricatures of the gushing interests of the spa guests by letting loose (on one another) a group of well-to-do, piously observant, love-crazy Warsaw Jews. In enamored *billet-doux* love notes, clandestine small cards from the adoring to the adored, and explanatory letters to their spouses back home, the author describes a narrow circle of acquaintances and neighbors who totally reorder their relations in the liberated atmosphere of Marienbad.

All the evil begins in the novel *Marienbad* when Shlomo Kurlander, a house owner now along in years, allows his second wife, the beautiful young Beltzi, to travel to Marienbad to take the cure. With her beauty and naivete, Beltzi brings spa society, or more precisely the circle of her Warsaw acquaintances, into a state of total confusion. Faithfully she reports to her husband back home in numerous letters about every flirt and encounter with charming young men. At the same time, Chaim Soroker, writing to his concerned friend at home, describes Marienbad as a place of medical asceticism, where the only pleasure is a game of cards: "In a word, it's hell, believe me."[44] While Soroker like all the others tries to get something going with Beltzi, the bon vivant Meyer Mariomchik from Odessa is at the same time on the erotic tail of Madam Sherentzis and Madam Pekelis, the wives of two strictly Orthodox Warsaw merchants, whom he addresses in the following words: "Do I deny that I have a wife? I only say that it doesn't keep me from being friendly with pretty, bright, educated ladies whenever possible. Accept the advice of a well-meaning friend and take advantage of your stay in Marienbad."[45] He tries to persuade the two pious ladies to go together on a jaunt by explaining to them that Marienbad can't be compared with the Warsaw Nalevkis: "A spa was meant for pleasure not for moralizing."[46] And indeed: "What would you say if you were to see our own pious women from Nalevkis, Madam Sherentzis and Madam Pekelis, strolling about, boldly and brazenly, with utter strangers, young men, and at night too?"[47]

In the novel, along with the married young women travelers coming unaccompanied, who once in Marienbad allowed themselves to have a playful flirtation, there are those who came with serious intentions: "Marienbad this season is full of wives. Everywhere you turn, wives—young wives, old wives, countless wives. Most of them are the ordinary sort from Bialystok, Kishinev, Yekaterinoslav, Kiev, Rostov and Odessa. Wherever they are from, they are here for the so-called 'cure.' But their main purpose is to corral husbands for their daughters, their ripe mam'selles."[48] Circling around these chaperones—"dressed in rich silks and satins," their necks bedecked with pearls, seeking to bring their daughters "to market," is an intent broker: "Buzzing around these mamas like a bee around honey, is this character with a top hat who is called Svirsky. This Svirsky is a marriage broker, but he calls himself an international matchmaker. He's Jewish but he refuses to speak Yiddish, only German."[49] The young men or, as the future mothers-in-law like to term them, the "merchandise" must be negotiated for with correspondingly high amounts for the dowry, and the going sum depends on what is on offer. Since this year there are relatively few young men from good families on hand, but a larger number of young ladies, their price is ever on the rise.[50] Ultimately it doesn't matter, because the seemingly interested men turn out to be married or soon travel on to other spas.

At the end of the summer, everyone leaves to head back to Warsaw. None are now on speaking terms with one another; instead there are threats of lawyers and divorces. And Sholem Aleichem's summertime romances in Marienbad have once again been duly weathered, as people return to the orderly, more bland, bourgeois everyday world.

Written shortly before the outbreak of World War I, Sholem Aleichem's *Marienbad* is not only a heightened literary portrayal of the eroticized atmosphere in the shadows and concealed corners of the spa. Rather, he discusses there the traditional Jewish moral codes as they shaped the Eastern European Jewish middle class down into the twentieth century, along with the secular ideals of Western Judaism and the increasingly disinhibited relations between the sexes in the spa. Both are subjected to criticism, the traditional Jewish way of arranging a relationship and the antiquated practice of *shiduch*, as well as the hasty discarding of traditions in favor of a supposedly liberated world of flirtation and fast affairs.

Among Zionists, Poets, and Friendly Exotics

[. . .] where those suffering from excessive sugar seek a cure
and go there to synagogue as they flock to the theater in
Vienna, because in Vienna they don't attend the synagogues
[. . .]

—*Der Israelit*, July 1910[51]

In August 1894, a committee was formed by rabbis who were in Marienbad at the time taking the waters. Among them were the rabbis of Prague, Budapest, Lemberg, Iglau, and Marienbad, who together organized a festive banquet to honor Hermann Adler, the chief rabbi of Great Britain and Ireland. The evening event took place on a Sabbath with a hundred invited guests and a subsequent formal dinner in the dining hall of the orthodox Hotel Walhalla. It was, as the *Israelitische Gemeindezeitung* reported, a resounding success: "It was a magnificent, uplifting event, where the feeling of solidarity and belonging among Jews from all lands and nations was concretely manifest."[52]

The fact that Jews changed from a minority to a majority in the western Bohemian spas during the summer was reason for Jewish communal representatives and spa guests to stage encounters designed to provoke and strengthen a sense of shared ethnicity. The program intended to link up in network fashion, via conventional processes of socialization, the large, heterogeneous, and only fleetingly connected summer Jewish Community. It sought to present the spas in this way as spaces of encounter extending over national, cultural, and social boundaries. The Jewish "lack of a nation" between the various national camps in the spa was to be transformed on a representative level into internationalism and cosmopolitanism, in short, into a positive quality in that specific counter-world matrix. Locals and spa guests worked together in trying to bring the different circles in the spa in closer contact with each other, relying for this largely on the potential communicative capacity of associations.

The religious, cultural, and social life of the spa towns profited in particular from the integrative personality of the veteran Carlsbad chief rabbi Ignaz Ziegler, whose work also impacted the Jewish Communities in Marienbad and Franzensbad. Ziegler had come to Carlsbad as a young rabbi in 1888 at the age of twenty-seven and remained *Gemeinde* rabbi for fifty years until he fled to Palestine. After initial enthusiasm for Orthodoxy in his younger years, he turned toward a Jewish liberalism that he implemented in such radical fashion in Carlsbad that despite his fame, he was denied posts including that of chief rabbi in Vienna and rabbi of the Prague Temple Association.[53] Ziegler was renowned as a preacher and was an attraction that drew Jewish visitors to Carlsbad. "Whenever Ziegler preached," recalled Friedrich Thieberger, "the main synagogue was crowded to capacity long beforehand. The content of his speeches became material for discussion among the spa guests, and Jews returning home reported in detail on his sermons." Ziegler, who originally had wanted to become a stage actor, was reportedly well aware of his rhetorical abilities as a preacher and had made the pulpit his stage.[54] In an autobiographical sketch he wrote in his final years of life, he describes his success as a pulpit orator: "Jews and Christians by the hundreds poured into my synagogue to hear the sermon. High-ranking spiritual leaders often came and were pleased to take the seat offered to them."[55] In Orthodox circles, Ziegler was just as controversial because of his liberal religious views as he was because of his popularity, which supposedly drew people to the Carlsbad Temple who back home would not set foot in a house of prayer. The Mainz paper *Der Israelit* mocked him as the "Carlsbad prophet," after he had given lectures to large audiences in Vienna and other cities.[56] In the spa town, however, his integrative abilities and the open, almost folkloristic Judaism that he taught and embodied were much appreciated. The lively Jewish organizational activity in Carlsbad was also largely due to his dedicated engagement in Zionist and philanthropic organizations.[57]

In spa papers and Jewish newspapers, cultural and political events were announced and promoted, while networking in the Orthodox and Chassidic spaces followed other internal structures. Exclusive associations like the B'nai B'rith Lodge brought together local and outside members, while other organizations, in the main Zionist in orientation, worked in a more integrative way and with a broad impact in the public sphere.[58] Around the turn of the century, local Zionists in Carlsbad, in cooperation with spa guests, founded several associations or clubs, including the association *Emunah*, the *Tischgesellschaft Zion*, the *Einzelverein Zion*, and the *Jüdisch-Akademischer Klub*. In addition, they planned to establish a reading room as a Zionist center for the seasonal summer community. Along with Zionist conventions, Maccabee festivals, Herzl commemorative celebrations, and students' ceremonial drinking sessions, during the season there were well-attended lectures, entertainment, and literary evenings every week, where famous spa guests were often at the center of attention.[59] Already then, public Zionist events were considered an established part of the social and cultural life in Carlsbad and Marienbad.[60] As *Die Welt* reported, more than 150 guests were in attendance at the first Zionist event of the summer calendar 1902 in Carlsbad.[61] When the Marienbad Zionists that same season organized a lecture evening with international speakers in the large hall of Hotel Walhalla, 700 persons attended, while another 300 had to be sent home because seating capacity had been exceeded.[62]

Marienbad in particular had developed around the turn of the century into a notable meeting place for representatives of the European *Haskalah* and Zionism. In the footsteps of the great Russian writers Gogol, Turgenev, and Goncharov, Eastern European Jewish poets such as Judah Leib Gordon had discovered the spa in the 1870s. Since the beginning of the new century, one could now expect to encounter many of Gordon's colleagues on the summer promenades, among them Chaim Nachman Bialik, David Frischmann, Sholem Aleichem, Reuben Brainin, Shai Ish Hurwitz, and lesser-known writers.[63] They organized public lecture evenings when well-known Zionists were present in the spa, such as Chaim Weizmann, Yosef Klausner, or Nahum Sokolow, and discussed the "problem of Hebrew culture," in Hebrew and in the well-attended spa hall.[64] Right after the stay at the spa they then traveled together to the Zionist congresses in Basle, the Hague, or Hamburg, initially held every year and then bi-annually. This tradition of coming to Marienbad or Carlsbad unofficially as a kind of prelude—or finale—to the Zionist Congress remained alive down into the 1930s.[65] An active Zionist life developed even in the small and quiet spa of Franzensbad, with support from associations in Eger.[66] The exterritorial and seemingly depoliticized space of the spa was suitable in particular to taking part in a non-committal fashion in events and social activities. In addition, these activities profited from the fact that evenings in the western Bohemian spas were relatively quiet and boring, compared with other spas.

Figure 12. Meeting of the Histadrut Ivrit at the Café Schoenbrunn, Carlsbad, 1910. Front row, third from the right, is the Hebrew essayist and editor Shai Ish Hurwitz; beside him is the publisher and politician Shoshana Persitz (née Zlatopolski); standing behind her (third from the right) is her father, the Zionist and philanthropist Hillel Zlatopolski; and next to him (standing fourth from the right) is Reuben Brainin. Central Zionist Archives, Jerusalem. CZA 1024499.

A declared aim of the Zionist work in associations in the western Bohemian spas was to dissolve the polarization between Western European and Eastern European cultures and to address persons interested in Zionism from both camps. Periodicals such as *Selbstwehr* and *Ost und West,* established around 1900 and soon boasting a growing readership, prepared the ground for a certain curiosity and openness.[67] They sought to propagate the idea of cultural pluralism within European Jewry among their German-speaking readership, to inscribe old stereotypes with new meanings, and to rediscover in positive ways Eastern European Jewish culture.[68] Against this backdrop, Zionist associations in Carlsbad, Marienbad, and Franzensbad tried, on the one hand, to win over the Western and Eastern European middle classes as a public, and on the other to include protagonists of Eastern European culture in presentations and events or to make them their centerpiece.

"Morris Rosenfeld in Carlsbad. [. . .] Due to a physical malady, the singer of the ghetto was constrained on his doctor's orders to leave his desk in order to recuperate and regain his health at the Sprudel in Carlsbad," reported the Carlsbad correspondent of the *Selbstwehr* when Rosenfeld was a spa guest there in 1908.[69] The Yiddish poet from Russia was already living in New York at that point, and, after years of severe illness, his visit to Carlsbad was not only for reasons of health. He combined his stay at the spa with a reading tour across Europe, in the hope of increasing his popularity and thus improving his economic situation. In Carlsbad itself, Rabbi Ziegler arranged in conjunction with the Jewish Academic Club an evening of readings in the *Großes Kurhaus*. After Rosenfeld had read his poems in the Yiddish original, a German translation followed, though prudently only of two poems. "The evening brought the poet ample honors. And because as a result many Western European Jews became acquainted with modern Jewish literature at the same time in its greatest representative, there is no doubt that many a prejudice about Jewish language and culture was dispelled," commented the *Selbstwehr* after the well-attended event.[70]

Eastern European Jewish evenings were frequently organized in Carlsbad and Marienbad and enjoyed great popularity. Accompanied by song and music, there were poetry readings, by writers whom the spa guests knew not only from their books but also from the promenades: along with Morris Rosenfeld, that included inter alia Yitzchak Leib Peretz and Sholem Aleichem.[71] The educational intention of these evening get-togethers was articulated in subsequent reports in the paper that described the events not just as entertaining and "very enjoyable" but noting that they had also conveyed "positive values of Judaism" to the audience.[72] The cultural provisioning of entertainment in Yiddish also encompassed guest performances by Jewish theater groups from Germany and Eastern Europe, such as the troupe of Yitzchak Löwy.[73] The Warsaw Yiddish actor had likely been brought into contact with the Carlsbad Zionist group through the mediation of his friend Franz Kafka, whom Yitzchak had met during a guest performance in Prague, and he was repeatedly invited to perform in Carlsbad.[74]

At the beginning of the new century, Martin Buber had published the first three volumes of his Chassidic legends, a thoroughly idealized and romanticized reworking of the original Yiddish texts. Through this work, Buber popularized a new, positive albeit stereotypical image of Eastern European Jewry among many readers. As an authentic Other, this new image of Eastern European Jewry irradiated a revitalizing and emotionalizing power that impacted on increasingly assimilated and acculturated Western European Jews.[75] Even if this remained in the realm of phantasmagoria for most until the Great War blurred the boundaries between East and West, the search for "Jewish Jews" had started already now.[76] If one wished to meet self-confident Eastern European Jews in an environment they were familiar and comfortable with in the West, and possibly to even speak with a rebbe, then a trip to the western Bohemian spas was a readily obvious option. The growing interest in the Eastern European Jewish oligarchy, which spent part of every summer here, began to attract journalists such as the editor of the *Vossische Zeitung,* who in the summer of 1909 traveled to Carlsbad in order to meet the "miracle rabbi of Sadagora." Surprised, the journalist found no confirmation of his preconceived image of Eastern European Jewish poverty. He reported that the rebbe was quartered in an elegant hotel and that his followers made a "quite cultivated impression." The real-life encounter with the rebbe likewise was not in keeping with the image of a "miracle rabbi" in Germany at the turn of the century:

> The first impression we had was disappointing, since instead of a dignified, white-bearded patriarch as we had expected, we encountered a young man in his 30s, with a beautiful, Christ-like physiognomy, a somewhat tired facial expression, and a skin color that was strikingly white and like a young girl's. In a silk caftan and velvet cap, he sat enthroned upon the sofa, smoking, and invited us with a gracious gesture of his hand to be seated before him.[77]

After a short and extremely difficult talk with the rebbe, since neither seemed to speak the language of the other, a Chassid "who appeared to be a kind of senior aide or general secretary" and who had a sufficient knowledge of German, informed the journalist about Chassidic society. He was interested to hear that the rebbe neither headed a Community nor did he have an official government post; rather, he had inherited his position. The young rebbe was very friendly toward the journalist despite their difficulties in communicating, and practiced a "generous and truly Oriental hospitality."[78] If on the spa promenades they had only been exotics out for a stroll, the Eastern European Jewish majesties appeared in the hands of journalists and on closer acquaintance to be transformed into an Oriental object of art which at the time was reconstructed anew again and again.[79]

The search for a common basis for differing Jewish cultures seized the interest in the western Bohemian spas relatively early on and with some degree of intensity. The fact that the summertime enclaves were especially suited to experiment with a closer and more intimate nearness between people lay in their distinctive culture of sociability. On the one hand, it was the heterogeneity of the different groups that converged in a compacted space, and on the other it was the nature of their contact, which was temporary and in keeping with the vacation situation, very laidback and easygoing.

In Other Places

> Yesterday, Max's lecture, "Religion and Nation." Talmud
> citations. Eastern Jews. The girl from Lemberg. The
> Western Jew who has become assimilated to the Hasidim,
> the plug of cotton in his ear. Steidler, a Socialist, long,
> shining, neatly cut hair. The delight with which the Eastern
> European Jewesses take sides. The group of Eastern Jews
> beside the stove. Goetzl, in a caftan, the matter-of-fact
> Jewish life. My confusion.
> —Franz Kafka, *Diaries*, 25 March 1915[80]

During the summer of 1916, amid the backdrop of the Great War, Stefan Zweig traveled to St. Moritz and described his stay there in bitter terms as a "visit among the carefree, the insouciant, this community of our world soon to be extinct."[81] What he found in the spa was something he saw as the dwindling remainder of a formerly large community, of the multilingual, pleasure-seeking, and carefree privileged rich. Now homeless, they had found here a final space of retreat where they might continue living as was their wont—untouched by the worries and ravages of the war and "somehow too loud, too boisterous, too bold; as if one didn't sense the enormous contrast, in spite of which all this was happening."[82] They struck him as debonair decadents, people who even in a world war don't allow themselves to be distracted from their customary pleasures and amusements: "Oh, they're all there, the ones we know from Vichy and Oostende and Carlsbad. And we are already familiar with all these inanities, though one doesn't understand why these individuals are not as yet bored by all this: the Tango Teas and the *soirées dansantes*, the masked balls, tennis matches, the illusionist."[83] Despite his moralizing indignation, the demonstrative character of the idyllic prewar scene was unsettling for Zweig, it made him less secure in his judgment: "And the heart, the earthy heart, it falters. It longs for joy for all the world and is shamed of each joy it might call its own. It hates unconcern, and also despises its own bitterness, its aimless mourning, of no use to anyone."[84]

While the carefree were dancing at their "masquerade of the nations"[85] in the Swiss Alps, what was happening back in Carlsbad? Here too the continuity of the protected spa everyday life was largely maintained, and probably was likewise at risk of sinking into a kind of insouciant decadence. At the same time, the political situation was different, the war in many ways perceptible: "I am *writing from an idyll* which we, my wife and I, have defiantly and stubbornly created for ourselves, but which is continually being interrupted by the demands of the times," Sigmund Freud wrote on 30 July 1915 from Carlsbad to Lou Andreas-Salomé.[86] One year had passed since the assassination attempt on the heir to the throne Franz Ferdinand, and the Marienbad doctor Max Porges recalled the events of the summer of 1914, writing in the *Zeitschrift für Balneologie*: "The news likewise struck like a bombshell in the peaceful mix of peoples in our spa, and yet the public behaved strikingly quiet and composed: no outward signs of anxiety about one's personal future and safety. French, English, Russians—none thought of leaving, all faithfully resolute in pursuit of their cure."[87] During the ultimatum, none departed, not even the politicians who were at the spa. Only after the declaration of war had made many of them "hostile aliens" on Austrian soil did people start flocking to the train station. Unlike in the Silesian spas, where Polish and Russian spa guests were taken into custody and interned by the German authorities, the business-minded Carlsbad locals encouraged their guests to stay on until the end of their cure. But none had any interest in that.[88] Along with spa guests from the Entente countries, the men fit for military service from the axis powers also departed. Finally, when persons from the areas of combat stopped coming, the number of visitors plummeted to a crisis low never before experienced in the spas.[89]

Many years earlier, the Marienbad physician Enoch Heinrich Kisch had launched an initiative aimed at providing the spas during wartime with a neutral status in order to utilize their medical capacities more efficiently.[90] After this effort went nowhere, once the Great War broke out the idea was resurrected and battlefield hospitals were set up in all three localities. In

Marienbad, efforts were made right after the beginning of the war to establish ten field stations under the direction of local physicians, with a total capacity of 600 beds. In return the military administration guaranteed it would not send patients with infectious diseases into the area. Since the field stations were not located in spa houses or hotels, the Marienbad local population assumed that spa activities would be somewhat curtailed in the upcoming summer season, but would be able to take their accustomed course largely undisturbed, which indeed was the case.[91]

Yet not long thereafter, other unforeseen changes entered the picture: on 22 November 1914, the front page of the *Karlsbader Zeitung* announced, with anger and dismay, the arrival of war refugees from Galicia.[92] The first refugees had already arrived some time before in Carlsbad and had been given a warm welcome by the owners of the empty hotels, because in contrast with those now announced these refugees were all well to do. According to a local paper, the municipality learned only two weeks before about the impending arrival of the impoverished and needy Galician refugees and tried at the last minute to prevent them from coming.[93] When that failed and they were sent to Carlsbad, the authorities were caught unprepared. They decided to house the refugees in inadequate mass quarters: in basements and the empty rooms of the racetrack, without beds, bathing facilities, or heating. Although the population looked after food and clothing for the refugees, very few hoteliers took them into their properties. In January 1915, the *Jüdische Volksstimme* was indignant: "The city of Carlsbad, where now many thousands of bright rooms with beds and bathtubs stand empty, should remind itself of its time-honored calling: to properly accommodate strangers, even if by chance they happen to be displaced, impoverished, melancholy Galicians!"[94]

Residents of the combat areas in Galicia and the Bukovina had been displaced and in flight since September 1914. Among them was a large proportion of the Jewish population who were more fearful than others of a Russian occupation. Once they arrived in Austria, the majority of those refugees dependent on state welfare were distributed to provisional collection camps and smaller towns and villages in Bohemia, Moravia, and Upper and Lower Austria.[95] In this way, a large number of Jewish and other refugees were sent to Carlsbad, Marienbad, and Franzensbad, where there the necessary infrastructure for Orthodox Jews was in place, and the Jewish Communities looked after the new arrivals.[96] According to unofficial statistics of the Jewish Communities in Prague, at the beginning of 1915 the Jewish refugees in

Carlsbad numbered already 3,654, and another 1,342 were housed in Marien-bad. Yet many more were still to come.[97]

Although in many localities the presence of Jewish refugees had exacer-bated anti-Semitism, to the dismay of the local Jews, that problem did not play a large role in the western Bohemian spas, given the insecure and iso-lated position of the Jewish Community in any case.[98] In Carlsbad, Jewish and non-Jewish residents even cooperated to put on an evening of entertain-ment in the vaudeville theater *Orpheum* for the benefit of the soldiers at the front and the refugees in town. The event proved a success: it had such a uniting and integrative character that the Carlsbad Jewish Community for-mulated cautious hopes for better times to come.[99]

During the first winter of the war, middle-class women and girls took care of 500 troops in Franzensbad, where they were receiving basic treatment for "battlefield neurosis, rheumatism, and gout" at the Medical-Mechanical Institute and also taking mineral and mud baths before being dispatched back to the front.[100] Armin Wilkowitsch, cantor in Eger, reported in the *Oes-terreichische Wochenschrift* about the situation in the small spa:

> The landscape painter usually depicts the scene of "Franzensbad in winter" as a "Blessed Isle," seemingly peaceful and quiet, with scarcely a soul visible on the white broad avenues. However, in the first winter of the war 1914/1915, the large town park shimmered in a motley array: Austro-Hungarian and German troops in various uniforms, dragging themselves on their crutches, or pushed about in wheelchairs. [. . .] Yet interwoven with these many colors is the black of the caftan, since some 1,200 war refugees have been displaced to the Franzensbad par-ish where they are recipients of the town's hospitality.[101]

Together with the Jewish Community, the municipality looked after supplies and accommodation for the refugees, while the local population assisted by do-nating clothing and food. In the meantime, the spa made preparations for the return of the summer guests in the 1915 season, many of whom had announced their intention to come despite the war. The spa activities were to go ahead nor-mally, even if with fewer visitors, while some of the refugees and soldiers stayed on in the city and others were replaced by new arrivals. Since here too field hospitals and refugee quarters were not located in the spa houses, there would be no direct interference. Only the Jewish Hospital was to be put exclusively at the disposal of Jewish soldiers during the summer of the war.[102]

In Marienbad, already in October 1914, members of the Jewish Community had set up an aid committee for refugees from Galicia and the Bukovina. When in November 1914 refugees of various religions and nations arrived, they were immediately housed in private homes in the Marienbad district and provided with basic necessities. Along with a separate primary school for the children, a prayer house and a Talmud Torah school were set up.[103] If refugees were returned to combat areas taken back from the enemy, other refugees arrived immediately in their place, and with time their infrastructure was expanded by a canteen, an outpatient clinic, and a home for the sick and childbearing women.[104] Members of the Jewish community founded a recreation home for Jewish war orphans in a Marienbad spa house, under the medical supervision of Enoch Heinrich Kisch, now age seventy-five.[105] A sewing and knitting school was set up for the women and girls where they made socks and caps for the soldiers in the field.[106]

A Marienbad banker by the name of Buxbaum directed the committee on whose initiative all these facilities were established. He had opened an administrative office that all refugees could turn to if they needed a place to stay, basic necessities, or spa medical therapy.[107] The work of the committee, as stated at a meeting in the kosher Hotel National, was mainly financed by the *Israelitische Allianz zu Wien* (Jewish Alliance Vienna), but it also received state funding, donations from spa guests, and members of the Jewish Community, as well as the German Orthodox organization *Agudas Jisroel*.[108]

When Franz Kafka and Felice Bauer stayed in Marienbad in the summer of 1916, a relatively pleasant and undisturbed spa life was still possible, now as before, and with a doctor's prescription even white bread was available instead of the customary "war bread." Nonetheless, the presence of the war was very perceptible:[109] injured soldiers were a common sight in the bathhouses and around the mineral springs, and in the evening they would sing patriotic songs on the promenades.[110] Numerous refugees were staying in the spa district. Although the women were hardly distinguishable from locals by their clothing, since the committee had provided for them quite well, the men in their caftans naturally struck the eye. However, they differed also for other reasons from the Marienbad local citizenry and especially from the spa guests, as described by the journalist and author Ida Barber in an August 1916 report for the *Jüdische Volksstimme*: "You see them, the demoralized, driven from their homes and farms, here among the Marienbad spa guests. The latter, on the sunny side of life, know nothing of distress and deprivation. [. . .] In the grief-lined faces of these pour souls, stooped as they creep along the pathways, we can read the tale of their suffering, more than a human can bear."[111] During this time, as in all the summers of the war, the buoyant mood on the promenades was tinged with sadness.

At some point during their days together in the spa in the summer of 1916, the conversation between Franz Kafka and Felice Bauer turned to the Berlin Jewish People's Home (*Jüdisches Volksheim*). The idea arose in Marienbad that alongside her professional work in Berlin, Felice would like to look after refugee children. The Jewish People's Home had been opened just two months before, on 18 May 1916. Along with the main initiator Siegfried Lehmann, a Berlin cultural Zionist, its promoters included Martin Buber, Gustav Landauer, Chaim Arlosoroff, and Max Brod.[112] Located in the Scheunenviertel in Berlin, the home was to assist the needs of the many refugees then resident in Berlin. The *Volksheim* conception was not one-sided: along with welfare and education for the refugees and their children, it also placed emphasis on learning from one another. As Landauer had declared at the opening, the idea was to create a space for "encounters and ties between East European and West European Jewries."[113] In this conception, the initiators of the *Volksheim* distanced themselves from the educational tendencies of the general social work with refugees.[114]

After Felice had left, Franz Kafka wrote to Max Brod and asked him to send her a flyer of the *Volksheim*: "We talked about it and she wanted very much to have it."[115] All the letters he wrote her in the following days from Marienbad now ended with a question about the Jewish People's Home.[116] At the end of July, he recommended to her very emphatically that she should not miss this opportunity:

> With the exception of walking and gymnastics, there is no better way of spending the little free time you have than there; it is a hundred times more important than the theater, than Klabund, Gerson, or whoever else there may be. Besides, it is one of the most self-interested of occupations. One is not helping, but seeking help; more honey can be gathered from these exertions than from all the flowers in all the Marienbad woods.[117]

Thus, Felice decided in August to apply to Lehmann for a volunteer job, in this way pleasing Kafka, who continued to encourage her. In September, he wrote: "That's why I was so pleased in Marienbad when, without my having expected or intended it, you tackled the idea of the Home quite independently and very well, and now intend to let it lead you on."[118] Soon after she started to teach literature to a group of girls in the Home. To give her moral support, Franz wrote her letters replete with motivating questions, references to literature, and also sent packages of books containing the anthologies of Sholem Asch and Yitzchak Leib Peretz.[119]

In thinking about the *Volksheim*, many questions arose for Kafka about Jewish identity, Eastern or Western European. He feared that the helpers could probably do nothing but try to align "the wards—at best respecting their individual characters," with their own attitudes toward living and their own mode of life. Despite caution and reserve, the wards would be adapted to the helpers and their spirit of life: "One will try to raise them to the standard of the contemporary, educated, West European Jew, Berlin version," though in his view, "with that, not much would be achieved."[120] In his reflections, he concluded that actually it was not the Eastern European Jews who needed guidance and education, but rather those "educated Western European Jews" who served as helpers at the Home. He went on: "If, for instance, I had to choose between the Berlin Home and another where the pupils were the Berlin helpers (Dearest, even with you among them, and with me, no doubt, at the head), and the helpers simple East European Jews from Kolomyja or Stanislawow, I would give unconditional preference to the latter Home—with a great sigh of relief and without a moment's hesitation."[121]

Since the time he had made the acquaintance of the actor Yitzchak Löwy during his guest performance in Prague five years earlier, Kafka began to interest himself more deeply in and reflect upon Eastern European Jewish cultures. In wartime, there were Jewish refugees from Galicia and the Bukovina on the streets in Prague as well, and he noted these observations in his diaries.[122] Together with Max Brod, in September 1915 he visited the Grodecker Rebbe, who had fled with his followers to Prague and was now housed in a humble apartment in Prague-Žižkov, where he held court.[123] On the occasion of this visit, which left a powerful impression on Kafka, it was likely that he met Jiři Langer.[124] Langer, eleven years younger than Kafka and who later gave him Hebrew lessons as well as to Max Brod and Felix Weltsch, was to exercise a powerful influence on the young generation of Prague Jews.[125]

Jiři or Georg Mordechai Zev Langer, son of a Prague liquor dealer, had dropped out of high school at age nineteen in the summer of 1913 in order to travel to Belz in Galicia. He lived there for half a year at the court of the Belzer Rebbe, until the difficult round of everyday life among the Chassidim became too burdensome for him and he returned to Prague, exhausted and emaciated.[126] Langer's appearance upon returning to Prague alarmed his family—the youngest son had within a few months become in effect a barely recognizable stranger. As his brother František wrote, he not only dressed like a Chassid in caftan and *shtreymel*, with beard and *peyes*, but also had adopted the fast-paced gait of young Chassidim and ate nothing but bread and onions: "My brother had not come back from Belz, home to civilization. He had brought Belz with him."[127] In the bourgeois Vinohrady quarter where the family lived, Jiři Langer appeared as an exotic, a person who was an embarrassment for his parents. While one could see large numbers of Chassidim before the war in Carlsbad and Marienbad, in Prague it was extremely rare to encounter them, and thus "the appearance of a solitary Polish Jew on the streets of Vinohrady in 1913, belonging to a well-known Vinohrady family, positively called out" for much attention.[128] The family suffered from this change in their son, and their attitude to Jiři "seemed to us at the time to resemble the situation in Kafka's novel *Die Verwandlung*," František Langer commented.[129]

Jiři Langer soon left Prague again, since he too was suffering because of his middle-class family and their indifference to religion. He stayed in Belz until the war broke out and the rebbe fled with his court to Hungary, while he himself was drafted in Prague into the Austrian army. His strict religious Orthodoxy and refusal to fight on the Sabbath landed him in a military jail, from where with the help of his brother he was released on the grounds of "mental confusion" and discharged from the military. At this time he met Kafka, who began to interest himself not only in Jiři Langer's metamorphosis, but also in Chassidism.[130]

In 1916, Langer joined the Belzer Rebbe for the third and last time when the latter was still living in Újfehértó in Hungarian war exile. During this period, Langer, Kafka, and the rebbe met, after the rebbe had earlier decided to take the waters during the summer. Years later, after he had finally left the Chassidim, Langer recalled this journey in an autobiographical text:

> The saint of Belz has fallen ill. After a great deal of persuasion, he has decided to visit Marienbad. We are carrying him there along the paths through the forests. At other times he is separated from us by his secretaries and servants, as God is separated from our souls by myriads of spheres and worlds. But here among the forest trees we can all approach him. Although he is seriously ill, he talks cheerfully

to everybody. We are conscious that his are no ordinary words even when he is talking about things that appear to be everyday matters. All his words, however small, are to be understood metaphorically. The whole time his thoughts are concentrated exclusively on supernatural matters. [. . .] When he is not speaking to anyone, he repeats the Talmud to himself, which he naturally knows by heart in its entirety—all thirty-six tractates in their twelve mighty volumes! Once, as we were walking through the forest, he remarked: "If I didn't have you, I would pray with these trees here."[131]

Never before and never again did Langer experience such a closeness to the rebbe, who was one of the most powerful Chassidic leaders of his day. Issachar Dov Rokeach, the third Belzer Rebbe, caused a great stir wherever he went in Eastern Europe. His trips to Marienbad, which brought him regularly to the West, also made him an exotic famous personage in the town.[132]

On 20 July 1916, Julius Elias reported from Marienbad for the *Berliner Tagblatt*:

The center of great interest, however, is a strange foreigner who is known in popular parlance only as the Miracle Rabbi of Belz: a, huge, strong, remarkable man, with a fabulous beard and mysterious eyes. He is like a prince among his blood relatives. This magus from Galician lands is said to own extensive rich tracts of land in his homeland. And it is not only his power of word and his erudition that is said to contribute to his fame, but also the suggestive way in which he treats the souls of human beings. He is here with a large following of family members and devotees, and has rented 21 rooms in a hotel. [. . .] Here he is sought out and visited by all sorts of ecstatics and emotionally ill persons: his "miracles," however, do not consist of visions, for example, of prophecies, prayer mysticism, or regulations for lay medicine—but rather his "advice." The rabbi is a man of knowledge and great gifts. He knows the people and speaks; his words come forth from a soul full of God, and have an immediate effect on the mental constitution of those who seek his wisdom with their heart.[133]

The presence of Issachar Rokeach generated particular attention and enthusiasm among one group in Marienbad: the refugees. They respected his authority and sought his counsel and advice. During her stay in Marienbad,

Ida Barber observed the rebbe and the refugees: "'Wandering! Wandering!' says an old man to me (dressed in a traditional Jewish costume, the large sable *shtreymel* on his white head, looking like a genuine patriarch), 'it is Israel's fate.' They call him the Great Rabbi of Belz, listen attentively to his every word, wherever he appears, and like him bear their destiny with dignity, the unhappy descendants of Ahasverus."[134]

About this time Felice Bauer had returned to Berlin, leaving Kafka alone in Marienbad. Kafka, who spent the days walking in the woods and reading in coffeehouses, received some news from Max Brod a bit later: the Belzer Rebbe and Jiří Langer were staying in Marienbad.[135] On one of the following evenings, Kafka went out looking for Langer and, as he wrote to Felice, for the "most distinguished visitor to Marienbad, a man in whom so many place their trust."[136]

That same night he began a long letter to Max Brod to tell him the details of the evening's events. "I shall only describe the externals, since I cannot speak of more than I could see. But all one actually sees is the most minute details; and this is significant in my opinion," he began. "It testifies to sincerity, even to the worst idiot. Where truth is, all one can see with the naked eye is such minute details."[137] Searching for Langer, he wandered into the Marienbad Judengasse, where he lost his way among densely built hotels and restaurants with names all sounding very similar. He inquired in the most humble guesthouses for Langer, but no one knew him anywhere. "After a moment, though, a girl remembered some young people who lived in the attic. If I were looking for the son of the Prague brandy dealer, I might find him there."[138]

From Langer Kafka learned that the rebbe went out in a carriage every evening at about 7:30 or 8:00. "He drives slowly toward the forest, some of his entourage following along on foot. Once in the woods he stops at a more or less predetermined spot and walks here and there along the forest paths with his entourage until nightfall. He returns home in time for prayers, at about ten."[139] Together with Langer Kafka stood waiting at 7:30 at the entrance to the Hotel National, the most elegant hotel on the Judengasse. To escape from the rain, they were just about to enter the hotel vestibule when suddenly Langer jumped back to one side:

The rabbi is coming. No one must ever stand in front of him, there must always be a free passage before him, which is not easy to provide, since he often suddenly turns around and in the throng it is not

Figure 13. The Belzer Rebbe on a stroll in Marienbad in the early 1920s.
Courtesy of Richard Svandrlik, Nuremberg.

easy to take evasive action speedily. [...] This custom makes everything very solemn, the rabbi literally having the responsibility—
without leading the way, since there are people to the right and to the
left of him—of setting the pace for everyone. The group is continually
reshaping itself so the rabbi's view will not be blocked.[140]

On this evening, the rebbe decided not to go to the forest but instead to take
a walk through the town. Because there was a light shower he replaced his
silver cane with an umbrella, and the walk commenced. Since Kafka was in
Langer's company, he followed the walk in the group of the devotees and very
close to the rebbe. During the slow pace, he not only had an opportunity to
ask Langer for explanations, but also was able to observe the rebbe quietly,
taking in every detail:

He is of medium height and rather broad of beam, though not slug-
gish in his movements. Long white beard, unusually long sidelocks.
[...] One eye is blind and blank. His mouth is twisted awry, which
gives him a look at once ironic and friendly. He wears a silk caftan
which is open in front; a broad belt about his waist; a tall fur hat,

which is the most striking thing about him; white stockings; and, according to L., white trousers.[141]

The appearance of the old man made as powerful an impression on the young writer as the enthusiastic gleam in the eyes of the Chassidim:

> He looks like the Sultan in a Doré illustration of the Münchhausen stories which I often looked at in my childhood. But not like someone masquerading as the Sultan, really the Sultan. And not only Sultan but also father, grammar-school teacher, gymnasium professor, etc. The sight of his back, the sight of his hand as it rests on his waist, the sight of his broad back as he turns—it all inspires confidence. I can detect this peaceful, happy confidence in the eyes of everyone in the group.[142]

The group consisted of about ten Chassidim, who were walking next to and behind the rebbe. One carried his silver cane, another a chair he might sit on, a third the cloth to wipe the chair dry, a fourth a bottle of mineral water, and a fifth the glass from which the rebbe would drink. In the rebbe's retinue were also four *gabba'im* or secretaries, and, as Langer explained, they were not good people. One couldn't, however, reproach them for that, Kafka commented, because "people cannot bear the continual presence of the rabbi without suffering damage. It is the contradiction between the deeper meaning and the unrelenting commonplaceness that an ordinary head cannot sustain."[143]

The group proceeded very slowly through the spa park and the streets of the town, since the rebbe was frail and in addition wished to see and admire everything—"but especially the buildings, the most obscure trivialities interest him."[144] He was particularly charmed by the New Bathhouse, commenting and asking about every architectural and technical detail of the huge neo-Renaissance building embellished with columns. He could not take his eyes off the steam pipes that went all around the building and led to the baths. The rain gutters also interested him, and he asked for an explanation about the purpose of the whole apparatus, while touching the pipe, "delighted at the water's thumping inside." Repeatedly he said, with "that characteristic East European Jewish wonderment: 'A handsome building.'"[145]

After two and a half hours, during which it had not stopped raining, the strollers reached the Hotel National once again and hurried to the evening prayers, while Kafka returned to his hotel to write to Max Brod. He summed up the talk of the rabbi as he walked through the town:

> All in all, what comes from him are the inconsequential comments and questions of itinerant royalty, perhaps somewhat more childish and more joyous. At any rate they reduce all thinking on the part of his escort to the same level. Langer tries to find or thinks he finds a deeper meaning in all this; I think that the deeper meaning is that there is none and in my opinion this is quite enough. It is absolutely a case of divine right, without the absurdity that an inadequate basis would give to it.[146]

The next day he continued the letter, the report reaching almost seven pages, but suddenly in the middle Kafka stopped.[147] That same evening found him wandering again through Marienbad among the devotees of the Belzer Rebbe.

Compared with his visit to the Grodecker Rebbe in Prague a year earlier, the strolls in Marienbad had been far more relaxed and offered Kafka greater opportunity to observe: although he was in the group's midst, he was not a part of it. Old images of Eastern European Jewry merged together with new ones in his mind, and in the end the image of the rebbe that remained was a positive jumble of childlike innocence, fatherliness, intensity, and various surface impressions.[148] On one of those days he wrote almost enthusiastically to Felix Weltsch, who was taking the cure in Carlsbad: "Yes, Langer is here, since at the moment Marienbad is the center of the Jewish world, for the Rabbi of Belz is here. I have twice joined his retinue for evening walks. He alone would justify the trip from Karlsbad to Marienbad."[149]

Franz Kafka and Jiří Langer stand as representatives of a generation of sons and daughters whose fathers were in their eyes weak, especially when the talk was about their Judaism.[150] By contrast, the rebbe can be read as a surrogate for these fathers, as representative of a patriarchal society and religious authority.[151] The weakness of his father, Kafka wrote, was not an "isolated phenomenon. [. . .] it was much the same with a large section of this transitional generation of Jews, which had migrated from the still comparatively devout countryside to the cities."[152] After arrival in Prague, this generation turned its back on its provincial Czech Judaism, bowed their heads under a German culture and language that was in the process of de- and re-territorialization, and began in the eyes of their sons and daughters to appear weak.[153] Kafka reproached his father for this move of assimilation, which in his view had surrendered so much and gained so little. "You really had brought some traces of Judaism with you from the ghetto-like village community; it was not much and it dwindled a little more in the city and during your military service; but still, the impressions and memories of your youth did just about suffice for some sort of Jewish life."[154] But, as Kafka wrote, "it was too little to be handed on to the child; it all dribbled away while you were passing it on."[155]

Symbolic of this generational conflict that had begun before the Great War and that erupted into full flare as the war broke out was a change that occurred in the Jewish places of Carlsbad, Marienbad, and Franzensbad. The experience of the war and its reality as personified by the refugees transformed the seemingly protective sanctuary of the bourgeois luxury spas, and that sanctuary appeared increasingly more decadent. With the end of the Habsburg Monarchy, the prewar idyll of the health spas belonged to a past now recalled with powerful nostalgia. The new Jewish places, however, were not merely spaces of remembrance of the good old days of the monarchy; they were scenes and mirrors of a process of nationalization taking place across the continent. The same generation of young Jews in search of utopias, solutions, and ways out, which had stood at the center of that sanctuary in the spas before the war, was now to define its national space.

Part III

Odradek

Chapter 8

A Story

Bohemia lies by the sea. Don't you want to be Bohemians,
all you Illyrians, Veronese and Venetians. Play the comedies
that make us laugh until we cry.
— Ingeborg Bachmann, "Böhmen liegt am Meer," 1964[1]

In its Hanukkah issue of 1919, the Zionist paper *Selbstwehr* published a short story by Franz Kafka.[2] "Die Sorge des Hausvaters" (The Cares of a Family Man) had been written in 1916–1917 and was being published now for the first time. The story begins:

> Some say the word Odradek is of Slavonic origin, and try to account for it on that basis. Others again believe it to be of German origin, only influenced by Slavonic. The uncertainty of both interpretations allows one to assume with justice that neither is accurate, especially as neither of them provides an intelligent meaning of the word. No one, of course, would occupy himself with such studies if there were not a creature called Odradek.[3]

Odradek looks like a "flat star-shaped spool for thread," and one "is tempted to believe that the creature once had some sort of intelligible shape and is now only a broken-down remnant." Yet there is no place of fracture in the surface to be found and "the whole thing looks senseless enough, but in its own way perfectly finished."[4]

In any case, closer scrutiny is impossible, since Odradek is extraordinarily nimble and can never be laid hold of. He generally stays at
home, and if asked where he lives, he gives no information: "No fixed
abode," he says and laughs; but it is only the kind of laughter that has
no lungs behind it. It sounds rather like the rustling of fallen leaves.[5]

And the narrator wonders:

I ask myself, to no purpose, what is likely to happen to him? Can he
possibly die? [. . .] Anything that dies has had some kind of aim in life,
some kind of activity, which has worn out; but that does not apply to
Odradek. Am I to suppose, then, that he will always be rolling down
the stairs, with ends of thread trailing after him, right before the feet
of my children, and my children's children? He does no harm to anyone that one can see; but the idea that he is likely to survive me I find
almost painful.[6]

This sentence finishes the short tale about a strange being, a story that since
publication has spawned a number of different interpretations.[7] Does the odd
creature called Odradek point to the existential situation of the writer? Or
does it refer to the alienated son of the *paterfamilias*? And how did the readers of the paper *Selbstwehr*, not a literary but a Zionist weekly, understand the
"star-shaped" being? Were they reminded of their own situation, surrounded
by the postwar economic depression and pressing questions of languages and
nationalities? The word "Odradek" does not exist either in German or Czech,
but it could be formed in Czech with a meaning of "something created by
discouragement, alienation."[8] Aside from the person of the writer, this seems
a very apt metaphor to describe the situation of the German-speaking Jews
in Bohemia, and even more so in the almost exclusively German townships,
to which Carlsbad, Marienbad, and Franzensbad belonged. The situation in
these supposedly international localities near the German border was difficult right from the beginning, and down to the end it remained marked by
alienation, and often discouragement, as the example of the Carlsbad Jewish
Community shows.

When the first Jewish families began to settle in Carlsbad in the first half
of the nineteenth century, their influx brought social advancement, yet was
also mixed with isolation within the local situation. The dominant, almost
exclusively German local population demanded from the new in-migrants

that they be absolutely loyal to the German language and culture, though without reciprocation by the Germans to accept them as a separate nationality. Although the Jewish community was very much involved in developing the flourishing spa, and its members played an important role in the local economic networks, its initiatives were nonetheless barely recognized as contributions; rather, they tended to be seen largely as unwelcome competition. There was a decline in the economy of the western Bohemian spas, conjunct now with an escalating conflict between Germans and Czechs. In the predominantly German spa towns, only a minuscule minority declared its loyalty to the Czech language and nationality. Although the number of Czechs in residence all year long was very low, the Czech community expanded significantly every summer season, when hotel staff, waiters, and servants were in demand, and women and men from the surrounding countryside gravitated for work to the spa towns. Within the smoldering German-Czech conflict, which at times flared into open confrontation, the Jewish communities remained somehow more to one side and yet a third party still an integral part of the picture, which simply by dint of its presence questioned this national conflict. The upshot was that they were rejected by both sides of this local deepening divide.

The independence of the Jewish communities initially was concentrated on a limited but vibrant sphere of organizational activities flourishing especially in the summertime, while the winters were marked by seclusion and privacy. While the generation of the parents, in significant measure driven by a powerful need for economic security, subordinated itself to the local hegemonies, a generation of self-confident sons and daughters was growing up, young adults who largely distanced themselves from the small-town atmosphere and its values. The Jewish communities had grown substantially and rapidly over the years, but every summer their numbers soared, reaching figures more common to large urban areas, as spa guests, seasonal spa doctors, hoteliers, and merchants flocked into town. Although these temporary communities were only in part connected internally, a consciousness of a summertime Jewish community crystallized via the dynamic interplay of diverse processes of socialization between locals, seasonal workers, and spa guests.

These amoeba-like Jewish communities, constantly changing their form, had both positive and negative effects for the local Jews in Carlsbad, Marienbad, and Franzensbad. Since the summer communities were perceived by the others as homogeneous, the permanently resident Jews never acquired the full status of indigenous locals. The existence of the summertime Jewish community served as a pretext to accuse them of a lack of local loyalty, proof they were still a community of temporary transients.

Yet the Jews who had settled there had long since abandoned a wandering existence and had decided to stay. But to stay on not as the stranger, as Simmel expressed it in a classic formulation, "not as one who arrives today and leaves tomorrow, but as one who comes today and stays tomorrow—the potential wanderer, so to speak, who has not completely overcome the loosening of coming and going, though not moving on. [...] This position of the stranger is intensified in consciousness when the stranger becomes fixed permanently in the place instead of again leaving the place of the business activity."[9] Thus, the insecure situation of the local Jews deteriorated every autumn, when thousands of strangers once again left the town. These different modes of existence as a stranger displaced and recalibrated presumably simple binarisms like distance and nearness, complicating the local relations.

The Jews in Carlsbad, Marienbad, and Franzensbad retained their status of the stranger as "an element whose immanent presence and membership include at the same time an externality and opposition"[10]—a position also ascribed to them in the conflict between Germans and Czechs. Utilitarianism and hypocrisy liberated them in a superficial and temporary way from the local isolation during the summer, but the role of a kind of Odradek with "no fixed abode" remained for the Jewish communities—this despite all the changes that occurred during the time of their existence.

The relations between Jews, other Germans, and Czechs will be explored in the chapters below on the history of Carlsbad, with excursions into Marienbad and Franzensbad supplementing the picture or providing contrast in some important way.[11]

Chapter 9

The City in the Hills

Becoming "Winter Jews"

... Carlsbad, a very beautiful spot with a society that is
lacking in unity, replete with conflicts and dissatisfaction.
—Lily Pincus, *Verloren—Gewonnen*[1]

Peddlers and traders who for many years had spent the summer and worked in Carlsbad established the Jewish community, when after a prolonged struggle over several decades they finally won the right to set up a formal *Gemeinde*.[2] As elsewhere, a battle of interests between the municipality and local merchants also preceded the settlement of Jews in Carlsbad; the former expected certain advantages from the presence of Jews in town, the latter feared for their businesses. But here the matter was a bit different in historical terms, given that the city since 1499 had had a so-called *Judenprivilegium* (Privilege for Jewry) that the municipal authorities stubbornly demanded to be reconfirmed by every ruler.[3] This "privilege" gave Carlsbad the right to decide on its own about any Jews settling there, which in practice meant to deny them that right. But since the town had a long-standing interest in Jews as paying spa clientele, the upshot was in effect a rather grotesque situation. It arose long before the founding of a Jewish Community and remained unchanged for the duration of its existence. In his analysis of the legal conditions of Jews in Carlsbad, Meir Lamed describes the situation right from the beginning as decidedly "peculiar." "This city has always oscillated between Jew-hate in regard to the presence of Jews in town for the entire year—and toleration, more or less promoted, for the summertime season."[4]

From May to September, Jews like all other spa guests were free to rent hotel rooms and apartments in town. But with the onset of the autumn, they had to leave the place once again. This possibility of temporary residence was also utilized by peddlers and merchants who came from the surrounding Jewish Communities to Carlsbad to engage in commerce. Since during the season the spa had the legal status of a "fair," no one could prohibit them from offering their wares for sale in stands and shops. Their presence and that of a constantly rising number of Jewish spa guests necessitated the establishment of Jewish kosher cook shops or food stands, whose operators likewise settled in for the duration of the season.[5] One of these restaurant owners was successful in arguing that his services were needed all year round, since sometimes in the winter as well Jews came for the cure and were tolerated as spa patrons off-season; in effect they were becoming "winter Jews."[6]

One consequence of this "peculiar" situation was that already at the beginning of the nineteenth century, long before the abolishment of the general prohibition on settlement for Jews, there were Jewish house owners in Carlsbad.[7] Although every autumn they were ordered to leave town, they did not always abide by the municipal directive, or did not adhere to its full letter. Since a number of these residents were under the protection of local spa physicians who prescribed for them a necessary regimen of Carlsbad therapeutic applications for the entire year, the municipality sent a strongly worded warning to the doctors in question in the fall of 1833: they were to provide no assistance if Jewish traders gave reasons of health as an argument for settling in town for the entire year, and were, in this way, "transforming the famous city of Carlsbad from a clean and tidy spa into a filthy nest of Jews." Only one of the physicians so addressed reacted to this open reproach of bribery and defended himself not only against the accusation, but confirmed with biting irony the inconsistency of the policies of the municipal authorities.[8] Since businessmen envious of competition constantly complained about the Jews, asking the municipality to be consistent about implementing the prohibition on residence out of season, Jewish families were repeatedly expelled from the town in the autumn.[9]

The establishment of the Jewish Hospital and the events of 1848 passed without any change in the regulation, while in the meantime ever more Jews were settling illegally in Carlsbad. The Imposed March Constitution in 1849 provided for civil equality of all religious communities in the Austro-Hungarian Monarchy, but the Bohemian Jews were not given full civil rights until the Basic State Act in December 1867.[10] After decades of attempts to circumvent the law, the Carlsbad Jewish merchants decided now to engage in open protest, and after several confrontations in 1869 they were finally given permission to establish a formal *Gemeinde*.[11] From that juncture on, many Jews decided to move into town, since Carlsbad held out the promise of rapid economic advancement. Whoever was able left the small, sometimes predominantly Jewish villages in the nearby countryside, relocating to settle in the "elegant spa."[12]

Proportionally with the growth of the city of Carlsbad as a thriving tourist center, the small Jewish Community also grew rapidly in the second third of the nineteenth century: the number of residents in Carlsbad more than doubled between 1869 and 1900; over and above the nearly 15,000 residents, every summer season there was an influx of an additional 5,000–6,000 waiters, servants, and other seasonal workers in the city.[13] In that same period, the Jewish community grew from a handful of families to 10 percent of the population, a proportion it would maintain for the duration of its existence. On the occasion of its fiftieth anniversary, in 1919, the Jewish community in Carlsbad was delighted to announce that it had now become the fourth largest Jewish *Gemeinde* in the former Bohemia.[14]

Like all other residents, the Jewish Carlsbaders also had a livelihood based on the spa and its operations, and as doctors, hoteliers, merchants, and owners of spa houses they generally belonged to the upper-middle and middle classes. Like all others at the beginning of the summer season, they moved from the more spacious bel-etage apartments on the second floor of their houses into the upper stories and the attic quarters so as to make room for the spa guests. Like all others, they worked during the summer around the clock, closed their business premises at 10 P.M., opened them very early the next morning, and dedicated their entire attention and time to the well-being of their guests.[15]

Nevertheless, the change in the season brought more change for the Jewish Carlsbaders than for others. This was because during the summer, the comparatively small community connected via multifaceted networks and circles with the incomparably larger number of Jewish spa guests. Many years before the establishment of the *Gemeinde*, this cooperation had facilitated the building of the Jewish hospital and continued to constitute the central and vital element of Jewish life in the town. Although or perhaps precisely because the ensemble of spa guests was so heterogeneous, it found diverse interfaces conducive for financial or other non-material investments. The activities in Jewish organizations thrived throughout the summer, while in winter these moved into virtual hibernation. The new synagogue, whose costly and spacious construction was geared to the needs of a Community in a large urban center, was only utilized during the summer, since it was far too large for the tiny Carlsbad *Wintergemeinde*.

Peaking at a majority of those in town during summertime, the number of Jews in Carlsbad shrunk to a minority every autumn. Then the seasonal workers also left along with the spa guests: many physicians returned to Vienna or Prague, or set up a practice during the winter months further south, in spas in Italy or Egypt. Orthodox and Chassidic merchants and hotel operators also departed, since the Orthodox *Wintergemeinde* was much too small for them.[16] Those remaining behind, generally liberal middle-class, German-speaking families, spent the winters mainly socializing among themselves, to the extent that was possible in a small town.[17] This was because due to their unchanged "peculiar" situation, most did not have any intensive friendly contacts with the majority of the non-Jewish Germans, aside from business ties. By contrast, the Czech minority was barely present in the local social landscape, since it was both marginalized and extremely small in number. Official figures around the turn of the century indicate that less than one percent of the population in the township identified itself as Czech.[18]

When the young Czech Marie Riegerová took the cure in Franzensbad in the second half of the nineteenth century, the twenty-three-year-old woman felt so out of place that she wrote to her sister: "I'm as if banished to a distant land here . . . this is such a German, a German-minded corner of Bohemia [. . .]. I feel even sadder when I think I'm at home and nonetheless a stranger in a foreign place."[19] From the turn of the century on, Czech travel guidebooks began to recommend that potential spa guests seek out the small number of hotels with staff that could speak Czech and the Czech spa doctors, sometimes only the sole Czech doctor in town.[20] Readers of Czech-Jewish papers were offered similar information services by *Rozvoj* and *Židovské Zprávy*, and the western Bohemian health spas sometimes were not even featured in their recommendations.[21] Menachem Ussishkin, who was in Franzensbad in 1889 and 1896 to take the waters, recalled later that he had not met any Czech guests in his kosher hotel: "To tell the truth, I encountered many Polish, Russian, and German Jews there, but not a single Czech Jew."[22] After a reader of the newspaper *Rozvoj* had complained that Czech Jews generally registered in German spas as Germans, Czech-Jewish newspapers issued an appeal that Czechs, quite apart from religion, should always and everywhere present themselves as "proud, self-confident Czechs."[23] Despite this, the Czech infrastructure for Jews in the spas did not improve until the 1930s, when kosher hotels began to target Czech-Jewish spa guests in their advertising.[24]

In the meantime, the German population was propagating an image of the spas that was exclusively German, especially since the conflict between

German and Czechs had flared into public confrontation. The Carlsbader Franz Zatloukal wrote in his 1908 guidebook: "The *residents* of the city are almost all German in nationality, and most are Roman Catholics. Their cheerful demeanor, cleanliness, friendly and courteous approach in dealing with foreign guests are well-known and greatly appreciated."[25] Neither the Czech nor the far greater Jewish minority were ever mentioned in such contexts; the Jews were simply subsumed under the Germans, and frequently their institutions were deliberately shrouded in a blanket of silence.[26]

The smoldering conflict between Germans and Czechs had flared into a first provisional high point in April 1897 after the Badeni government issued a language ordinance for Bohemia and Moravia. This new ordinance gave equal status to Czech and German, and demanded that all officials use both languages in conducting administrative affairs. The uncertainty that spread in the wake of the announcement of the decree in the German-speaking areas of Bohemia was utilized by the German nationalist politician Georg von Schönerer for his own political ends. After his All-German Movement had lost substantial influence in previous years, he now thought he discerned a new opportunity at hand to press forward with his anti-liberal, anti-Semitic, and anti-Catholic agenda. The "Teutonic fury," street violence that broke out in many parts of the Habsburg Empire, was largely due to Schönerer's agitation against the ordinance and its implications for the German-speaking population in Bohemia.[27] After the Badeni government was toppled and the ordinance rescinded later that year, there were street protests by Czech nationalists, venting their anger at the Germans, and most especially the German Jews.[28] In retrospect, the *Oesterreichische Wochenschrift* summed up the chronology of events from the perspective of Bohemian Jewry with a sense of resignation: "In Carlsbad, Eger, Saaz, and other localities in the predominantly German language area, they are persecuted because they have been declared harmful parasites feeding on German culture, while in Prague, Kolin, and Jungbunzlau, they are under attack because they supposedly support German culture."[29] In numerous predominantly German-speaking towns in Bohemia, liberal political and organizational life and Jewish participation in this social sphere now dwindled. To a large extent, it disappeared.[30]

Relations between Germans and Czechs had also deteriorated in Carlsbad, Marienbad, and Franzensbad. German feelings of resentment and anger were directed not only against the tiny and relatively weak Czech minority but even more against the established Carlsbad Jewish Community. The old attitude of rejection now found new life in a specifically German identity that defined itself far more through language and nation than via shared cultural attributes.[31]

When about ten years later practical efforts were undertaken from Prague and Vienna to improve the situation of the Czech minority in the German-speaking areas, the fight erupted into the open in Carlsbad, marked by an aggressive vehemence. There were furious protests among the Germans in response to setting up of Czech minority schools, the appointment of Czech postal and railroad officials, and the threat of the introduction of official government forms in two languages. Although the spa season had already begun and the spa district was deemed a pacified territory, violent protests erupted on Carlsbad's streets in May 1908. The spark for this had been a Czech sign that a hotel owner had mounted on his premises, while the target of the attacks were the numerous Czech domestic and hotel employees. The demonstrators were not subdued until the municipality issued an appeal to spare the spa city—and thus themselves—from more serious damage. But immediately after the season had concluded, the conflict exploded once more with such vehement controversy that the municipality saw itself forced to issue a ban on public gatherings and introduced nightly curfews.[32]

At the suggestion of the German-Bohemian Chancellery of Municipalities (*Deutschböhmische Städtekanzlei*), the predominantly German towns prepared lists of their Czech residents. Discrimination against Czech residents in Carlsbad now reached a high point: house owners and hoteliers stopped hiring Czech employees and renting to Czech tenants. The municipality even instructed its officials to stop hiring Czech domestic servants for "national reasons." It was only natural that the official number of Czechs in the town declined as a result. For the time being, the German municipal administration emerged from the conflict satisfied, as the autonomy of the spas was expanded from bureaucratic and administrative matters to encompass concerns about language rights.[33]

However, this situation proved short-lived. After the founding of the Czechoslovak Republic, the Czech spa guests gained in self-assurance and started to defend themselves against the disadvantages they had previously been subjected to in the western Bohemian spas. The spa administrations recognized the need for a rapid response and immediately sent their employees to courses to learn Czech.[34] But the majority of the German hoteliers and merchants still refused in the 1920s to serve their guests in Czech.[35] This constituted a blatant discriminatory measure against Czech spa patrons, since it was well known that almost every resident of the spa towns had a basic knowledge of a number of languages and could use that proficiency when needed.

The fledgling Czechoslovak Republic reacted to the aggressive behavior of the western Bohemian spas, which were acting as though they were ex-territorial German enclaves, by broaching the idea of nationalizing the baths and springs in Marienbad. The expropriation of the German monastery Tepl, which had owned the springs since their discovery, was to be a first step toward the transformation of the German national character of the spa. The dispute that this plan triggered dragged on for several years, bringing the German spas in northern and western Bohemia closer together. Heading the initiative was the German nationalist mayor of Carlsbad, Hermann Jakob, who feared that his spa town could be the next on the list of plans for nationalization.

Together with the mayors of Marienbad, Franzensbad, Teplitz-Schönau, Johannisbad, and Joachimsthal, Jakob drew up a petition in 1924 that was submitted to the League of Nations.[36] In response to an official declaration by the Czech authorities and press reports, their petition stated that the nationalization of Marienbad did not have in mind the good of the spas, but represented their forcible adaptation to the "Czechoslovak character of the state."[37] The central and at the same time paradoxical argument of the German nationalist opposition against the expropriation stressed the distinctively international character of the spa, which could only be guaranteed, they argued, under German executive direction. A declaration by the Carlsbad municipal council put it bluntly:

> The previous flourishing development of Marienbad as a world-class spa in its present size is due solely to the fact that it has always had a purely German management. Yet that management took the interests of all visitors to Marienbad into proper consideration to such an extent that there was never any justified complaint possible. Rather, its work was always lauded and given recognition by an international spa public.

Once again, the municipal administration proved successful, and although the autonomy of the spas was somewhat reduced, their nationalization was postponed indefinitely.[38]

For the Jews in Carlsbad, Marienbad, and Franzensbad, the exclusive manner in which the German nationalist majority populations waged these conflicts left them little latitude for response. There was but scant possibility for them to come closer to the local Czechs, some of whom harbored feelings of resentment against the Jews and accused them of representing specifically German culture and values.[39] Thus, the majority of the Jewish population, as the Carlsbad resident Lily Pincus wrote in her memoirs, viewed themselves "as standard-bearers of German culture, and could not be German enough."[40] In most Jewish families, only German was spoken, and many children continued to attend German schools even after the founding of the Czechoslovak state; this only began to change toward the end of the 1920s.[41] In general, most of the liberal middle-class families lived quite removed from any political and religious activities.[42] Though the children at school had classes in religion and learned biblical history and Hebrew, many parents and grandparents had long since ceased to attend services at the synagogue.[43]

We can assume that a substantial segment of local Jewish behavior was attributable to the decidedly "peculiar" political and social situation in which they lived. It demanded that they profess loyalty to German culture and the German nation, yet in return it denied them full social acceptance. Thus, for example, the Jewish Community was not officially invited in October 1913 when the Carlsbad municipality celebrated the hundredth anniversary of the Battle of the Nations near Leipzig as a German patriotic national holiday with choir singing, participation by members of the German Association of Gymnasts (*Turnverein*) and the paramilitary *Schützencorps*. Nonetheless, the municipality instructed Rabbi Ziegler to deliver a special festive sermon at the synagogue to mark the *Völkerschlacht* festivities. Well versed in dealing with the Carlsbad municipal administration, Ziegler replied diplomatically, saying unfortunately that would not be possible since the congregation was celebrating the Feast of Tabernacles (Sukkoth) on that same day. But he promised to mention the important event in his Sukkoth sermon.[44]

Ignaz Ziegler served as Carlsbad chief rabbi for over five decades, representing the Community almost from its start until its demise. His engaging integrative personality and the decided liberalism he espoused had a huge impact on the reality of Carlsbad Jewry. However, Ziegler was also powerless in the face of developments since the turn of the century, as ever more *Gemeinde* members succumbed to the everyday pressures and converted to Christianity. Around the turn of the century, conversions to Christianity were still rare in Carlsbad, but already in 1910, the weekly *Selbstwehr* published a polemical column entitled "Baptized Jewish Spa Doctors," in which a number of converted doctors in Carlsbad, Marienbad, Franzensbad, and several other German spas in Bohemia were listed.[45] In Marienbad, even the son of Enoch Heinrich Kisch, the longtime director of the Jewish Spa Hospital, had converted on the occasion of his marriage. To the astonishment of spa guests from Germany, the young Dr. Kisch nonetheless retained his post as his father's successor at the Jewish hospital.[46] Although the actual number of conversions in the western Bohemian spas can no longer be accurately determined, it was clearly a massive social trend, and in the 1920s already was an established target for jokes and ridicule in the pages of the Carlsbad satirical magazine *Karlsbader "Kikriki."*[47]

At the beginning of the 1930s, there were occasional meetings in Carlsbad between Rabbi Ziegler and Chaim Nachman Bialik. During the last years of his life, the Zionist poet traveled repeatedly to Carlsbad and Marienbad to take the waters, although at that time he was already living in Tel Aviv.[48] During one stay he paid a visit to the Carlsbad Temple, but the celebrated preacher Ziegler did not make a positive impression on Bialik. In a letter he wrote in September 1931 to his wife, Mania, he sketched a polemic picture of the charismatic Carlsbad rabbi: "A smart man, but his sermons are '*parve*' and don't touch the heart. They could be delivered in any church. On the basis of such sermons, over the last 40 years things have reached a point where 70 percent of the Carlsbad Jews no longer have their children circumcised, and mixed marriages are becoming ever more common from year to year." When Ziegler visited Bialik a short time thereafter, he himself painted a depressing picture of Czechoslovak Jewry, declaring that the Jewish identity of the local Jews was nearing its end. Bialik closed his report on the conversation with the comment: "Only a miracle or a proper pogrom can save them."[49]

Enduring Wintertime Anti-Semitism

Recently the "Alliance of the Racially Pure" organized
a festivity in the peach orchards of the Indischer Hof.
Chinese, Jews, and other foreigners were not issued any
tokens for participants. Japanese women with a pixie cut
coiffeur were also thrown out.

—*Karlsbader "Kikriki," "*Japanischer Brief,"
September 1925[50]

To be too German and yet not quite German enough—that was the pro-
filed and not particularly grateful role ascribed to Carlsbad Jewry during
the events of 1897. In the course of that year, expressions of repressed resentment mounted. These had shaped relations since early on, but now
were being reformulated, acting to finally codify the status of outsider for
Jews within the small-town society of the spa. The economic reasons that,
prior to Jewish settlement in town, had already served to underpin the anti-
Semitism of competing hoteliers and merchants now acquired, in the matrix
of concrete discussion, a new dimension that was increasingly ideological in
its motivation.[51]

In November 1897, the weekly *Oesterreichische Wochenschrift* published a
front-page article entitled "Carlsbad—Anti-Semitic," which angrily discussed
the recent events in the spa town: "Yes indeed, Carlsbad has become anti-
Semitic, the famous health resort, to which members of all peoples across
the planet flock as pilgrims, whose power to enhance life and health is the
common heritage of all human beings without distinction of faith, tribe and
social class, has hoisted the banner of Jew-hatred on the flagpole before its
city hall." According to the paper's Carlsbad correspondent, the turn in communal politics was the result of a nasty hate campaign. After the candidate
from Schönerer's All-German Party had found many new adherents among
the Eger electorate, but nonetheless had lost the election to the Social Demo-
crat candidate (by coincidence a Jew), the Carlsbad Jews were accused of "national treason."[52]

Heading up this vituperative campaign was the physician and chair of
the Carlsbad German Association of Gymnasts, August Hermann. On his
initiative, the local *Turnverein*, which had in the past admitted Jewish members, passed a resolution stating that "members of the Association can only
be Germans of Aryan extraction." As the *Oesterreichische Wochenschrift* reported, this decision was conceived as a personal attack on the Jewish councilor and lawyer Ferdinand Fleischner:

> One day before this questionable resolution, the Christian councilor
> Dr. Hermann paid a visit to the Jewish councilman Dr. Fleischner. He
> informed him in his own name and that of four members of the Gym-
> nastic Council that the purpose of the "Aryanization" of the Associa-
> tion of Gymnasts was to combat the influence of the Jews in general,
> and in the Collegium of Alderman (*Stadtverordneten-Collegium*) and

of the Jewish councilman Dr. Fleischner in particular. The events in the *Turnverein* had thus taken on a character that went beyond the limited framework of the association, directly impinging on the equal civil status of the Jews throughout all public life in Carlsbad.[53]

Councilman Fleischner reacted to the open attack by tendering his resignation to the Collegium of Alderman, since under these circumstances he did not wish to continue to sit at the same table with his colleague Hermann. If up until that moment people could have assumed that an anti-Semitic clique of some kind was at work, the correspondent commented on the incident from another vantage. He stated that as the subsequent session proved, "the poison of Jew-hatred had already penetrated into broad circles, and the supposedly liberal mayor and the entire body of municipal representatives were now already infested with this." Significantly, the *Stadtverordneten-Collegium* accepted Fleischner's resignation without any comment. Neither the mayor nor any of the alderman, all themselves members of the Association of Gymnasts, rose to defend him. The article closes: "I can only conclude this truthful report with the local-patriotic wish that anti-Semitism in Carlsbad, which is now beginning to thrive in such rank profusion, shall not lead to the sad economic consequences which unfortunately we must so sorely fear."[54]

The reports on the events in Carlsbad spread like wildfire through the press in Vienna and Berlin, triggering vehement reactions among the local politicians addressed. Mayor Ludwig Schäffler tried to avoid any responsibility by declaring in an open letter to the *Wochenschrift* that Fleischner had "resigned because he had raised suspicions about his own anti-Semitic tendencies, in that he had allowed much to transpire which he should have sought to prevent from happening." The paper commented on Schäffler's rectification, only noting that the Carlsbaders claimed "a status of national exclusivity for communal life and internationalism when it came to spa life. [. . .] We are revealing an open secret in asserting that Carlsbad has after all been anti-Semitic for quite some years."[55]

Since this open confession of an anti-Semitic communal politics, which not coincidentally came in the period when the German nationalist movement in Bohemia was on the upsurge, Jewish newspapers in Prague, Vienna, and Berlin reported regularly on the situation in Carlsbad. In 1901, the periodical of the *Centralverein deutscher Staatsbürger jüdischen Glaubens* reported with alarm on current developments in the spa town:

The question whether Carlsbad is anti-Semitic is dismissed by many of our co-religionists, but is affirmed by anti-Semitic circles. And this view is substantiated by the fact that the "international spa" is now being represented by a "German-national anti-Semite" in the Bohemian parliament, recently elected by a margin of 1,407 votes to 406. The fact that the *Staatsbürger Zeitung* explains this attitude among Carlsbaders by pointing to the behavior of the Jews in the Bohemian spa is pretty irrelevant. Because in comparison with the hooliganism which the anti-Semitic press has reared there, the most uneducated spa guest from the depths of southeastern Europe [*Halbasien*] is a veritable gentleman! But it would not hurt those "winter anti-Semites," who show their little cat's paws in the summer, if the Jewish patients would let the Sprudel spring flow over with all its anti-Semitism, and would preferably look for recovery elsewhere: for example in Neuenahr, which is supposed to have equally effective mineral springs.[56]

The phenomenon of Carlsbad wintertime anti-Semitism had in the meantime become proverbial. It was strange that this escalation occurred at a time when other long established spas popular with a Jewish clientele had aroused no suspicions of anti-Semitism in their communal politics.[57] It was no secret that such criticisms could seriously damage a successful tourist center over the longer term were it not for the fact that it was about petty bourgeois localities which for strategic reasons had in fact nurtured an image of being anti-Semitic.[58] However, the Carlsbaders insulted a large proportion of their clientele with their overtly anti-Semitic local politics. Lines of continuity led back to the grotesque tradition of institutionalized seasonal Jew hatred, according to which Jews were only welcome as paying spa guests.

During the summer, when the spa district, as a socially and politically pacified space, protected both spa guests and locals under its canopy of cooperation, the community of convenience between Jewish and other Carlsbad residents also functioned with relative harmony. However, the moment the last spa guest left town in the autumn the situation radicalized, and the summertime tolerant town shifted to attack mode, channeling its German nationalism against the locally resident Jewish Community. The humorist Julius Stettenheim, a veteran spa guest in Carlsbad, described the ambivalence of this seasonal extreme as a schizoid experience even for the visitors:

Anti-Semitism in Carlsbad is particularly comical. Of course, in the summer they have their hands full just trying to plunder the visitors. Just as farmers have no time for dancing during the harvest, the anti-Semite has no time for agitation. [. . .] Then Carlsbad is packed with gentlemen "von Cohn," and especially in the shops, everyone is treated as a baron—who come winter, is at the very least set ablaze verbally, or beaten to a pulp.[59]

Even when the radical violent disturbances subsided across Bohemia at the beginning of the century, the situation in Carlsbad did not improve. According to the *Selbstwehr*, nowhere in the German lands were things as bad as here, where Jews were formally excluded from most associations and pushed into social isolation.[60] This was because it belonged to the good social form of the nationalistic "Egerlanders"[61] to be anti-Semitic and to be a member of an "Aryan" association, as Walter Klemm described the non-Jewish society in Carlsbad around the turn of the century. In the memoirs of his youth published in 1936, having been raised in Carlsbad, he noted that one of the most important experiences of his schooldays was his entry as a member in a forbidden, color-carrying dueling fraternity: "We were arch-patriots, gave political speeches; it was a point of honor to be a foe of the Jews, a friend of the 'break free from Rome' movement and an arch-enemy of the Czechs."[62]

The Prague paper *Selbstwehr* regularly expressed its astonishment and dismay over the prevailing situation in Carlsbad, accusing the Jewish Community of hypocrisy, a lack of self-assurance, and a total misreading of their own situation.[63] Regularly in the run-up to elections, the Zionist journal would criticize the "wealthy and intelligent Jewry of Carlsbad," which despite its isolation still clung to and espoused the values of the once strong tradition of German liberalism.[64] Yet the German Progressive Party, formerly the strongest political force in the spa, was long supported only by Jewish voters, while all the others had flocked to the German nationalists and their DNP (*Deutsche Nationalpartei*).[65] With a touch of cynicism, *Selbstwehr* commented that the Carlsbad Jews wanted to rescue German liberalism, "although the Germans neither wish nor need such saviors."[66] It stressed that the fact that Jews were increasingly being pushed from official positions and replaced by supporters of the DNP should also finally open the eyes of the Carlsbad Jews to what was actually transpiring.[67] The paper stressed that the real tragedy lay in the split between the generation of the fathers and their children. In order to escape the narrowness and constraints of Jewish reality in Carlsbad, their sons and daughters were turning toward Zionism, a decision that horrified the fathers. The paper went on to note that in the meantime, the distance between young, self-confident Zionists and old, assimilated "German" Jews was especially great in Carlsbad.[68]

The *Oesterreichische Wochenschrift* also described the situation of the local Jews in Carlsbad as being fraught with difficulty. A correspondent who came in the winter of 1910 to the town observed a total "separation of society into Christians and Jews," which was also evident to an outsider:

> Already upon entering Carlsbad you can readily see that the beautiful spa town likewise knows how to find diversion in wintertime. Because there are large posters announcing that all sorts of associations are putting on big amusements, balls, theater performances and the like, open to all, except for one category of individuals, the Jews. Almost all associations in Carlsbad have excluded Jews, and they are barred from entry to any of their amusements and events.[69]

The journalist asked how things could have developed to this extreme degree in a place that was so popular among Jews in the summer. And the answer he got was as follows: "When anti-Semitism reared its head about twelve years ago in Carlsbad and across the Egerland, the Jews in Carlsbad tried to defend themselves. But now a peculiar phenomenon arose here. The liberal municipal representatives put such huge pressure on the Jews to 'keep quiet' that those who wished to fight against the exclusionary anti-Semitism ran the risk of suffering the worst economic consequences."[70] Worse than the isolation of the Carlsbad Jews, the correspondent reported, was the multiple internal division of the Jewish Community. The upshot was that the various religious and social groups shared neither a common forum nor any real sense of solidarity and cohesion.[71]

A few weeks later, the *Oesterreichische Wochenschrift* published a reply to this report. In an open letter, Rabbi Ignaz Ziegler and the deputy head of the Community, Adolf Rosenfeld, rejected the assertion that the Carlsbaders did not invite Jews to winter events nor accept them as association members:

> Of the nearly 200 associations here in our town, a small number, probably three at the most, declared themselves in times past to be Aryan. That regrettable current of the times came to a stop as little before our gates as it did before those of other international spas and

tourist spots in Germany, Austria, and Switzerland—but the exclusion of Jews from all associations in Carlsbad is a pure invention. [. . .] The regrettable social separation between Christians and Jews in Carlsbad is no worse than elsewhere. The public and economic life in our town is at present completely peaceful and quiet.[72]

It is possible that this defensive assertion actually reflected a reality that was perceived this way by many Carlsbad Jews of an older generation. In any event, as a response, it remained a rare if not indeed unique statement. Because in actual fact, the Carlsbad Jewish Community lived within a far more complicated network of dependencies than previously discussed. Every article that focused on wintertime anti-Semitism damaged the image not only of the German nationalist and all-German Carlsbad citizens; it also impacted to the same degree on the Jewish hoteliers, merchants, and doctors who lived not only off of the seasonal *Sommergemeinde* but together with it. However, Carlsbad was well enough established in Jewish circles to absorb the reproach of anti-Semitism, especially since many spa guests presumably never heard such criticism. They did not come in wintertime nor did they have subscriptions to Jewish papers.

The situation differed in the nearby and smaller spa of Franzensbad. In the winter of 1909, a spa guest who came to Franzensbad every season complained in a letter to the monthly *Oesterreichisch-Israelitische Union* about the "existence of two souls" that had in the meantime become a common phenomenon in all Bohemian spas. Carlsbad with its exceptional mineral springs could cope with such criticism, but Franzensbad, which up until then had always been considered very liberal, had to definitely avoid such tendencies: "The official personalities in the municipality ought probably to carefully consider that more than 50 percent of all spa guests are Jews, and that if the struggle should take on more acrimonious forms, it would be a true debacle for Franzensbad should Jewish spa guests decide to stay away." Jewish spa guests would, he stressed, tolerate neither a "quiet" nor an "open anti-Semitism, neither a wintertime nor a summer agitation against Jews." Instead, they would seek out another spa.[73]

The reply from a local was not long in coming. In his response, he declared with outrage that although there were anti-Semitic tendencies in Franzensbad, both Jewish spa guests and locals were treated with great cordiality. The writer of the original letter, in this reader's opinion, "evidently had a too one-sided view of the situation in the Bohemian spas," and was "particularly misinformed when it came to the situation in Franzensbad." Because, as the reader stressed, the fact was that the problem lay not in Franzensbad but in Carlsbad and Marienbad, where "almost half of the municipal representation consisted of open or clandestine anti-Semites."[74]

The emotional tone pervading this letter suggests that its purpose was not only to prove what the situation in Franzensbad really was. Since the spa was the smallest among the spas in western Bohemia, and its mineral springs were not especially important, such an accusation could have drastic consequences. And in actuality, there was little talk about Franzensbad in regard to manifestations of anti-Semitism, even if German nationalist spa guests praised the locals as "German to the core, and healthy to the bone."[75] On the contrary: peaceful Franzensbad was denounced as being too "Jew-friendly" in the nearby district center of Eger, where there was an aggressive anti-Semitism. With a tone of evident chagrin, the *Egerer Nachrichten* reported in August 1899 that "refined Jewish patrons" were being treated very well indeed in Franzensbad. "Oh, German city of Franzensbad," lamented the German nationalist paper, "what has become of your Germanness?"[76]

Even in the 1920s, when there were ever more frequent warnings to avoid anti-Semitic hotels in Carlsbad and Marienbad, Franzensbad remained unmentioned. Evidently the small spa, especially popular with women, could not afford or did not wish to frighten off its numerous Jewish visitors. In the meanwhile, the "existence of two souls" became more visible in Marienbad and Carlsbad, and the clear boundaries between summertime season and the exclusionary winter became increasingly blurred.[77] Ever more frequently, the features of a Germanizing "Egerlander" provincial town near the German border intruded onto the perfectly orchestrated stage of the refined international cosmopolitan city.

Chapter 10

Warmbod Grotesques

Scylla and Charybdis

Peoples, languages, colors intermingle
At the coffeehouse tables.
Extreme Paris fashion
Side by side with caftan
Simple provinciality in wool loden
rubs elbows with the spruced-up dandy.
—Max Nordau, *Karlsbader Anblicke*, 1911[1]

Professor Hermann Neumann from Potsdam was not only addressing a warning to his colleagues when he published an article in 1910 in the *Zeitschrift für Balneologie*. His opinions constituted a rare public statement in a controversy that had been raging in Germany since the turn of the century:

There has been serious criticism both from physicians and from the spa administrations [. . .] about the level of noise in spas. The time has finally come to say something about the 'noise' being generated in our spas by politics, class and racial hatred, and which do harm to the sick. [. . .] In these health spas, which serve mainly for the care and recovery of the ill, the weak and those in need of rest and recuperation, we need an end to the curious inquiries and classifications based on race, religion, party affiliation and political views. This has to cease once and for all, simply because of their unspeakable inhumanity and indescribable intolerance. We physicians, who unswervingly follow the banner of humanity, perceive such narrowness of mind as a slap in the face [. . .]. However, we doctors, in the interest of the general well-being of all, have an ineluctable duty to emphatically

warn against such spas, fortunately still few in number. And we must
guard against sending patients to those spas where mental confusion
threatens to inflict incalculable harm on them.[2]

The discourse on "spa anti-Semitism" as a phenomenon was generally limited to the awareness of a Jewish readership and was rarely discussed in the
broader public society. Yet in contrast with Neumann's assessment, this phenomenon was anything but "rare": since the end of the nineteenth century,
the travel service of the *Centralverein,* the *Israelitisches Familienblatt,* the
journal *Selbstwehr,* and the Association for Combatting Anti-Semitism (*Verein zur Abwehr des Antisemitismus*) had been issuing regular warnings at the
beginning of every summer season not just regarding anti-Semitic hotels and
guest houses. They also alerted people to explicitly anti-Semitic localities: on
the North Sea islands Juist and Borkum, in the Baltic spas Zinnowitz and
Bansin, in Kitzbühel and Rupolding, and in a whole slew of other health resorts, Jewish spa patrons and summer vacationers were deemed undesirable.[3]

The nationalizing of the neutral soil of the spas, which was conceived as
a socially and politically pacified protective space, triggered a sense of dismay and indignation in many places: "We've grown accustomed to many
perversities and often no longer sense the sheer absurdity of what surrounds
us," wrote the *Mitteilungen aus dem Verein zur Abwehr des Antisemitismus* in
May 1903: "Nonetheless, there's hardly a more unnatural phenomenon than
anti-Semitic health spas. If anything ought to lay back and take a rest during
vacation time, it's the political differences."[4] In many spas and vacation spots
in Austria-Hungary, tourism played a key role in the formation of national
and regional identities, against the backdrop of mounting ethnic tensions.[5]
Quite often, spas in the Habsburg Empire around the century's turn took on
cultural, ethnic, or linguistic definitions where the components "friendly to
Jews" or "hostile to Jews" played a key discursive role.[6]

Already before World War I, an aggressive "summertime vacation spot
anti-Semitism" was widespread in Austrian tourist centers.[7] Czech holiday
resorts in the Prague area also practiced a "rude and crude anti-Semitism"
that basically excluded Jewish summer guests and was similar to the situation in Austria. The *Selbstwehr* noted in 1912 that Germans were far more
welcome around Prague and environs than Jews.[8] The anti-Semitism predominant in many health resorts in Poland and Galicia was noxious and at
times coupled with violence, while in spas in Russia and the Caucasus Jews
had long been barred from entry: not until World War I was this regulation

abolished, but now as before Jews had to subject themselves to a humiliating ritual of screening by a special government commission set up for this purpose.[9]

Yet the dominant ideology in tourist centers was one of economic utilitarianism. Anti-Semitic health resorts on the German North Sea and Baltic coasts were for the most part latecomers. Lacking a prestigious history or luxurious reality, they sought to appeal to a new clientele drawn largely from the petty bourgeois strata.[10] By contrast, similar utilitarian reasons were responsible for the fact that summertime anti-Semitism at vacation spots in Austria began to disappear at the end of the 1920s, and especially after 1933, when many German Jews fled to Austria or at least chose to spend their vacations there.[11]

Since the turn of the century, relative security and a guaranteed quiet stay were only promised by more traditional, costly, and international spas; these already had tended to attract visitors from the middle and upper-middle Jewish social strata.[12] Among such health resorts were the old German spas such as the established resorts Bad Kissingen, Wiesbaden, or Bad Ems.[13] Carlsbad and Marienbad played a special role in this group, since the two spas, due to their location and infrastructure, attracted Jews from all over Europe, while at the same time being considered the birthplaces of wintertime anti-Semitism. Tacit agreements between spa administrations and municipalities were intended to offset these extremes, creating in a sense ex-territorial localities for the duration of the summer: during this period, political statements and agitation were deemed taboo throughout the spa district.[14] Local papers eager to find a readership among the spa public, such as the *Karlsbader Fremdenblatt* or the *Karlsbader Badeblatt*, adopted a non-political air until the season's end—but then quickly shifted gears and were acrimonious in their anti-Semitic attacks on the local Jews.[15]

In the summer of 1922, Stefan Zweig declined an invitation to the North Sea island Langeoog: "I don't need to ask for a pardon and 'toleration,' especially where I'm paying the bill. Preferable to go to a spa with 700,000 Galician Jews! No, I don't need that—better for me to go to Marienbad."[16] But despite their widespread reputation that there was no danger in Marienbad of running into some "all-German boys,"[17] unlike the situation in many German coastal resorts, the wall against local anti-Semitism occasionally sprang a leak. Since the beginning of the century, local anti-Semitism was no longer expressed solely in the form of caricatures on picture postcards. Now there were ever more personal attacks reported, in the main targeting Orthodox

Jews from Eastern Europe.[18] In the summer of 1903, the liberal *Karlsbader Tageblatt* carried a story on an incident in the spa district:

> Last Wednesday on Egerstraße, a frail old man wearing the tradi-
> tional dress of the Polish Jews was leaning against the garden fence
> of the Villa Mattoni. He had apparently had a serious attack of short-
> ness of breath. In front of him stood two adolescents, "adorned"
> with cornflowers and a black-red-gold belt, they mumbled and ges-
> ticulated as they mocked the poor harassed Jew. Passers-by were
> indignant about the crude behavior they witnessed, and since no
> policeman was anywhere in sight, one gentleman took the initia-
> tive to notify the police so as to put an end to this disgusting scene,
> which even found approval from several German-national business-
> men who were walking past. [. . .] It is characteristic of the entire
> 'national' movement in Carlsbad that the 'German' courage of these
> boys is vented specifically only against poor Jews. In our opinion,
> the whole anti-Semitic movement in Carlsbad is a blot of shame for
> the entire town.[19]

A year later, in June 1904, a Carlsbad innkeeper put up signs in his tavern stating, "No Jews admitted," and he had glasses ready in the event that some Jewish spa patrons nonetheless entered his premises; these were inscribed "For Jews only." When the bureau of the District Chief Officer heard about the incident, it threatened to take measures, stating: "The proprietor of a tav-ern is required by virtue of the license granted him to serve food and drink to all guests, without distinction of nationality and religion."[20] The *Mitteilungen aus dem Verein zur Abwehr des Antisemitismus* were pleased that the "au-thorities in Carlsbad [. . .] had set a good example."[21] What the paper did not report was the reaction of the innkeeper. In response to this warning, he put up another sign: "Only because of official pressure are Jews tolerated on these premises."[22]

Although anti-Semitic statements were considered undesirable by the au-thorities, Carlsbad hotel owners advertised in anti-Semitic newspapers and guidebooks, openly espousing their ideology. Regularly at the beginning of the season, readers of Jewish papers were warned about these hotels. In the summer of 1902, twenty-one Carlsbad hotels and spa houses whose owners were well known anti-Semites were already on the exceptionally long list.[23] A journalist commented:

Imagine if all the hotels in Carlsbad were to come down with the pestilence of anti-Semitism, and the spa administrations as well. Is it permissible to close the doors of a unique spa to people looking for a certain kind of recovery and cure and who have done nothing wrong, [. . .] or to cause a situation where the patient who must of course avoid all excitement should find, instead of the cure he seeks, that his suffering instead is made worse?[24]

Frequently, at the end of these lists warning spa guests was a notice that one or another hotel owner had asked for the opportunity to respond and provide a correction.[25] Thus, the owner of the Carlsbad *Sanssouci* was astounded to learn from a regular reader of the *Mitteilungen* that his hotel had been labeled anti-Semitic. He explained that his shop tenants were Jews and that Jews, "as our informant has clearly established," were among his "best guests. The innkeeper believes that this rumor arose only because of a competitor's envy." His hotel was then removed from the list.[26]

Although Carlsbad and Marienbad already before World War I were considered by attentive travelers as localities with some tendency to anti-Semitism, not only in wintertime, complaints remained within reasonable limits. Yet at the beginning of the 1920s, things began to change, and Jewish spa guests and summer vacationers came to feel deeply insecure. After the war, anti-Semitism in spas and summer resorts in Germany and Austria took an increasingly radical turn, and many localities now decided not to take in any more Jewish visitors.[27] Although the situation in Bohemia was comparatively quiet and protected, travelers had become especially attentive. Jewish spa patrons in Carlsbad and Marienbad continued as before to be treated in a cordial and friendly manner, especially since the spas had been particularly hard-hit by the postwar economic situation. Yet the seasonal polarization had worsened: in the 1923 elections, the German-National Party, with its anti-Semitic mayoral candidate Hermann Jakob, won the poll by a large margin. The Social Democrats remained the second strongest party but had lost many votes in their traditional area of electoral support, the industrial zones of the town. The party in third position now was the DNSAP (*Deutsche Nationalsozialistische Arbeiterpartei*), which already since 1920 maintained close fraternal ties with the National Socialists (NSDAP) in Germany. Meanwhile, the Carlsbad Liberals had shrunk to insignificance, as had the sole Czech party.[28]

While the winter anti-Semitism tended to get worse and the summers apparently remained unchanged, ever more ambivalent experiences were increasingly preoccupying the spa guests. Although most probably a large segment of the Jewish spa patrons did not have much idea of the local arrangements, a growing group observed the changes with apprehension. The distance to other spa guests was increasing and it was felt important to identify and make public anti-Semitic hoteliers, innkeepers, and doctors. The difficulty inherent in this undertaking is illustrated by an extensive correspondence between members and staff of the *Centralverein deutscher Staatsbürger jüdischen Glaubens (CV)*. The inconsistencies in the situation in Carlsbad and Marienbad left both CV members seeking answers and CV staff trying to respond in a state of relative helplessness. The product of the seasonal change between radical German-national anti-Semitism and hypocritical depoliticized hospitality shown to tourists was an ensemble of accusations, investigations, corrections, even disputes and polemics inside the CV.[29] Although there were also ambivalent experiences in other health spas, the situation was nowhere as thorny as here.

Unlike in Germany, the CV beyond its borders did not make direct contact with potentially anti-Semitic hoteliers and innkeepers, but rather relied on a network of informants.[30] In the main, these persons were year-round residents who were considered to be in a position to assess the local situation and if necessary to make inquiries. Thus, the CV did not only have to depend on the short-term impressions of spa guests and their sometimes contradictory statements, but instead instructed the informants to check on the hotels that were recommended in anti-Semitic travel guidebooks or had been reported by CV members. If an informant confirmed that an innkeeper or hotelier was indeed known to be anti-Semitic, or did not treat Jewish spa guests with the necessary friendly hospitality, the name of the establishment was included in the red lists of the *CV-Zeitung* and in special brochures published by the CV.[31]

This system of informants also had its weak points and embroiled those involved at times in conflicts of interest. In the sensitive situation of the Jewish Communities in Carlsbad and Marienbad, several informants tried to deescalate the tensions there, for the good of the *Gemeinde*. Thus, one of the most important on-the-spot informants in Carlsbad was Rabbi Ziegler himself, whose diplomatic and balancing position within the context of the town generally was manifested in recommendations he made to the CV to remove certain hotels from their list of anti-Semitic establishments.[32]

The CV offered its members an information service that accepted personal reports on experiences, or replied to individual inquiries about the anti-Semitic institutions and facilities in a particular locality. This correspondence documented not only anti-Semitic experiences while a guest at a spa, but also covered attempts by members to defend hotels and spa houses listed as anti-Semitic by the *Centralverein* or the *Israelitisches Familienblatt*.[33] In its replies, the Berlin CV central office sought to explain the complexity of the situation and to specify the reasons why a given hotel had been included in the red lists:

> In answer to your inquiry as to the reasons why the Abbazia in Carls-
> bad is listed in our list of anti-Semitic spas, we respectfully wish to
> inform you that the owner of this spa house, Herr Löw, was already
> many years ago the leader of the nationalistic anti-Semites in Carls-
> bad. It is not surprising for us that you and other Jewish spa patrons,
> while staying in Carlsbad, have noticed nothing in regard to the anti-
> Semitic attitudes of individual hotel owners. That can be adduced
> from the fact that most of the hoteliers in Carlsbad on the list are so-
> called "winter anti-Semites," who during the summer season pocket
> the money of Jewish spa guests with a friendly face, yet otherwise
> at every opportunity, elections and the like, do not make any secret
> whatsoever of their anti-Semitic attitudes and ethos.[34]

The decisions of the CV were rarely as clear as in the case of the owner of the *Abbazia*. But in most of the other situations, the boundaries were fuzzy and the context difficult to assess. After the *Israelitisches Familienblatt* had reported on regular anti-Semitic meetings taking place in a Carlsbad spa house, the local informant there explained: "The leaseholder of the spa house opens his premises to anyone who pays the bill, his party is his pocket."[35]

One of the main reasons for the helplessness of the CV in these matters was the situation of the local Jewish Communities, since reports on anti-Semitism in their town damaged them as well as all others. Even more, the threat of a decrease in the size of the summer Community meant not just the loss of financial and moral support, but also endangered local Jewish identities, which were in any case fragile. For that reason, many members of the local Communities opposed such criticisms, because they rightly had good reason to fear that not only would they suffer in the summer from the boycott against anti-Semitism, but the following winter would face the anger of the other residents in Carlsbad. Their position in the society of their small town was insecure enough without repeatedly having to be reconfirmed and consolidated anew. Asked for his personal view on the situation, a Carlsbad physician told the CV in May 1930:

> In my entire 25 years of practice, I know of no case where Jews any-where in Carlsbad were attacked because of their religion. [. . .] That is also impossible, because the authorities here would take forceful ac-tion immediately in such an eventuality. Anti-Semitism here is latent and too clever to neglect any opportunity for material advantage. In spa houses where the owners are German-national aldermen, even the most shabby Polish Jew, if he pays, will be treated with the greatest of respect.[36]

As peculiar and complicated as the work of the CV in Carlsbad was, it re-mained all the more difficult in Marienbad. The idyllic small spa was men-tioned less often in connection with winter anti-Semitism, and had a greater reputation than Carlsbad for being a preferred holiday retreat for Eastern European Jews. Only in isolated instances did the *Abwehrverein* or the CV warn about anti-Semitic hotels and guesthouses in Marienbad, which at first glance seemed almost as peaceful and inviting as Franzensbad. But a second glance was enough to reveal a situation comparable to that in Carlsbad. In fact, the correspondence on the situation in Marienbad is far larger in the files of the CV than that on Carlsbad. In paradoxical discussions, these letters combine reports on anti-Semitic facilities, retractions of the reports, lengthy investigations, cautious processes of decision making, and often in the end conflict and disputes.

The main reason put forward by the *Centralverein* for this complicated balancing act was the exceptionally high proportion of Jews among the spa clientele of Marienbad. Given this situation, the CV repeatedly found itself saddled with the peculiar task of defending the hotel or medical practice of a declared anti-Semite, and not putting said individual on its red lists of en-terprises to avoid. This was because if his clientele, as so often in Marien-bad, was almost exclusively Jewish, the mere accusation of anti-Semitism could demolish the proprietor's business.[37] But in any case, the CV wished to prevent endangering the precarious position of the local Marienbad Jews, to whose evident detriment such an event would be interpreted. For that reason, Marienbad was also not included in the general warning lists of the *CV-Zeitung* and the *Israelitisches Familienblatt*, but rather only advertised as a mailbox notice: interested CV members could personally request a confidential list that had been put together on the basis of anti-Semitic travel guidebooks and statements by spa guests and informants if they so desired. Since the situation in Marienbad was especially sensitive, the CV asked its informants to be very careful in checking all data in order to avoid the numerous subsequent demands for a correction and retraction.[38]

Despite all precautionary measures, the *Centralverein* would only rarely appear to please its members in connection with these conflicts, and often had to retract data it had given on anti-Semitic facilities or provide reasons why there should not be a more consistent crackdown on such offenders. Many guests who visited Marienbad stated in their letters what was a widespread view within the Jewish spa public: namely, that Jewish newspapers should emphatically warn spa patrons about a hotel "whose owner was happy to take Jewish money but otherwise, and especially during the winter, was an active anti-Semite."[39] Other members alerted the CV office to anti-Semitic public events and meetings that took place during the season but toward its end, asking the CV to observe the establishment more carefully.[40] Still others complained that the hotel they were staying at or the doctor they had consulted was listed as anti-Semitic, although they had had a positive experience.

If the hotel owners or physicians learned from their clients that they were on the warning lists, they reacted with letters of complaint sent to the CV office in Berlin, often declaring that they had been fighting for years "against these suspicions spread by competitors."[41] Some even went so far as to attach character references from the Jewish Community or from a Jewish alderman ensuring they were neither members in any anti-Semitic association nor politically active.[42] The informants were then asked to check the association and party memberships of these persons. But that often turned out to be a difficult task, since concepts such as "Aryan paragraph" and "registered member" suddenly became subject to flexible explanation and interpretation. If membership in an association was established that was "not just a-Semitic, but as we know from a reliable source, anti-Semitic," the hotel or doctor's practice remained on the warning list.[43]

These processes of decision making repeatedly triggered conflict within the CV, and there were instances where a member of the CV resigned from the organization due to a sense of solidarity with his hotelier or physician, who in the member's view had always behaved with integrity beyond any doubt. Ludwig Holländer, the director of the CV, tried to explain the difficult role of the association to such a former member:

Fundamentally speaking, the area of economic anti-Semitism, under which I wish to classify the question under consideration here for the sake of clarity, belongs to the most important but most difficult areas of activity of our association. [. . .] We are caught here between Scylla and Charybdis. [. . .] Sometimes it is a matter of the personal hyper-sensitivity of a reporter, sometimes, conscious or not, the envy of competition, sometimes unjustified generalizations of individual facts, either incriminating or exonerating.[44]

As a result of these conflict situations, the view developed for a time among the CV staff that it was not the ideological conviction of the proprietor that was decisive, but rather the question of whether a spa guest felt comfortable and safe in his establishment. Ultimately, it was no secret that almost the entire locality in Carlsbad consisted of anti-Semites, and that the town mayor was at the top of the local list of the anti-Semitic *Deutschnationale Partei*. Yet during the high season, even the local Jews did not suffer in any way because of that.[45] Only toward the end of the 1920s did the CV begin to include all hotels and guesthouses in its lists categorically, and without a further check, if they were recommended in the *National Socialist Yearbook*.[46]

Fighting Cockerels

Artistic caricature is only convincing where existence itself is already a caricature—of what should it otherwise convince us of?

—Georg Simmel, "Über die Karikatur"[47]

As bright summers and foggy cold winters followed one after the other on the black River Tepl in a round of change charged with politics and emotion, critical voices began to be heard among the residents of Carlsbad. In the fledgling Czechoslovak Republic—the successful heyday years of the world-class spa were now over, and would perhaps never return—individual voices spoke out against the dominant opinion in the German enclave. They openly formulated their misgivings about the artificially depoliticized atmosphere of the special arrangements, speaking against the taboos and falsehoods that had served to completely divide the society of the town. Admittedly, such voices were few, they have left little in published form, and they expressed their views exclusively in a vein of humor, adapted to the local logic, and thus ambivalent and hard to fathom.

One such voice was that of the *Karlsbader "Kikriki,"* a satirical paper founded in 1924 and probably discontinued sometime in 1930. The thin monthly publication was published on cheap newsprint with low-quality types. Behind the misleading name of the paper ("Cock-a-doodle-do") lay concealed a "barbed ironical polemic paper against one and all." The *"Kikriki"* itself was a satirical take on the Christian Socialist Viennese paper *Kikeriki* and sought to counter its pan-German and anti-Semitic agenda. The target of the attacks was the moral degeneration of the spa town and its politics, the utilitarianism of its residents and their hypocrisy. As the local scandal sheet, *"Kikriki"* probably had a relatively large readership, whose different factions regularly took the main editor to court—most of the time without much success, since after all this was only a humor magazine.

The paper was in effect a muckraking sheet, a small local monthly in the tradition of the satirical tabloid. Its publisher and most prominent editor was the Carlsbader Poldi (Leopold) Weiß: he was featured on the front page, next to the obligatory cockerel, as a portly, vengeful journalistic cowboy, sporting a pistol in one hand and a pen in the other—or portrayed as a grinning intellectual, with rotund face, spectacles, and a crown of thorns. Although Weiß was the central personality of the paper, little is known about him other than that he lived in the Carlsbad suburb of Drahowitz and is recalled by the former German population of the town as a local original.[48]

Poldi Weiß loved to play a satirical game of deliberate confusion that wrapped his identity in a haze of true and invented allusions. Thus, he sometimes refers to himself as an "infamous Jewish rascal," and at another time declares that he is "thank God, of the same tribe" as the Carlsbad Jews, even if he had "signed a pact with Hell."[49] On another occasion, he described the *"Kikriki"* as a "purely Aryan sheet" that would only hire staff of "Aryan descent [. . .] blond, blue eyes—but with the abilities of a Jewish journalist. In the main, he has to be in full and complete possession of his powers of irony. However, we believe that up to now, such a phenomenon has never seen the light of living day."[50]

Poldi Weiß positioned himself, independent of his actual family background, outside the mutually hostile groups in Carlsbad society. Instead he was in solidarity with the downtrodden in society—the poor, weak, and oppressed. He ignored taboos and wrote against the abuses and social injustices in the town. That included the still largely customary exploitation of domestic female servants and waitresses, forced into prostitution by their employers, along with the prostitution of many young men.[51] In line with this, he formulated the program of the satirical sheet at the beginning of 1926 as follows: "We avenge all the downtrodden, the victims of society or of certain sections of society, getting back at those who were the cause of this. We avenge the despised and ridiculed poor by also laughing a bit at the wealthy of Carlsbad grubbing in their money and filthy fat, because the sweetest taste of revenge is successful scorn."[52]

In his satirical articles, Weiß describes everyday life in Carlsbad as an unending, ridiculous, and a bit sad farce: the place of action is *Warmbod,* a kind of cross between a health spa and the "fools of Gotham," a "cretinopolis" whose residents *"bei uns z'Warmbod"* are the protagonists in this never-ending drama of annoyance. The central concern and topic running like a red thread through the pages of the *"Kikriki"* is the everyday ambivalence of life in Carlsbad, especially among the Jews. In his satire, Poldi Weiß strikes out in nearly all directions: against the *Deutsche Nationalpartei,* which discriminates against Jews and Czechs as "alien peoples," against the "swastika crowd" and their dense-witted *Deutschtum*; against the mendacious "racialist anti-Semites," who are only keen on raking in personal profit and love to make life tough for the "Jew still unbaptized"; against the "assimilationists" and the converted Jews, who cozy up to the German nationalists and would sooner jettison their Jewish identity today than tomorrow. And also significant, and certainly not least, he satirized the municipality and the Jewish *Kultusgemeinde,* which bore direct responsibility for the impossible situation.[53] One of his worst enemies was the immediate adversary, the anti-Semitic press. Poldi Weiß accused it of pretending to be un-political while seeking to silence Jewish and Czech residents in Carlsbad, and refusing to accept their ads and announcements. At the start of the 1927 summer season, he scoffed: "The Carlsbad media landscape has grown poorer by the loss of one sheet propagating anti-Semitism. The *Deutsche Tageszeitung,* which not so very long ago was sharpening its snout lambasting Poldi Weiß's 'Jewish ways of fighting' against the racially pure gentleman Josephus Lindner, now is even listing the schedule for the Jewish services at the synagogue."[54]

In his texts, Poldi Weiß provided a caricature of the discourse and language of his German-national adversaries as a concatenation of anti-Semitic stereotypes, and he presented the language of the Jews as a parody of Yiddish, admixed with a few select Hebrew words more or less depending on the topic. He enjoyed working with the effect of estrangement or *Verfremdung,*

likening Carlsbad to Japan and Jews to Chinese. He predicted that the Carlsbad Jewish "assimilationists" were going to come down with diabetes from
all their sweet talk, while the Eastern European Jews were derogatorily labeled as "parasites," "beggars" (*Schnorrer*), and "thieves" (*Ganoven*) in the local jargon—individuals who nevertheless deserved to be defended and given
proper warning about the dangers and pitfalls of Carlsbad society. In short
sketches and stories, he expostulated on their cousins who had emigrated to
America, and who, as parvenu ladies or crafty small-time criminals, like the
imaginary figure Leib Pelzlaus, showed up on the promenades in Carlsbad.[55]

Whenever there were elections, "*Kikriki*" shifted into high gear, bringing
detailed analyses of the political mood in the town. Weiß repeatedly accused
the party representatives, whether on the liberal or German-national side of
the spectrum, of trying to woo the votes of the

> Jews, often spit at and pummeled both physically and morally, who no
> matter what their class, are supposed to vote for the candidate recom-
> mended by the leadership of the Jewish Community, alone for reasons
> of requisite discipline and religious solidarity. The Jewish leadership
> has spoken, and the Jew must obey. [. . .] Up in the higher echelons of
> this leadership sit the richest co-religionists and fellow members of
> the folk, there's no wheeling and dealing, the order is: obey.

Poldi Weiß was acrimonious in his comments on the role of the Jewish Community in the race for Jewish votes during the elections in the spring of 1927.[56]

The behavior of the Jewish *Kultusgemeinde* remained for him a constant
source of disappointment and annoyance, which is why its influential members seldom come off in a good light in his portrayals:

> We (Poldi Weiß) divide the Jews of Warmbod into three classes: the
> elite, the traders and the beggars. Belonging to the elite are the bank
> directors, industrialists, merchants and university graduates who
> were clever enough to transform their knowledge into big money.
> Traders include smaller businessmen, and the category of *Schnor-
> rer* or beggars comprises tramps and vagabonds, panhandlers, office
> workers, small shopkeepers and university graduates who saw their
> knowledge solely as a means for promoting the general well-being,
> and due to this idealism completely forgot and neglected their own
> material selves. Also part of the elite are the members of the Executive

Board of the Jewish community, who will never tolerate that someone from a lower class will ever sit in their august ranks.[57]

A lack of solidarity and community identity is Poldi Weiß's diagnosis of what ails Carlsbad Jewry. And on the occasion of a candidature in a Jewish electoral list, he stated: "A large, let's say very large proportion of our Jews" would be ashamed to "show even any snippet of sympathy for the Jewish list, for which the shopkeeper or, according to their notions, the beggar casts his ballot."[58] But it was precisely those shopkeepers and beggars who demonstrated Jewish consciousness and pride, and "finally wanted to make a clean slate of things, and by casting their ballot for their own candidate, sought to sidestep the kick in the ass of wanting to be tolerated, and to form a Jewish bloc." And a Jewish bloc that "both the religious and racist anti-Semites would badly break their teeth on." Deeply disappointed, he described these Community members who take part in German-national gatherings and seek dubious entry into these circles: "Fellow Jews, we ask you again and again: Let your enemies have their machinations. Don't constantly humiliate yourselves with your intrusive familiarities. Instead, turn your social abilities to the good of your own people, because that is your duty."[59] Poldi Weiß believed that if they did this, anti-Semitism in Carlsbad would disappear overnight, "were the Jews with capital to prohibit the Warmboders from making use of this game previously permitted. This entire anti-Semitic fuss is nothing but the envy of a witless mass toward shrewd Jews, and the politics of a few people who depend on this."[60] He saw potential for change and a few reasons to remain loyal to his mission, solely in the growing self-confidence of the young Carlsbad Jews and the financial clout and size of the Jewish Community.

The "*Kikriki*" was less optimistic in describing perspectives for a change among other Carlsbad residents, whose mendacious and aggressive character he lambastes with acrimony. The paper energetically endeavored to uncover the ruses and devices of the Carlsbad "economic anti-Semites" and to make public the sundry ambivalent aspects of their behavior. Although they had no respect for Jewish businessmen, they cut deals with them and served as hosts in the summer even to Orthodox observant Jews from Eastern Europe—who during the rest of the year functioned as the most popular image of the adversary in their German-national attitudes and ethos. And every autumn, "once the last spa guest has departed, and those still left belong to the rabble," the courteous and accommodating business partners and polite hoteliers are transformed at the stroke of the season once again into aggressive Egerlander nationalists, who at times do not shrink back even from anti-Semitic violence.[61]

> It's autumn again. [. . .] Quickly open the lowest drawer of the bug-infested leather sofa and pull out the cloth of our national conscious-ness, carefully stored there over the summer. Freshly iron the crease of anti-Semitism, because now we can allow ourselves to think and feel once again along German radical lines. And, if the opportunity arises, beat up the Jew. Oh, we're sure the times were heavenly when you could just burn the Jew. But nowadays he won't put up with that anymore, and the most awful thing is that the stinker won't even allow you to give him a solid thrashing. Because often what happens is that the swastika boys are the ones who get beaten up if they were bold enough to make some trouble for a Jew. So in the autumn people have the courage once again to stage the good old German masquerade. This means, well, people don't yet quite dare, yet in order not to stand on ceremony with the big shots and to satisfy our customs and tradi-tion, people send children dressed in costumes out into the streets. [. . .] The crowd of children, large and small, bellows and hoots. But when among the spectators on the street they spot a Jewish face, then calls of phoey or 'hep-hep' resound from the delighted throng.[62] Yes, they've trained the youngsters well. They'd never curse a Czech, be-cause then they might get arrested. But a Jew, the member of a mi-nority, it's all right to hurl some uncouth remark at the guy or maybe even a stone at his head.[63]

The "crease of anti-Semitism" was most likely too old and deep for the pro-minority policies of the new Czech Republic to be able to protect the Carls-bad Jews from the mounting German nationalism of the Egerlander. As a satirical sheet, the "*Kikriki*" definitely exaggerated the actual situation, pre-senting it in the full subjectivity of Poldi Weiß's perspective. At the same time, however, he reported on spaces of possibility and discourse that during the 1920s already reflected a tense situation in the annual round of everyday life in Carlsbad.

Chapter 10

Peculiar Adverts

> This man's lines are meant to cheer and delight you. With
> Democritus, he ridicules humanity (and not like Heraclitus,
> bemoaning humankind). And he does so with equanimity
> and understanding.
>
> —Mentullus, *Intimacies from an International Spa*[64]

Josef Steiner, a lawyer and long-time informant for the *Centralverein* in
Marienbad, sent the CV main office in Berlin an article in August 1928 that
had been published shortly before in a local spa paper.[65] In his enclosed letter,
Steiner remarked that the article, entitled "The Poles," gave a vivid description about how observant Orthodox Jews from Eastern Europe were being
treated in Carlsbad. He suggested that people in Berlin could form a quite
exact picture of the comparable situation in Marienbad from this article. It
begins:

> Who doesn't know them, the disciples from the East? You can see
> them in large numbers in Carlsbad. They have their fixed quarters at
> the Morgenzeile, and in nice orderly fashion, in twos and threes, they
> stroll from there to the Sprudel, to Mühlbrunn and the other min-
> eral springs. [. . .] You can't say that the men in caftan are a welcome
> sight in Carlsbad, they're tolerated according to the old adage: "Beg-
> gars can't be choosers." The Polish Jews stroll along their way between
> glances chilly and taunting.[66]

The article stated that the Orthodox Jews did not let the hostile atmosphere
disturb them in any way. Situated at a distance from Carlsbad society, they
moved only between the prayer house, the hotel, and their favorite meeting
place, the Elisabethpark. They became, the article stressed, far more unpopu-
lar and "the horror of the hotelier" the moment they "took off their caftan
and then looked apparently quite civilized and very American." Changed in
external appearance, "striking figures almost all,[67] elegant in their demeanor,"
they would then meet their "Orthodox relatives" in Carlsbad and invite
them to the expensive hotels they were staying at. Appalled, the Carlsbad
hotel owners felt they had been deceived and swore never again to accept an
"Amerikohner" as a guest.[68]

The author continues by noting that the city is doing its Eastern European

guests an injustice, since with their precise knowledge of the medical facilities in Carlsbad, they are after all the best source of publicity for the town in
Eastern Europe. Moreover, the life of the "Polish Jews" was closely bound
up with an interest in business, which is why they were playing a key role in
the expansion of the circles of commerce in Carlsbad. Upon returning home
after every trip, they took a number of the newest products of Czech industry
with them, and "quite often, we then have large orders placed from there,
which provide good business for our local commerce in times of terrible economic stagnation."[69]

Nonetheless, Carlsbad hotel proprietors felt it was a debasement and loss
of status for their establishment if "Polish Jews" registered as guests. "And
here the illogical element emerges. The hotel owner is proud of a Negro, Arab
or Indian—naturally with a princely title—but a Polish Jew for him is a horror." The observant Orthodox Jews would even respect these incomprehen-
sible negative feelings against them, and only if there were an acute shortage
of rooms would they try to get a room in some better hotel. The author is
annoyed:

> How pathetic when contrasted with this true cultural mission of the
> East European Jew is the role of many a princely impostor from Egypt,
> Sudan or No-Man's Land. [. . .] An old towel wrapped around the
> head has more importance in Carlsbad than the dignified silk caftan
> of the East. [. . .] But our "Poles" are not fazed by this at all. They come
> to Carlsbad not because of the Carlsbaders but for the springs, and
> there is not a spa administration anywhere on the globe that could
> persuade them to visit a spa whose utility for their physical health and
> business they fail to see.[70]

This partly ambivalent article appears to have been a success with its readers, because the author, Gustav Wack-Herget of the Carlsbad *Hotel Jägerhaus*,
included it a few years later in a collection of articles entitled *Karlsbad. Wie
es die wenigsten kennen* (Carlsbad as But Only a Few Know the Place). The
thin volume that appeared in 1933 in Carlsbad appealed to potential spa patrons as a kind of alternative travel guide, and sought to provide them with
an unusual window onto local special characteristics: "Why don't you go to
Carlsbad?—Yes, indeed, why *don't* you go to Carlsbad?" is the way the book
begins. It is a guide lacking in all the essential features of a conventional
guidebook: it has no practical information, historical introductions, or medi-

cal recommendations. The author addresses two fictive "tourists," male and female, who would like to get to know another Carlsbad, mysterious and unknown. After the sufficiently popular tales of Carlsbad evidently fail to excite the two, Wack-Herget suggests that he can present the city and its residents to them quite apart from that familiar battery of clichés comprised of "old customs," "narrow streets," "high prices," and a town "frugal, precocious and snobbish." When they finish reading, they are supposed to shout: "Carlsbad is really charming, a town only just a few really know!" And then they immediately hop on the next train to the city.[71]

The book is not written very professionally, and is most probably the only one that Gustav Wack-Herget ever published. Although the slim volume saw only a small print run and was read by a limited readership at best, it pursued the same goal as all other travel guides, at a time when Carlsbad had long since ceased to be the magnet it once was: namely to lure as many people as possible to the town. But the book did that in a rather strange way.

In the first third of the book, the readers encounter a chapter entitled "Distinctive features you simply have to know." This is a chapter they should read right at the outset, since it is indispensable for understanding what precedes and follows it. It notes that any city has its characteristics, "but aside from these distinctive features, Carlsbad has special and quite entertaining facilities and customs, which are in often striking contrast with general European customs." Included in the description of these special features is the demand to keep to the right on all streets. And the odd fact that nowhere are there so many public clocks as here, although apparently none display the correct time. Wack-Herget mentions another completely different topic as a further special feature of the town:

> You'll ask me: "Are there Jews here?" [...] Probably the Jews elsewhere are far less popular than they are here in Carlsbad. I don't intend here to write about the Jewish problem, but simply wish to call your attention to the peculiar views on this question which you can encounter in Carlsbad. It has nothing to do with politics or anti-Semitism. Because one question can be heard on the lips of everyone in Carlsbad, just as often from Jews as from Nazis: "Is he Jewish?"—all other questions are of secondary importance. Whether the actor or composer has visible talent, whether the well-known doctor is successful in treating patients, whether the spa guest gives a generous tip—the first question is always: is he a Jew? One thing is absolutely

certain: the merit of the composer or doctor or whatever a person may be is assessed without any consideration of that person's religion. None whatsoever. Let me give you some good advice for taking the waters when in Carlsbad: don't talk so much about this stuff. Otherwise people here will try to find out whether you too "are a Jew."[72]

One may wonder: do the "peculiar views on this question which you can encounter in Carlsbad" actually have "nothing to do" with politics or anti-Semitism? During the high season, probably not. Everything else remains shrouded in the winter fog, as the months march on quietly, in a kind of monotony, interrupted at the most by the patriotic event of the church fair. As the author notes with a touch of sarcasm: "The Carlsbaders are genuine Egerlanders, and like all Egerlanders, they're pretty robust," coarse and lumbering, reactionary and a just bit greedy for money.[73] The author fails to mention that every tenth winter resident of Carlsbad was also Jewish, and that people knew very exactly who these persons were, to say nothing of the rapidly growing Czech population group.

Wack-Herget's somewhat alternative travel guide was not the only book of this kind that one might find in Carlsbad at the beginning of the 1930s. One year before, a local humorist by the name of Arthur Mendl had published a volume of poetry under the pen name Mentullus, which promised its readers a glance into local "intimacies."[74] In uniformly poor rhyme, Mentullus jokes about the international public, and invokes the city as a cosmopolitan center, which is not unusual. However, it is a striking fact that almost all his spa guests have stereotypically Jewish names, and that they become embroiled in a relatively harmless game that makes a caricature of them as stingy petty bourgeois, arrogant parvenus, or eccentric Eastern European Jews.[75] In the poem *"Am Sprudel"* (At the Sprudel), for example, he ridicules a man "dressed in a black caftan" who moves helter-skelter around the spring, drinking seven glasses of water per hour. Asked if he wasn't overdoing the cure a bit, he answers that he has been preparing his tea with saline Sprudel water in order to save money by not buying the far too costly Carlsbad coffee.[76] The highlighting of the almost exclusively Jewish protagonists places the book in a questionable light, suggesting two possible target readerships: one with a leaning toward anti-Semitism or a Jewish readership with more than a touch of self-irony.

Although the global economic crisis was now a few years in the past, the economic situation in the expensive upscale spas in western Bohemia was still far from recovery at the beginning of the 1930s.[77] The economically strapped situation was probably one of the main reasons why locals decided to experiment with alternative advertising strategies. In addition, this kind of humoristic presentation of surprising insights also was more on the offensive in dealing with Carlsbad realities. It presented ambivalences and discrepancies as "human qualities" that wished to be viewed as just as attractive and pardonable as the coarseness of the robust German Egerlander.[78] Against the backdrop of the "peculiar" situation in Carlsbad, these texts were perhaps actually directed to all and wished to please everyone, both anti-Semitic and Jewish spa guests. That was because in its "peculiar" logic, the spa town had a permanent need to offer explanations to both groups.

The "Carlsbad" envisioned as "but only a few know the place" wanted to be seen as an especially charming locale because of all its distinctive characteristics, but in retrospect, and from what must be a fragmentary and incomplete perspective, it appears to have been too hypocritical and utilitarian to have struck others as a really friendly spot for a special health vacation. On the other hand, the continuity of its popularity among Jewish spa guests supports the assumption that during the summer months, the place was more pleasant than other health spas—and nicer than the respective places travelers journeyed from to congregate in Carlsbad. It was quite as possible, here as elsewhere, to overlook or fail to hear anti-Semitic attitudes and remarks—action that suggests they were constantly exposed to this, long since a part of everyday experience back home. It is not surprising that after Hitler's seizure of power, the western Bohemian health spas became sanctuaries for German Jews who wished for a few weeks to have a relaxing respite from the realities of National Socialism. It astonishes even less that people knew quite well just how to exploit this situation in Carlsbad and Marienbad at the expense of ideology, and in so doing to promote the local economy.

Part IV

Jutopia

Chapter 11

A Map

Port Visa—New York—Beersheba—Grunewald—
Wannsee—Pollackia—Kfar Yeladim—the Epstein—
St. Moyshe—Isle of the Blessed—at Auerbach—Graetz . . .
—"Jutopia," A. Isr. Gutfeld, 1939[1]

As a staff member of the *Hilfsverein für die Juden in Deutschland (*Relief Association of Jews in Germany*)*, Dr. Gutfeld had the task of locating potential emigration possibilities and destinations for persecuted German Jews. This was an especially difficult job, and Gutfeld and his colleagues could in fact only assist a very limited number of people. In 1939, when the *Hilfsverein* was finally dissolved, Dr. Gutfeld drew several extraordinary fictional maps of a utopian island state that he dubbed *Jutopia*.[2]

As a colony of the *Hilfsverein*, this country, in its fantastic regions and landscapes, combines the past and a possible future for the refugees: familiar German localities appear there side by side with distant port cities, all closed to the refugees in the real world. In *Jutopia*, they form a common protective sanctuary, an island of refuge and a safe Jewish colony open to all.

The map *Jutopia—H.-V. Kolonie, nach neuesten Forschungen gezeichnet* (Jutopia, Relief Association Colony, draft based on the latest research) is a kind of mental map of European Jewry in 1939, when its world had shrunk to a small island of points of departure and arrival. The places and cities in *Jutopia* are mainly real or defamiliarized places in Germany, Palestine, and around the world. They are located on imaginary rivers, such as Milk and Honey, *Parnasse,* and *Mesumme*, and are surrounded by fantastic mountain ranges and islands:[3] the mountain town of *St. Moische* lies in the mountains of the *Jüdische Schweiss,* which might be read as both Jewish Switzerland or Jewish Sweatland, while stretched along the coast are the cities of London, Brussels, Venice, Prague, and Cape Town; offshore is the island group *Per-*

mitzvoth.[4] The small country is populated by human beings and all kinds of familiar, exotic, and fantastic animals: with its cows, sheep, deer, elephants, turtles, and dragons, fanciful *Jutopia* is slightly reminiscent of Noah's Ark.

The cities in the country appear only once, aside from several exceptions, such as Carlsbad, which is on the map twice: once in the Gallstone Mountains near the *Tsores* (Trouble) range, and the other Carlsbad situated on *Überfluss* (Affluence) River, downstream from the localities of *Basle, Zion, Ruppin*, and *Poznan*, and not far from the *Blumenfeld*.[5] Although much in the geography of this fictional-fanciful colony may be accidental, this double placement of Carlsbad reflects precisely the image that the spa town embodied in the Jewish world at the beginning of the 1920s, and especially in Zionist circles. Soon after World War I, the Zionist Executive in London decided to hold the first World Zionist Congress in many years in Carlsbad.[6] It was not coincidental that the Zionist movement returned to the Jewish place of yesteryear: not just the image and well-developed Jewish infrastructure made the town suitable as a venue for the Congress, but also its geographical location at a kind of midpoint between Western and Eastern Europe. Carlsbad now would remain for several more years a surprisingly well-functioning locale for Zionist meetings and events.

At first glance it may seem a bit astonishing that this health spa, as a symbol of assimilation and the social and physical illnesses of the Diaspora, should advance to being the temporary sanctuary of the Zionist utopia. However, against the backdrop of the transition from the multi-ethnic Austro-Hungarian monarchy to a Czechoslovak nation-state, there had been a semantic shift in the imagined Jewish place that was Carlsbad: after the experience of World War I, when the regular clientele comprising Russian, Polish, and Galician Jews stayed away from the Bohemian health spas, and instead Jewish refugees from the war zones were quartered there, the protective sanctuaries of the Diaspora were no longer functioning in the way they did before. In the face of the misery that the war had brought upon so many Jews and continued to inflict upon them, concern for one's own self appeared to be a decadent choice, irresponsible and egoistic. Predominant now was concern for a collective self and the realization of the national utopia that, since the Balfour Declaration in November 1917, had been a tangible space of possibility.[7] The need for a Jewish place could now no longer tarry in the chimerical space of a summertime place for encounter, dalliance, and protection.

If the place Carlsbad in the Gallstone Mountains and the range of Trouble

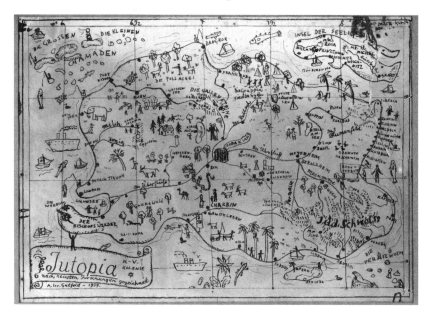

Figure 14. Map of *Jutopia*, A. Isr. Gutfeld, Germany, 1939. Courtesy of the
Jewish Museum, Frankfurt/Main.

(*Tsores*) symbolized the problems of a satisfied yet at the same time insecure life in the Diaspora, the other Carlsbad, located between Ruppin and
Blumenfeld, Basle and Zion, symbolized the utopian spaces of possibility of
a Jewish state. The simultaneous presence of the two places in *Jutopia* disturbed the viewer but little and, likewise, the two images blended well in the
spa town of the 1920s. Although it is certain that some residents or visitors
in the one Carlsbad rejected the other, most lived in both places. Those who
only shortly before had come to take the waters now came to speak on behalf of the envisioned new state and would soon after come back again as
patients. Strangely enough, the two places do not seem to have contradicted
but rather mutually determined one the other. The Zionist presence changed
the image of the Jewish place Carlsbad to such an extent that the decadent
spa was rehabilitated in the eyes of many. The old Carlsbad had made the new
one possible, and only through the new town did the old still survive. The
complexity of Jewish experience in Europe between the wars was reflected in
this duality in precisely the way that Dr. Gutfeld had depicted it in his imaginary cartography.

Chapter 12

Traveling to Bohemia

Heal the Heart (the Body) . . .

Herzl and all the respected gentlemen
Put the foundation of the Jewish State, in Basle
Wolfsson and Nordau and bubbly Ussishkin
And Motzkin and all members of the Congress
Wolfsson brought the funds to the land
Nordau gave the respect and fame
Ussishkin gave the energy of the generation
and Bialik brought "El Hatzipor"
Only Herzl walked there hurting
Because Herzl gave his heart to the land.

—Yoram Teharlev, "Herzl"[1]

It was 3 May 1904. The proprietor of the *Villa Impériale* in Franzensbad, an elegant hotel near the Kurpark, was surprised by an unannounced guest at the reception desk.[2] The bearded gentleman from Vienna was the first patron in this new season, and she had to have a bed brought up to the room she offered him. That same day the gentleman sent two letters to Vienna, one to his wife, Julie, and a second to his mother, Jeanette, in order to tell them he had arrived safely. "My dearest darling," he wrote to Julie, "I have a splendid and cheap room, am staying right in the middle of the park in this elegant hotel, in a salon with four windows up on the first floor," and from this vantage he even had a direct view of the spa orchestra.[3] Franzensbad, still abuzz with preparations for the impending beginning of the summer season, seemed to him to be dead, like Altaussee in November: the merchants were getting ready to put a new coat of paint on their shops, the book dealer had started to unpack his stock, you couldn't even find a copy of the *Neue Freie Presse* from Vienna, and with the exception of the local lending library, there was little diversion for the guest from the capital. He set Julie's mind at ease regarding her worries that Franzensbad was full of women of all ages, since it was recommended especially as a spa for ladies with gynecological ailments: "In general here at the moment, I'm not just the only man but also the only woman. The spa music is already playing, but since it wasn't certain that I'd come by, they stopped early, at 4:30 P.M."[4]

Unexpectedly but a few days earlier, Theodor Herzl had found it necessary to take a sudden trip to Franzensbad. In a diary entry of 2 May 1904, his forty-fourth birthday, he mentioned in passing that he had had a "medical consultation" two days before. Dr. Bondy's diagnosis appeared to be serious, because he ordered his patient to leave immediately for six weeks at the spa to treat an acute heart ailment. Herzl cancelled a planned trip to London on business matters for the Zionist movement, and three days later he left for Bohemia, about ten hours by train from Vienna.[5]

Before departure, he sent a request to his closest associate, David Wolffsohn: "I'm going tomorrow for the cure to Franzensbad, where I have to stay six weeks. During this time I'm not permitted to deal with any business. So just don't write me anything more about business stuff until I come back from the cure."[6] With this restriction on himself, Herzl was dutifully following the regulations laid down for the successful application of a spa cure, as a contemporary popular travel guide for Carlsbad described it. In the chapter "Preparing for your trip," it stated:

> Novices to the spa should put all their affairs in order before leaving in such a way that later at the spa they will be spared strenuous or upsetting tasks, such as business correspondence, etc. In short, the spa guest should leave all worries at home, and dedicate the time of his spa stay solely to the purpose of healing. He should keep this aim alone squarely in sight, and for that reason, should also obey unconditionally the orders of the doctor to whom he has entrusted his treatment. Then he will not need to have any fears about taking the cure in Carlsbad.[7]

Rest and relaxation were regarded as especially important as a means of healing for neurasthenic maladies like the neurological components diagnosed in Herzl's heart ailment. The balneological treatment of these illnesses, as the Berlin professor Alfred Goldscheider explained in the framework of a series of popular scientific lectures in Carlsbad, generally showed good therapeutic results.[8] For chronic nervous ailments and cardiac functional disorders, carbonic acid baths in particular had proved beneficial, since part of their effect was to stimulate cardiac activity.[9] The physician Herzl summoned to his salon at the hotel immediately after arrival in Franzensbad also had trust in this mode of treatment and prescribed mineral baths with high carbonic acid content.[10]

During the first few days, as he assured his wife, Herzl actually believed in the efficacy of the treatment and had set about his "matters of recuperation with the same seriousness of purpose that you know quite well I apply in all serious undertakings."[11] He asked her to please be patient and not to phone him until he could take a break and be "cure-free" for a day: "I have to unbuckle everything that makes me nervous, you can certainly understand that, I'm sure."[12] During this time he was dedicating himself, as he wrote her, solely to the prescribed regimen of his daily bath, long walks, the regular spa concerts, and the reading of a novel by Dickens from the lending library.[13] With the lack of anything happening in the still empty and very quiet spa town, Herzl experienced a "profound quiet, devoid of thought, and an indescribable boredom. I suck on this boredom like someone else on some pleasure. I want to take a long rest from kings, popes, ministers, politics and newspapers. I don't want to hear about anything. By the way, people treat me here with the greatest courtesy. The few people around all know me."[14] Although known by all and greeted by the mayor, the town prior to high season had precious little to offer him. The expected summertime guests had not yet arrived, and the city had not as yet assumed its later role as a hub within a supra-regional and cosmopolitan communication network. "Today there was a distraction for the seven spa guests here," joked Herzl in a letter to Julie, "the spa hall burned down. The weather is lousy. I'm reading a lot."[15]

Already by the third day of the cure, his doctor raved that the success of treatment was "excellent!" and was able to note a small decrease in the size of his expanded heart.[16] Herzl wrote the two women repeatedly that for the first time in many years, he was really resting and recuperating well. Franzensbad was having a "remarkably good" effect, "the color of gray blotting paper" on his face had vanished, and his cheeks were always rosy—without, he swore facetiously, putting on any makeup.[17] It seemed to be very much the case that the everyday round of life in the spa, with its rituals and regularities, was having the desired effect on the patient Herzl. It provided security and structure and helped to sublimate fears about suffering and death.[18]

In these letters, Herzl never mentioned just how serious his condition actually was. He had been suffering for years from a heart ailment that he downplayed to his wife and that he had kept a total secret from his mother.[19] Long before his stay in Franzensbad, he had been informed about the critical condition of his heart, as documented by a comment of his friend Heinrich York-Steiner: "About six years ago, he used to ride the bike all the time. We met on bicycles in the Prater, and he told me that the well-known clinical physician Prof. Nothnagel had seen him riding his bicycle. 'He warned me, he said; Doctor, pay attention to your heart.' In a very melancholy tone, he added: My heart is not strong, the doctors can't find any illness, but I'm not completely healthy."[20]

Already back then Herzl began telling friends that he had "premonitions of an early death."[21] When, two years after the appearance of his heart ailment, his father Jacob died of a sudden and unexpected heart attack, the loss was a hard blow for him, reminding him at the same time of his own physical weakness.[22] For that reason, he had concealed from his mother that his heart was the real reason for taking the cure. Instead he had told her he was going to Franzensbad because of "exhausted nerves" in order to "take a good rest."[23] In the meantime, he allayed Julie's fears with the convincingly formulated story of an unusually rapid therapeutic success.

Letters that Herzl wrote while at Franzensbad to friends and colleagues in the Zionist movement, however, reflect a quite different picture of the situation. After the first few days filled with hope, his mood quickly changed, and he appeared to have less and less faith in any improvement in his condition. "Writing makes me weary," he wrote to conclude a short letter to Wolffsohn, signing it: "Your sick Benjamin."[24] In letters to Israel Zangwill and Alfred Klee, he described his condition as "broken down," and wrote that he was feeling "so so,—la, la. More so-so than la la."[25]

The initial enthusiasm for the cure had also long since evaporated. Even before a week had passed, Herzl received a visit from Nissan Katzenelson, who arrived directly from London to give him a report on the events transpiring there.[26] Katzenelson noted in recollection of his visit that Herzl had been waiting for him at the station in a good mood and apparently not suffering from any malady, but after a short stroll he had a bad attack of weakness and shortness of breath. At 5:30 A.M. he came to Katzenelson's room to pick him up and go to the morning imbibing of the mineral waters, and Herzl joked about the earnestness with which he was pursuing his cure. But in his hand he held a thick pile of paper, an extended memo he wanted Katzenelson to take along to Petersburg, and which he had worked on all night. "I looked at him reproachfully: 'That's how you want to get healthy again? This is what you call a cure?!' 'Yes, my friend. You saw yesterday, after all, we no longer have any time to lose. The last weeks or days. [. . .] We need to hurry.' "[27] After that Herzl returned to his work for the Zionist movement, which until the beginning of his trip he had devoted himself to as if obsessed and without a break. He resumed correspondence that had nearly been broken off, and he even tried to arrange a meeting with the Archduke Eugen of Austria, who happened to be in Carlsbad at the time.[28]

But that meeting never occurred. On 20 May, just two and a half weeks after his arrival in Franzensbad, Theodor Herzl abruptly terminated his cure therapy, planned to last for six weeks. He returned to Vienna, where he was bed-ridden as a result of his poor health, because in hindsight the cure had turned out to be disastrous and his health had worsened.[29] From Herzl's sickbed, Wolffsohn wrote to a friend: "Our Herzl is feeling better. He returned from Franzensbad very ill and it's lucky he interrupted the cure there, because it appears it was not in the least suitable for him."[30] Hoping that mountain air might help, Herzl went with Julie to Edlach near Semmering in the high mountains. Despite initial improvement, after some days of severe shortness of breath, he fell ill with pneumonia and died shortly later at age forty-four.[31]

Although the cause of death has never been unequivocally established, the myth spread that Herzl had died of a heart attack as a result of his dedicated work for Zionism and thus that he had sacrificed "his heart" to the cause. Although Herzl's work within the Zionist movement had not been without controversy, his early death was a huge shock for many. Herzl himself had apparently tried to prepare Wolffsohn for this eventuality when shortly after his arrival in Franzensbad he wrote his successor a short letter: "Don't do anything stupid when I'm dead. Greetings from your friend Benjamin, worked to death."[32]

. . . and the "Soul of the Nation"

> . . . on up to the statue of Herzl. Heads above more heads,
> they hang there like some miracle.
> —Zalman Shneour, "Kongresskolumne," Carlsbad, 1921[33]

Many years later, toward the end of the summer 1921, an unusual transformation, never before seen, occurred in nearby Carlsbad before the astounded eyes of attentive observers: "Although we have a few days to go until the start of the Congress, its atmosphere can already be felt throughout the city," reported the correspondent of the Hebrew newspaper *Ha-aretz*. "Carlsbad is now on the cusp between two seasons: the time of those who came to heal their body has come to an end, and they are slowly leaving town. And the people of the Congress, who are coming here to heal the soul of the nation, are filling up the hotels and private rooms."[34]

In the late summer of 1921, the 12th Zionist Congress convened in Carlsbad. It was a special event for all the participants because this was the first congress not only after the painful rupture of the Great War, but also after the issuing of the Balfour Declaration. Expectations were running high and there was great excitement both among the organizers and among the several hundred delegates and thousands of guests.

There was also some nervousness among the local Carlsbaders, since it was one of the largest congresses that the spa town had ever experienced. The event was a welcome boon for the hoteliers and innkeepers, since the crisis after the war had still not been overcome and visitor figures remained low.[35]

In the Jewish Community, there was a uniformly shared sense of enthusiasm as the Congress approached. A substantial number of young Carlsbaders, who were rebelling against the generation of their parents and their role in the everyday political life of the spa town, had become members of one of the now numerous Zionist associations.[36] In addition to long-established organizations such as *Emunah, Zion,* and the *Jüdisch-Akademischer Klub,* the aftermath of the war saw the founding of the *Jüdischer Sportverein Karlsbad,* the *Wanderbund Techelet-Lavan,* the association *Binjan Ha-aretz,* and the cultural alliance *Tarbut.*[37]

Significantly, as well, many of the spa guests present, intentionally or coincidentally, were also awaiting the Congress with great interest. The Jewish spa public was not only intensively involved in the Zionist associations in town and their activities, but materially as well: in the postwar period, Carlsbad had also become one of the most important sources of funding for the Jewish National Fund anywhere in Czechoslovakia. During a few months in the summer season, the Carlsbad *Sommergemeinde* managed to collect and donate twice as much for construction in Palestine as had Jews in the capital city of Prague.[38]

The news that the Executive Committee of the World Zionist Organi-

zation had decided to hold the 12th Zionist Congress in Carlsbad reached
the municipal council in early April 1921. In a letter to the council, Walter
Kohner, spa physician and chair of the local association *Zion,* informed the
municipality of the decision, which had come in response to an invitation by
the Zionist convention in Brünn. Kohner wrote: "Bearing in mind that hold-
ing this congress will be of exceptional importance for the spa city (regarding
frequency of guests, publicity, reputation of the town, etc.), I wish to take this
opportunity to officially inform the worthy Municipal Council of the intention of the Zionist Organization."[39] This piece of news held out the promise
of a badly needed economic lifesaver to the Carlsbad municipal council, and
there was an immediate positive response.

For symbolic and practical reasons, the Executive in London welcomed
the prospect of what most probably would be a significant Zionist congress
on the soil of the fledgling Czechoslovak state. The success of the national
movements in Czechoslovakia and the positive and supportive attitude of the
new nation-state toward Zionism were just as inviting as was its inflation-
ary currency. The choice of Carlsbad, despite its German-national communal
politics, was likewise certainly due to the international reputation of the city
as a world-class spa, but there were other reasons as well: for one, prices in
the western Bohemian spas had fallen significantly as a result of the war, and
this was appealing to numerous congress participants coming from countries
with weak local currencies. Another positive factor was the ready availability
of some 3,000 hotel rooms in Carlsbad, in contrast with Prague, coupled with
the good rail links the city enjoyed with both Western and Eastern Europe.[40]

The Zionist Executive moved quickly to set up a Congress office in Carlsbad that would handle all questions of organizing the event. Its staff reserved
hotel rooms, organized cheap lodgings and cooking facilities for young
people expected in large numbers from Palestine, Germany, and Eastern
Europe, and negotiated with the municipality for sports grounds, meeting
rooms, and discounts for public transport and spa visitor's taxes.[41]

The chosen venue was the *Grandhotel Schützenhaus,* the building of the
former Austrian *k. u. k. Schützenkorps.* This was the largest available meeting hall in the city. It had been designed by the Vienna architects Fellner and
Helmer at the beginning of the century in neo-Renaissance style, and since
1909 it had housed the vaudeville house *Orpheum.*[42]

Now the entire building including its spacious side rooms was transformed into a Congress center. All around the large hall were the press bureaus of international papers and the two official Congress papers, which

reported daily in German and Czech.[43] A kosher buffet was set up in the other rooms, along with a number of exhibitions. In a Palestine exhibit, the Jewish National Fund put photos, maps, fruits, trees, and flowers on display, meant to provide a striking impression of *Eretz Israel*. Next door, the Ewer Society and the *Jüdischer Verlag* had a book exhibition, and in another room Hermann Struck, Lesser Ury, and a number of other Jewish artists put on an art exhibition.[44]

Already a few days before the beginning of the Congress, numerous Zionist organizations and parties gathered in town and held their own conferences in the spa hall and various hotels. Along with conferences of the *Hitachdut ha-poel ha-tsair ve-tseirey Tsion*—the Union of Young Workers and Young Zionists—the International Zionist Students, and the Jewish National Fund, there were conferences of the Orthodox Zionist organization *Mizrachi*, the pioneer movement *He-chalutz*, and Hebrew writers and Zionist doctors. The Makkabi World Federation, the umbrella organization of Zionist sports, organized its first constituting conference in Carlsbad, where the statutes and the aims and nature of the organization were reformulated. And the Women's International Zionist Organisation, founded a year earlier in London, held its first conference that summer as well.[45]

On 1 September, the Congress was finally opened. Gathered on the main floor in the grand hall of the Schützenhaus were 540 delegates from forty-two countries, dressed in Herzl's tradition in a cutaway coat or dark suit, while roughly a thousand guests crowded into the boxes. After the opening speeches in Hebrew by Chaim Weizmann, the president of the Zionist Organization, and Nahum Sokolow, the chair of the Zionist Executive, there was an address of welcome by the English ambassador to Prague. Then telegrams conveying greetings were read from the Czech government, the Jewish National Council, the Zionist Central Committee, the Carlsbad Municipal Council, the Jewish Community of Carlsbad, and the Carlsbad Zionist associations. A total of sixty-nine press bureaus, mainly of British and American papers, reported on the evening.[46]

The Congress convened for a full two weeks, with a great throng of people and activities extending often into the late-night hours.[47] As the organizers had foreseen, it would become one of the most significant congresses in the history of the Zionist movement.[48] After its official political recognition by the British government, the Zionist movement was suddenly confronted with political realities instead of utopian fantasies.[49] Since the last meeting, before the war, the number of Shekel-paying members had increased fivefold and

Figure 15. Main entrance to the Congress Building, 13th Zionist Congress, Carlsbad, 1923. Central Zionist Archives, Jerusalem, CZA 1052783

had reached one million, a fact that impressed on the Congress its growing responsibility.[50] As the writer and essayist Arthur Holitscher reported, their "utopian desires" were confronted by numerous problems of internal politics and pragmatic questions about building the state. But if the sense of reality left discussion even for a short moment, then "Eretz Israel shimmered like a soap bubble—an impassioned breath pushed the amusing creation, hovering above, through the hall."[51]

One of the key topics at the Congress was the question of the relations with the Arab population in Palestine.[52] The Congress denounced the violence of a few months before in Jaffa, Judea, and Samaria when Jewish settlers, including the writer Yosef Chaim Brenner, had been murdered. Despite this, Chaim Weizmann underscored the need for a "good amicable arrangement and peaceful cooperation between the Jews and the Arabs for the well-being and blessing of the land and its entire population."[53] Under the influence of Martin Buber, the Congress passed a "Resolution on the Arab Question," in which a peaceful life together of Jews and Arabs was formulated as the goal of the new state:

The enmity of a part of the Arab inhabitants, incited by unscrupulous elements to commit deeds of violence, can weaken neither our resolve to construct a Jewish national home nor our will to live at peace and in mutual respect with the Arab people, and together with them to make our home in a flourishing commonwealth whose reconstruction will assure undisturbed national development for each of its peoples.[54]

The official Congress language was Hebrew, along with Yiddish the language most spoken by delegates and participants.[55] Although the Congress was on principle opposed to Yiddish, espousing the spread and promotion of Hebrew language and literature in Palestine and the Diaspora, many discussions continued to be held in Yiddish, the shared vernacular.[56] Arthur Holitscher noted with amusement: "In any case, you have to suppress more than smile when university graduates with whom you've just been conversing in standard German step up to the rostrum and make use of Yiddish, in their passionate speeches words recurring like *dafke*, *efsher* and *machloike*. And when after especially persuasive arguments by some speaker, the packed house breaks out in cries of '*emes*'!"[57]

After twenty-seven sessions and fourteen days of deliberation and discussion, the 12th Zionist Congress was concluded on 15 September 1921, at 3 A.M., with a very positive summary followed by the singing of the anthem *Ha-tikva*.[58] During the two weeks of the Congress, the presence of several thousand participants had dominated the Carlsbad townscape. The liberal *Karlsbader Tagblatt* was euphoric in prophesizing a flourishing future for Carlsbad as a convention city:

And this year the confirmation is there, since right at the moment within our walls we probably have the largest convention that Carlsbad has ever seen. [. . .] Many thousands of supporters of the Zionist idea have gathered together in Carlsbad in recent days, and the spa list of patrons has names almost exclusively of Zionists who have come to attend the Congress. A huge machinery has been set in motion to organize and put on this Congress. [. . .] In the Schützenhaus, the main Congress center, there is a swarm of activity from morning to evening, it resembles a bustling beehive. Upstairs on the first and second floors, we find office after office, where numerous typists sit at their labors into the late hours of the night in order to take smooth care of all Congress affairs. [. . .] Wherever you go, you see the white-blue flower or the Congress badge adorning people's garments.[59]

The Congress office had borrowed all available blue-white banners from the Carlsbad municipality in order to decorate the streets of the town for the duration of the event. Near the Schützenhaus, a special Congress post office was set up, offering picture postcards with Czech and Hebrew texts.[60] Between the sessions, an entire array of events was planned for amusement and social networking and was also meant to appeal to and involve the broader spa public. Along with a "flower day," there were many sports events, including a relay race through town involving 600 Jewish gymnasts, a swimming contest, a bicycle relay race from Prague to Carlsbad put on by *Hagibor Prag*, and gymnastic performances and festivals staged by the *Jüdische Turnerschaft* (Association of Jewish Gymnasts). But the biggest sensation was a soccer tournament with a match between *Hakoah Vienna* and the Jewish Football Federation of the Czechoslovak Republic (*Jüdischer Fußballverband der ČSR*), which the famous Austrian team won 4-0.[61]

In the evenings there were lectures by Max Brod and Martin Buber in the large spa hall, and "East European Jewish song evenings" and concerts with Lia Rosen and the Hakoah Orchestra as gala events. Delegates, participants, and guests could choose among "Hebrew meetings," invitations by Carlsbad Zionists, and a festive religious service at the synagogue, or they could decide to see the documentary movie chronicling the lives of Jewish settlers in Palestine, *Shivat Zion* (1921), by filmmaker Yaacov Ben-Dov at the Apollo Theatre. The film proved so popular it was shown five times.[62]

For Carlsbad, events of this kind were not part of the everyday round; at the same time, the setting of the spa city formed an unusual backdrop for the Zionist convention. Zalman Shneour, who reported on the Congress for the Hebrew paper *Ha-olam*, described all the details of Carlsbad for his readers in a daily "Congress Column." He discussed its geographical and mineralogical special features, as well as its atmosphere and rituals. With a touch of humor, he described the spa public, promenading through the colonnades, drinking cups and glass straws in hand: "Would you like to know how bearded Jews and honorable ladies once looked sitting on their mother's lap? Then go down to the Mühlbrunnen and you can see for yourself."[63]

Other Congress participants encountered daily life in Carlsbad less with

Figure 16. Mass display of female Jewish gymnasts. 12th Zionist Congress, Carlsbad, 1921. Central Zionist Archives, Jerusalem, CZA 1001116.

a sense of bemused curiosity and more with derisive rejection: "The good old Sprudel! It'll probably last out a few more upheavals, until one fine morning the astonished public will let their glass straws slip from the mouth, because the spring has dried up or is blocked. And the hot stream will have found another exit point into a Carlsbad of the future!" This was the wry comment by Arthur Holitscher, deriding the town as the very symbol of a decadent, outdated past. He felt that the "spa bourgeoisie, driven to Carlsbad by worries about their worthy state of health," was "scarcely tolerable" in view of the political changes the Congress symbolized.[64]

During the Zionist presence over several weeks, the atmosphere in the spa town changed ever more, as enthusiastic reports document. The Czech-Jewish paper *Židovské Zprávy* commented:

One could write much more than the framework of a newspaper permits about the Congress, its typical and grand personalities, life in the session hall, in the commissions, in the vestibule, out in front of the main building, on the streets, in the various different localities. But it is indisputable: there is no other Jewish organization which could succeed to such an extent, as has the Zionist Congress, to penetrate with its distinctive physiognomy into the townscape of the host locality, the well-chosen, world-renowned spa of Carlsbad, leaving its shaping stamp upon the city. The Congress was seen and felt everywhere: at the railway station, in the streets, the shops, on the posters, in the bookstores, travel bureaus, movie houses, in the entertainment spots and public halls.[65]

In actual fact, for a short span of time in the early autumn of 1921, there was a city in Europe in which on the streets and in all its facilities, in restaurants and inns, and in stores and shops, you could hear Hebrew being spoken.[66] The changes were clearly visible in the public sphere of the spa district, where the gaze focused on representation and the staging of physicality. In contrast with Basle, Vienna, or other large cities where Zionist Congresses had been held, Zionist functionaries, intellectuals, athletes, and young pioneers populated a space here that was intimate and compact. Writing in his diary, Arthur Ruppin noted: "I saw half of Palestine and many old acquaintances from other countries."[67] Their different look and character, especially the appearance of the young pioneers, were perceived with a sense of astonishment, as Holitscher noted: "A totally new type never seen before: the outdoor Jew, the chalutz returned from the Galut of exile to the Land of Israel," young women "tanned by the sun of the Orient, quiet jubilation in the steeled contours of their limbs, no longer the effete heavy-set harem types of the ghetto."[68] The stage of the spa district, usually occupied with the ever-repeated routines of the everyday spa round of life, was now taken over by the rituals of the Zionist movement: "Young adults were moving in a strange Oriental round folk dance, young boys, girls, some still almost children. And among them also some who were elderly, white-haired—completely free, buoyant, their movements loose and relaxed, delighting in the rhythms of their liberated muscles."[69]

Zesi Rozenblit, born and raised in Berlin, describes in her memoirs how powerfully this atmosphere of Zionist youth culture during the Congress was perceived and experienced as a source of liberation by the sons and daughters from protected bourgeois families. After some initial resistance from her parents, Zesi traveled to the Congress together with a girlfriend. Already on the train, the third-class compartments were filled with young Zionists, among whom Zesi was to meet her future husband: "We arrived in Carlsbad. Not only did I fall in love with Felix Rozenblit, but with the whole city. The joy of youth I had previously repressed [. . .] was suddenly released, it gushed out."[70] Late at night, when the final session of the Congress was over, she wandered together with a few friends into the Carlsbad hills to greet the dawn, while Alfred Berger, a "stocky socialist" and atheist, sang Chassidic melodies. After the small group had returned to town to have coffee, Zesi met a friend of her parents. "When did you go to sleep?" he inquired. "I didn't," she replied with a proud laugh.[71]

Writing in his "Congress Column," Zalman Shneour believed the pacified ambience of the spa had had a positive influence on the Congress. "Charles IV made an effort for us to build a city and sanctuary, a place to which we are called, and where we gather in congresses."[72] The importance of Carlsbad as a place of refuge was different from before, since the expectation of salvation was no longer centered on the physical body and its individual recuperation. In Shneour's view, the neutral soil of the spa town had paved the way for the Zionist utopia to Palestine and forged linkages on levels other than just the political. The international network of spas that had always situated Carlsbad closer to Oostende than Prague had created a neighborly bond between *Eretz Israel* and the young Czechoslovak state: "The hot springs of Carlsbad remind one very much of the hot springs of Tiberias [. . .]. Isn't it a greeting from afar, a reference from the depths, to the respected delegates: 'Remember to rescue the springs of Tiberias!' because distances like these, from Tiberias to Carlsbad, are actually just a small trifle on this wide planet."[73]

Meanwhile, Theodor Herzl had returned in spirit to Bohemia seventeen years after his unfortunate and fateful stay in Franzensbad. Since he had been a presence in the spas for many years in innumerable celebrations of his memory, his spirit and vision along with recollections of his stays in Franzensbad and Carlsbad were invoked with deep emotion during the Congress.[74] Delegates and participants regularly made the short pilgrimage up to a bench on the *Freundschaftshöhe*, a popular vantage point in the hills, where Herzl supposedly liked to sit.[75] And above the Congress itself, his bust rose resplendent as an image of the utopia he had envisioned, patterned on Michelangelo's statue of Moses:[76]

Between two large green myrtle bushes the bust protrudes, in pure white, Theodor Herzl. His upright glance is marked by a slight reserved smile. This gaze hovers over the heads of those presiding, spreading through the great hall with all its galleries and box seats. It appears

Figure 17. Congress Presidium and Executive of the Zionist Organization, 13th Zionist Congress, Carlsbad, 1923. In the background is a bust of Theodor Herzl. Central Zionist Archives, Jerusalem, CZA 1052822.

as if he is thinking to himself: really a large public, unbidden!—A really impressive public! All the seats are occupied, all the aisles full of people. Crowds throng into all the vestibules. [. . .] The large and motley-colored crowd of visitors flows and moves forward on its way, rising toward the stage and on up to the statue of Herzl. Heads above more heads, they hang there like some miracle.[77]

Chapter 13

To Bohemia and Beyond

Zionist Summers at the Sprudel

... and now my wife and I are strolling in the Marienbad
paradise, eating manna, drinking from *be'erah shel Miryam*.
And sometimes, on foggy days, we are even surrounded
by the *ananei ha-kavod*, which sink down upon the hills. A
wonderful place!

—Chaim Nachman Bialik to Yehoshua Rawnitzki,
27 August 1929[1]

After the 12th Zionist Congress concluded its work and all those involved left
Carlsbad, the spa town returned to its daily rounds, though not completely.
The previous weeks of publicly experienced Jewish culture had left perceptible traces. Jews, both spa patrons and locals, now began to behave more
self-confidently and to define themselves with changed demeanor as a separate ethnic group out on the promenades. The Congress had rehabilitated
the spa town in the eyes of a Jewish world in transition, exonerating it of the
accusation of decadence. The old and new Carlsbad, prewar nostalgia and
Congress romanticism, existed side by side in harmony. Doubtless practical
considerations also played a role, as Carlsbad after the Congress advanced
to becoming a preferred venue of the Zionist movement. The fact that this
came to pass, despite the nationalistic politics and the worsening reputation
of the majoritarian German towns in Bohemia, was attributable to Carlsbad's
position as a center within the topography of Jewish places in the prewar era.

Already a year prior to the Congress, the Zionist public presence in Carlsbad emerged in prominent fashion when the First Jewish World Relief Conference convened there in the summer of 1920. In the spa grand hall, before a
large audience, Leo Motzkin, Zwi Peretz Chajes, Anitta Müller-Cohen, Berta

Pappenheim, Menachem Ussishkin, and others presented reports on the misery of the Jewish war refugees in Europe and the settlers in Palestine.[2] Three years later, the Central Council of the Jewish World Relief Organization met in Marienbad, and the following summer the Second Jewish World Relief Conference convened in Carlsbad with a large number of participants.[3] After the Zionist Annual Conference convened in the Carlsbad spa hall at the end of August 1922 to formulate a position on ratification of the Palestine mandate granted by the League of Nations to Great Britain, the Zionist movement decided in 1923 to hold its next Zionist Congress once again in Carlsbad.[4]

In terms of organization, the 13th Zionist Congress was as devoid of problems as its predecessor but characterized somewhat more by routine.[5] Yet just as the Congress sessions this time were marked by considerable conflict and controversy, cooperation with the municipality and the population also proved more difficult and conflict-ridden than in 1921.[6] The Executive in London had long hesitated to make a firm decision on Carlsbad as a Congress venue, despite the fact that at the 12th Congress everything had gone smoothly and prices in the spa city had in the meantime dropped even further. Their hesitation can be attributed, on the one hand, to the overall political situation in the town and, on the other, to rumors that had spread to the Executive during the negotiations. In a letter sent in February 1923 to the leaseholder of the *Grandhotel Schützenhaus*, Richard Lichtheim wrote that numerous cities were vying to be considered as hosts for the Congress, since the event promised the presence of several thousand visitors. Although Carlsbad was a frontrunner, he said that he had recently received some news that raised a serious obstacle: "We've been informed that the Carlsbad Municipality has recently included the swastika in the municipal coat of arms." The municipal council replied quickly, claiming that was a false rumor and completely untrue.[7] The Executive was satisfied, and the Congress took place in Carlsbad after all.

It is not surprising that the local population and the municipality under Mayor Hermann Jakob, known for his anti-Semitic views, regarded the event more positively in economic than in ideological terms. The *Deutsche Tages-Zeitung,* the German-national paper in the town, got to the very heart of the matter when at the beginning of its report it declared that the World Zionist Congress was "of exceptional propagandistic value for our world-class spa, and this is the viewpoint from which we wish to see the Congress." The editor openly criticized the Congress organizers for having put the name "Karlovy Vary" first before "Karlsbad" in official releases and statements.[8] In actual fact, this regulation about the name of the place was not yet in effect two years earlier, suggesting that now there was an increasing political awareness of the situation in Carlsbad among the Zionist organizers.

During the Congress, disturbances broke out when "young people" tried to distribute anti-Semitic flyers and news reports in the city.[9] In addition, the Prague weekly *Selbstwehr* quoted an anti-Semitic article entitled "Palestine in Carlsbad," which had appeared on the occasion of the event in a local Carlsbad paper. The article noted: "World Jewry is having a general rehearsal. If otherwise the streets of the Sprudel town are generally teeming with Jewish faces on a usual day, [. . .] during the Zionist Congress, Carlsbad seems downright repugnant and disgusting for any anti-Semite."[10]

This and other conflicts were responsible for the fact that there was never another Zionist Congress held in Carlsbad, even though every two years the municipal council regularly submitted a proposal to be considered again for the venue. With hopes to bring this major event back once more, local politicians not only accepted all the wishes of the Zionist Executive, but also sought the mediation of members of the Jewish community and a staff member of the Propaganda Department of the Spa Administration in Paris, dispatched to London to lobby for Carlsbad, though to no avail. Although there were repeatedly drawn-out negotiations and near agreement, the Executive again and again declined to select Carlsbad, due to prevailing "political circumstances," if reasons were given at all.[11]

Despite these difficulties, the five Zionist summers of the years 1920–1924 had left their mark, bringing the health spas into discussion and recalling their past role. From now on, political and medical reasons for a stay there began to intermingle: those who had come to take the cure also attended events at the Congress, and those who came specifically for the Congress took advantage of the opportunity to stay on afterward to take the healing waters.[12] The organizers, responding to requests from Congress participants, were able to arrange discounts with the spa administration for all those who wanted to take the cure before, during, or after the conferences.[13] Many who had never set foot in Carlsbad before started coming regularly after the two Congresses, and even doctors in the Jewish settlements in Palestine now began sending their patients for the cure to Bohemia.[14]

Menachem Ussishkin, who had been in Franzensbad earlier, came almost every summer to Carlsbad for therapy after the Congresses.[15] The journal *Die jüdische Welt*, which Sami Glücksmann had brought out in 1933 in Carlsbad, urged participants of the 18th Zionist Congress in Prague in 1933 to come to the western Bohemian health resort to relax and recuperate afterward, and many followed that advice.[16] Two years later, in June 1935, a group of leading Zionists, including Weizmann and Ussishkin, accidentally met out on the Carlsbad promenades. They all intended after the end of their cure to travel to Lucerne to participate in the 19th Zionist Congress.[17] Prior to that, they went to see the special plaque mounted on a panel recounting the historical events in the town; a Hebrew text recalled the Carlsbad Congresses.[18]

Among those who repeatedly returned to the spa was the poet Chaim Nachman Bialik. After he had been to Marienbad in the late 1920s with his wife, he traveled several times alone to take the cure in Carlsbad.[19] Although he liked Marienbad far more, regarding Carlsbad as noisy and dirty, he remembered the city positively after the Congresses. Because his doctor had also specifically prescribed a Carlsbad water and bath cure, he had no choice but to spend several weeks there. At the beginning of his first stay he had felt a bit lonely, until he learned that quite a number of "Eretz Israel Jews," known and not known to him, were in town.[20] The following year as well, during a cold and rainy September, Bialik began his stay with chagrin. He wrote to his wife, Mania: "I really would not have been able to cope with my melancholy and would have run from here, had several excellent Maskilic and Zionist Jews among the spa guests not joined me. We met in coffeehouses and on the streets in order to wile away some time together."[21] When some friends and acquaintances from Marienbad also arrived, he was delighted, as he wrote to Mania: "A pleasant piece of good fortune that God has sent me a few fresh Jews."[22]

Travelers who came to western Bohemia during these years were greeted by a Jewish spa tourism that was self-confident, often also tinged with a bit of folklore. In travel guides, traditional kosher hotels now targeted spa guests without the customary coded messages, openly advertising their Jewish facilities: "The finest, strictly kosher restaurant on the premises," proclaimed the Marienbad Hotel National in a travel guide in the Grieben Series in 1930, "60 elegantly appointed rooms, with hot and cold running water, central heating, elevator, all the comforts, *minyan*, *mikva* on the premises, expert service, reasonable rates. Brochure available on request."[23] A growing sense of confident self-awareness among Jewish tourists could also be observed elsewhere, but it rarely found such distinct expressive forms as here, where for a time there was a special paper published just for Jewish spa patrons.

As a supplement to the Brünn-based *Jüdische Volksstimme*, the *Jüdische Bäder- und Kurortezeitung* (Jewish Spa & Health Resorts Journal) appeared

Figure 18. Carlsbad, 1931. From left to right: Chaim Nachman Bialik; József
Patai, Hungarian and Hebrew poet, translator, and editor; and Izhak Leib
Goldberg, Russian Zionist leader and philanthropist. Central Zionist Archives,
Jerusalem, CZA 1030603.

for the first time in the summer of 1929. During the season, Armin Wilkowitsch, cantor in Eger and publisher and main author of the supplement, provided a weekly fare of entertaining and informative news for a Jewish readership. In the first issue, he explained the need for the paper by pointing to the resilient popularity of Carlsbad, Marienbad, and Franzensbad with Jewish spa guests, who continued to frequent these watering places despite the mounting political tensions in the region:

> It is not my intention here to announce the arrival in the western Bohemian spas of that epoch which the prophet Isaiah predicted, when they shall beat their swords into ploughshares. I mean, a time when anti-Semitism will have completely vanished and died out—far from it! [...] But the spa guest, no matter who he may be, is treated as though he were a saint in those spas. [...] This truce during the spa season induces Jewish patrons from all corners of the world to gladly come to the western Bohemian health resorts.[24]

As a platform for Jewish interests, the supplement wished to provide a space to forge ties between patients, tourists, doctors, and hoteliers, and in addition promised "never to neglect what moves the Jewish people." Full of pride over the unique character of this Jewish spa newspaper, Wilkowitsch concluded his first editorial with the words: "With a fearless call *forward!*, with a hearty wish of '*rak chazak!*', we send this paper out into the wide world!"[25]

In the manner of a casual, light, entertaining newspaper, the *Jüdische Bäder- und Kurortezeitung* informed readers about local events and new books on Jewish topics, as well as the presence of Jewish writers, artists, and "miracle rabbis" in Carlsbad, Marienbad, and Franzensbad.[26] Novels in installments and short stories, such as *Dr. Einpfennigs Erholungsreise—Eine Franzensbader Kurnovelle* (Dr. One-Penny's Holiday Trip—A Franzensbad Spa Novella) offered diversion and amusement, along with pages on fashions and reports on life in Palestine. At the same time, the paper propagated an idealized image of the health cure as a folkloristic experience: in places where on sunny afternoons the spa orchestra played "Kol Nidre," where there were "more kosher kitchens [...] than in the large world metropolises," and where Jewish women were requested not to appear in synagogue wearing "evening dress or theater robe" and expensive jewelry, even if these synagogues were as liberal as in the western Bohemian spas.[27] Articles on topics such as "Jewish Carlsbad" or "The Jews in the Spas" sought to knit the heterogeneous spa public closer together. They hoped to bridge over differences between "the Western Jew, who dresses like a European and stays at the better and best spa establishments, and who tries to discard the Jewish *signum-metsuyonim*," and the "Jew in East European dress, his facial features telling a tale of poverty and sickness."[28]

A special concern of the paper was to inform its middle-class and largely secular readership about the life, customs, and rituals of Orthodox observant Jews, who came to Bohemia for the most part from Eastern Europe. Since they were much in evidence on the promenades and pathways, but at the same time were withdrawn and isolated among themselves in their own restaurants, hotels, and synagogues, the *Kurortezeitung* wished to provide some insight into these supposedly exotic places. In the summer of 1929, it published an article entitled "Sabbath Evening: Oriental Intermezzo in Western Bohemia," dealing with the Judengasse in Marienbad as an exclusively pious neighborhood for observant Orthodox Jewry:

> There is a small lane in Marienbad, there the dark Eastern caftan flutters around the walking figures. Long often wonderful beards, silver-white, frame honorable patriarchal faces; even the small boy who sits strangely still and shy, playing at his serious games, wears a round hat, side-curls and caftan. It is a friendly ghetto over there. While all around it, the grand procession of the international world surges. It is a self-chosen corner of togetherness of the East European Jews, the most observant and pious of Europe's Jews. A ghetto which stamps, quietly but resolutely, the distinctive mark of original Jewish character upon the neighboring surroundings.[29]

The report continued with a romantic picture of the prayers and dances in well-attended Chassidic prayer halls and kosher restaurants, noting that especially on this evening, as the Sabbath begins, a visit would be worth considering.

Occasionally the *Kurbäderzeitung* also published letters to the editor from prominent spa guests, especially if they documented the Jewish life in the spas with empathy and affection. In the summer of 1930, Mayer Ebner, a journalist and leading Zionist in the Bukovina, playfully described how Jewish spa guests would "occupy" the Marienbad hills and mountains:

Israel is rising. Literally. Years ago Jews were a people of the flat plain. The number of Jewish spa patrons dropped in ratio to rising altitude above sea level. [. . .] Up on the heights of Nimrod, Jägerheim, Wolfstein, Pfarrsäuerling, Podhorn, etc., the others could expect to be more or less among their own. Once that was the way it was. Things have changed. The Jewish spa guests are leaving the plain and climb into the mountains. Now here, now there, one can see Jews in long gowns stepping forth from the shadows of the forests and striding up toward the heights.[30]

The *Jüdische Bäder- und Kurortezeitung* was published only for four summers, and was discontinued in 1932 at the end of the season. As droll and trivial as it may appear to today's readers, it nonetheless reflected a moment of transition: the growing felt need among Jewish spa guests to be among themselves corresponded to their simultaneously increasing sense of isolation. The fact that individual spas that earlier were popular among a Jewish clientele were now changing into spaces of exclusivity and isolation reflected the radicalization of the general social situation at the time.

In the summer of 1933, the *Jüdische Volksstimme,* which had included the *Kurortezeitung* as a supplement, reported several more times on the new and altered situation in the health resorts: "The time is past when in a Jewish restaurant there was an audible clash between the most diverse and sundry nationalisms. Zionism is now the *dernièr cri.* At each and every table where Jews are sitting, you now will often hear discussions about Palestine and its problems." As in the past, the spa society talked playfully and a bit superficially about innocuous topics. If politics was mentioned, it was usually in the form of a funny joke: "The talk is about clothes, photographs and Hitler. There's no railing about Hitler's politics. Instead people tell each other the latest political jokes. [. . .] —The most sought-after woman in Germany now is an Aryan grandmother."

The *Volksstimme* concluded its "Spa Reflections" by noting: "In any event, if nowhere else, in the Czechoslovak spas the Jews should not only be always welcomed, but also be seen in large numbers."[31] A short time later, in 1934, the *Jüdische Volksstimme* also ceased publication.

In the Border's Dark Shadow

> ... then I decided never ever to leave my room again. But
> rather like Bacon of Verulam, to stay in bed all the time,
> may the world outside go to wrack and ruin.
>
> —Theodor Lessing, Marienbad, summer 1933[32]

In the summer of 1933, the Jewish philosopher and feature writer Theodor Lessing wrote an ironic essay in his Marienbad exile entitled *"Mein Kopf"* (My Head).[33] The long unpublished manuscript begins: "Suspecting nothing, I was walking along the Kreuzbrunn, my head empty of any thought, when suddenly I caught sight of an ad printed in bold in a spa paper, and my eyes remained riveted: '80,000 Reichsmark for the head. Will they try to bring him by force to Germany?' 'Wow!' I thought. 'That's interesting! Eighty thousand marks! No small sum.'" But when he reads on, he discovers the head mentioned there is in fact his own, which is to be brought alive back to Germany, in order "to answer for the content of his writings." Perplexed, Lessing looks for a lawyer and asks him for advice. Dr. Kohn-Schanzer, at the same time chairman of the Marienbad Jewish Community, immediately threatens the newspaper editor responsible with a lawsuit and forces him into an immediate retraction.[34]

His own path of suffering, Lessing continues ironically, did not begin until the point he started fantasizing about his potential murderers, suspecting them in a kind of cabal—"Murder Lessing, Inc."—as well as in the person of his driver, the hotel director, the policeman who has been assigned to protect him, impostors, and close friends. They all appear to be lured by the reward placed on his head.

What I've had to listen to about my head all my life. At school they said it was no head for study. At the university, they said: a scatterbrain. Colleagues said: a maverick head. A critic wrote: not a head that could think politically. Another: not a head that could think historically. Still others said: my head lacked certain capacities. Like the proper organ for metaphysics. For myth. For humor. For math. In short: everything about my head was negative. I racked my brain and earned nothing for the effort. And now: 80,000 Reichsmark!

So now the whole spa town was looking with longing at this head: ladies, young girls, distinguished gentlemen. "A Polish Jew I walked past look at me tenderly and murmured: '*Gebenshtes Ganefkeppele* (blessed little head of a thief).'" In his unhappy state, Lessing decides not to leave his room anymore in the future. Then suddenly, in his narrative, Albert Einstein appears at the door and suggests that Lessing should hand himself over directly to Goebbels. Then the two could split the reward money. "After I'd heard these noble and helpful words, I broke down in a flood of redeeming tears, crying out like Schiller's noble robber Charles Moor, who had had the same friendly experiences in these Bohemian woods: 'That man shall be served.'"[35]

Despite the sarcastic undertone and the unexpected final punchline from Schiller's play as Charles Moor decides to turn himself in to the authorities, it is likely that Lessing's essay largely reproduces the tenor of those days with all the fears and fantasies he had gone through, subsequent to the appearance of this brief piece on 28 June in the *Marienbader Neueste Nachrichten* and the *Tschechoslowakische Bäderzeitung*:

> The dear Professor Lessing. Germany increases the bounty to 80,000 marks. As we have learned from several sources, the previous bounty reward of 40,000 marks for the person who brings Prof. Lessing alive back to Germany has already been raised to 80,000 RM.—Who would like to cash in on this reward? Here among us probably not a soul. Professor Dr. Lessing, the well-known writer and journalist, is currently in the Czechoslovak Republic as a refugee, and has to answer in Germany for the content of his writings.[36]

After Lessing had consulted with Dr. Kohn-Schanzer, just as he had described it in his essay, a retraction was published two days later in both papers as well as in the *Reichenberger Zeitung*:

> 80,000 Reichsmark for a head. A bad joke. The news that the German government has raised the reward for the handing over of Prof. Dr. Lessing to 80,000 marks has proven after more detailed inquiries to be totally incorrect and a pure invention. Professor Lessing, who is currently staying as a spa guest in Marienbad, is a scholar who has nothing to do with politics. Professor Dr. Lessing says the story that has been circulated is a crude piece of nonsense, and wishes to take legal steps against those who invented and spread the story.[37]

Theodor Lessing had been staying in Marienbad since the spring of 1933, after he had left Germany as a dissident and regime opponent and initially fled to Prague. During his time in exile, Lessing occasionally wrote in the Czechoslovak press against National Socialism, and felt—for that reason among others—that he was being spied on and under surveillance already in Prague and later in Marienbad.[38] For some time previously, Lessing had been involved in Hanover with adult education for workers and was planning now with his wife, Ada, to open a rural boarding school for German and Czech teenage girls in Marienbad.[39] For that purpose, the couple left the *Hotel Miramare* in Marienbad and moved into an apartment at the *Villa Edelweiß* at the edge of town. They intended to rent the entire house, which was owned by a Social Democratic town councilor, and to open the school they planned that same autumn.[40]

At the end of July 1933, Sofie Leffmann received a letter from her brother in which he told her about the incident: "The local papers here have reported that there is a large bounty on my head. That's nonsense, of course, but it excites the imagination of criminal elements."[41] Lessing rejected all offers to leave Czechoslovakia and emigrate to Palestine, China, or London and also rejected the request from Kohn-Schanzer that he move into a house in the center of town. He was under police protection and said he felt safe. "I'll stay where I am," he wrote to his sister. "I wouldn't be able to stand a situation where I have to suspect my murderer is hiding behind every tree. I'm in God's hands. If a fanatic tries to kill me, I only pray that it may be quick."[42]

Scarcely a month later, the night of 30 to 31 August 1933, Theodor Lessing was murdered in his flat in the *Villa Edelweiß*. He had only shortly before returned from the 18th Zionist Congress in Prague and had not yet reported to the Marienbad police that he was back. About 9:30 P.M. he was shot by two men through the window of his study, which faced the woods. They had used a ladder to climb up to the third floor. Toward 1 A.M. that night, Lessing succumbed to his head wounds and died in the local hospital.[43] As became clear after some investigation, the two perpetrators were from the immediate environs of Marienbad and had close connections with the *Deutsche Nationalsozialistische Arbeiterpartei* (DNSAP). That same night they fled across the border into Germany, which they reached on bicycle in less than half an hour. The murder, carried out on orders from Joseph Goebbels and likely long in planning, unexpectedly resulted in only a small monetary reward for the two men after the assassination.[44]

Lessing was buried on 3 September in the Marienbad Cemetery. Since disturbances were feared, the funeral was not officially announced.[45] The murder also met with approval among locals. After National Socialist papers had commented that the killing was the product of an "outpouring of emotion" in regard to the "goings-on among the emigrants," the atmosphere in the town remained tense.[46] For months, the stones laid on his gravestone during the day as a token of remembrance disappeared every night.[47]

On the occasion of the memorial for Lessing in the Marienbad Temple, Chief Rabbi Diamant announced that the Jewish Community "would establish, in honor of the memory of Prof. Lessing, a home that will be open to all refugees, without distinction of nationality, religion or political conviction. The institution will bear the name of Professor Lessing."[48] Kohn-Schanzer worked together with the widow Ada Lessing to implement the creation of this sanctuary, placing ads in domestic and foreign newspapers calling for donations. The aim of the fund was to set up a home for emigrants, not in Marienbad but in Palestine. However, the sad reality was that the Theodor Lessing Memorial Fund—although supported by intellectuals such as Albert Einstein, Romain Rolland, Max Brod, and Hugo Bergmann—received only enough contributions to finance the gravestone.[49]

Marienbad had seemed a space of retreat and sanctuary in the eyes of Theodor and Ada Lessing. In the text of the proposal for the planned boarding school for teenage girls, they explained the choice of Marienbad: it was not only "one of the most beautiful and healthiest places in Europe," but also combined the "advantages of a world-class spa with those of country living."[50] In addition, geographically the place was centrally located and easy to reach for the German girls (presumably mostly Jewish refugees) who would be educated together with young Czechs. It is also likely that the presence of numerous German refugees in this border area and the existence of Social Democratic exile newspapers in Carlsbad were also among the reasons for the Lessings to set up a school of this kind in Marienbad. Yet the seemingly peaceful, depoliticized atmosphere in the spa town proved to be just as deceptive as its immediate proximity to the German border.[51]

The closeness to the border brought numerous Jewish tourists into the region every summer. They temporarily fled the growing insecurity and discrimination in Germany, seeking relaxation and recuperation in the free and protected atmosphere of the summertime health resorts. Already in the summer of 1933, an aggressive policy of exclusion and ghettoization against Jewish patrons had been instituted in many German spas and summer vacation resorts.[52] By 1935, there were but a few German spas whose doors still stood open to Jewish guests. In the summer of 1937, a year before official segregation was imposed through the *Judenbann*, Jews in a small number of German health spas were granted entry, but they were only permitted to visit specifically designated bathhouses during special limited hours. As a consequence, German Jews who could afford it journeyed abroad.[53]

One upshot of this was that the western Bohemian health spas, still weakened from the effects of the Great Depression, experienced a renewed increase in prosperity.[54] They were easy to reach from Germany, offered a well-developed Jewish infrastructure, and guaranteed, at least during the summer season, friendly and courteous treatment. Max Stingl, director of the Jewish Spa Hospital in Marienbad, wrote in April 1936: "Words fail me when I try to describe how beneficial the work of our institution is. Just think of the many of our co-religionists from the Reich who have so little means at their disposal that they cannot afford taking the cure in Marienbad. We actually help them preserve their health."[55]

Ultimately, so many Jews were coming over from Germany at this juncture that the spas in West Bohemia took on an atmosphere of places of protective sanctuary and refuge and retained that sense of a temporary counter-world until the summer of 1937.[56] Paradoxically so, however, since the aggression against the local indigenous Jewish community was all the while worsening from winter to winter.

Thus it was that in the summer of 1937, an event was organized in Marienbad that involved the most important Jewish congress that the spa town had ever hosted, and also the largest single congress gathering it had ever seen. In August, the *Agudas Jisroel* (founded in 1912)—the international umbrella organization of the Orthodox Jewish political parties—issued a call for the 3rd World Congress of Orthodox Jewry. Akin to the Zionist Congresses earlier held in Carlsbad, the *Agudas* event dominated the town's landscape, with the sole difference that Marienbad was smaller and the participants were easier to spot in its topography. Despite the fact that in the 1930s many Chassidim continued to travel to Carlsbad and Marienbad, this 3rd *Knessiah Gedola* or *Kenessio Gedaulo* constituted something special for Marienbad.[57] Hundreds of delegates and guests now predominated in the cityscape, "for the most part Orthodox Jews, with long cloaks and donning black felt hats."[58] Flags decorated the hotels, while banners festooned the main streets and embellished public transport vehicles. Congress and press offices were set up, a Congress paper was issued, special postmarks were designed in Hebrew and Czech, and photos of famous rabbis were sold all over town.[59] Marienbad, wrote the daughter of a Chassidic hotel owner, looked like "old Jerusalem," even if associations with Warsaw and Lvov seemed closer to the mark.[60]

Some 700 delegates from eighteen countries and 2,000 guests took part in the Congress, among them Chassidic leaders such as the Gerer, Aleksander, Czortkower, and Sohaczower Rebbes.[61] The liberal *Marienbader Zeitung* reported:

> The Spa Hall, in which conferences are being convened, had an unusual appearance at the opening session. Along the marble walls of the great hall, there were banners in Hebrew lettering with slogans. The crowded hall was filled with some 700 delegates of Orthodox Jewry from throughout the world. Up on the platform were the members of the Great Rabbinic Council and leading personalities of Orthodoxy. Most had long flowing beards, wore large, black hats or small skullcaps, and two top hats were also in evidence. The women were gathered with a large audience in the small spa hall, where speeches were carried over loudspeakers. The total number of participants at the opening session was estimated to be some 1,700.[62]

The Congress discussed in Yiddish, Czech, and German the importance of the impact of the *Agudas* on developments in Palestine. Over against images of the foes of Orthodoxy such as liberalism, individualism, nationalism, and Zionism, the Congress called for a return to tradition. "There is only one infallible means for national existence, tested in the past, and that is the teachings of Judaism," the Congress paper stated in reporting on the sessions. It was resolved during these sessions that only the *halakha* could constitute the true foundation for a possible state of Israel in its biblical borders.[63]

The 150 female delegates participated in the sessions solely as listeners to the deliberations via loudspeakers, situated together in an adjoining room; after the Congress, they held their own conference. The main issue they discussed there was how they could prevent Orthodox women in Eastern Europe, who existed in a space of isolation between the world of their husbands and secular Judaism, from turning away from religion.[64] Alongside the women's conference, sixty writers and journalists met to found the World Association of Religious Jewish Writers and Journalists as an organ and mouthpiece of Jewish Orthodoxy, which they felt was urgently needed.[65] During this time, the Grand Spa Hall hosted a rally of *Agudas Jisroel* youth, which began with speeches by rabbis and ended with exuberant Chassidic dancing.[66]

The Zionist paper *Selbstwehr* in Prague, true to its nature, reported polemically on the Congress, viewing it as an imitation of the Carlsbad Zionist Congresses. "And for that reason, actually only that reason, they chose to convene their world congress to demonstrate their strength and to state: now, we too are for regaining Palestine, but only under our leadership, and only if Zion will be 100 percent as *Agudas Jisroel* wants it."[67] The journal felt that the Congress had been a failure in terms of content, since the on-the-ground practical work of the *Agudas* in the Yishuv in Palestine was still half-hearted and devoid of success, even in the face of the catastrophic situation developing in Germany. Despite its fundamental political opposition, the *Selbstwehr* conceded that the Congress had convincingly dominated the Marienbad townscape:

> They stood at the Marienbad springs and prayed in small groups. Likewise in the reading room. Likewise in the city park. Likewise out in front of the forest cafés. They walked majestically, in Sabbath regalia, through the main streets. Now and then they greeted each other and kissed warmly. They demonstrated some of their unshakable spiritual attitude to life, thus drawing around themselves a magic circle. The well-groomed spa idlers, a bit ashamed, a bit anxious, tried to sneak on past them along the waysides.[68]

In Marienbad, where the municipality had decided to approve the event for economic reasons, the debates that raged around the presence of the *Agudas* Congress pointed up local anti-Semitic attitudes and biases. The hotelier and former chair of the Jewish Community, Siegfried (Fritz) Buxbaum, was deputy mayor at the time, and in that capacity had opened the Congress.[69] Buxbaum declared:

> Given the democratic structure of our beloved fatherland, the Czechoslovak Republic, it goes without saying that we take the greatest care in Marienbad to welcome and host each and every visitor, no matter what country he comes from, no matter what political views he may hold, no matter what religion he may belong to. There was not a single voice in the Municipal Council that spoke against convening this Congress here. And for me, as a faithful son of Judaism, it is not only a great honor to represent our mayor, the municipality and the Municipal Council in expressing to you my most heartfelt words of

welcome, but also to convey these greetings in the name of our entire local population.[70]

Buxbaum closed his welcoming address with the dictum that "where there is Torah, there is wisdom." This all-embracing speech was followed by a public statement of complaint by the nationalist German *Sudetendeutsche Partei* (SdP). As the *Selbstwehr* and *Die neue Welt* reported, the SdP publicly distanced itself from the words of welcome of a "non-Aryan deputy mayor" spoken in the name of the Marienbad population.[71] The *Selbstwehr* asked: "What impact do they (the hoteliers) think such an anti-Semitic campaign will have on the Jewish spa guests?" as it wondered about the supporters of the Marienbad SdP, who were all profiting from this large-scale event. "Isn't the anti-Semitic gesture of the SdP an election ploy that may well prove too costly? [. . .] These circles apparently can only see as far as the upcoming elections, not the seasons to come."[72]

Despite this conflict that had finally erupted into the open, *Selbstwehr* recommended to its readers half a year later, at the beginning of the summer season 1938, to travel again to Carlsbad, Marienbad, or Franzensbad:

> The western Bohemian spas are suffering from the lowest level in visitors ever seen. Observers everywhere agree that this is due to the unmistakably political coat of paint these cities have given themselves, or allowed others to apply to them. After the National Socialist program of the SdP was proclaimed specifically in an international spa, then no one should be surprised if people here in the country and abroad now make certain associations with the beautiful spas in western Bohemia which cannot be too beneficial in encouraging the public to pay them a visit. But the Jewish spa guest who is contemplating where to spend the coming summer should also keep in mind that Carlsbad, Marienbad, and Franzensbad have numerous excellent Jewish hotels, spa houses and doctors who at the moment are especially hard hit by a situation they are not responsible for. And that the Jewish spa patron here will find a cordial and heartfelt welcome that is outstanding in its quality and exacting professionalism.[73]

Ever since 24 April 1938, when Konrad Henlein, leader of the SdP, had presented his Carlsbad Program, calling for full autonomy for the Sudetenland

Dies waren unter tschechischer Herrschaft die
Kurgäste der sudetendeutschen Bäder

Das Schuhhaus Bata in Marienbad
Die drei riesigen Schaufenster sind gähnend leer.
Sudetendeutsche Nationalsozialisten schrieben darauf
„Die Vergangenheit"

Sämtliche Bilder Schirner-Archiv

Die Flucht der Juden
Das ganze Judengesindel verließ fluchtartig die
sudetendeutschen Badeorte. In riesigen Schwärmen
kommen sie von allen Richtungen nach Prag, der
verjudeten Hauptstadt der Tschechei

Verlassenes jüdisches Ladengeschäft mit
Aufschrift

Ohne Lösung der Judenfrage keine Erlösung der Menschheit!

Julius Streicher

Figure 19. Images in the anti-Semitic paper *Der Stürmer* depicting the
history and demise of the Jewish spas of Bohemia. The paper reprinted two
photographs of Chassidic leaders in the western Bohemian spas that had been
published in the *Daily Forward* in the 1920s and early 1930s. One of them,
showing the Belzer Rebbe's departure from Marienbad in 1932, was chosen to
illustrate a mass flight of Jews from the Bohemian spas. *Der Stürmer* 16 (42)
October 1938.

and the reinstatement of the forbidden National Socialists, the local Jewish Communities felt increasingly more isolated and believed that Jewish spa patrons were urgently needed.[74] After the first boycotts against local Jews, their situation deteriorated further during and after the Sudeten crisis in August 1938, and many started to leave the region.[75] In mid-September, after Hitler's speech to the Nuremberg *Reichsparteitag*, there were violent anti-Semitic disturbances across the entire Sudetenland. In Carlsbad, shop windows of stores owned by Jews or Czechs were smashed, and the government in Prague immediately introduced martial law and assembly ban.[76] Many Jews and Czechs, but also Germans with oppositional political views, now left the spa towns in great haste, often leaving all their belongings behind.[77] Maurice Hindus, an American travel writer who had come to Carlsbad shortly before the German occupation, described the spa town as abandoned and "ghostly as a funeral parlour." The entire summer long, tourists had stopped coming, and Carlsbad now had the "reputation of a cheap and brawling beer hall."[78]

On 16 November 1938, six weeks after the Nazi invasion, the *Marienbader Zeitung* triumphantly announced the spa town now to be *judenfrei*. The paper declared the Jewish past of the town finished and concluded that "everything that today is still reminiscent of Jewish dominant power in a past time will soon be eliminated."[79] How many Jews who had lived in town or had owned a house, medical practice, or law office soon would be forgotten? It should also be forgotten that 80 percent of the spa patrons in Marienbad were Jews, as were the numerous émigrés who had settled here after 1933. "Marienbad's darkest times are now finally a thing of the past."[80]

The image of the western Bohemian spas as Jewish places was publicly conjured up for the last time when the anti-Semitic smearsheet *Der Stürmer* carried a series of editorials between October 1938 and the summer of 1939 about the former Jewish presence in the "world-class spas" of Marienbad, Carlsbad, and Franzensbad.[81] These printed invectives were illustrated by many photos of Chassidic groups in the spas, as these photographs had been appearing regularly in the New York Yiddish newspaper *Forverts*. Not only the actual places had been "Aryanized," but now also the memory of their Jewish character only a few weeks and months earlier.

Figure 20. Preparing Carlsbad Wafers at the Carlsbad Water Factory in
Nahariya, Israel, 1952. Central Zionist Archives, Jerusalem, CZA PHKH
1260771.

World-Class Spas in Palestine

Wie schön, wie schön auf Urlaub zu geh'n!
Man schickt ins Haus vielerlei Prospekte!
Deauville, Trouville ist niemals mein Ziel,
denn ich bleib treu der Tschechoslowakei.

Das größte Wunder ist für mich der Sprudel
in Ka-Ka-Ka-Ka-Karlsbad,
dort herrscht im Sommer stets ein Kudelmudel
in Ka-Ka-Ka-Ka-Karlsbad!
Man hört das Na-Na-Nikatoseli
und manch andre schöne Melodie.
Zum Schluss singt dann alles den Refrain:

„Das Moor hat seine Pflicht getan,

jetzt kannst Du wieder geh'n!

[...]

—*"Karlsbader Sprudelfox,"* Hermann Leopoldi/

Peter Herz, 1931[82]

Eric Reisfeld, who was born in Vienna and emigrated as a young man to the United States, left the Leo Baeck Archive in New York a collection of early literary pieces he wrote in Europe during the 1930s. In the unpublished sketch *"Frühlingsabend in der Galuth"* (Spring Evening in the Diaspora), Reisfeld, then age twenty, enthusiastically describes a trip to Marienbad in the summer of 1937:

> A mild spring evening: soft, warm winds blow through the old trees, here and there revealing one of the hidden electric bulbs shining in their treetops. At small tables, whose white table setting stands out in sharp contours over against the dark green of the backdrop, people sit, laughing, talking, speaking about the day's events—although these topics concern only such existentially crucial matters as the course of their cure, the baths and excursions.

Like other young men there, the narrator asks a girl to dance. They start talking and discover they both know a bit of Hebrew and share a dream: to emigrate soon to Palestine. "For us, the world all around us has disappeared, we could also just be dancing somewhere in a cafe on the beach in Tel-Aviv, which acquaintances have so often told us about—and not in some European spa or other."[83]

The beach in Tel Aviv as a place of longing and a counter-site against the spa was an oft-cited symbol for comparing the circumscribed, restricted life in the Diaspora and the comparatively free life in *Eretz Israel*. This beach symbolized the Zionist dream of a liberated youth, which no longer had to search for Stefan Zweig's shadows and hideaways, but rather could move naturally and self-confidently under the bright dazzling sun.[84] Likewise, when the Berlin sexologist Magnus Hirschfeld traveled for the first time to Palestine in the summer of 1932, he invoked this polarity in looking at Tel Aviv. "Very seldom—much more seldom, anyway, than in Carlsbad or Marienbad—one sees the characteristic 'Struck' heads," no "so-called 'Jewish nose[s],'" but noses "of 'western' or 'northern' form predominate," and blond children playing among "hundreds of swimmers of both sexes."[85] Tel Aviv's population had shed all the supposedly racially distinctive features as stigmata of the Diaspora, and moved their bodies, erect and self-confident, under the open skies of Palestine: "Tel Aviv has become a place of deliverance for approximately 50,000 Jews who had grown weary of persecution and contempt in their native lands. The wide, white bathing-beach at Tel Aviv is quite magnificent. It is as though it were created for an international health-resort—a Palestinian counterpart of Ostend, Biarritz and Miami."[86]

But since even in the Zionist idyll, there were sicknesses to be cured, Hirschfeld conceded that Tiberias would have to be expanded. If the small spa on the shores of the Sea of Galilee were finally modernized, it would be able to compete with all the large European spas: "If every Jewish rheumatic or arthritic in the world who could afford it, took a thermal cure in Tiberias followed by a period of convalescence in Tel Aviv, much money would flow into the land and both the invalid and the country would be helped. And a third group would also be benefited—the physicians in Palestine with the best European training, of whom there are now too many."[87] Fantasizing about future "world resorts in Palestine," Hirschfeld wanted to start a new tradition and help people to forget the decadent old places.

He was not alone in that regard. Others, like the Zionist spa physician Dr. Lachmann from Bad Landeck, prophesized for Tiberias not only a thriving future as a "first-class international spa," but also pointed to its history over 2,000 years as proof of a continuous Jewish presence in the land.[88] If Tiberias was not comparable with Carlsbad, the wish was nonetheless often expressed that it might one day supplant it. Max Buchmann, a physician of German origin who had emigrated to Palestine, noted in 1928: "The still popular comparison with Carlsbad, that chemically is associated with a completely different category of mineral springs, was probably borrowed from the rabbinic literature, where already in the seventeenth century we find Tiberias compared to Carlsbad. But we can hope that someday in the Jewish world, Tiberias will have the reputation as a spa that Carlsbad enjoys today."[89]

Since the 1920s, German, Austrian, and Czech emigrants had brought the specific reputation that Carlsbad enjoyed in the Jewish world to Palestine, where now Carlsbad mineral salt and other specialties were on sale.[90] As a longtime spa doctor in Carlsbad and a staunch Zionist, Walter Kohner also dreamed in the 1930s of emigrating to Palestine and launching a new career in Tiberias, at the Dead Sea or in a climatic spa on Mt. Carmel.[91]

That never came to pass, perhaps because after World War II the medical importance of spas increasingly declined or because social changes rendered these bourgeois sanctuaries superfluous. Unlike what Theodor Herzl had predicted in 1902 in his utopia of the Jewish state in Palestine, the decadent middle-class health spa was not transferred to *Altneuland*. In Herzl's novel, a traveler comments on the spa park in Tiberias with the following, somewhat ambivalent remarks: "Ah, here they are at last! The Jewesses with the diamonds, I mean! I really missed them. I had said to myself that this whole thing must be a hoax—that perhaps we were not really in Jewland at all. Now I see it's real. The ostrich feather hats, the gaudy silk dresses, the Israelitish women with their jewels."[92]

Whether it was due to the Israeli climate or the therapeutic effect of the young state, its poverty and everyday cares and worries—there was no longer any place in Israel for a phenomenon like what Carlsbad, Marienbad, and Franzensbad had been among Jewish cultures for more than five decades. In many respects, it was probably no longer necessary.

Afterword

Return to Bohemia

> Spring returned to Badenheim. In the country church
> next to the town the bells rang. The shadows of the forest
> retreated to the trees. The sun scattered the remnants of the
> darkness and its light filled the main street from square to
> square. It was a moment of transition.
> —Aharon Appelfeld, *Badenheim 1939*[1]

On the hotel facade, a blue-white flag flutters in the wind. Small blue-white flags decorate the tables in the dining hall. In the lobby one overhears guests speaking Hebrew, Czech, and Yiddish. There are some Orthodox Jews in silk caftans, some wear a *shtreymel*. Zevi Hirsch Wachsman comments on the scene: "Marienbad is a kind of traditional Jewish health spa and a place for international Jewish congresses."[2] It is September 1947.

The journalist and writer Wachsman was on an extended trip through Czechoslovakia and was reporting for *Der Vidershtand*, a small Yiddish paper in New York founded in 1940 for the interests of Czechoslovak Jewry. In several travel letters, Wachsman described his impressions of the changes in the country and Jewish life in the early postwar era. Prague was not the only city that he found was a temporary place of refuge for thousands of Jews. He also discovered to his surprise that Jewish life was present once more in several other localities.[3]

Together with a group from Palestine that, according to Wachsman, was in Czechoslovakia in part for business, in part for pleasure, he traveled in mid-September to Marienbad to celebrate the Rosh Hashanah holiday there and "to create a little corner of *Eretz Israel* for the Jewish New Year."[4] There they encountered some larger groups of Jews, not the "old Jewish clientele of Marienbad," but now, mixed among groups of pious Jews and of travelers from the Yishuv in Palestine, there were several American soldiers. The

Jewish officers and officials had come over from the nearby American Zone of Occupation to celebrate the Jewish New Year and enjoyed the festive holiday atmosphere together with the others: "There is a mood of *Erev Rosh Hashanah* here that you can only feel in *Eretz Israel*."[5]

Wachsman had already visited the western Bohemian spas more than ten years earlier. The trip then—as a Jew and socialist—had led him right across Czechoslovakia. He was attracted on the one hand by the Jewish settlements, and on the other by the new industrial regions. Afterward he brought out a travel book in a Warsaw Yiddish publishing house, and then a short time after he issued a much-revised German version.[6] He was fascinated at that time by the realities he found in the western Bohemian spas, which appeared to do full justice to their lingering image as Jewish places:

> Why describe Carlsbad anyhow? After all, it's a very specific Jewish spa. Or even write a report about Franzensbad, which not only doctors but also rabbis recommend to childless women to visit? But not to mention these spots at all would mean omitting an interesting part of my reportage. It's based on the truth. The whole world knows these localities. But that is why, I think, that this truth is just as interesting for those who learn about it for the first time as for those for whom these descriptions just bring back pleasant memories.[7]

At the same time, he described this world also as strange and decadent. Among the "Jews from all over the world" who filled the promenades, among the scholars and rabbis, he also thought that many had come not only because of their health, but for reasons of prestige.

Wachsman joked:

> Just like so many states organize maneuvers and military exercises, here the miracle rabbis go around with their retinue of followers. Naturally, this entourage is not as ready and imposing as a bunch of soldiers. But one rabbi tries to outdo the other with a larger throng of followers. Who doesn't come to Carlsbad? But our dear Jews need the place more badly than all the others! They are much too fond of the fine goose livers and goose gizzards. They burden their bellies too much in the course of the year with pepper carp and sweet pastries, and the numerous other Jewish specialties so hard to digest.[8]

During his stay, Wachsman also visited the municipal archives, where he copied texts by Max Nordau and other Jewish spa guests for his book, selecting passages from among the hymns of praise and letters of gratitude over several centuries and in many languages stored there.[9] Ironically he observed: "Whoever's been to Carlsbad once is bound to come again. Because the miracle rabbis say: Carlsbad is a fountain of youth, where you can extend your life, and on that one, they are very close to the truth."[10] The fact that he now agreed with the Chassidim's appreciation of the spa, though on other occasions he tended to make fun of them, was due to an experience he had had in the industrial zone of Carlsbad. Shortly before his departure from town, Wachsman visited one of the large Carlsbad porcelain factories. This industry seemed to him one of the genuine lifelines of the locality, and he was overjoyed when the director presented him with a small porcelain ashtray: it was inscribed in Hebrew as a memento.[11]

In 1947, when Wachsman returned more than a decade later to western Bohemia, there was less irony in his voice than nostalgia, memories of past spaces of possibility lost forever.[12] It was not the same people, not the same Jewish place. Nonetheless, he emphasized again and again, the different groups of Jews who came to western Bohemia felt they were "at home" once again. "Karlovy Vary, as it is called in Czech, or Karlsbad, as it used to be known in German, is today once again a center of Jewish life, international Jewish congresses, and a contemporary Jewish reality. Now there are a few Jews less here than before, but the Carlsbad 'Yiddishkayt' hasn't disappeared."[13] Carlsbad remained *Karlsbad* for Wachsman, just as Marienbad did not become *Mariánské Lázně*—because these were the names of the Jewish places of before, which stirred memories not of a German-Bohemian or Sudeten-German past, but that of Habsburg Austria-Hungary.

Carlsbad was used in part as a field hospital during the war and survived largely unchanged, at least in terms of architecture.[14] Wachsman noted that on the promenades one could now hear Yiddish and the refugee English of the newly naturalized Americans, as well as snippets of Russian and Hebrew. There were kosher hotels once again, but you could also get a good non-kosher meal. "The spas are the same and the air is just as good as before. Only the Germans are absent from town, and it's good that way,"[15] wrote Wachsman in the conclusion of his reportage for New York readers.

One year later, in 1948, Karlovy Vary was nationalized. The Mühlbrunnen Colonnade was renamed Colonnade of Czechoslovak-Soviet Friendship and the spa facilities were put theoretically at the disposal of all workers, but in practice they were reserved for the new oligarchy. Many hotels and guesthouses were converted into apartments for the new population that had moved in, and in 1951 the Grandhotel Pupp was converted into a convalescent home for senior army officers and renamed Grandhotel Moskva.[16] "What had once been the Grand now bore the name 'Baikal,'" as the dissident Czech writer Milan Kundera described this Sovietization in his novel *The Unbearable Lightness of Being*. "As a result, a Czech spa had suddenly metamorphosed into a miniature imaginary Russia."[17]

Since 1989 and the Velvet Revolution, there have been attempts to link the city with the heyday long since past, with buildings being renovated and in some cases being repainted in the old Schönbrunn yellow, even if now as before many houses stand dilapidated and are up for sale. The actual town center is now located outside the spa district, which today is extremely costly and unaffordable for the local population. In nearby Mariánské Lázně, still the most idyllic of the three spas, changes are taking place at a slower pace than in Karlovy Vary or in Františkovy Lázně, which now is being managed by the highly efficient *Bad Franzensbad AG*. In Mariánské Lázně a few years ago, one could still find the red wallpaper of the Communist era and hear Russian and German pop hits from the 1970s and 1980s. And at every odd-numbered hour of the day, the Singing Fountain, a mineral spring illuminated in bright colors on the square in front of the Colonnade, offers a small water show to the public while playing melodies by Dvořák, Smetana, or Mozart over the loudspeakers. On Hlavní třída, the main street, a well-kept lawn emerges as an unexpected and unexplained void in the long row of hotels and restaurants, a reminder of the former site of the Marienbad Temple.

In recent years, Karlovy Vary has for the first time reached the number of visitors of its heyday before World War I.[18] Today the spa guests arrive from Germany, Russia, the United States, Israel, Japan, the Arab Middle East, and elsewhere.[19] Marienbad, Carlsbad, and Franzensbad are often still alive in the memory of Jewish families. This is because emigrants and survivors frequently have recollections different from those of their own hometowns in Europe: they recall the health spas and vacation resorts full of nostalgia and positive feelings.[20] As strange as it may seem, many who were born in Carlsbad and Marienbad have also retained memories of their most beautiful days in their native towns, despite negative experiences. It is as if it was always bright and sunny here, the buns more golden, the ham tastier, and the pastries and coffee *sans pareil*.[21]

Once again, blue-white flags and banners hang from the hotels, and many Israelis come to take the cure or for a pleasant detour on the way to Prague. The places apparently remain enscribed in Jewish memory. Once again? Perhaps, still, just a bit as before: "*L'schonnoh habbo!* To beautiful Marienbad"— as the cantor Armin Wilkowitsch put it in 1929 in the *Jüdische Bäder- und Kurortezeitung.*[22]

Abbreviations

AJA	American Jewish Archives, the Jacob Rader Marcus Center, Cincinnati
CAHJP	Central Archives for the History of the Jewish People, Jerusalem
CV	Centralverein deutscher Staatsbürger jüdischen Glaubens (Central Association of German Citizens of the Jewish Faith)
CZA	Central Zionist Archives, Jerusalem
DNSAP	Deutsche Nationalsozialistische Arbeiterpartei (German National Socialist Workers Party)
INJOEST	Institut für Geschichte der Juden in Österreich, St. Pölten (Institute for the History of the Jews in Austria, St. Pölten)
JMF	Jüdisches Museum Frankfurt (Jewish Museum Frankfurt am Main)
JMW	Jüdisches Museum der Stadt Wien (Jewish Museum Vienna)
LBI	Leo Baeck Institute Archives, New York
MmML	Městské museum Mariánské Lázně (Municipal Museum Marienbad)
SdP	Sudetendeutsche Partei (Sudeten German Party)
SOAKV	Státní okresni archiv Karlovy Vary (Archive of the Carlsbad District)
SUA	Státní ústřední archive v Praze (Central State Archive Prague)
YIVO	YIVO Institute for Jewish Research, New York
ŽMP	Židovské museum v Praze (Jewish Museum Prague)

Notes

Introduction

1. Carroll, *Through the Looking-Glass*, 8–9.

2. Agnon, *Only Yesterday*, 23.

3. *Eretz Israel* (Heb.), the Land of Israel.

4. Agnon, *Only Yesterday*, 25.

5. Second Aliyah (Heb.), migration wave of Jewish settlers to Palestine, comprising mainly Eastern European youth, 1904–1914.

6. Singer, *Brothers*, 230–231. Chassidim are members of a mystical religious movement that arose in Eastern European Jewry in the eighteenth century.

7. Ibid., 240. On the Chassidim in Carlsbad, see Singer, *Yoshe Kalb*, 9–10, 14.

8. Wilkowitsch, "Das jüdische Karlsbad," 4.

9. Kisch, *Erlebtes*, 225–296; *Marienbad. Die Perle*, 8, 13. In 1911, the number of spa guests peaked at 70,935 in Carlsbad. *Die tschechoslowakische Republik*, 43. Even after the construction of the airport in Espenthor/Karlsbad, which offered daily flights to Prague and Marienbad starting in the 1920s, the overwhelming majority of visitors continued to arrive by rail. "Wissenswertes für den Kurgast," 38, 56; Wack-Herget, *Karlsbad*, 4.

10. *Die tschechoslowakische Republik*, 43.

11. Sölch, *Orient-Express*, 23–24, 199, 205; Reichardt, "Schlaf- und Speisewagen," 96; Schlögel, *Berlin*, 25.

12. According to an advertising leaflet, Le Corbusier is said to have described the town this way. Karlsbad—Carlsbad—Karlovy Vary.

13. The number of guests from the nobility in Carlsbad in 1911 was only one percent. Charvát, "Analytische Betrachtung," 418; see also Geisthövel, "Promenadenmischungen," 211; Steward, "Spa Towns," 91; Kaschuba, "Deutsche Bürgerlichkeit," 41–42.

14. Brenner, "Zwischen Marienbad"; Triendl-Zadoff, "Herzl im Kurbad"; Triendl-Zadoff, "L'schonnoh habbo!"

15. Lichtblau, "Die Chiffre Sommerfrische"; Kanfer, *Summer World*. For other U.S. resorts, such as South Haven in Michigan, which in its heyday in the 1940s was known as the "Catskills of the Midwest," see Cantor, *Michigan*, 40; Cutler, *Chicago*, 230–231.

16. Teplitz (Teplice), likewise situated in northwestern Bohemia and very popular with a Jewish spa clientele (see Lässig, *Jüdische Wege*, 542), was not part of this "spa tri-

angle" and lost ever more of its importance from the middle of the nineteenth century. It boasted the largest synagogue in all of Bohemia.

17. Wachsman, *In land*, 210.

18. Kos, "Amüsement," 226.

19. Local spa newspapers published advertisements from other spas as well as the timetables of the spa trains: see, for example, the *Karlsbader Fremdenblatt* 32 (1912): 1, 1–2.

20. Among the former were personalities such as Arthur Schnitzler and Richard Beer-Hofmann, among the latter, the author Sholem Aleichem. Schnitzler, *Briefe*, 264–265, 387–388; LBI, Miriam Beer-Hofmann Lens Collection; Landmann, "Nachwort," 235.

21. On the position of the Jews in the German middle classes, see Gotzmann/Liedtke/van Rahden, *Juden, Bürger, Deutsche*, 13.

22. See Schlögel, *Im Raume*, 371–378.

23. The *Gemeinde*, or Jewish Community, was a statutory body under public law. In many German and Austrian cities, it was a key long-standing Jewish institution regulating Jewish life in its respective locality. It went by a number of names, inter alia *Synagogengemeinde, Israelitische Gemeinde, Jüdische Kultusgemeinde*. In most towns, it was governed internally by an elected Executive Board *(Vorstand)*, on which various religious and political currents were represented, and it obligated members to pay an annual communal tax. The *Israelitische Gemeinde* in Carlsbad was established in 1869. In 1890, there were 206 organized Jewish *Gemeinden* in Bohemia (Barkai, "Population," 33).

24. Algazi, "Kulturkult," 118–119.

25. Mann, *Magic Mountain*, 1995, 102.

26. See Geppert/Jensen/Weinhold, "Verräumlichung," 48–49.

27. See inter alia Soja, *Thirdspace*, 154–163.

28. Defert, *Raum*, 77.

29. Foucault, *Heterotopien*, 9. This is the German translation of the text of two radio broadcasts on heterotopia by Foucault, 7 and 21 December 1966; issued in 2004 in France as *Utopies et Heterotopies*.

30. Foucault, "Of Other Spaces."

31. Ibid.

32. Defert, *Raum*, 76.

33. Foucault, "Of Other Spaces."

34. On the concept of liminal and liminoid spaces, see Turner, *Ritual*, 20–61.

Chapter 1

1. *Divrei Torah* (Heb.), words of the Torah. Letter, 18 July 1883, Gordon, *Igrot*, vol. 2, 50.

2. Solomon Rubin (1823–1910), Hebrew writer and *maskil*. Kressel, "Rubin."

3. Heb.: *tit ha-yaven*.

4. Heb.: *ruʾah ha-kodesh.*

5. Heb.: *shehina.*

6. Heb.: *beʾera shel Miryam.* Letter, 17 August 1883, Gordon, *Igrot*, vol. 2, 53.

7. Ibid.

8. *Haskalah* (Heb.), the Jewish Enlightenment.

9. Marienbader Kurliste 1883; Spicehandler, "Literature."

10. Ben-Yishai, "Gordon." The poetic practice of utilizing metaphors with a religious connotation to describe places as sites of vital significance was not unusual among modern Jewish authors: Eshel, "Cosmopolitanism," 124; Zadoff, "Writers."

11. Shamir, *Sadan*, 48.

12. The development of Marienbad (Cz., Mariánské Lázně) as a spa goes back in part to the initiative of the Abbot Karl Kaspar Reitenberger (1779–1860), a Premonstratensian priest at the Teplá Abbey; as a result, the town was declared an official spa in 1818. *Marienbad. Die Perle*, 11–12; Kisch, *Curort*, 220.

13. *Aggadah* (Heb.), non-legalistic exegetical stories and legends in the Talmud.

14. Tosefta, Massekhet Sota, Perek 11, Halakha 1, 8, ed. Saul Lieberman (New York, 1955–1988); Midrash Ba-Midbar Rabba, ed. Vilna, Parasha 1, Dibur ha-matkhil "davar akher va-yedaber," and Parasha 18, Dibur ha-matkhil and Parasha 22, "Yitbarakh shemo"; Talmud Bavli, Shabbat, 35,1; Talmud Yerushalmi, Ketubot, 12,35, 2.

15. *Maskil* (Heb.), supporter of the Jewish Enlightenment (*Haskalah*).

16. *Marienbad und seine Heilmittel*, 11–14.

17. Psalms 40:3–4, *The Holy Scriptures According to the Masoretic Text* (Philadelphia: Jewish Publication Society, 1917).

18. Numbers 5:12–31.

19. Letter, presumed to be dated 6 August 1883, Gordon, *Igrot*, vol. 2, 51–52.

20. *Marienbad und seine Heilmittel*, 8.

21. See also Zadoff, "Writers," 82–86.

22. Of the 8,667 spa guest parties (so-called *Kurparteien*), comprising a total of 13,063 individuals, who visited Marienbad in 1881, 2,673 came from the Austro-Hungarian empire, 2,363 from Prussia, and 1,140 from czarist Russia, the latter some 13 percent. *Marienbad und seine Heilmittel*, 4–5.

23. Lamed, "Marienbad." A Russian church was in construction at the time and was dedicated in 1902. Kisch, *Erlebtes*, 261–270; *Marienbad und seine Heilmittel*, 10.

24. This restriction applied in all spas in the Caucasus and many spas in Russia. Not until 1916 were Jews allowed again to visit spas in the Caucasus, though not until they had submitted to a degrading ritual of examination by a special government commission set up for this purpose. "Die Juden in den Kurorten des Kaukasus," 534; *Selbstwehr* 10 (1916) 3:3; *Mitteilungen aus dem Verein zur Abwehr des Antisemitismus* 13 (1903): 46:366; *Israelitisches Familienblatt*, 20 July 1911, quoted in Bajohr, *Hotel*, 152.

25. Steiner, "Geschichte," 396; Křížek/Švandrlik, *Marienbad*, 92–93.

26. "Secularization occurs when man turns his attention away from worlds beyond

and toward this world and this time (saeculum = 'this present age'). It is what Dietrich Bonhoeffer in 1944 called 'man's coming of age.'" Cox, *Secular City*, 2.

27. Chaim Nachman Bialik is said to have called Yalag one of the greatest magicians of Hebrew literature. Ben-Yishai, "Gordon."

28. On this procedure, see LBI, Lalla Kaden (née Bondi), "Akt," 167–168.

Chapter 2

1. See John Urry, *Consuming Places*; the term "consuming places" encompasses both the meaning of "to consume places" and "places of consumption." Letter, 10 July 1895, Schnitzler, *Briefe*, 265.

2. Kisch, *Curort*, 1.

3. *Marienbad und seine Heilmittel*, 6; Kisch, *Curort*, 1.

4. At the beginning of the twentieth century in Marienbad, there were thirty-eight active mineral springs. Diem, *Bäderbuch*, 425.

5. *Marienbad. Die Perle der böhmischen Weltbäder*, 31–32.

6. See König, *Kulturgeschichte*, esp. 214–223.

7. See Fuhs, *Orte*, 80–136, here esp. 89–92 and 98.

8. Simmel, *Philosophy*, 508.

9. Kisch, *Erlebtes*, 225–296.

10. *Marienbad. Die Perle der böhmischen Weltbäder*, 8, 13.

11. See Föhl, "Klassizismus"; Nicolai, "Lebensquell."

12. The Viennese architectural firm Fellner & Helmer, known for its theater buildings, constructed a number of buildings in Carlsbad: not only the Municipal Theatre and large concert halls, but also the so-called Sprudel Colonnade and the Emperor Baths. Föhl, "Klassizismus," 66–67; Linke, *Kunstgeschichte*, 110.

13. Nicolai, "Lebensquell," 104–106.

14. *Marienbad. Die Perle der böhmischen Weltbäder*, 43.

15. Ibid., 44.

16. Around 1900, there were some 8,000 room rentals. Kisch, *Curort*, 216; *Kurorte, Heilanstalten, Sommerfrischen in der Č.S.R.*, xxiv–xxix; Lucca/Lang, *Orientierung*, 77.

17. Rubritus, *Kurstadt*, 44–50; *Marienbad. Die Perle der böhmischen Weltbäder*, 38–40; Kisch, *Curort*, 217–218.

18. *Die tschechoslowakische Republik*, 28–36.

19. *Beilage zur Marienbader Kurliste für die Saison 1906*, 15–16; Rubritus, *Kurstadt*, 77–78; *Marienbad und Umgebung*, 40; *Amtliche Nachrichten 1906*.

20. Before the moviehouse opened in 1910, a traveling cinema had regularly visited the town. Křížek/Švandrlik, *Marienbad*, 134–135; *Marienbad. Die Perle der böhmischen Weltbäder*, 36–37, 55; Kisch, *Curort*, 217–218; *Marienbad und Umgebung*, 27; Lucca/Lang, *Orientierung*, 75.

21. Marienbad. *Die Perle der böhmischen Weltbäder*, 58–59; Lucca/Lang, *Orientierung*, 41.

22. See Knoch, "Grandhotel," 139.

23. According to an advertisement, some 35,000 spa guests and 100,000 transient visitors came to Marienbad before World War I. *Zeitschrift für Balneologie, Klimatologie und Kurort-Hygiene* 7 (1915), 7/8, binding. By contrast, in Carlsbad the spa guests made up two-thirds of all visitors, the transient tourists one-third. Rompel, *Wiesbaden*, 136.

24. Henisch, *Tanz*, 218.

25. Lucca/Lang, *Orientierung*, 58; Zörkendörfer, "Gesundheitspflege," 65.

26. *Ärztlicher Führer von Marienbad*, 31–33; Kisch, *Marienbad*, 42; *Marienbad und Umgebung*, 37; Glax, "Hygiene," 418–423; Slokar, "Bedeutung," 159–160.

27. Lucca/Lang, *Orientierung*, 57, 61–63.

28. Ibid., 56–57.

29. Rubritus, *Kurstadt*, 119; Lucca/Lang, *Orientierung*, 41.

30. Kisch, *Erlebtes*, 225–296; Macpherson, *Baths*, 264.

31. Lucca/Lang, *Orientierung*, 54.

32. Riehl, *Land*, 99–100; Fuhs, *Orte*, 334–335.

33. Riehl, *Land*, 99–100; Fuhs, *Orte*, 334–335.

34. Fuhs, *Orte*, 335.

35. Torberg, *Tante Jolesch*, 64.

36. LBI, Lalla Kaden (nee Bondi), "Akt," 166.

37. The first branches of the *Wiener Werkstätte* of Josef Hoffmann and Kolo Moser were opened in 1909 in Carlsbad and in 1917 in Marienbad. *Wiener Werkstätte*; Palmer, *Life*, 127; ads in *Feller's Carlsbader Omnibus oder Ganz Carlsbad für 30 kr.*

38. Henisch, *Tanz*, 216–218; Spitzer, *Hereinspaziert*, 84; Baedecker, *Österreich*, 303; see also Baedecker, *Austria-Hungary*, 317–336. The term *kurgemäß* was central to spa discourse, meaning "appropriate for the spa."

39. Letter to Elsa and Max Brod, before 22 August 1916, Kafka, *Letters*, 128. In the English edition of these letters, the letter is identified as written inside the *Guide* sent to Kafka's uncle Siegfried Löwy. Later research (Kafka, *Briefe*, 209–210) has established that this attribution was mistaken.

40. Letter to Felice Bauer, 20/21 July 1916, Kafka, *Briefe*, 184–185.

41. Landau, *Kindheitserinnerungen*, 125, quoted in Kaplan, *Making*, 125.

42. Mann, *Magic Mountain*, 1979, 73.

43. Berg, *Mann*, 17.

44. *Kalender für Israeliten für das Jahr 5656* = 1895/96.

45. SUA, B'nai B'rith

46. See, for example, the *Marienbader Kurliste*, 1867; *Karlsbader Zeitung* (1914): 1:3; *Karlsbader Eisenbahnzeitung* 15 (1903): 2:2; *Karlsbader Saisonanzeiger* 6 (1894): 1:2.

47. *Jüdische Bäder- und Kurortezeitung* 1 (1929): 24:13.

48. Only exterior views of the Marienbad synagogue have been preserved. It was destroyed in November 1938. The Wehrmacht occupied the so-called Sudetenland in October 1938, annexing a large area in Bohemia including Marienbad, Carlsbad, and Franzensbad.

49. Lucca/Lang, *Orientierung*, 72–73.

50. Steiner, *Geschichte der Juden*, 396.

51. *Jeschurun* 17 (1884): 34:539.

52. Černoch, *History*. The Reform movement preferred the term "temple" to express the idea that the center of the Jewish world was not Jerusalem and its former Temple but rather the local place of residence and worship, such as Marienbad.

53. Wilkowitsch, "Mode," 2.

54. There are contradictory data regarding the architect: the building is attributed by some to Adolf Wolff from Stuttgart, by others to Edwin Oppler from Hanover. Kokkelink/Lemke-Kokkelink, *Baukunst*, 545–555; Linke, *Kunstgeschichte*, 13.

55. Gnirs, *Topographie*, 58; The *Encyclopaedia Judaica* mentions 2,000 seats, which cannot be verified because construction documents are not extant; s.v. "Carlsbad."

56. Linke, *Kunstgeschichte*, 14.

57. *Kaiser Franz Josef Jubiläumshospital für arme Israeliten*; Steiner, "Geschichte der Juden," 396; Kisch, *Marienbad*, 252.

58. Kohn, "Brief," 1; Lucca/Lang, *Orientierung*, 79.

59. Letter to Max Brod, mid-July 1916, Kafka, *Letters*, 120.

60. The necessary infrastructure for supplying kosher meat, milk, and bread was present in Marienbad. Private archive of the author, letter from Ruth Shaingarten, 8 February 2003; Lucca/Lang, *Orientierung*, 79; *Marienbad und Umgebung*, 18.

61. Private archive of the author, letter from Ruth Shaingarten, 8 February 2003; Kisch, *Erlebtes*, 266. In his novels, Israel J. Singer also describes rebbes and rich Chassidim, who travel with servants and ritual slaughterers to a watering place in order not "to rely, for kosher food, on strangers." See Singer, *Yoshe Kalb*, 107. and Singer, *Brothers*, 108.

62. *Eruv* (Heb.), Sabbath boundary allowing Jews to carry objects beyond four cubits on the Sabbath, otherwise forbidden. The *eruv* traditionally comprises walls, doorways, fences, wire, and posts and is often barely visible to the eye as a connecting "enclosing" boundary.

63. Schlör, *Stadt*, 155; Černoch, "History."

Chapter 3

1. Zatloukal, *Karlsbad*, 128.

2. *Ärztlicher Führer von Marienbad*, 4.

3. Spitzer, *Hereinspaziert*, 205; see also Julian, "Marienbader Saison."

4. See Steward, "Spa Towns," 91.

5. Kaplan, *Making*, 124–125; Sallis-Freudenthal, *Land*, 52–53.

6. The interests of the doctors often collided with those of the business people. Kos, "Amüsement," 220.

7. Kisch, *Umgebung*, 183.

8. Thus, for example, Zatloukal, *Karlsbad*, 3–13.

9. Letter to Friedrich Engels, 18 September 1874, Marx/Engels, *Werke*, vol. 33, 116. In the summer of 1895, a casino was opened in Marienbad, but it was soon thereafter

shut down by the office of the Austro-Hungarian Governor General (*k.k. Statthalterei*) in Prague. Kisch, *Erlebtes*, 272–273.

10. Howells, *Silver Wedding*, 175.

11. Palmer, *Life*, 127.

12. Private archive Gabriel Kohner, Walter Kohner, Karlsbad, 30.

13. *Ärztlicher Führer von Marienbad*, 38–39.

14. Ibsen, *Enemy of the People*, 6.

15. Enoch Heinrich Kisch (1841–1918). Kisch, *Erlebtes*, 215; Deutsch/Kisch/Singer, "Kisch."

16. Kisch, *Erlebtes*, 215–217, 225–296.

17. Ibid., 235–240.

18. Ibid., 118, 131–133.

19. Ibid., 118, 297–304. He also wrote regularly for the *Karlsbader Fremdenblatt*.

20. *Ärztlicher Führer von Marienbad*, 36.

21. Ibid., 36.

22. Kos, "Amüsement," 229–230.

23. *Marienbad und seine Heilmittel*, 3.

24. Buttlar, *Landschaftsgarten*, 134–135; Fuhs, *Orte*, 96.

25. Bacon, "Rise," 184; Steward, "Spa Towns," 92. On the medicalization of the French spas, see Mackaman, "Tactics."

26. *Jahresbericht des Wiener Stadtphysikats über seine Amtstätigkeit*, 1891–93 and 1897–99, quoted in Krauss, *Medizin*, 28–29. See also Lesky, *Schule*.

27. Krauss, *Medizin*, 2–4.

28. Ibid., 7–9.

29. Ibid., 17–19; Teicher, "Anteil," 22.

30. Krauss, *Medizin*, 19.

31. See Fuhrmann, *Jahrbuch*.

32. Diem, *Bäderbuch*, 280–281, 406–407, 435–436, 752; Rubritus, *Kurstadt*, 4, 44–50; *Marienbad. Die Perle der böhmischen Weltbäder*, 38–40; *Marienbad und Umgebung*, 37; *Ärztlicher Führer von Marienbad*, 28–30; *Marienbad und seine Heilmittel*, 5; Herz, *Sommertage*, 42–44.

33. Of twelve lecturers (*Dozenten*) of the first generation who took their habilitation degree in the predecessor subdisciplines of physical medicine, seven were from a Jewish background. By contrast, all the lecturers who obtained habilitation in another field, but who worked as spa doctors or the heads of institutes for physical medicine, were of Jewish extraction. Krauss, *Medizin*, 9.

34. Ibid., 42; Efron, *Medicine*, 250.

35. Winternitz, "Hydrotherapie," 29.

36. See Beller, *Vienna*, 35–38.

37. Volkov, "Ursachen," 158.

38. Ibid.; Volkov, *Germans, Jews*, 238.

39. Volkov, "Ursachen," 162. As Volkov emphasized in a revision of her article ten

years later, it is problematic to generalize the discrimination of Jewish scientists "as the decisive factor for their scientific creativity." Volkov, "Mandarine," 12. In the specific case of physical medicine at the University of Vienna, her original argument certainly retains its validity.

40. Krauss, *Medizin*, 3.

41. Ibid., 48.

42. Thus, for example, Theodor Fritsch, *Handbuch der Judenfrage*, Hamburg 1919, quoted in Efron, *Medicine*, 247–248. Fritz Ringer argues that the tendency to marginalize innovation in the German and probably likewise in the Austrian university system was widespread. Ringer, *Decline*; see also Ash, "Innovation," 241–252.

43. Efron, *Medicine*, 251.

44. "Der Beruf des Arztes," 337.

45. "Jüdische Ärzte," 338.

46. Gustav Gärtner (1855–1937), Samuel von Basch (1837–1905), and Julius Schütz (1876–1923) in Marienbad, Marcus Abeles (1837–1894) and Rudolf Kolisch (1867–1922) in Carlsbad. Krauss, *Medizin*, 36–37, 59–61; Singer/Haneman, "Rudolf Kolisch."

47. Private archive Gabriel Kohner, Walter Kohner, Carlsbad, 1.

48. "Lotus" and "Neu-Klinger" are the names of the houses where he was practicing and residing. Fuhrmann, *Jahrbuch*, 402.

49. Max Löwy (1875–1948) was interned from 1942 to 1945 in the Theresienstadt concentration camp, and survived.

50. Statistics indicating 56 percent of doctors being Jewish in Carlsbad (Schönbach, "Aufstieg") are unreliable because they stem from a National Socialist source (*Deutsche Tageszeitung*, 20 November 1938.) See also the polemic column "*Getaufte Jüdische Kurärzte*" (Baptized Jewish Spa Doctors) in the Prague-based Zionist periodical *Selbstwehr*, where mention in the main is of spa physicians in Carlsbad, Marienbad, and Franzensbad. *Selbstwehr* 4 (1910): 25:5.

51. Supplement, *Marienbader Kurliste für die Saison 1937/1938/1939.*

52. Kisch, *Erlebtes*, 132–133.

53. Ibid., 62.

54. *Ausweis über die Einnahmen und Ausgaben des Marienbader israel. Spitals 1889.*

55. His younger brother Alexander was chief rabbi in the Meisel Synagogue in Prague. Kisch, *Erlebtes*, 16–17.

56. Johann Schnitzler, 10 December 1884, on the occasion of his appointment as director of the General Polyclinic in Vienna, quoted in Schnitzler, *Briefe*, 717.

57. LBI, Gerald Meyer, Sprudel, 1.

58. Engländer, *Krankheitserscheinungen*, 34.

59. Jacobs/Fishberg, "Diabetes."

60. Even still at the end of the 1930s, in many places treatment by taking the waters was preferred to insulin treatment. Jurecký, *Diabetesbehandlung*.

61. Lucca/Lang, *Orientierung*, 118–119; Lüthje, "Behandlung," 38–39.

62. Ibid., 37–38.

63. Fleckles, *Diabetes*, 22–23.

64. Ibid., 29.

65. Seegen, *Handbuch*, 364–365.

66. Lüthje, "Behandlung," 51.

67. Ibid., 48.

68. Ibid., 36, 57.

69. Seegen, *Diabetes*; adverts in *Feller's Carlsbader Omnibus oder Ganz Carlsbad für 30 kr.*

70. Krauss, *Medizin*, 9–10; *Feller's Carlsbader Omnibus oder Ganz Carlsbad für 30 kr.*, 59.

71. Seegen, *Diabetes*, 125–126.

72. Jacobs/Fishberg, "Diabetes"; Becker, *Nervosität*, 7.

73. Efron, *Medicine*, 132; for an excellent overview of the debate, see 132–142.

74. Ibid., 106.

75. For example, in the Medical Reading Room in Carlsbad. Private archive Gabriel Kohner, Walter Kohner, Carlsbad, 18; *Beilage zur Marienbader Kurliste für die Saison 1906*, 15–16.

76. Among the former, for example, Noorden, "Diabetes," 1118; among the latter, Singer, *Allgemeine Krankheitslehre*. See Efron, *Medicine*, 135–136.

77. *Karlsbader Adress-Buch 1888*, 83.

78. All quotes of Pollatschek in his "Aetiologie," 478–481. Ottomar Rosenbach already before him had arrived at similar findings, after establishing in his practice that he could find virtually no differences whatsoever between Jewish and Christian patients. However, it did not surprise him that other doctors had come up with different results, since they had after all only investigated well-to-do patients, and done so mainly in spas where most of the spa guests stemmed from one social class or religion. Rosenbach, "Lehre," quoted in Efron, *Medicine*, 136.

79. The studies mentioned are Friedrich Theodor von Frerich, *Über den Diabetes*, Berlin 1884, and Rudolf Eduard Külz, *Klinische Erfahrungen über Diabetes Mellitus*, Jena 1899.

80. Noorden, *Zuckerkrankheit*.

81. Thus, for example, by Arnold Lorand and Adolf Magnus-Levy. Efron, *Medicine*, 137 n.119.

82. Jacobs/Fishberg, "Diabetes."

83. Ibid. Joseph Jacobs had expressed similar ideas already some years earlier, shifting the discussion in a new direction. Jacobs, *Statistics*, Appendix X. On the specific situation of German Jews, see Fishberg, *Jews*, 300–301. Both quoted in Efron, *Medicine*, 137, 139.

84. See Becker, *Nervosität*, 11, 16, 25–30; Besser, "Einfluss," 8.

85. Engländer, *Krankheitserscheinungen*, 15. Engländer (39) draws his data on a disposition for developing diabetes from M. Gerstl, the former physician of the Jewish Community, Curaçao, and in the meantime spa doctor in Carlsbad.

86. Ibid., 29, 46. About the same time as Engländer's lecture, Willy Hellpach's *Nervenleben und Weltanschauung* was published, in which the Karlsruhe neurologist analyzed neurasthenic disorders as a disease of the era among the middle classes, which had its origin in capitalism and materialism of the bourgeois world view, in the economic struggle for survival, and in consumption and representation. Hellpach, *Nervenleben*, 26–44, 50–53.

87. Mezan, "Morbus," 91.

88. Gilman, "Gemeinschaft."

89. Kessler, "Disposition," 8.

90. Private archive Gabriel Kohner, Walter Kohner, Carlsbad, 14.

Chapter 4

1. Singer, *Brothers*, 88.

2. Jellinek, "Mensch," 5–7.

3. Efron, *Medicine*, 251.

4. Sarasin, *Maschinen*, 173. Somewhat later on, in the 1920s, this literature was also widespread in the Jewish life worlds of Eastern Europe. Bley, *Vi azoy*; Mats, *Kurerter*.

5. Goldscheider, "Erkrankungen," 112–113.

6. Mann, *Magic Mountain*, 1995, 213. In Carlsbad, Ignaz Zollschan among others operated an X-ray lab. Fuhrmann, *Jahrbuch*, 393; *Ärzteverzeichnis der Amtstelle Karlsbad 1937*.

7. Postcard to Felice Bauer, 31 May 1916, Kafka, *Letters to Felice*, 595.

8. Sebestyén, "Kurpromenade," 37–38.

9. Kos, "Amüsement," 221.

10. LBI, Lalla Kaden (nee Bondi), "Akt," 168.

11. Kisch, *Umgebung*, 201–202; Lucca/Lang, *Orientierung*, 162.

12. Nordau, *Degeneration*, 9. Max Nordau (1849–1923) was a physician, writer, and leading Zionist politician.

13. Gay, *Schnitzler's Century*, 129.

14. Sicknesses such as diabetes, gout, and stomach, intestinal, and heart ailments were often described as causing nervous disorders, such as neuralgias, neurasthenia, and hysteria. Goldscheider, "Erkrankungen," 90.

15. Joachim Schlör analyzes this stereotype in all its aspects in *Stadt*, here esp. 213.

16. Ernst Bloch, letter to his wife Karola, 26 June 1936, in Bloch, *Abenteuer*, 211.

17. Arthur Schnitzler, *Paracelsus. Versspiel in Einem Akt*, Scene 11, quoted in Gay, *Schnitzler's Century*, xxxi.

18. Zweig, *World*, 1–2; see also Wagner, *Krankheit*; Hödel, "Armut," 311.

19. Goldscheider, "Erkrankungen," 90, 99–110.

20. Bauman, *Life*, 108.

21. Berg, *Mann*, 17.

22. Letter to Friedrich Engels, 1 September 1874, Marx/Engels, *Works*, vol. 45, 37–38.

23. Ibid., 37.

24. Letter to Ludwig Kugelmann, 4 August 1874, ibid., 331.

25. Letter to Friedrich Engels, 17 August 1877, ibid., 277.

26. Kisch, *Marx*, 5–6.

27. All further data on the prescribed course of the day for Karl and Eleanor Marx in Letter to Friedrich Engels, 18 September 1874, Marx/Engels, *Works*, vol. 45, 45–47.

28. Baedecker, *Österreich*, 304; Baedecker, *Austria-Hungary*, 326; LBI, Lalla Kaden (nee Bondi), "Akt," 167.

29. LBI, Lalla Kaden (nee Bondi), "Akt," 166. Photos of the morning promenades in Carlsbad and Marienbad are reminiscent of pedestrian malls in large cities at rush hour. A short movie captures some of this: "Karlsbad 1930–1939," available via tinyurl.com/c4r6wt2 (retrieved 15 August 2011). For this reason, signs were put up in Carlsbad, telling pedestrians to "keep to the right!" Steward, "Spa Towns," 106; *Die Tschechoslowakische Republik*, 32; Rubritus, *Kurstadt*.

30. Zatloukal, *Karlsbad*, 128; Kisch, *Umgebung*, 185–189; Rubritus, *Kurstadt*, 78; Spitzer, *Hereinspaziert*, 84.

31. Zatloukal, *Karlsbad*, 67, 173.

32. See the ad for the *Kurgemäße Bäckerei* of Ferdinand Sander, Carlsbad, in *Die Tschechoslowakische Republik*, 193; Zatloukal, *Karlsbad*, 173.

33. Zatloukal, *Karlsbad*, 175; LBI, Lalla Kaden (nee Bondi), "Akt," 167–168.

34. Lucca/Lang, *Orientierung*, 158–159; Zatloukal, *Karlsbad*, 78, 177; Nordau, "Karlsbader Anblicke," 210.

35. Torberg, *Tante Jolesch*, 83–84; Spitzer, *Hereinspaziert*, 85.

36. Zatloukal, *Karlsbad*, 174.

37. LBI, Lalla Kaden (nee Bondi), "Akt," 170–171. Siechenhaus—old, now obsolete term for hospice or infirmary.

38. Letter to Friedrich Engels, 21 August 1875, Marx/Engels, *Works*, vol. 45, 82–83.

39. Letter to Friedrich Engels, 8 September 1875, ibid., 87–88.

40. Letter to Friedrich Engels, 21 August 1875, ibid., 82.

41. Lucca/Lang, *Orientierung*, 159.

42. Letter to Friedrich Engels, 8 September 1875, Marx/Engels, *Works*, vol. 45, 89.

43. Letter to Friedrich Engels, 19 August 1876, ibid., 137.

44. Heinrich Graetz to Karl Marx, 1 February 1877, Graetz, *Tagebuch*, 336–337; Baron, *History*, 266, 447.

45. Letter to Friedrich Engels, 18 September 1874, Marx/Engels, *Works*, vol. 45, 46–47.

46. Letter to Jenny Longuet, late August/early September 1876, ibid., 143.

47. Letter to Friedrich Engels, 18 September 1874, ibid., 47.

48. Letter to Wilhelm Bracke, 11 October 1875, ibid., 96.

49. Kisch, *Marx*, 44–46.

50. Singer, *Brothers*, 195–196.

51. Ziegler, *Dokumente*, 104–105. In Marienbad in 1861, the Jewish Spa Hospital was established, in part by the same benefactors. See also ŽMP, *Tätigkeitsbericht des Israeliti-*

schen Kurhospitals in Marienbad für das Jahr 1934; ŽMP, *Ergänzung des Tätigkeitsberichtes für das Jahr 1935*; Lamed, "Marienbad"; Kisch, *Curort*, 221–222; Kisch, *Marienbad*, 39–40. In Franzensbad, needy Jewish spa guests were provided for on an individual basis until the construction of the *Kaiser Franz Josef-Jubiläumshospitals für arme Israeliten* in 1897. Kisch, *Marienbad*, 252–253; *Kalender für Israeliten für das Jahr 5656–1895/96 zugleich Führer durch die israel. Cultusgemeinden in Oesterreich-Ungarn*, 263.

52. "Geschichte der Juden in Karlsbad," 255.

53. Ziegler, *Dokumente*, 104–105.

54. The *Repräsentanz der Landesjudenschaft in Böhmen* was the main organization of Jewry in Bohemia outside Prague.

55. *Jahres-Bericht des Carlsbader israelitischen Armen-Hospitals.*

56. *Kalender für Israeliten für das Jahr 5656–1895/96 zugleich Führer durch die israel. Cultusgemeinden in Oesterreich-Ungarn*, 221, 244–245.

57. *Jahres-Bericht des Carlsbader israelitischen Armen-Hospitals.*

58. Sachs, *Opfer*, 22.

59. The Carlsbad Jewish Community (*Israelitische Gemeinde*) was established in 1869. Although the Imposed Constitution of March 1849 had already stipulated civil equality for all religious communities in Austria-Hungary, Jews there did not acquire full civil rights until the Basic State Act of 21 December 1867. Friedländer, *Juden*, 36; Ziegler, *Dokumente*, 104–105, 140–141.

60. See also Kolski, "Lassar," 78–83; Pirhofer/Reichert/Wurzacher, "Bäder."

61. Slokar, "Bedeutung," 161.

62. *Israelitischer Frauen-Wohltätigkeits-Verein Karlsbad*, established 1870. *Statuten des Israelitischen Frauen-Wohltätigkeits-Vereins in Karlsbad*, 3–4. In many Jewish Communities, women's associations were established early on or simultaneous with the modernization of traditional male associations. Lässig, *Wege*, 532–533.

63. SOAKV, Vereinsregister. *Chevra kadisha* (Heb.), the traditional Jewish institution dealing with arrangement and rituals for burial.

64. *Humanitätsverein B'nai B'rith*, founded in 1894. In 1932, a sisters' association of the B'nai B'rith was established. Ziegler, *Dokumente*, 141. The B'nai B'rith also supported the Carlsbad Jewish Hospital for the Poor. SUA, B'nai B'rith, 1926, 1932.

65. *Wohltätigkeits- und Geselligkeitsverein Eintracht*, founded in 1897. Ziegler, *Dokumente*, 141.

66. *Jahres-Bericht des Carlsbader israelitischen Armen-Hospitals*; Lang, "Israelitenhospital," 478, 481; *Karlsbader Adress-Buch*, 80; [*Israelitische*] *Gemeindezeitung* [*Böhmen*] (1888): 5:8.

67. "Das Kaiser Franz Josef-Regierungs-Jubiläums-Hospiz für arme Israeliten," 482.

68. *Selbstwehr* 7 (1913): 26:7.

69. Ziegler, *Dokumente*, 141; "Das Kaiser Franz Josef-Regierungs-Jubiläums-Hospiz für arme Israeliten," 483.

70. SUA, B'nai B'rith, 1926, 266–267.

71. Other religious welfare networks in Carlsbad operated with far less extensive coverage. Zatloukal, *Karlsbad*, 170.

72. The springs that were nationalized after 1945 again were given the name Mattoni, under which Carlsbad mineral water is sold to the present day.

73. LBI, Ledermann, Familienstiftung, 7–13; *Karlsbader Adress-Buch 1888*, advert section.

74. *Geschäfts-Bericht der Städt. Armen-Kommission Karlsbad in den Jahren 1910, 1911 und 1912*, 8; *Gedenkschrift anläßlich des 25jährigen Bestehens des Ersten Karlsbader Kranken-Unterstützungs-Vereines*, 8–9; *Gedenkschrift anlässlich seines 25-jährigen Gründungs-Festes herausgegeben vom Verein Gesellschaft Kinderfreund in Karlsbad*, 37.

75. Rappaport, "Leben," 155.

76. Jellinek, *"Rede."*

77. Lässig, *Wege*, 530; see also Katz, *Ghetto. Mitsvot* (Heb.), religious commandments.

78. Rappaport, "Leben," 147.

79. Baum, "Zedakah," 96.

80. Caspary, "Wurzel," 93–94.

81. Stark, "Krankenexpositur," 553–555.

82. Baum, "Zedakah," 97.

83. See Hödl, "Armut," 325–332.

84. Quoted in *[Israelitische] Gemeindezeitung [Böhmen]* (1889): 12:95.

85. *Mitteilungen aus dem Verein zur Abwehr des Antisemitismus* 16 (1906): 37:282; Bajohr, *Hotel*, 37–45.

86. Rappaport, "Leben." *Mizrachi* (Heb.), the name of an Orthodox Zionist organization.

87. Zibbell, Berman, and Einhorn, "Philanthropy"; *gabba'ei tsedakah* (Heb.), charity collectors.

88. *Galut* (Heb.), Diaspora.

89. Rappaport, "Leben," 153–154.

90. Support also necessarily covered the return trip back home. Rappaport, "Leben," 154–156.

91. "Das Kaiser Franz Josef-Regierungs-Jubiläums-Hospiz für arme Israeliten," 482.

92. See Lässig, *Wege*, 555.

Chapter 5

1. Robbe-Grillet, *Letztes Jahr*, 31.

2. The original Hebrew title *Badenheim ir nofesh* [Badenheim Summer Health Resort] was changed to *Badenheim 1939* in the English translation by Dalya Bilu, and in the German version shortened to *Badenheim*.

3. Roth, *Shop Talk*, 26.

4. Appelfeld, *Badenheim*, 13f.

5. Ibid., 12f.

6. Ibid., 12–14.

7. Ibid., 36.

8. Ibid., 33.

9. Ibid., 38f.

10. Ibid., 65.

11. Ibid., 37, 39, 41f., 52.

12. Roth, *Shop Talk*, 28–29.

13. Ibid., 29–30.

14. Bernstein, *Conclusions,* 58, 61.

15. Steward, "Spa Towns," 119.

16. Fuhs, *Orte*, 460.

17. Private archive of the author, interview with Aharon Appelfeld, 21 March 2005.

18. Singer, *Brothers*, 240; letter to Felix Weltsch, 19 July 1916, Kafka, *Letters*, 123.

19. Something similar was observed for Wiesbaden by Burkhard Fuhs and for Bad Ems by Hermann Sommer. Fuhs, *Orte*, 372; Sommer, *Kur*, 485–492.

20. LBI, Gerald Meyer, Sprudel, 2–3.

21. Letter to Emilie Zöllner, 19 August 1893, Fontane, *Werke*, 276.

22. See Rahden, *Jews*, Introduction, especially 6–9.

23. On the concept of "miscounter" or mismeeting ("*Vergegnung*" in Buber's sense), see Buber, *Meetings*, 22.

24. Private archive of the author, interview with Aharon Appelfeld, 21 March 2005.

Chapter 6

1. Bauman, *Life*, 92.

2. Already in April 1916, Kafka had been in Carlsbad for two days officially and in the accompaniment of his sister Ottla. Letter to Felice, 9 April 1916, Kafka, *Briefe*, 155.

3. Kafka's parents also frequently spent the summer in Franzensbad, as his father had a nervous heart problem. For example, Kafka, letter to Oscar Baum, 16 July 1922, Kafka, *Letters*, 342; see also Kafka, *Briefe*, 447.

4. Letter to Felice Bauer, 25 April 1916, Kafka, *Letters to Felice*, 591–592.

5. Letter to Felice Bauer, 14 May 1916, Kafka, *Letters to Felice*, 592.

6. Letters to Felice Bauer, 19 April 1916 and 14 May 1916, Kafka, *Letters to Felice*, 591, 592; diary entry, 11 May 1916, Kafka, *Tagebücher*, 785–786.

7. Postcard to Felice Bauer, 15 May 1916, Kafka, *Letters to Felice*, 593–594.

8. In the story "The Great Wall of China," the Chinese are a kind of coded symbol standing for the Jewish people. See Robert, *Kafka*, 20–21; Alt, *Kafka*, 579–582.

9. China played a central role in Jewish Orientalist discourse. Thus, for example, Martin Buber saw Judaism as an "Oriental" culture closer to Chinese, Persian, or Indian traditions than to the Occident. Buber, "Spirit." In addition, the rediscovery of the Jews living in China played a role (see series of articles on this in *Jeschurun, Die Welt, Ost und West*, et al.). Another factor was the importance of China as a potential land of migra-

tion, for example for 3,000 Romanian Jews who wished to leave Romania in 1902 due to the rising wave of anti-Semitism there. See "Nach China!," 4.

10. See lecture by Prof. Christian Ehrenfels, German University Prague, *Selbstwehr* 5 (1911): 48:1.

11. See among others the stay by the Persian Shah Mussafer ed Din in September 1900. Pustejovsky, "Politik," 22; Kisch, "Kurorte," 1.

12. *Karlsbader "Kikriki"* 2 (1925): 8:2.

13. Zilcosky, *Travels*, 7.

14. Kaplan, *Questions*, 33–35.

15. Letter to Tile Rössler, 3 August 1923, Kafka, *Letters*, 375.

16. *Marienbad. Die Perle der böhmischen Weltbäder*, 27.

17. Sennett, *Fall*, 17.

18. Ibid., 117–118.

19. Ibid., 19.

20. Geisthövel, "Promenadenmischungen," 218–227.

21. Kuhnert, *Urbanität*, 17–18.

22. Mackaman, *Leisure*, 123–124.

23. Sennett, *Fall*, 195, 217.

24. Böttcher, *Brunnengeister*, cited in Geisthövel, "Promenadenmischungen," 227.

25. Sennett, *Fall*, 26–27, 153.

26. Kisch, *Blätter*, 19–20.

27. "Antisemitismus in Badeorten," 271.

28. Geisthövel, "Promenadenmischungen," 206.

29. Sennett, *Fall*, 19, 161–163.

30. See Knoch, "Grandhotel," 139.

31. Letters to Max Brod, 12, 14, 17, and 18 July 1916, Kafka, *Briefe* 172, 177.

32. Letter to Hugo von Hofmannsthal, 10 July 1895, Schnitzler, *Briefe*, 265.

33. In general, the attitude of social mixing in spas tends to be idealized, and in reality contacts between different social groups were rather unusual. See Blackbourn, "Meeting Places," 452; see also Kaplan, *Making*, 126; Philipp Loewenfeld, *Memoiren*, in Richarz, *Life*, 235. This was different when spas where still more exclusive around 1800 and the aristocracy enabled relationships between classes, religions, and sexes. See Naimark-Goldberg, "Health."

34. Kaplan, *Making*, 126.

35. When confronted with impoverished Eastern European Jewish immigrants at the turn of the century, local Jews in Berlin or Vienna often felt a need to distance themselves from these Jews. On the one hand, the society regarded them as racially deviant and outsiders; on the other, bourgeois Western Jews felt reminded by them of their own past, and they viewed these new arrivals as impediments to their own complete integration. Brenner, *Renaissance*, 142; Hödl, "Migration," 154; Aschheim, *Brothers*; Wertheimer, *Strangers*.

36. Sennett, *Fall*, 27, 159.

37. See Deleuze, *Difference*, 135f.; Lacan, "Mirror Stage."

38. *Israelitische Wochenschrift* 10 (1879): 36:307; Graetz, "Leben," 761–764.

39. *Selbstwehr* 2 (1908): 32:6.

40. Henisch, *Tanz*, 199.

41. INJOEST, Norbert Toller, Erinnerungen. Only women traveling alone frequently took along a child, generally a daughter of any age, to the spa. LBI, Lalla Kaden (nee Bondi), "Akt," 165–166; INJOEST, Egon Basch, Erinnerungen.

42. LBI, Philipp Loewenfeld, *Memoiren*, undated manuscript, written in New York between 1940 and 1945, translated into English in Richarz, *Life*, 234.

43. Singer, *Brothers,* 240.

44. Ibid., 123.

45. Gilman, "Rediscovery," 360–361.

46. This went on until their emigration to the United States in 1914. According to his correspondence from this period, Sholem Aleichem lived in Nervi/Genoa, Bern, Lausanne, Lugano, Badenweiler, Wiesbaden, and the Black Forest. Sholem Aleichem, *Briv.*

47. Landmann, "Nachwort," 235.

48. Sholem Aleichem, *Marienbad*, 61.

49. Ibid., 92, 93, 103.

50. Singer, *Brothers*, 88; Sholem Aleichem, *Marienbad*, 56–57. On the actual significance of western Bohemian health spas as advertising media for the industry of Bohemia in Eastern Europe, see Slokar, "Bedeutung," 161.

51. Auslander, "Taste," 300.

52. Sholem Aleichem, *Marienbad*, 88.

53. Agnon, "Aufstieg und Abstieg," in *Gemeinschaft*, 15–16. It was written in the early 1920s and published by Martin Buber in his journal *Der Jude* 8 (1924): 1:31–57, and later included in Agnon's collection *In der Gemeinschaft der Frommen*, published by Schocken in 1935. According to Dan Laor, an English version of this tale by Agnon has never been published.

54. Langer, *Nine Gates*, xvi.

55. Franz Kafka on the Belzer Rebbe, letter to Max Brod, 17 and 18 July 1916, Kafka, *Letters*, 122.

56. Private archive of the author, letter from Ruth Shaingarten, 8 February 2003. For images of Chassidim in the West Bohemian spas, see YIVO, *People of a Thousand Towns.*

57. Private archive of the author, letter from Ruth Shaingarten, 8 February 2003.

58. This motif is also used by, among others, Israel J. Singer in his novel *Yoshe Kalb*, 105–106.

59. "Der Wunderrabbi von Sadagora in Karlsbad," 2; Kisch, *Erlebtes*, 266.

60. Philipp Loewenfeld, *Memoiren*, in Richarz, *Life*, 234.

61. *Persermesse*, disorderly, chaotic crowd of people.

62. Here he used the expression *pólisi*, a term of opprobrium for Polish Jews in Hungary. The Yiddish *peyes* is the term for sidelocks.

63. Private archive of László A. Magyar, letter from Siegmund Deutsch to his sister Adél, April or May 1912. Siegmund (Zsigmond) Deutsch (ca. 1885–1944), dentist and cellist, practiced as a dentist in Vienna and during the summers of 1912–1914 in Carlsbad. In 1944, he was murdered together with his wife by the SS in the Slovakian mountains.

64. Sholem Aleichem, *Marienbad*, 60–61. The German edition has some additional sentences omitted in the standard English version: "But that's based on mutuality. They hate us Russian Jews more than pork. A poor man who comes from among us—they call him a 'shnorrer'—they'd tear the guy to pieces if they could." *Marienbad, Kein Roman*, 48.

65. Lalla Kaden, quoted in Richarz, *Leben*, 335–336.

66. LBI, Gerald Meyer, Sprudel, 18.

67. Philipp Loewenfeld, *Memoiren*, in Richarz, *Life*, 235.

68. LBI, Meyer, Sprudel, 29–30.

69. Letter, Aline Bernstein, 22 July 1928, in Wolfe/Bernstein, *Loneliness*, 163. Wolfe dedicated his novel *Look Homeward, Angel* to her ("A.B.") in 1929.

70. Edward VII came to Marienbad in 1897 and 1899 (still as the Prince of Wales), and then every summer from 1903 until his death in May 1910. Münz, *King Edward*.

71. Ibid., 236–237, 253–258.

72. Ibid., 237.

73. LBI, Philipp Loewenfeld, Memoiren, 23.

74. "King Edward Smiles on Maxine Elliot."

75. Sholem Aleichem, *Marienbad*, 61–62.

76. The American novelist William Dean Howells visited Carlsbad in 1899 and set parts of his novel in the Carlsbad scenery. Howells, *Silver Wedding*, 126.

77. Bajohr, *Hotel*, 21.

78. Sennett, *Fall*, 48–49.

79. Ibid., 161.

80. Palmer, *Life*, 126–127.

81. "Bäderantisemitismus," 105–106.

82. Ibid., 106.

83. Letter to Martha Fontane, 21 August 1893, Fontane, *Werke*, 278–279.

84. Letter to Friedrich Paulsen, 2 September 1897, Fontane, *Werke*, 663.

85. Fleischer, *Cohn*, 124–139.

86. Letter to Martha Fontane, 17 August 1893, Fontane, *Werke*, 275–276.

87. Mecklenburg, "Portugiesen," 95, 99.

88. Benz, "Antisemitismus," 166.

89. Letter to Martha Fontane, 21 August 1893, Fontane, *Werke*, 279; letter to Martha Fontane, Bad Kissingen, 15 July 1889, quoted in Fleischer, "Cohn," 128.

90. Letter to Karl Zöllner, 21 August 1894, Fontane, *Werke*, 379–380.

91. Letters to Martha Fontane, 24 August 1893, and to Karl Zöllner, 21 August and 6 September 1894, Fontane, *Werke*, 283–285, 379–380, 383.

92. Benz, "Antisemitismus," 167.

93. Jannidis/Lauer, "Baruch," 103–106, 116; Balzer, "Zugegeben," 203.

94. Letter to Paul Schlenther, 13 August 1895, Fontane, *Werke*, 481. On the stereo-type of the "beautiful Jewess" in Fontane's work, see Klüger, *Katastrophen*, 102–104.

95. See Hax, "Isaac," 99–100.

96. One marked exception are the numerous picture postcards from the German spa Borkum, an island in the North Sea, which aggressively called for barring Jews from spa society.

97. JMW, collection Martin Schlaff; Dipper, "Mensch"; Hornemann/Laabs, "Bär."

98. "Der Sammler Wolfgang Haney," 156.

99. Hax, "Isaac," 97–98.

100. Dipper, "Mensch," 198.

101. Geisthövel, "Promenadenmischungen," 210.

102. Dipper, "Mensch," 201; see also Leiskau/Geppert, "Thaler."

103. Hornemann/Laabs, "Bär," 176–177.

104. Dipper, "Mensch," 197.

105. "Antisemitische Bade-, Kur- und Erholungsorte" (1902).

106. CAHJP, Collection CV, No. 2353, letter to Ignaz Ziegler, 17 August 1926.

107. Hornemann/Laabs, "Bär," 176–177; Hax, "Isaac," 110.

108. Hax, "Isaac," 115–116; Baeumerth, *Fremden*, 41–52.

109. Dipper, "Mensch," 198.

110. "Antisemitische Postkarten," 82–85.

111. See Bajohr, *Hotel*, 16–21.

112. "Mein Freund, der Althändler Kohn," 184.

113. Hax, "Isaac," 104.

114. Ibid., 105; Backhaus, "Cohn," 314.

115. Schäfer, *Judenbilder*, 70–71.

116. Kaulbach, *Karikaturen*.

117. Twain, "Marienbad," 116.

118. Clemenceau, *Foot*, 62.

119. Ibid., 63f., 71–73.

120. Ibid., 68.

Chapter 7

1. Postcard to Felice Bauer, 18 July 1916, Kafka, *Letters to Felice*, 598.

2. Letter to Max Brod, 5 July 1916, Kafka, *Letters*, 116; see also Zadoff, "Reichweite."

3. Kafka, *Briefe*, 494.

4. Letter to Max Brod, 12 and 14 July 1916, Kafka, *Letters*, 118.

5. Diary entry, 6 July 1916, Kafka, *Tagebücher*, 795.

6. Letter to Max Brod, 12 and 14 July 1916, Kafka, *Letters*, 118. When Franz Kafka fell ill in December 1917 with tuberculosis, he also broke off the second engagement to Felice Bauer.

7. Letter to Ottla Kafka, 12 July 1916, Kafka, *Briefe*, 171.

8. Letter to Felice Bauer, 15 July 1916, Kafka, *Briefe*, 474.

9. Letter to Felice Bauer, 22 July 1916, Kafka, *Briefe*, 478.

10. Letter to Felice Bauer, 28 July 1916, Kafka, *Letters to Felice*, 602.

11. Diary entry, 29 January 1922, Kafka, *Diaries*, 409.

12. Mackaman, *Leisure*, 135–141.

13. Diary entry, 3 July 1916, in Franz Kafka, *Tagebücher*, p. 790.

14. Zweig, *World*, 89–90.

15. Ibid., 76.

16. Mackaman, *Leisure*, 137; Zweig, *World*, 81; see also Gay, *Passion*; Flemming, "Krise."

17. Zweig, *World*, 71.

18. Johannes Dück, "Aus dem Geschlechtsleben unserer Zeit," quoted in Flemming, "Krise," 43–44.

19. Fred, "Gesellschaft," 104, quoted in ibid., 55.

20. Mackaman, *Leisure*, 136.

21. Sholem Aleichem, "Hot Springs," 357.

22. Ibid., 138.

23. Palmer, *Life*, 127.

24. Mackaman, *Leisure*, 135–141.

25. See Fuhs, *Orte*, 120–121.

26. Gabriele Reuter, *Aus guter Familie* (1895), quoted in Kaplan, *Making*, 125.

27. Hanel, *Geschichte*, 94; trans. Iggers, *Women*, 182. Hanel confused the Marienbad spring Kreuzbrunnen as being in Carlsbad.

28. Hanel, *Geschichte*, 95; trans. Iggers, *Women*, 183.

29. Hanel, *Geschichte*, 99, 101; trans. Iggers, *Women*, 185.

30. In his novel *Große, kleine Schwester*, Peter Härtling develops this motif by having the daughter of a bourgeois Jewish family from Brünn, while at Franzensbad in the summer of 1927, meet a National Socialist. Härtling, *Schwester*, 112–128.

31. For example, in Stefan Zweig's *Brennendes Geheimnis* (*Burning Secret*), a novella published in 1914; see also Singer, *Brothers*, 243–244.

32. Sacher-Masoch, *Venus*, 9.

33. Simmel et al., *Culture*, 174. The changed social conditions of beginning mass tourism prompted Simmel further: "An acquaintanceship made while travelling [. . .] often develops an intimacy and openness for which no inner reason can actually be found. Three factors appear to me to work together here: the separation from one's accustomed milieu, the momentary impressions and encounters held in common, and the consciousness of an imminent and definitive separation once more." Ibid., 162.

34. LBI, Rudolf D. Keller Collection; see Fuhs, *Orte*, 241–245.

35. Henisch, *Tanz*, 203–206; Petrescu, *Vamps*, 8–11.

36. Křížek/Švandrlik, *Marienbad*, 82.

37. On a more general image of the Bohemian spas as marriage markets, see Howells, *Silver Wedding*, 163.

38. Kaplan, *Making*, 86.

39. Ibid., 108–109; Gay, *Passion*, 9.

40. Gay, *Passion*, 3.

41. Kaplan, *Making*, 111. In his novel *Jüdinnen* (1911), Max Brod describes precisely this milieu in nearby Teplitz. See on this Zimmermann, "Distanzliebe," 238–241.

42. Isidor Hirschfeld, Erinnerungen, quoted in Richarz, *Life*, 232–233.

43. Kaplan, *Making*, 92.

44. Ibid, 48–54.

45. Ibid., 107.

46. Ibid., 105–106.

47. Ibid., 87.

48. Ibid., 51.

49. Ibid.

50. Ibid., 65–70, 82.

51. Quoted in "Ueber Rabbiner Dr. Ziegler in Karlsbad," 4.

52. [*Israelitische*] *Gemeindezeitung* [*Böhmen*] 22 (1894): 16:185.

53. Ziegler, "Skizzen," 218–220; Thieberger, "Vorbemerkung," 211–212.

54. Thieberger, "Vorbemerkung," 211–212.

55. Ziegler, "Skizzen," 212.

56. Quoted in "Ueber Rabbiner Dr. Ziegler in Karlsbad," 4.

57. Thieberger, "Vorbemerkung," 212.

58. *Das dreissigjährige Gründungsfest der Loge "Karlsbad" I.O.B.B*, 56–62.

59. *Die Welt* 4 (1900): 33:16; 4 (1900): 38:15; 4 (1900): 40:10; 5 (1901): 44:13; 6 (1902): 16:6; 6 (1902): 35:11–12; *Selbstwehr* 1 (1907): 23:5; 1 (1907): 42:5; 3 (1909): 22:3; 3 (1909): 30:6; 3 (1909): 39:5; 7 (1913): 34:6. The Jewish Academic Club (*Jüdisch-Akademischer Klub*) was founded on the initiative of the Prague student dueling fraternity *Barissia*. Wlaschek, *Juden*, 74–75.

60. Diary entry, 22 June 1907, in Brainin, *Works*, 122.

61. *Die Welt* 6 (1902): 32:12.

62. Ibid.

63. See Zadoff, "Writers."

64. Diary entry, 27 July and 2 August 1910, in Reuben Brainin, Diaries [Heb.], CAHJP, File no. P8/8, 2–3; partially torn poster, Shai Hurwitz file at the Hebrew University Archives, as cited in Nash, *Search*, 150.

65. Charney, *Barg*, 223; see on this Chapters 11–13 below.

66. *Selbstwehr* 2 (1908): 35:6.

67. *Ost und West* was founded in 1901, *Selbstwehr* in 1907. See Spector, *Territories*, 160–194; Brenner, *Identities*.

68. Brenner, *Identities*, 159; Gilman, "Rediscovery," 351–352.

69. *Selbstwehr* 2 (1908): 30:4.

70. *Selbstwehr* 2 (1908): 32:5.

71. *Selbstwehr* 1 (1907): 15:4; 1 (1907): 16:6; 1 (1907): 18:5.

72. *Selbstwehr* 7 (1913): 37:6.

73. Kohn, "Brief," 1.

74. Letter to Yitzchak Löwy, June–July 1914, Kafka, *Letters*, 108, 135, 148; Stach, *Kafka*, 64–65.

75. Brenner, *Renaissance*, 142; Gilman, *Self-Hatred*, 270–271; Mattenklott, "Ostjudentum," 297.

76. Brenner, *Renaissance*, 143; Aschheim, *Brothers*; Gilman, "Rediscovery," 359.

77. "Der Wunderrabbi von Sadagora in Karlsbad," 2.

78. Ibid.

79. Langer, *Byli a bylo*, 244–245; Mattenklott, "Ostjudentum," 294.

80. The "Western Jew who has become assimilated to the Hasidim" was a reference to Jiři Langer, whom Kafka had presumably seen for the very first time that evening, 24 March 1915. Entry of 25 March 1915, Kafka, *Diaries*, 334, translation there slightly revised.

81. Zweig, "Sorglosen," 40.

82. Ibid., 43.

83. Ibid., 43–44.

84. Ibid., 46.

85. Ibid., 46.

86. Letter to Lou Andreas-Salomé, 30 July 1915, Freud and Andreas-Salomé, *Letters*, 32. Freud had already been in Carlsbad in 1911, 1912, and 1914, and in Marienbad in 1913 to take the cure.

87. Porges, "Brief," 44.

88. Ibid., 45; LBI, Ledermann, Familienstiftung, 12.

89. See the Carlsbad figures for visitors: 71,000 spa guests in 1911, 51,000 in 1914, 22,000 in 1915, 32,000 in 1916, and 15,000 in 1919, constituting a drop of over 75 percent in eight years. Gitschner, "Kurstatistik," 43.

90. Kisch, *Erlebtes*, 252.

91. Porges, "Brief," 44.

92. *Karlsbader Zeitung* (1914): 47:1.

93. "Galizien in Karlsbad," 5.

94. Ibid.

95. By the end of 1915, 385,645 refugees had arrived in Austria, among them 157,630 Jews, 41 percent of the total. That figure rose by 1917 to approximately 200,000 Jewish refugees, 72,000 just in Bohemia alone; of the latter, 49,730 were indigent. Rozenblit, *Identity*, 66; Rozenblit, "Fatherland," 205; Hoffmann-Holter, *Abreisendmachung*, 31–34.

96. *Selbstwehr* 11 (1917): 6:6.

97. Kudela, "Emigration," 125.

98. On anti-Semitism during the war, see Hoffmann-Holter, *Abreisendmachung*; "Die Ostjudenfrage," 77–92. On anti-Semitism in the western Bohemian spas, see Chapters 9 and 10 below.

99. "Unterhaltungsabend in Karlsbad," 864.

100. Wilkowitsch, "Franzensbad im Zeichen," 356.

101. Ibid.

102. Ibid.

103. *Selbstwehr* 10 (1916): 32:6; Barber, "Flüchtlinge," 518–519.

104. Rand, "Versammlung," 334.

105. *Selbstwehr* 10 (1916): 25:7.

106. Barber, "Flüchtlinge," 518–519.

107. Ibid.

108. Rand, "Versammlung," 334. The *Agudas Jisroel* was an association of Orthodox Jewry founded in 1912.

109. Kafka was declared indispensable by the Workers' Accident Insurance Institute where he worked, and thus was exempted from military service. Kafka, *Briefe*, 513; Kafka, letter to Felice Bauer, 5 April 1915, Kafka, *Letters to Felice*, 577–578.

110. Porges, "Brief," 45–46. After Felice had departed, Kafka planned to participate in the laying of the foundation stone for the Field Marshal Archduke Friedrich Sanatorium for War Veterans with Kidney and Heart Ailments, but then decided not to. Kafka, *Briefe*, 536.

111. Barber, "Flüchtlinge," 518.

112. See Schäfer, *Zionistenkreise*.

113. Kafka, *Briefe*, 534–535; Richarz, *Leben*, 206.

114. Rozenblit, *Identity*, 77–78.

115. Letter to Max Brod, 12 and 14 July 1916, Kafka, *Briefe*, 175.

116. Letter and postcard to Felice Bauer, 25 and 26 July 1916, Kafka, *Letters to Felice*, 601–602.

117. Postcard to Felice Bauer, 30 July 1916, Kafka, *Letters to Felice*, 603, translation there slightly corrected.

118. Letter to Felice Bauer, 12 September 1916, Kafka, *Letters to Felice*, 616.

119. Letters to Felice Bauer, 26 and 29 September 1916, Kafka, *Letters to Felice*, 623–626; letter to Felice Bauer, 2 October 1916, Kafka, *Briefe*, 244; Alt, *Kafka*, 445.

120. Letter to Felice Bauer, 12 September 1916, Kafka, *Letters to Felice*, 617, translation there slightly amended.

121. Ibid.

122. Diary entry, 24 November 1914, Kafka, *Tagebücher*, 698–699.

123. Diary entry, 14 September 1915, Kafka, *Tagebücher*, 751–752; Kafka, *Briefe*, 538–539.

124. Kafka, *Briefe*, 538–539.

125. Singer, "Hebräischstunden," 151; Alt, *Kafka*, 425.

126. Vízdalová, "Langer," 112–113.

127. Langer, *Byli a byalo*, in Iggers, *Jews*, 250.

128. Langer, *Nine Gates*, xvi.

129. Ibid., xvii.

130. Vízdalová, "Langer," 112–113; Langer, *Nine Gates*, xxiii.

131. Langer, *Nine Gates*, 20.

132. After his death in 1927, his son and successor Aaron likewise traveled to Marienbad to take the waters. Miškovský, *Marianskolázeňské obrásky*; Alfassi, "Belz."

133. Elias, "Marienbad," quoted in Kafka, *Briefe*, 538.

134. Barber, "Flüchtlinge," 519.

135. Postcard to Felice Bauer, 18 July 1916, Kafka, *Letters to Felice*, 598.

136. Ibid.

137. Letter to Max Brod, 17 and 18 July 1916, Kafka, *Letters*, 119–120.

138. Ibid., 120.

139. Ibid.

140. Ibid., 121.

141. Ibid.

142. Ibid.

143. Ibid., 122.

144. Ibid.

145. Ibid., 123.

146. Ibid., 122.

147. Ibid., 123.

148. In his biography, Peter-André Alt interprets Kafka's experience in Marienbad as entirely negative, an analysis that seems unconvincing against the backdrop of his attentive and partly highly sympathetic report: "He sees the ritual order which determines how to deal with the holy man as a form not accessible to him. It remains closed because the path of tradition is blocked. By contrast, he thinks to perceive here a structure of power that appears as threatening as modern bureaucracy." Alt, *Kafka*, 429–430.

149. Letter to Felix Weltsch, 19 July 1916, Kafka, *Letters*, 123–124.

150. Gilman, *Kafka*, 88–100; Zadoff, "Reichweite."

151. Gilman, "Rediscovery," 351–352.

152. Kafka, *Letter to His Father*, 200. František Langer formulated similar reflections in *Byli a bylo*, 241.

153. Deleuze/Guattari, *Kafka*, 14–15, 26.

154. Kafka, *Letter to His Father*, 199.

155. Ibid., 200.

Chapter 8

1. Bachmann, *Darkness*, 177.

2. *Selbstwehr* 13 (1919): 51/52. Kafka published several short tales in this paper and frequently mentioned it in his letters and diaries. Hartmut Binder ("Franz Kafka and the Weekly Paper 'Selbstwehr'") explores his special relation with this weekly and the nature of the paper.

3. Kafka, *Stories*, 427–428.

4. Ibid. According to Marek Nekula, the detailed description of Odradek's body yields

a Star of David. Nekula, *Sprachen*, 15–18. Willi Goetschel suggests that "maybe Odradek is actually memory in the form of tradition." He notes: "The last line is very biblical: it's not just the children but the children's children. I think that's where the fear of the family man comes in: When he's gone, Odradek will still be there. In that way Odradek is almost an objectification of that memory." Goetschel, "Dis/Enchanted World," 1.

5. Kafka, *Stories*, 427–428.

6. Ibid., 428–429.

7. Such as Malcolm Pasley, based on Höllerer, "Odradek"; Benjamin, "Kafka," 810f.; Nekula, *Sprachen*, 15–18; Zizek, "Odradek."

8. Nekula, *Sprachen*, 16.

9. Simmel, "Excursus," 601.

10. Ibid.

11. The files of the Jewish Communities (*Kultusgemeinden*) in Carlsbad, Marienbad, and Franzensbad were destroyed during the German occupation and cannot be found. Files of the municipalities in relation to the Jewish Communities have only survived in fragments or are only partially accessible as such.

Chapter 9

1. Pincus, *Verloren*, 18.

2. Many Jewish Communities in Bohemia and Moravia came into being in this way. Wasserman, "Peddling"; "Geschichte der Juden in Karlsbad," 255.

3. Lamed, "Gesetz," 306–307. Franzensbad and Marienbad had no similar *Privilegium* at their disposal; Jewish settlement there was similar to patterns in most other towns in Bohemia.

4. Ibid.

5. LBI, Ottilie Bondy, Beitrag.

6. The term "winter Jews," a translation of *Winterjuden*, is used by Gotthard Deutsch and Ignaz Ziegler in their entry "Karlsbad" in *The Jewish Encyclopedia* (1901–1906); see also LBI, Hoenig Family Collection, 14.

7. Lamed, "Gesetz," 307; "Geschichte der Juden in Karlsbad," 255.

8. Ziegler, *Dokumente*, 70–72.

9. Ibid., 74.

10. Friedländer, *Juden*, 36.

11. Ziegler, *Dokumente*, 104–105, 139–140; "Geschichte der Juden in Karlsbad," 258–259.

12. LBI, Rudolf D. Keller Collection.

13. The population soared from 7,291 in 1869 to 14,637 in 1900. Ahnelt, "Verhältnisse," 488–489.

14. In 1900, 1,405 Carlsbad residents designated themselves as Jews (9.6 percent of the total population), in 1921, the figure was 2,115 (10 percent of the total), and in 1930 about the same, 2,120 (8.9 percent of the total). However, the figures remain problematic, since up until 1918 this data was for religious affiliation, yet afterward was under

the rubric of nationality. Ziegler, "Bestand," 659–660; "Geschichte der Juden in Karlsbad," 259; *Statistisches Gemeindelexikon des Landes Böhmen*; Friedmann, "Ergebnisse," 4; Lang, "Israelitenhospital," 493; "Carlsbad."

15. Pincus, *Verloren*, 17; Křížek/Švandrlik, *Marienbad*, 78–79.

16. Many observant religious hotel owners and merchants left the spas during the winter, but the rabbis, ritual slaughterers, and the owners of kosher grocery stores did not. Private archive of the author, letter from Ruth Shaingarten, 8 February 2003.

17. Pincus, *Verloren*, 17; see on this Gary B. Cohen's analysis of everyday German-Czech relations in Prague, especially in regard to the mixed neighborhoods in the city. Although the concrete situation in the spas can be compared with Prague only to a limited degree, the everyday realities in a small city generated numerous points of contact between the various groups. Cohen, *Politics*, 123–139.

18. At the turn of the century, 129 Carlsbad residents indicated Czech as their everyday vernacular, while 14,000 identified themselves as German-speaking. Ahnelt, "Verhältnisse," 493. Even after 1918, the situation changed but haltingly. In the census of 1930, of 23,901 Carlsbad residents, 20,856 gave their nationality as German (87.2 percent), 2,120 as Jewish (*Israelitisch*, 8.8 percent), and 1,446 as Czech (6 percent). *Statistisches Gemeindelexikon des Landes Böhmen*.

19. Quoted in Bubriski, "Bäder," 569.

20. *Průvodce po letních sídlech, lázeňských a léčebných místech.*

21. *Židovské Zprávy* (1909): 13:6; *Rozvoj* 15 (1921): 15:2.

22. Ussishkin, *Devarim*, 247.

23. *Rozvoj* 20 (1926): 34:6.

24. Bouda, *Průvodce*, 45, 48–50, 64; *Karlsbad. Klimatische Kurorte und Touristik in der ČSR, Annoncenteil* (adverts).

25. Zatloukal, *Karlsbad*, 32.

26. Jewish associations and physicians generally went unmentioned in publications of the municipality, such as the brochure on social life issued on the occasion of the 74th Convention of German Natural Scientists and Physicians held in Carlsbad in 1902. SOAKV, AM KV G–3–II; see also Zörkendörfer, "Gesundheitspflege," 66.

27. See Whiteside, *Schönerer*, 160–187.

28. Kieval, *Languages*, 166; Kieval, "Jews," 23; Judson, "Frontiers," 391–393; "Die Judenhetze in Böhmen," 1001.

29. Ibid.

30. Cohen, "Jews," 59.

31. See Judson, "Frontiers," 384. Dimitry Shumsky analyzes the worsening anti-Semitism in nearby Eger around the turn of the century as part of a program directed against multi-ethnicity and bilingualism—an observation I cannot confirm for the situation in the health spas. Shumsky, "History."

32. SOAKV, AM KV A-18-I-1; *Karlsbader Fremdenblatt* 3, 25 May 1908.

33. SOAKV, AM KV A-18-I-1.

34. SOAKV, AM KV A-I-1-6-1.

35. *Deutsche Tages-Zeitung* 148, 4 July 1923.

36. *Dritte Eingabe der Bürgermeister [. . .] an den Völkerbundrat*, 1–4.

37. Ibid., 5–7.

38. SOAKV, AM KV A-18-I-1. The spas were in fact not nationalized until 1948. *Karlovy Vary*, 36–37.

39. Henisch, *Tanz*, 54; compare the situation in Prague, where Jews felt many elements in the new Czech national culture were not attractive and the mounting wave of Czech anti-Semitism rejected them completely. Cohen, *Politics*, 81–82.

40. Pincus, *Verloren*, 18.

41. Private archive of the author, letter from Mimi Ormond, 16 July 2001; LBI, Robitscher Family Collection. When Emanuel Engel, Czech politician and physician in Carlsbad, offered a course in Bohemian in 1907 for German-speaking children, interested parents enrolled more than 300 children. However, after various newspapers, such as the *Reichenberger Zeitung, Karlsbader Badeblatt,* and the paper *Vaterland*, expressed their indignation over the supposed "Slavicization" of the children, the municipal authorities stopped the course. SOAKV, AM KV D-IV-43-10.

42. Private archive of the author, letter from Kurt Reichert, 12 July 2002.

43. *Jahres-Bericht der Knaben und Mädchen-Bürgerschule in Karlsbad für das Schuljahr 1897–98*, 37.

44. SOAKV, AM KV A-18-I-1.

45. Wlascheck, *Juden*, 48; *Selbstwehr* 4 (1910): 25:5.

46. CAHJP, Collection CV, No. 2365.

47. "Wir rächen!," 1.

48. Marienbader Kurliste, 12 August 1929; letters to Mania Bialik, 25 July 1930 and 22 September 1931, Bialik, *Igrot el ra'ayato*, 78–81, 213–214, 241–246.

49. In kosher dietary laws, *parve* (Yid.) food is neutral, without dairy or meat ingredients. Letter to Mania Bialik, 22 September 1931, Bialik, *Igrot el ra'ayato*, 241.

50. *Karlsbader "Kikriki"* 2 (1925): 8:2. The pixie cut as a hairstyle around 1925 became a symbol for the new and emancipated woman.

51. There were repeated cases where anti-Semitic arguments were employed to alienate clients from Jewish firms, such as in the case of the grocery store owner Alfred Zentner and the Catholic sisters of the local hospital. SOKAV, AM KV A-I-18-1.

52. "Karlsbad—antisemitisch," 941. Already at the end of the 1880s, Schönerer, in the framework of a public campaign of incitement against Jewish physicians, had issued a list of spa doctors from Carlsbad and Franzensbad with a notation after every name as to whether the person was a Jew. "Jüdische und antisemitische Ärzte," 298; "Das 'Vaterland' gegen die jüdischen Ärzte"; "Herr Georg Schönerer und die jüdischen Ärzte."

53. "Karlsbad—antisemitisch," 941.

54. Ibid., 942.

55. "Karlsbader Sprudelsalz," 961.

56. *Im Deutschen Reich* 7 (1901): 11:642.

57. "Karlsbad—antisemitisch," 941.

58. See Fellner, "Judenfreundlichkeit," 69–70.

59. Kohut, "Stettenheim," 266.

60. *Selbstwehr* 2 (1908): 4:5.

61. Egerland was the historical region surrounding the administrative center of Eger/Cheb, and also a synonym for the German-speaking popular folk culture of the region.

62. Klemm, *Jugend*, 80.

63. *Selbstwehr* 2 (1908): 4:5.

64. *Selbstwehr* 1 (1907): 1:5.

65. *Selbstwehr* 1 (1907): 13:6.

66. *Selbstwehr* 1 (1907): 7:6.

67. *Selbstwehr* 3 (1909): 2:4–5.

68. *Selbstwehr* 1 (1907): 7:6; 1 (1907): 4:5; 4 (1910): 8:5.

69. *Oesterreichische Wochenschrift* 27 (1910): 5:93.

70. Ibid.

71. Ibid.

72. Ibid., 12:208.

73. "Antisemitisches Treiben in Franzensbad," 46.

74. "Antisemitische Treibereien in böhmischen Kurorten," 113.

75. "Reisebeilage," *Vossische Zeitung*, 1 June 1910, quoted in *Franzensbader Tagblatt* 6, 7 June 1910, 2.

76. Quoted in *Mitteilungen aus dem Verein zur Abwehr des Antisemitismus* 9 (1899): 35:272.

77. Near Chicago on Lake Michigan, where a "miniature Catskills *borsht* belt—without the mountains" had evolved in the 1930s and 1940s, Cutler notes something similar in the summertime season: "South Haven developed as the major Jewish summer vacation center in the Midwest despite what many Jews perceived to be underlying anti-Semitism in the town." Cutler, *Chicago*, 230.

Chapter 10

1. Nordau, *Anblicke*, 178.

2. Quoted in "Gegen das Hineintragen von Rassen- und Klassenhaß in die Kurorte," 244.

3. Thus, for example: *Im Deutschen Reich* 9 (1903): 3:246; "Antisemitische Bade-, Kur- und Erholungsorte"; *Selbstwehr* 4 (1910): 19:3; "Wo Juden unerwünscht sind!"; see also Bajohr, *Hotel*, and Wildt, "Antisemitismus."

4. "Die Juden in den Bädern," 242.

5. Steward, "Tourism," 5; Judson, "German."

6. See Steward, "Spa Towns," 119.

7. Bajohr, *Hotel*, 143–149; Lichtblau, "Chiffre."

8. *Selbstwehr* 6 (1912): 29:3; 6 (1912): 35:3.

9. "Die Juden in den Kurorten des Kaukasus," 534; *Selbstwehr* 10 (1916): 3:3; *Mittei-*

lungen aus dem Verein zur Abwehr des Antisemitismus 13 (1903): 46:366; *Israelitisches Familienblatt*, 20 July 1911, quoted in Bajohr, *Hotel*, 151–152.

10. See the analysis by Bajohr in *Hotel*, 35–37.

11. "Judenreine Sommerfrischen," 9; Bajohr, *Hotel*, 147–149.

12. "Die Juden in den Bädern," 243.

13. Bajohr, *Hotel*, 18–20.

14. SOAKV, AM KV A-I-18-1.

15. *Im Deutschen Reich* 19 (1913): 3:135; *Selbstwehr* 4 (1910): 8:5–6.

16. Letter to Victor Fleischer, 29 June 1922, Zweig, *Briefe*, 70–71.

17. Ibid.

18. See Bajohr, *Hotel*, 37–45.

19. Quoted in *Im Deutschen Reich* 9 (1903): 9:549–550.

20. *Mitteilungen aus dem Verein zur Abwehr des Antisemitismus* 14 (1904): 24:190.

21. "Das Reich und die konfessionellen Bäder und Sommerfrischen," 220.

22. *Deutsch-soziale Blätter* (1904): 653:765, quoted in Bajohr, *Hotel*, 47.

23. Marienbad was mentioned much more rarely, and Franzensbad not at all. *Mitteilungen aus dem Verein zur Abwehr des Antisemitismus* 12 (1902): 34:259.

24. "Antisemitische Bäder und Sommerfrischen," 186.

25. "Antisemitische Bade-, Kur- und Erholungsorte" [1911], 116.

26. "Antisemitische Bade-, Kur- und Erholungsorte" [1904], 280.

27. Bajohr, *Hotel*, 53–115, 145–149.

28. *Deutsche Tageszeitung* (*Karlsbader Badeblatt*) 64 (1923): 211:1.

29. CAHJP, Collection CV, Nos. 2353 and 2365.

30. Borut, "Antisemitism," 23.

31. *Verzeichnis der judenfeindlichen Erholungsorte, Hotels und Pensionen nach ihrer geographischen Lage.*

32. CAHJP, Collection CV, No. 2353, letters to Ignaz Ziegler, 9 July 1927 and 16 March 1928.

33. CAHJP, Collection CV, No. 2353.

34. Ibid., letter to A. Friedberg in Hamburg, 9 August 1921.

35. Ibid., letter to Ludwig Steinberger, 18 May 1927.

36. Ibid., letter from Rudolf Roubitschek, 16 May 1930. For comparison, see an almost identical statement about Marienbad in CAHJP, Collection CV, No. 2365, letter from J. Schermant, 14 May 1931.

37. CAHJP, Collection CV, No. 2365, letter to Paul Waldstein, 7 October 1925.

38. CAHJP, Collection CV, No. 2365.

39. Ibid., letter from the CV Pommerania, 4 July 1927.

40. Ibid., letter from Dr. Cohn, 13 August 1930.

41. Ibid., letter from Ernst Wallach, 27 June 1929.

42. CAHJP, Collection CV, No. 2365.

43. Ibid., letter from Dr. Jonas, 12 February 1926, and letter from Hans Schicker, 22 June 1927.

44. Ibid., letter from Dr. Jonas, 12 February 1926.

45. Ibid., letter to *Israelitisches Familienblatt*, 26 June 1927, and letter to attorney Nathansohn, 19 March 1925.

46. Barkai, "Centralverein," 177–178.

47. Simmel, "Über die Karikatur" [1917].

48. Schubert, *Karlsbad*, 161.

49. "Hilfe! Polizei! Der Weiß-Poldl will uns beißen!," 1; "Salvete medici !?!," 1.

50. "Was ist in Karlsbad los?," 2; *Karlsbader "Kikriki"* 4 (1927): 9:5.

51. "Der Mädchenhandel in Karlsbad," 2; "Was unsere Leser erfahren müssen," 2; "Die sexuelle Ausbeutung in Karlsbad," 3; "In Memoriam Haarmann," 1; "Zur Sexualgeschichte Karlsbads," 2.

52. "Wir rächen - - -!," 1.

53. *Karlsbader "Kikriki"* 2 (1925): 7:3; "Wir rächen - - -!," 1; "Götzendienst und Ahnenkultus," 2–3.

54. "Bei uns z'Warmbod," 2.

55. Leib/Löw stands for a typical Jewish name, and Pelzlaus means fur-louse. *Karlsbader "Kikriki"* 4 (1927): 11:5; "Ostjuden passt auf!," 3; "Nebbich, der Juwelier," 3.

56. "Bei uns z'Warmbod," 1.

57. Ibid.

58. "Wie Karlsbad wählt," 2.

59. "Wir wählten - - - -," 1; "Skandalia," 3.

60. "Wir wählten - - - -," 2.

61. "Wahlahnungen," 1.

62. "Hep-Hep" is a rallying cry for anti-Semitic violence, as in the Hep Hep Riots of 1819 across Germany.

63. "Der Herbst ist wieder da," 2.

64. Mentullus, *Intimitäten*, 9.

65. CAHJP, Collection CV, No. 2353, letter from Josef Steiner, 11 August 1928.

66. Wack-Herget, *Karlsbad*, 75–76.

67. In the original its says, "Rasseköpfe fast durchwegs."

68. Amerikohner refers to the Jewish name of Kohn. Wack-Herget, *Karlsbad*, 75–76.

69. Ibid., 75–78.

70. Ibid., 77.

71. Ibid., 1–2.

72. Ibid., 18–20. This paragraph is a rewriting of the text by Ludwig Hirschfeld, *Wien . . . was nicht im Baedeker steht*, Munich 1927, quoted in Riedl, *Wien*, 18.

73. Wack-Herget, *Karlsbad*, 108–110.

74. Mentullus, *Intimitäten*.

75. Ibid., 14, 19–20, 22–23.

76. Ibid., 59–61.

77. "Wiederaufstieg unserer Weltkurorte," 1.

78. Mentullus, *Intimitäten*, 9; Wack-Herget, *Karlsbad*, 108.

Chapter 11

1. LBI, Arthur Prinz Collection; see also Hanak, *Eden*, 150–151.

2. LBI, Arthur Prinz Collection; see also Hanak, *Eden*, 150–151.

3. *Parnasse*, from *parnose* (Yid.), livelihood, income; *Mesumme*, from *mezumen* (Yid.), cash.

4. *Permitzwoth*, possibly a humoristic variant on *mitzwot* (Heb.), religious commandments.

5. *Tsores* (Yid.), difficulties, trouble; Arthur Ruppin (1876–1943), German Zionist and sociologist; Kurt Yehudah Blumenfeld (1884–1963), German Zionist.

6. The First Zionist Congress was convened in 1897 in Basle at the initiative of Theodor Herzl and formulated the goal of creating a Jewish state in Palestine. Until the outbreak of World War I, further such congresses were held annually or every two years.

7. In 1917, the British foreign minister Arthur James Earl of Balfour, in a letter to Lionel Walter Rothschild, the second Baron Rothschild (1868–1937), announced the acceptance by the British government of the eventual "establishment in Palestine of a national home for the Jewish people," promising to "use their best endeavours to facilitate the achievement of this object." Mendes-Flohr and Reinharz, *Jew*, 458.

Chapter 12

1. Israeli popular song, lyrics by Yoram Teharlev; see http://www.hebrewsongs.com/?song=hertzel (retrieved 19 March 2012). "*El ha-tsipor*" is a Zionist poem by Chaim Nachman Bialik. The song elaborates a play on Herzl's name, which in German means "little heart." Wolffsohn is misspelled in the translated lyrics from Hebrew into English online.

2. On the Villa Impériale, see LBI, Lalla Kaden (nee Bondi), "Akt," 165–166. The Villa Imperial is still today one of the most luxurious old smaller hotels in Franzensbad.

3. Letter to David Wolffsohn, 6 May 1904, Herzl, *Briefe*, 577. All translations of Herzl's letters here are directly from the German.

4. Letter to Julie Herzl, 3 May 1904, Herzl, *Briefe*, 576.

5. Letter to David Wolffsohn, 2 May 1904, Herzl, *Briefe*, 575.

6. Ibid., 575.

7. Zatloukal, *Karlsbad*, 4.

8. Goldscheider, "Erkrankungen," 96–97.

9. Zatloukal, *Karlsbad*, 148–149.

10. Letters to Julie Herzl, 4 and 8 May 1904, Herzl, *Briefe*, 577, 581.

11. Letters to Julie Herzl, 4 and 5 May 1904, Herzl, *Briefe*, 577–578.

12. Letter to Julie Herzl, 4 May 1904, Herzl, *Briefe*, 577.

13. Letter to Jeanette Herzl, 6 May 1904, Herzl, *Briefe*, 579.

14. Letter to Jeanette Herzl, 8 May 1904, Herzl, *Briefe*, 580.

15. Letter to Julie Herzl, 10 May 1904, Herzl, *Briefe*, 582.

16. Letter to Julie Herzl, 7 May 1904, Herzl, *Briefe*, 580.

17. Letters to Jeanette Herzl, 11 May 1904, and Julie Herzl, 12 May 1904, Herzl, *Briefe*, 582–583.

18. Kos, "Amüsement," 221.

19. York-Steiner, "Herzl," 621.

20. Ibid. Hermann Nothnagel (1841–1905), internist and head of the Medical Clinic I in Vienna. Neuberger, *Lexikon*, 158. Heinrich Elchanan York-Steiner (1859–1935), Austrian journalist and Zionist.

21. York-Steiner, "Herzl," 621.

22. Ibid.

23. Letters to Jeanette Herzl, 4 May 1904, and David Wolffsohn, 6 May 1904, Herzl, *Briefe*, 576–578.

24. Letter to David Wolffsohn, 15 May 1904, Herzl, *Briefe*, 584–585. Binyamin Ze'ev was Herzl's given Hebrew name.

25. Letters to Israel Zangwill, 6 May 1904, and Alfred Klee, 16 May 1904, Herzl, *Briefe*, 579, 587. Israel Zangwill (1864–1926), English writer and Zionist. Alfred Klee (1875–1943), leading German Zionist.

26. Nissan Katzenelson (1862–1923), Russian Zionist and a close associate of Herzl.

27. Katzenelsohn, "Tage," 2.

28. York-Steiner, "Herzl," 624; Herzl, *Briefe*, 584–587; letters to Julie Herzl, 10 May 1904, Wjatscheslaw Plehwe, 13 May 1904, and to Berthold Dominik Lippay, 14 May 1904, ibid., 582, 584.

29. "Theodor Herzls Krankheit, Tod und Begraebnis," 625.

30. Letter to Gustaf G. Cohen, 30 May 1904, Herzl, *Briefe*, 589, 802.

31. Ernst Pawel, *Labyrinth*, 522–526; "Theodor Herzls Krankheit, Tod und Begraebnis," 625.

32. Letter to David Wolffsohn, 6 May 1904, Herzl, *Briefe*, 578.

33. Shneour, "Me-pinat," 619.

34. "Lifnei ha-kongres," 2. On the history of the Zionist congresses in Carlsbad, see Augustin, "Kongresse."

35. It was not until 1925 that visitor numbers once again reached a level close to figures on the eve of the war. Gitschner, "Kurstatistik," 43.

36. Pincus, *Verloren*, 17.

37. SOAKV, Vereinsregister. In the course of the 1920s, the *Jüdischer Verein Jeschurun* (1926) and *Jüdischer Volksverein Zion* (1929) were added.

38. *Selbstwehr* 14 (1920): 41:9.

39. SOAKV, AM KV C-VI-91.

40. CZA, S1/67, "Bericht des Hauptbureaus des Keren Kajemeth zur Direktoriumssitzung," 22 August 1922; *Židovské Zprávy* (1921): 22:2–3.

41. *Kongreß-Führer*, 27–29.

42. Linke, *Kunstgeschichte*, 41; *Karlsbader Fremdenblatt* 29 (1909): 2:4.

43. *Kongress-Zeitung*; *Věstník XII sionistického kongresu*; *Kongreß-Führer*, 41; *Židovské Zprávy* (1921): 22:1.

44. Hermann Struck (1876–1944) and Lesser Ury (1861–1931), German Jewish artists. *Kongreß-Führer*, 32, 37–39, 40–41.

45. SOAKV, OkÚ KV 18/11, Kart. 553; CZA, F49/3062, "The WIZO Conferences and Minutes of the 1st Wizo Conference held in Karlsbad 4th to 8th September 1921," 1935; *Karlsbader Tagblatt* 30 (1921): 199, 3; *Makkabi Weltverband*; Shapiro, "Ha-ve'idot," 6–8; Shapiro, "Mi-saviv," 4–5; "Asefat ha-rofim be-Karlsbad," 606; *Kongreß-Führer*, 36–37.

46. *Der XII. Zionisten-Kongress. Karlsbad*, 7, 9; *Kongress-Zeitung* (1921): 1:1; *Deutsche Tageszeitung*, No. 194, 26 August 1921, 2; *Kongreß-Führer*, 34–35.

47. Holitscher, "Karlsbad/Palästina," 144.

48. Lavsky, "Brit Shalom," 174.

49. CZA, Bodenheimer Archive, Zionist Correspondence; Diesendruck, "Zionismus," 216.

50. "The Zionist Congress [1921]," 194. The Shekel was the annual dues for the World Zionist Organization, and members were also termed "Shekel-payers."

51. Holitscher, "Karlsbad vor Palästina," 1152–1153, 1157.

52. "The Zionist Congress and Co-operation with the Arabs," 195–197.

53. *Der XII. Zionisten-Kongress. Karlsbad*, 164–165.

54. Ibid., 166. See also Mendes-Flohr, *Land*, 62–63; Lavsky, *Catastrophe*, 157. Significantly, Mendes-Flohr (62) notes that Buber was upset with the compromise proposal that emerged from the Congress committee set up to deal with the Arab question and other matters; chagrined, he "held that it fully emasculated the principal intent of his proposal" and had "no deep commitment to reach an accord with the Arabs."

55. Diesendruck, "Zionismus," 217.

56. *Der XII. Zionisten-Kongress. Karlsbad*, 133.

57. *Dafke* (Yid.), precisely, specifically; *efsher* (Yid.), possibly, maybe; *mahloyke* (Yid.), debate; *emes* (Yid.), exactly, that's right. Holitscher, "Karlsbad vor Palästina," 1162.

58. *Ha-tikva* (Heb.), "The Hope," title of the Zionist movement hymn and later the national anthem of the State of Israel. *Stenographisches Protokoll [. . .] XII. Zionistenkongresses*, 739–774.

59. *Karlsbader Tagblatt* 30 (1921): 202:2.

60. Ibid.

61. *Kongreß-Führer*, 29, 36–37; SOAKV, AM KV C-VI-91, 1907–1938; *Kongress-Zeitung* (1921): 1: 1; *Karlsbader Tagblatt* 30 (1921): 2.

62. *Shivat Zion* (Heb.), return to Zion. *Kongreß-Führer*, 29, 36–37; SOAKV, AM KV C-VI-91, 1907–1938; *Kongress-Zeitung* (1921): 1:1; *Karlsbader Tagblatt* 30 (1921): 199:3. Ben-Dov was a filmmaking pioneer in the Jewish Yishuv (Jewish settlement area) in Palestine.

63. Shneour, "Me-pinat," 618.

64. Holitscher, "Karlsbad vor Palästina," 1163.

65. *Židovské Zprávy* (1921): 24:3.

66. "Lifnei ha-kongres," 2.

67. Ruppin, *Briefe*, 329.

68. Holitscher, "Karlsbad vor Palästina," 1161–1162.

69. Ibid., 1164.

70. Rozenblit, *Mi-Berlin*, 35.

71. Ibid., 36–37.

72. Shneour, "Me-pinat," 619.

73. Ibid.

74. *Selbstwehr* 3 (1909): 30:6; 27 (1933): 30:10; 27 (1933): 33:10; *Franzensbader Tagblatt*, no. 1, 1 June 1910, 3; *Židovské Zprávy* (1921): 22:8.

75. Ussishkin, *Devarim*, 248.

76. Holitscher, "Karlsbad vor Palästina," 1157.

77. Shneour, "Me-pinat," 619.

Chapter 13

1. *Be'erah shel Miryam* (Heb.), Miriam's well (see Part I); *anan ha-kavod* (Heb.), cloud of glory (in which the glory of the Lord appears), from Exodus 16:10; Bialik, *Igrot Chaim Nachman Bialik*, 283.

2. AJA, Zweite Jüdische Welthilfskonferenz, *Bulletin* 6, 2–4, and *Bulletin* 8, 2; see also Hecht, "Jewish World Relief Conference."

3. "Die Tagung des Zentralrates der Jüd. Welthilfsorganisation in Marienbad," 5. The *Comité Exécutif de la Conférence Universelle Juive de Secours*, as organizer of these conferences, worked together neither with the Joint nor with the Jewish Colonial Association, the most important philanthropic institutions at the time. This is perhaps a reason why the *Comité* was dissolved after a few years. AJA, Zweite Jüdische Welthilfskonferenz; CZA, S81/13, Agenda of the Second Jewish World Relief Conference.

4. "Die Zionistische Jahreskonferenz in Karlsbad," 4; Ruppin, *Briefe*, 341.

5. *Deutsche Tages-Zeitung* 64 (1921): 177:2–3; SOAKV, AM KV C-VI-91.

6. "The Zionist Congress [1923]," 1.

7. SOAKV, AM KV C-VI-91.

8. "Der Zionisten-Kongreß in Karlsbad," 2.

9. *Karlsbader Tagblatt* (1923): 187:7.

10. "Kongreß-Spreu," 2.

11. SOAKV, AM KV C-VI-91.

12. Walter Kohner treated so many Zionist patients in his medical practice that he planned to write a treatise entitled *Zionists from Within*, but his collection of case histories remained in Carlsbad after he fled, and was destroyed. Private archive Gabriel Kohner, Walter Kohner, Carlsbad, 9, 10, 13.

13. SOAKV, AM KV C-VI-91.

14. Thus, for example, Hillel Oppenheimer, son of the economist and sociologist Franz Oppenheimer, was sent in the 1920s, only shortly after his migration to Palestine, to take the cure in Carlsbad. His doctor had diagnosed a gallbladder infection as a result

of improper nutrition. Oppenheimer, *Mabat*, 129; Private archive Gabriel Kohner, Walter Kohner, Carlsbad, 21.

15. Ussishkin, *Devarim*, 248; Private archive Gabriel Kohner, Walter Kohner, Carlsbad, 24.

16. *Die jüdische Welt* 1 (1933): 3, adverts; Private archive Gabriel Kohner, Walter Kohner, Carlsbad, 2.

17. Weitz, *Yomani*, 105–109.

18. Ussishkin, *Devarim*, 248.

19. "Marienbader Kurliste," 12 August 1929 [archive, Municipal Museum Marienbad]; Wilkowitsch, "Brief," 1.

20. Letters to Mania Bialik, 25 July 1930 and 22 September 1931, Bialik, *Igrot el raʾayato*, 213–214.

21. Letter to Mania Bialik, 22 September 1931, Bialik, *Igrot el raʾayato*, 241–242.

22. Ibid., 242.

23. *Marienbad und Umgebung*, VII.

24. "Ein Geleitwort," 1.

25. *Rak chazak* (Heb.), version of the greeting common in the Zionist youth movement, *chazak veʾemats*, "be strong and of good courage," from Joshua 1:18. "Ein Geleitwort," 1.

26. Thus, for example, Pataky, "Interview," 1; Wilkowitsch, "Schriftsteller," 1.

27. *Kol Nidre* (Aram.), traditional solemn declaration in Aramaic recited on the evening of the beginning of Yom Kippur, the Day of Atonement, also arranged for cello and orchestra (1881) by Max Bruch; Grob, "Spaziergänge," 1; Wilkowitsch, "Erholungsreise," 3; Wilkowitsch, "Karlsbad," 4; Wilkowitsch, "Mode," 2.

28. *Signum-metsuyonim* (Heb.), special marker, badge. "Der Jude in den Kurorten," 3.

29. "Sabbat-Vorabend," 1.

30. Ebner, "Brief," 1.

31. Falk, "Kurort-Reflexionen," 5.

32. Baco of Verulam–Francis Bacon. LBI, AR 980, Theodor Lessing, "Mein Kopf," ms.

33. LBI, AR 980, Theodor Lessing, "Mein Kopf," ms. Excerpts published in Lessing, *Mein Kopf*, 69–71.

34. LBI, AR 980, Theodor Lessing, "Mein Kopf," ms., 1.

35. Ibid. At the end of Schiller's play "The Robbers," Charles Moor decides to turn himself in so that a day laborer he met with eleven children can receive the large reward for his capture, and he proclaims, "Dem Mann kann geholfen werden" (That man shall be served), a classic Schillerian quotation.

36. LBI, AR 980, Copy, article from the *Tschechoslowakische Bäderzeitung*, no. 144, 28 June 1933.

37. LBI, AR 980; "Die Mordwaffe gefunden," 1.

38. LBI, AR 980, letter from Sofie Leffmannn, 7 January 1957; "Wie Professor Lessing in 'Edelweiß' ermordet wurde."

39. Lessing, "Töchter- und Landerziehungsheim," 166.

40. Kotowski, "Philosophie," 138–139, 153; "Wie Professor Lessing in 'Edelweiß' ermordet wurde," 1.

41. LBI, AR 980, letter from Sofie Leffmannn, 7 January 1957.

42. Ibid.

43. "Hakenkreuz-Mord an Professor Lessing," 1.

44. Rudolf Zischke died in World War II. Max Eckert was convicted in 1946 and sentenced to thirteen years in prison. He was deported in 1958 to the Federal Republic of Germany. LBI, AR 980, letter from Arnold Hindl, 28 April 1968.

45. "Bisher zehn Verhaftungen," 1.

46. "Neue Verhaftungen in Marienbad," 1; "Lessings stilles Begräbnis ein lauter Ruf an die Welt," 1.

47. LBI, AR 980, letter from Sofie Leffmannn.

48. "Neue Verhaftungen in Marienbad," 1.

49. LBI, AR 980, letter of 2 September 1933. Wollenberg, "Rückkehr," 226.

50. Lessing, "Töchter- und Landerziehungsheim," 165–166.

51. Henisch, *Tanz*, 68; Ussishkin, *Devarim*, 250; Bauer, *Jude*, 96.

52. As, for example, in resorts on the North Sea and Baltic. Wildt, "Antisemitismus," 19–25.

53. Bajohr, *Hotel*, 116–141; Maurer, "Everyday," 335–336, 338.

54. "Wiederaufstieg unserer Weltkurorte," 1; Private archive Gabriel Kohner, Walter Kohner, Carlsbad, 2.

55. ŽMP, 51966, letter to Emil Ascher, Prague, 1 April 1936,

56. Such as Betty Scholem, Salman Schocken, and many others. Scholem/Scholem, *Briefwechsel*, 430–434; David, *Patron*, 241; LBI, Herta Seidemann Collection, postcard from Alice Meschitzy sent from Marienbad to Lodka Honigmann, 7 July 1934; Kohl, *Maiden*; INJOEST, Jaegermann, Erinnerungen; Private archive of Gabriel Kohner, Walter Kohner, Carlsbad, 9.

57. "Pictures of Jewish Life in Europe, 1923–1937"; YIVO, People of a Thousand Towns. *Knessiah Gedola* was the Hebrew designation for the "Grand Congress" or *Kenessio Gedaulo* in Ashkenazic pronunciation.

58. "Marienbad im Zeichen der Kenessio Gedaulo," 3; "Die Tage vor der Kenessio Gedaulo," 5.

59. "Die Tage vor der Kenessio Gedaulo," 5.

60. Private archive of the author, letter from Ruth Shaingarten, 8 February 2003.

61. "Dritte Kenessio Gedaulo eröffnet," 1; "Die Eröffnung der Kenessio Gedaulo," 3.

62. "Eröffnung des Juden-Weltkongresses," 1.

63. *Halacha* (Heb.), Jewish religious law. "Ganzes thoratreues Palästina," 1; "Marienbad im Zeichen der Kenessio Gedaulo," 3.

64. "Der Frauenkongress," 10.

65. Schachnowitz, "Bedeutung," 4.

66. "Große Jugendkundgebung im Rahmen der Kenessio Gedaulo," 4.

67. Steiner, "Kongreßgast," 6.

68. Carlebach, "Warburg," 3.

69. In 1925, Fritz Buxbaum (1874–1953) had founded the *Arbeits- und Wirtschaftspartei* (Labor and Economy Party), which he now represented in the Municipal Council. Along with him among the thirty-two councilors, there was another Jewish councilman, Stingl, from the *Zionistische Partei*. *Hamelika* 25 (2001): 10 and 22 (1998): 1. There were possibly two more Jewish councilmen. "Vertreibung der Juden aus dem Kurort," quoted in *Verfolgung*, 462–463.

70. "Begrüßungsansprachen bei der Eröffnung der Agudas Jisroel," 3.

71. "Auch in Marienbad," 4.

72. "Die SDP in Marienbad," 2.

73. "Wohin im Sommer?" 3.

74. Bauer, *Jude*, 141.

75. "Die aussäen unter Tränen," 15–23.

76. Osterloh, *Judenverfolgung*, 168–175; Wlaschek, *Juden*, 68.

77. Osterloh, *Judenverfolgung*, 180–183. The events after the transformation of western Bohemia into a part of the Reichsgau Sudetenland are beyond the scope of this study and are described elsewhere: Osterloh, *Judenverfolgung*; Hahn, *Kristallnacht*; Pincus, *Verloren*, 14; Wlaschek, *Juden*, 165–166; Schönbach, "Aufstieg."

78. Hindus, *Live*, 211–213, 224.

79. "Vertreibung," quoted in *Verfolgung*, 462–463.

80. Ibid.

81. *Der Stürmer. Deutsches Wochenblatt zum Kampfe um die Wahrheit* 16 (1938): 37, 42, 44, 47, and 48; 17 (1939): 3, 9, 18, and 30.

82. Hermann Leopoldi (Hersch Kohn, 1888–1959), Viennese composer and humorist, gave guest performances with his stage partner Betja Milskaja regularly from 1929 onward in Carlsbad. Peter Herz (1895–1987), Viennese cabaret artist and librettist. Approximate translation of the lyrics: "How beautiful, how nice to go on vacation! / We get lots of adverts sent right to the door! / Deauville, Trouville is never my destination, / 'cause I'm loyal to good old Czechoslovakia. / For me the greatest is the Sprudel / in Ca-Ca-Ca-Ca-Carlsbad, / In summer's there's always quite a mess / in Ca-Ca-Ca-Ca-Carlsbad! / You'll hear the Na-Na-Nikatoseli / And many another beautiful tune." Another version has here the line: "The program has such nice songs, for example 'Egerlander halt's Euch z'samm,'" a reference to the increasing German-national atmosphere in Carlsbad. At the end all chime in with the chorus: "The moor's done its job, now you can leave!" The play on the word "moor" in German (*Moor / Mohr*) is an allusion to a standing expression in German, based on a quote from a play by Schiller: "*Der Mohr hat seine Arbeit getan, / Der Mohr kann gehen*" (The moor has done his duty / The moor can go). Friedrich Schiller, *Die Verschwörung des Fiesco zu Genua* III, 4.

83. LBI, Eric Reisfeld Collection.

84. See Zweig, *World*, 89–90.

85. He is referring to the artist Hermann Struck, who among other things was famous for his sketches of Eastern European Jews done during World War I. Hirschfeld, *Women*, 273, 278.

86. Ibid., 277.

87. Ibid., 278.

88. Lachmann, "Mineralquellen," 223–224; Buchmann, "Thermen," 365. The "celebrated Hot Baths of Tiberias" were mentioned in the Baedecker guides to Palestine (1875 in German, 1906 in English). Baedecker, *Palästina*, 386; Baedecker, *Palestine*, 250.

89. Buchmann, "Thermen," 369.

90. See on this the regular ads in the *Palestine Post* and *Doar Ha-yom*.

91. Private archive Gabriel Kohner, Walter Kohner, Carlsbad, 4, 7.

92. Herzl, *Old New Land*, 171.

Afterword

1. Appelfeld, *Badenheim*, 1.

2. Wachsman, "Forhang," 1.

3. Ibid.

4. Wachsman, "Bloy-vays," 3.

5. Ibid. *Erev Rosh Hashanah* (Heb.), evening of the beginning of the Jewish New Year festival.

6. Wachsman, *Land*, 208–226; Wachsman, *Nachbarschaft*, 277–281.

7. Ibid., 278.

8. Ibid., 279; Wachsman, *Land*, 210.

9. Wachsman, *Land*, 212–220; Nordau, *Anblicke*, 177–178.

10. Wachsman, *Nachbarschaft*, 280.

11. Ibid., 280–281.

12. See Motzkin, "Possibility."

13. Wachsman, "Bloy-vays," 3. Thus, for example, in 1947, the Central Committee of *Agudas Jisroel* met in Marienbad. *Palestine Post*, 4 September 1947, 2.

14. Wachsman, "Forhang," 2; *Karlovy Vary*, 36.

15. Wachsman, "Forhang," 2. The German population of Carlsbad had been expelled from the Czechoslovak Republic a few months before, in 1946.

16. *Karlovy Vary*, 37. Conversation with Milan Augustin, SOAKV, August 2005; "Grandhotel Pupp, Evropa," 1.

17. Kundera, *Lightness*, 165–166.

18. In 2004, there were 73,911 spa guests and some 130,000 day tourists who visited Carlsbad. Conversation with Milan Augustin, SOAKV, August 2005. In 2009, according to official Czech government statistics, there were a total of 456,726 foreign guests in the entire Carlsbad Region, which includes most of the western Bohemian spas, with an average length of stay of 7.7 days. A total of 5,662 were from Israel, with an average

length of stay 12.6 days, topping the list for average length of stay by country of origin, along with Russian tourists; *Statistical Yearbook of the Karlovarsky Region.*

19. *Prager Zeitung*, 3 August 2005.

20. Brenner, "Marienbad," 134–136; Lichtblau, "Chiffre."

21. Private archive of the author, interview with Otto Meyer, 14 October 2002; Henisch, *Tanz*, 216–218.

22. The facetious phrasing "Next year! To beautiful Marienbad" is a play on the Passover final prayer asking for God's favor, "Next year may we be in Jerusalem!"—*le-shana ha-ba'a be-Yerushalayim*. Wilkowitsch, "Brief," 1.

Bibliography

Unpublished Sources

AMERICAN JEWISH ARCHIVES, THE JACOB RADER MARCUS CENTER, CINCINNATI
Zweite Jüdische Welthilfskonferenz, Karlsbad, press releases, August 1924. The World
  Jewish Congress Collection. Series A/1, Box A8/7

CENTRAL ARCHIVES FOR THE HISTORY OF THE JEWISH PEOPLE, JERUSALEM
Collection Centralverein deutscher Staatsbürger jüdischen Glaubens (CV), No. 2353
  Karlsbad and No. 2365 Marienbad
Reuben Brainin: Diaries [Heb.], File no. P8/6–8

CENTRAL ZIONIST ARCHIVES, JERUSALEM
A185/39; F49/3062; S1/67; S5/1913; S6/3674; S81/13
Bodenheimer Archive, Zionistische Korrespondenz, 2 (1921): 4, File 3/62
Bodenheimer Archive, Max Nordau, Karlsbad, 30 May 1905, File 65/23
List of Files of the Office of the 12th Zionist Congress, 1921. http://tinyurl.com/3uzlcxy
  (retrieved 15 August 2011)
Photograph collection
WIZO (Women's International Zionist Organization) Conferences [1935], F 49/3062

INSTITUT FÜR GESCHICHTE DER JUDEN IN ÖSTERREICH, ST. PÖLTEN (INSTITUTE FOR
THE HISTORY OF THE JEWS IN AUSTRIA, ST. PÖLTEN)
Egon Basch, Erinnerungen
Judith Jaegermann, Erinnerungen
Norbert Toller, Erinnerungen

JÜDISCHES MUSEUM DER STADT WIEN (JEWISH MUSEUM VIENNA)
Antisemitische Bäderpostkarten, Sammlung Martin Schlaff

LEO BAECK INSTITUTE ARCHIVES, NEW YORK
Arthur Prinz Collection, AR 5103, Series III, Subseries I 1/31
Eric Reisfeld Collection, AR 6951

Gerald Meyer: Sprudel, Strudel & Chassidim, in Samuel Echt–Bernhard Kamnitzer
    Collection MF 596, Folder 35
Herta Seidemann Collection, AR 25060
Hoenig Family Collection, AR 5076
Lalla Kaden (nee Bondi): Der erste Akt meines Lebens, ME 342; MM 42
Lisbeth Ledermann: Die Schottlaender'sche Familienstiftung, ME 576; MM 68.
Theodor Lessing Collection, AR 980
Miriam Beer-Hofmann Lens Collection, MF 492, reel 10 box 4/29–5/10
Nelly Berg: Memories of Nelly Levy Berg. Her Life in Germany and Her First Ten Years
    in America. ME1077; MM II 29
Ottilie Bondy: Ein Beitrag zu einer Familiengeschichte des Hauses M. B. Teller. ME 65;
    MM11
Philipp Loewenfeld: Memoiren ME 404; MM 51
Robitscher Family Collection, AR 25012
Rudolf D. Keller Collection, AR 7281/3/4

MĚSTSKÉ MUSEUM MARIÁNSKÉ LÁZNĚ (MUNICIPAL MUSEUM MARIENBAD)

Marienbader Kurliste, 1815–

PRIVATE ARCHIVE GABRIEL KOHNER, AMIAD/ISRAEL

Walter Kohner: Karlsbad. Aus dem Nachlass, vol. 5. (Posthumous papers, Kohner, vol. 5)

PRIVATE ARCHIVE LÁSZLÓ A. MAGYAR, BUDAPEST

Letter, Siegmund Deutsch to Adél Deutsch

PRIVATE ARCHIVE MIRJAM ZADOFF, MUNICH

Aharon Appelfeld, taped interview, 21 March 2005
Judith Jägermann, taped interview, 29 August 2002
Edith Kraus, taped interview, 27 August 2002
Kurt Reichert, letter, 12 July 2002
Otto Meyer, taped interview, 14 October 2002
Mimi Ormond, letter, 16 June 2001
Ruth Shaingarten, letter, 8 February 2003

STÁTNÍ OKRESNI ARCHIV KARLOVY VARY (ARCHIVE OF THE CARLSBAD DISTRICT)

AM KV A-I-18, 1907–1928, affairs of nationalities
AM KV A-I-1-6-1
AM KV C-VI-91, 1907–1938, Zionist Congresses
AM KV D-IV-43-10
AM KV G-3-II
OkÚ KV 18/11
Registry, Spolkový Katastr 1921–1940

Státní ústřední archiv v Praze (Central State Archive Prague)
B'nai B'rith, 1924–1937, Knih./A/C885
Jews in Czechoslovakia, 1919–1944, MZV-VA I., 2320

YIVO Institute for Jewish Research, New York
People of a Thousand Towns. The Online Catalog of Photographs of Jewish Life in Prewar Eastern Europe, http://yivo1000towns.cjh.org/ (accessed 15 August 2011)

Židovské Museum v Praze (Jewish Museum Prague)
Correspondence, Marienbad Jewish Hospital, 1931–1936, ŽMP 51966
Ergänzung des Tätigkeitsberichtes für das Jahr 1935, ŽMP 51966 (Supplement, Annual Report, 1935)
Tätigkeitsbericht des Israelitischen Kurhospitals in Marienbad für das Jahr 1934, ŽMP 51966 (Annual Report, Jewish Spa Hospital, 1934)

Periodicals

Amtliche Nachrichten
Ha-aretz
Beilage zur Marienbader Kurliste
Deutsche Tages-Zeitung
Doar Ha-yom
Dr. Bloch's Oesterreichische Wochenschrift
Forverts—Forward
Franzensbader Kurliste
Franzensbader Tagblatt
Hamelika
Im Deutschen Reich
[Israelitische] Gemeindezeitung [Böhmen]
Israelitisches Familienblatt
Jeschurun
Der Jude
Jüdische Bäder- und Kurortezeitung, Beilage der Jüdischen Volksstimme
Die Jüdische Welt
Karlsbader Eisenbahnzeitung
Karlsbader Fremdenblatt, Beilage der Neusten Nachrichten
Karlsbader "Kikriki"
Karlsbader Kurliste
Karlsbader Saisonanzeiger
Karlsbader Tagblatt
Karlsbader Zeitung
Die Kenessio Gedaulo
Kongress-Zeitung. Organ des . . . Zionistenkongresses

Marienbader Kurliste
Marienbader Zeitung
Mitteilungen aus dem Verein zur Abwehr des Antisemitismus
Ha-olam
Ost und West
Palästina
Palestine Post
Rozvoj
Selbstwehr
Der Stürmer. Deutsches Wochenblatt zum Kampfe um die Wahrheit
Vestnik . . . sionistickeho kongresu
Die Welt
Zeitschrift für Balneologie, Klimatologie und Kurort-Hygiene
Zidovske Zpravy

Published Source Material and Research Literature

First year of publication is indicated in brackets. For German titles, the intial articles "der/die/das" are ignored for the purpose of alphabetization.

Agnon, Shmuel Yosef. *Gestern, vorgestern*. Frankfurt/Main, 1996 [1946].
———. *In der Gemeinschaft der Frommen. Sechs Erzählungen*. Berlin, 1933 [1924].
Ahnelt, O. "Die demographischen Verhältnisse der Stadt Karlsbad." In *Festschrift zur 74. Versammlung Deutscher Naturforscher und Aerzte*, ed. Stadt Karlsbad. Carlsbad, 1902, 487–496.
Alfassi, Itzhak. "Belz." *Encyclopaedia Judaica*, ed. Michael Berenbaum and Fred Skolnik. 2nd ed. Vol. 3. Detroit, 2007, 308–309.
Algazi, Gadi. "Kulturkult und die Rekonstruktion von Handlungsrepertoires." *L'Homme. Zeitschrift für Feministische Geschichtswissenschaft* 11 (2000): 1: 105–119.
Alt, Peter-André. *Franz Kafka. Der ewige Sohn. Eine Biographie*. Munich, 2005.
Amtliches Fernsprechbuch für den Bezirk der Reichspostdirektion Karlsbad. Chemnitz, 1939.
Anderson, Benedict. *Imagined Communities. Reflections on the Origin and Spread of Nationalism*. London, 1991.
"Antisemitische Bade-, Kur- und Erholungsorte." In *Mitteilungen aus dem Verein zur Abwehr des Antisemitismus* 12 (1902): 26: 195; 13 (1903): 21: 166–167; 14 (1904): 19: 149–150; 35: 279–280; 15 (1905): 25: 191–192; 17 (1907): 21: 158–159; 18 (1908): 22: 164; 21 (1911): 15: 116.
"Antisemitische Bäder und Sommerfrischen." *Mitteilungen aus dem Verein zur Abwehr des Antisemitismus* 14 (1904): 24: 185–186.
"Antisemitische Postkarten." *Im Deutschen Reich* 4 (1898): 2: 82–85.
"Antisemitische Treibereien in böhmischen Kurorten." *Mitteilungen aus dem Verein zur Abwehr des Antisemitismus* 19 (1909): 15: 113.

"Antisemitisches Treiben in Franzensbad." *Mitteilungen aus dem Verein zur Abwehr des Antisemitismus* 19 (1909): 6, 46.

"Antisemitismus in Badeorten." *Mitteilungen aus dem Verein zur Abwehr des Antisemitismus* 16 (1906): 35, 271.

Appelfeld, Aharon. *Badenheim 1939.* Trans. Dalya Bilu. Boston, 1980 [Heb. ed., 1979].

———. *The Retreat.* New York, 1984.

Ärzteverzeichnis der Amtstelle Karlsbad. Carlsbad, 1937.

Ärztlicher Führer von Marienbad. Ed. Marienbader Ärzteverein. Marienbad, 1912.

Aschheim, Steven E. *Brothers and Strangers: The East European Jew in German and German Jewish Consciousness, 1800–1923.* Madison, 1982.

"Asefat ha-rofim be-Karlsbad." *Ha-Olam* 1921: 606.

Ash, Mitchell. "Innovation, Ethnicity, Identity. German-Speaking Jewish Psychologists and Social Scientists in the Interwar Period." *Jahrbuch des Simon-Dubnow-Instituts* 3 (2004): 241–268.

"Auch in Marienbad." *Die neue Welt* 11 (1937): 683: 4.

Augustin, Milan. "Die zionistischen Kongresse in Karlsbad." In Augustin Milan (ed.), *Karlsbader historische Schriften.* Vol. 1. Carlsbad, 2002, 167–180.

Auslander, Leora. "Jewish Taste? Jews and the Aesthetics of Everyday Life in Paris and Berlin, 1920–1942." In Rudy Koshar (ed.), *Histories of Leisure.* Oxford, 2002, 299–318.

Die aussäen unter Tränen, mit Jubel werden sie ernten. Die jüdischen Gemeinden in der tschechoslowakischen Republik nach dem Zweiten Weltkrieg. Ed. Rudolf Iltis, Rat der Jüdischen Gemeinden in den Böhmischen Ländern and Zentralverband der Jüdischen Gemeinden in der Slowakei. Prague, 1959.

Ausweis über die Einnahmen und Ausgaben des Marienbader israel. Spitals und den Vermögensstand desselben für das Jahr 1884, 1889. Prague, 1885, 1890.

Bachmann, Ingeborg. *Darkness Spoken. Ingeborg Bachmann. The Collected Poems.* Trans. P. Filkins. Brookline/MA, 2005.

Backhaus, Fritz. "'Hab'n Sie nicht den kleinen Cohn geseh'n?' Die Bilderwelt antisemitischer Postkarten vom Kaiserreich bis in die NS-Zeit–ein Ausstellungsprojekt." *Jahrbuch für Antisemitismusforschung* 6 (1997): 314.

Bacon, W. "The Rise of the German and the Demise of the English Spa Industry. A Critical Analysis of Business Success and Failure." *Leisure Studies* 16 (1997): 173–187.

"Bäderantisemitismus." *Mitteilungen aus dem Verein zur Abwehr des Antisemitismus* 22 (1912): 14, 105–107.

Baedecker, Karl. *Austria-Hungary. With Excursions to Cetinje, Belgrade, and Bucharest. Handbook for Travellers.* Leipzig, 1911.

———. *Österreich, ohne Dalmatien, Ungarn und Bosnien. Handbuch für Reisende.* Leipzig, 1907.

———. *Palästina und Syrien: Handbuch für Reisende.* Leipzig, 1875.

———. *Palestine and Syria with the Chief Routes through Mesopotamia and Babylonia. Handbook for Travellers.* Leipzig, 1906.

Baeumerth, Angelika. *"Es wimmelt von Fremden aller Nationen."* Ansichtspostkarten aus *Homburg 1888–1928*. Marburg, 1984.

Bajohr, Frank. *"Unser Hotel ist judenfrei." Bäder-Antisemitismus im 19. und 20. Jahrhundert*. Frankfurt/Main, 2003.

Balzer, Bernd. "'Zugegeben, daß es besser wäre, sie fehlten, oder wären anders, wie sie sind.' Der selbstverständliche Antisemitismus Fontanes." In Hanna Delf von Wolzogen and Helmuth Nürnberger (eds.), *Theodor Fontane. Am Ende des Jahrhunderts*. Würzburg, 2000, 197–209.

Barber, Ida. "Die Flüchtlinge in Marienbad." *Oesterreichische Wochenschrift* 33 (1916): 31: 518–519.

Barkai, Avraham. "Population Decline and Economic Stagnation." In Michael A. Meyer and Michael Brenner (eds.), *German-Jewish History in Modern Times*. Vol. 4. New York, 1998, 30–44.

———. *"Wehr dich!" Der Centralverein deutscher Staatsbürger jüdischen Glaubens (C.V.) 1893–1938*. Munich, 2002.

Baron, Salo W. *History and Jewish Historians*. Philadelphia, 1964.

Bauer, Stefan. *Ein böhmischer Jude im Exil. Der Schriftsteller Ernst Sommer (1888–1955)*. Munich, 1995.

Baum, Georg. "Zedakah und Sozialversicherung." In *Hygiene und Judentum. Eine Sammelschrift*. Dresden, 1930, 96–97.

Bauman, Zygmunt. "Broken Lives, Broken Strategies." In *Life in Fragments. Essays in Postmodern Morality*. Oxford, 1995, 72–104.

———. "A Catalogue of Postmodern Fears." In *Life in Fragments. Essays in Postmodern Morality*. Oxford, 1995, 105–125.

Becker, Rafael. *Die jüdische Nervosität, ihre Art, Entstehung und Bekämpfung*. Zürich, 1918.

———. *Die Nervosität bei den Juden. Ein Beitrag zur Rassenpsychiatrie für Ärzte und gebildete Laien*. Zürich, 1919.

"Begrüßungsansprachen bei der Eröffnung der Agudas Jisroel." *Marienbader Zeitung*, 18 August 1937, 3.

"Bei uns z'Warmbod." *Karlsbader "Kikriki"* 4 (1927): 11: 1–2.

Beller, Steven. *Vienna and the Jews. 1867–1938. A Cultural History*. Cambridge, 1990.

Ben-Yishai, Aharon Zeev. "Judah Leib Gordon." *Encyclopaedia Judaica*, ed. Michael Berenbaum and Fred Skolnik. 2nd ed. Vol. 7. Detroit, 2007, 769–772.

Benjamin, Walter. "Franz Kafka." In Michael W. Jennings, Howard Eiland, Gary Smith, and Rodney Livingstone (eds.), *Walter Benjamin. Selected Writings*. Vol. 2, 1929–1934. Cambridge/MA, 1999.

Benz, Wolfgang. "Antisemitismus als Zeitströmung am Ende des Jahrhunderts." In Hanna Delf von Wolzogen and Helmuth Nürnberger (eds.), *Theodor Fontane. Am Ende des Jahrhunderts*. Würzburg, 2000, 157–168.

Berg, Armin. *Der Mann mit dem Überzieher. Couplets, Conférencen und Parodien aus dem Repertoire*. Ed. Hans Veigl. Vienna, 1990.

Bergmann, Hugo. "Schulzeit und Studium." In Hans-Gerd Koch (ed.), *"Als Kafka mir entgegenkam . . ." Erinnerungen an Franz Kafka.* Berlin, 2005, 20–31.

Bericht der Exekutive der Zionistischen Organisation an den XIII. Zionisten-Kongress. Carlsbad, 1923.

Bernstein, Michael André. *Foregone Conclusions. Against Apocalyptic History.* Berkeley/CA, 1994.

"Der Beruf des Arztes." *Mitteilungen aus dem Verein zur Abwehr des Antisemitismus* 6 (1896): 337–338.

Besser, Max. "Der Einfluss der ökonomischen Stellung der deutschen Juden auf ihre physische Beschaffenheit." In Ausschuss der Jüdischen Turnerschaft (ed.), *Körperliche Renaissance der Juden.* Berlin, 1909, 7–9.

Bialik, Chaim Nachman. *Igrot Chaim Nachman Bialik.* Ed. Fischel Lachower. Vol. 4, 1928–1929. Tel Aviv, 1938.

———. *Igrot el raʾayato Mania.* Jerusalem, 1955.

Binder, Hartmut. "Franz Kafka and the Weekly Paper 'Selbstwehr.'" *Leo Baeck Institute Yearbook* 12 (1967): 1: 135–148.

"Bisher zehn Verhaftungen." *Marienbader Zeitung* 60 (1933): 199: 1.

Blackbourn, David. "'Taking the Waters': Meeting Places of the Fashionable World." In Martin H. Geyer and Johannes Paulmann (eds.), *The Mechanics of Internationalism: Culture, Society, and Politics from the 1840s to the First World War.* Oxford, 2001, 435–457.

Bley, Julia. *Vi azoy men darf zorgn farn gesunt. Geshriben far di, vos noytikn zikh in luft, in likht, in fayer, in vaser un in a shtikl broyt.* Warsaw, 1922.

Bloch, Ernst. *Das Abenteuer der Treue. Briefe an Karola 1928–1949.* Frankfurt/Main, 2005.

Böröcz, József. *Leisure Migration. A Sociological Study on Tourism.* Oxford, 1996.

Borsay, Peter. "Bath: An Enlightenment City?" In Peter Borsay, Gunther Hirschfelder, and Ruth-E. Mohrmann (eds.), *New Directions in Urban History: Aspects of European Art, Health, Tourism and Leisure Since the Enlightenment.* Münster/Westf., 2000, 3–17.

Borut, Jacob. "Antisemitism in Tourist Facilities in Weimar Germany." *Yad Vashem Studies* 26 (2000): 7–50.

Böttcher, Karl. *Brunnengeister. Marienbader Saisonbilder.* Carlsbad, 1885.

Bouda, Z. *Průvodce po Máriánských Lázních a okolí.* S.l., 1935.

Brainin, Reuven Ben-Mordecai. *Complete Works.* Vol. 3: *Monographs and Memoirs* [Heb.]. New York, 1940.

Brenner, David. *Marketing Identities. The Invention of Jewish Ethnicity in Ost und West.* Detroit, 1998.

Brenner, Michael. *The Renaissance of Jewish Culture in Weimar Germany.* New Haven/CT, 1996.

———. "Zwischen Marienbad und Norderney. Der Kurort als 'Jewish Space.'" In Gisela

Dachs (ed.), *Orte und Räume*. In *Jüdischer Almanach des Leo Baeck Instituts*. Frankfurt/Main. 2001.

Brod, Max. *Jüdinnen*. Leipzig, 1915 [1911].

Buber, Martin. *Meetings. Autobiographical Fragments*. Ed. Maurice S. Friedman. London, 2002.

———. "The Spirit of the Orient and Judaism." In Buber, *On Judaism*, ed. Nahum Glatzer. New York, 1967, 56–78.

Buber, Martin, and Rosenzweig, Franz. *Die Schrift*. 4 vols. Stuttgart, 1992 [1954].

Bubriski, Wanda. "Böhmens Bäder oder Eine Postkarte aus Böhmen (via Amerika)." In Walter Koschmal, Marek Nekula, and Joachim Rogall (eds.), *Deutsche und Tschechen. Geschichte, Kultur, Politik*. Munich, 2001, 569–574.

Buchmann, Max. "Die Thermen von Tiberias und Tiberias als Winterkurort." *Palästina* 11 (1928): 8: 364–371.

Buttlar, Adrian von. *Der Landschaftsgarten*. Munich, 1980.

Cantor, Judith Levin. *Jews in Michigan*. East Lansing/MI, 2001.

Carlebach, Esriel. "Von Felix Warburg zum Gerer Rabbi." *Selbstwehr* 31 (1937): 36: 3.

"Carlsbad." In *Encyclopaedia Judaica*, ed. Michael Berenbaum and Fred Skolnik. 2nd ed. Vol. 4. Detroit, 2007, 482–483.

Carroll, Lewis. *Through the Looking-Glass, and What Alice Found There*. London, 1991 [1872].

Cartellieri, Paul. *Bericht über die Wirksamkeit des Badehospitals für mittellose Kranke ohne Unterschied des Vaterlandes und der Religion zu Franzensbad bei Eger in Böhmen während des fünfzehnjährigen Zeitraumes 1842–1856*. Prague, 1857.

Caspary, Eugen. "Die doppelte Wurzel der modernen jüdischen Sozialhygiene." In *Hygiene und Judentum. Eine Sammelschrift*. Dresden, 1930, 93–95.

Černoch, Pavel. *Jewish History of Marienbad*. Leaflet. S.l., 2002.

Charney, Daniel. *Barg aroyf. Tsveyter teyl (partey-khronik)*. Warsaw, 1935.

Charvát, J. "Eine analytische Betrachtung der Karlsbader Kurfrequenz." In *Balneologia et Balneotherapia*. S.l. 1962, 407–421.

Clemenceau, Georges. *At the Foot of Sinai*. New York, 1922 [1898].

Cohen, Gary B. "Jews in German Liberal Politics. Prague 1880–1914." *Jewish History* 1 (1986): 1: 55–74.

———. *The Politics of Ethnic Survival: Germans in Prague, 1861–1914*. Princeton/NJ, 1981.

Cox, Harvey. *The Secular City: Secularization and Urbanization in Theological Perspective*. New York, 1965.

Cutler, Irving. *The Jews of Chicago: From Shtetl to Suburb*. Urbana/IL, 1996.

David, Anthony. *The Patron. A Life of Salman Schocken 1877–1959*. New York, 2003.

Defert, Daniel. "Raum zum Hören." In *Michel Foucault. Die Heterotopien–les hétérotopies. Der utopische Körper–le corps utopique. Zwei Radiovorträge*. Frankfurt/Main, 2005 [1966], 69–92.

Deleuze, Gilles. *Difference and Repetition*. Trans. Paul Patton. Chippenham, 1994.

Deleuze, Gilles, and Guattari, Félix. *Kafka: Toward a Minor Literature*. Trans. Dana Polan. Minneapolis, 1986.

Deutsch, Gotthard, Kisch, Alexander, and Singer, Isidore. "Kisch." In *The Jewish Encyclopedia*. New York, 1901–1906.

Deutsch, Gotthard, and Ziegler, Ignaz. "Karlsbad." In *The Jewish Encyclopedia*. New York, 1901–1906.

Diamant, Dora. "Mein Leben mit Franz Kafka." In Hans-Gerd Koch (ed.), *"Als Kafka mir entgegenkam . . ." Erinnerungen an Franz Kafka*. Berlin, 2005, 194–205.

Diem, Karl. *Österreichisches Bäderbuch. Offizielles Handbuch der Bäder, Kurorte und Heilanstalten Österreichs*. Berlin, 1914.

Diesendruck, Z. "Zionismus und nationale Bewegung. Zur Psychologie des Karlsbader Kongresses." *Der Jude* 6 (1921): 2: 126–128.

Dipper, Rachel. " 'Einmal muss der Mensch ins Bad!' Grüße aus Karlsbad und Marienbad." In Helmut Gold and Georg Heuberger (eds.), *Abgestempelt. Judenfeindliche Postkarten. Auf der Grundlage der Sammlung Wolfgang Haney*. Heidelberg, 1999, 194–204.

Das dreissigjährige Gründungsfest der Loge "Karlsbad" I.O.B.B. 1894–1924. Carlsbad, 1924.

Dritte Eingabe der Bürgermeister der Kur- und Badestädte Karlsbad, Marienbad, Franzensbad, Teplitz-Schönau, Joachimsthal und Johannisbad in der Tschechoslowakei an den Völkerbundrat wegen drohender Verletzungen des Minderheitsschutzvertrages von St. Germain-en-Laye vom 10. September 1919 durch ein bevorstehendes Kurortegesetz. Carlsbad, 1925.

"Dritte Kenessio Gedaulo eröffnet." *Die Kenessio Gedaulo* (1937): 2: 1–2.

Dück, Johannes. "Aus dem Geschlechtsleben unserer Zeit. Eine kritische Tatsachenschilderung." *Sexual-Probleme* (1914/15): 10: 470–484, 545–556, 713–766.

Ebner, Mayer. "Marienbader Brief." In *Jüdische Bäder- und Kurortezeitung* 2 (1930): 15: 1.

Efron, John. *Medicine and the German Jews. A History*. New Haven/CT, 2001.

Ehrke, Thomas Rainer. "Antisemitismus in der Medizin im Spiegel der 'Mitteilungen aus dem Verein zur Abwehr des Antisemitismus' (1891–1931)." Dissertation. Mainz, 1978.

Elias, Julius. "Marienbad." *Berliner Tagblatt*, 20 July 1916.

Engländer, Martin. *Die auffallend häufigen Krankheitserscheinungen der jüdischen Rasse*. Vienna, 1902.

"Die Eröffnung der Kenessio Gedaulo." *Die Kenessio Gedaulo* (1937): 2: 3.

"Eröffnung des Juden-Weltkongresses." *Marienbader Zeitung*, 18 August 1937, 1.

Eshel, Amir. "Cosmopolitanism and Searching for the Sacred Space in Jewish Literature." *Jewish Social Studies* 9 (2003): 3: 121–138.

Falk, Max. "Kurort-Reflexionen." *Jüdische Volksstimme* 34 (1933): 26: 5.

Feller's Carlsbader Omnibus oder Ganz Carlsbad für 30 kr. Verkehrs-, Lokal-, Personal- und Cur-Anzeiger. Carlsbad, 1873.

Fellner, Günter. "Judenfreundlichkeit, Judenfeindlichkeit. Spielarten in einem Fremdenverkehrsland." In Robert Kriechbaumer (ed.), *Der Geschmack der Vergänglichkeit. Jüdische Sommerfrische in Salzburg*. Vienna, 2002, 59–129.

Fishberg, Maurice. *The Jews*. London, 1911.

Fleckles, Leopold. *Ueber Diabetes mellitus mit besonderer Berücksichtigung balneothera-peutischer Erfahrungen in Karlsbad*. Prague, 1865.

Fleischer, Michael. *"Kommen Sie, Cohn. Fontane und die 'Judenfrage.'"* Berlin, 1998.

Flemming, Jens. "'Sexuelle Krise' und 'Neue Ethik.' Wahrnehmungen, Debatten und Perspektiven in der deutschen Gesellschaft der Jahrhundertwende." In Helmut Scheuer and Michael Grisko (eds.), *Liebe, Lust und Leid. Zur Gefühlskultur um 1900*. Intervalle Vol. 3. Kassel, 1999, 27–55.

Föhl, Thomas. "Von Klassizismus bis Neubarock." In Rolf Bothe (ed.), *Kurstädte in Deutschland. Zur Geschichte einer Baugattung*. Berlin, 1984, 49–87.

Fontane, Theodor. *Werke, Schriften, Briefe. Abteilung 4, Band 4: Briefe 1890–1989*. Ed. Walter Keitel and Helmuth Nürnberger. Munich, 1982.

Foucault, Michel. *Die Heterotopien—les hétérotopies. Der utopische Körper—le corps uto-pique. Zwei Radiovorträge*. Frankfurt/Main, 2005 [1966].

———. "Of Other Spaces." Trans. J. Miskowiec. S.l., 1967/1984. http://foucault.info/documents/heteroTopia/foucault.heteroTopia.en.html (retrieved 15 August 2011).

"Der Frauenkongress." *Die Kenessio Gedaulo* (1937): 2: 6.

Fred, W. "Die Gesellschaft." In Eduard Heyck (ed.), *Moderne Kultur. Ein Handbuch der Lebensbildung und des guten Geschmacks*. Vol. 2. Stuttgart, 1907.

Frerich, Friedrich Theodor von. *Über den Diabetes*. Berlin, 1884.

Freud, Sigmund, and Lou-Andreas-Salomé. *Letters*. Ed. Ernst Pfeiffer. Trans. W. and E. Robson-Scott. New York, 1972.

Friedenthal, Ludwig. *Der Kurort Karlsbad in Böhmen. Topographisch und medicinisch dargestellt*. Vienna, 1895.

Friedenwald, Harry. *The Jews and Medicine: Essays*. New York, 1944.

Friedländer, M. H. *Die Juden in Böhmen*. Vienna, 1900.

Friedmann, Franz. "Die Ergebnisse der ersten tschechoslowakischen Volkszählung be-treffs Juden." *Selbstwehr* 16 (1922): 38: 4.

Fuhrmann, Emil. *Ärztliches Jahrbuch für Österreich 1916*. Vienna, 1916.

Fuhs, Burkhard. *Mondäne Orte einer vornehmen Gesellschaft. Kultur und Geschichte der Kurstädte 1700–1900*. Hildesheim, 1992.

"Galizien in Karlsbad." *Jüdische Volksstimme* 16 (1915): 2: 5.

"Ganzes thoratreues Palästina. Die Beschlüsse des Juden-Weltkongresses in Marien-bad." *Marienbader Zeitung*, 24 August 1937, 1.

Gay, Peter. *The Bourgeois Experience. Victoria to Freud*. Vol. 2: *The Tender Passion*. New York, 1986.

———. *Schnitzler's Century. The Making of Middle-Class Culture 1815–1914*. New York, 2002.

Gedenkschrift anläßlich des 25jährigen Bestehens des Ersten Karlsbader Kranken-Unterstützungs-Vereines. Carlsbad, 1904.

Gedenkschrift anlässlich seines 25-jährigen Gründungs-Festes herausgegeben vom Verein Gesellschaft Kinderfreund in Karlsbad. Carlsbad [1902].

"Gegen das Hineintragen von Rassen- und Klassenhaß in die Kurorte." *Mitteilungen aus dem Verein zur Abwehr des Antisemitismus* 10 (1910): 32: 244.

Geisthövel, Alexa. "Promenadenmischungen. Raum und Kommunikation in Hydropolen. 1830–1880." In Alexander C. T. Geppert, Uffa Jensen, and Jörn Weinhold (eds.), *Ortsgespräche. Raum und Kommunikation im 19. und 20. Jahrhundert.* Bielefeld, 2005, 203–229.

"Ein Geleitwort." *Jüdische Bäder- und Kurortezeitung* 1 (1929): 1: 1.

Geppert, Alexander C. T., Jensen, Uffa, and Weinhold, Jörn. "Verräumlichung. Kommunikative Praktiken in historischer Perspektive, 1840–1930." In Geppert et al., *Ortsgespräche. Raum und Kommunikation im 19. und 20. Jahrhundert.* Bielefeld, 2005, 15–49.

Geschäfts-Bericht der Städt. Armen-Kommission Karlsbad in den Jahren 1910, 1911 und 1912. Carlsbad [1913].

"Geschichte der Juden in Franzensbad." In Hugo Gold (ed.), *Die Juden und Judengemeinden Böhmens in Vergangenheit und Gegenwart.* Brünn, 1934, 141–142.

"Geschichte der Juden in Karlsbad." In Hugo Gold (ed.), *Die Juden und Judengemeinden Böhmens in Vergangenheit und Gegenwart.* Brünn, 1934, 255–259.

Gilman, Sander. *Difference and Pathology: Stereotypes of Sexuality, Race and Madness.* Ithaca/NY, 1985.

———. *Franz Kafka: The Jewish Patient.* New York, 1995.

———. "Die Gemeinschaft der genetischen Risikofälle." In *Die Welt*, 13 June 2001. http://goo.ge/gbicf (accessed 29 June 2012).

———. *Jewish Self-Hatred. Anti-Semitism and the Hidden Language of the Jews.* Baltimore, 1986.

———. "The Rediscovery of the Eastern Jews. German Jews in the East, 1890–1918." In David Bronsen (ed.), *Jews and Germans from 1860 to 1933: The Problematic Symbiosis.* Heidelberg, 1979, 338–365.

Gitschner, Rudolf. "Kurstatistik." In *Die tschechoslowakische Republik. Teil 1. Karlsbad.* Ed. Stadtrat Karlsbad, Berlin, 1927, 42–45.

Glax, J. "Hygiene der Kurorte." In Stadtrat Karlsbad and Edgar Ganz (eds.), *Balneologie und Balneotherapie.* Jena, 1914, 418–437.

Gnirs, Anton. *Topographie der historischen und kunstgeschichtlichen Denkmale in dem Bezirke Karlsbad.* [Prague, 1933]. Munich, 1996.

Goetschel, Willi. "Kafka's Dis/Enchanted World." *Fathom* 2002.

Gold, Helmut. "Stimmungsbilder. Die Postkarte als Medium des (frühen) Antisemitismus." In Helmut Gold and Georg Heuberger (eds.), *Abgestempelt. Judenfeindliche Postkarten. Auf der Grundlage der Sammlung Wolfgang Haney.* Heidelberg, 1999, 13–19.

Goldscheider, Alfred. "Die Erkrankungen des Nervensystems und ihre Beziehungen zur Balneotherapie." In Stadtrat Karlsbad and Edgar Ganz (eds.), *Balneologie und Balneotherapie.* Jena, 1914, 90–114.

Gordon, Judah Leib. *Igrot Judah Leib Gordon (1858–1892).* Vols. 1 and 2. Ed. Yitzchak Yaakov Weissberg. Warsaw, 1894.

"Götzendienst und Ahnenkultus." *Karlsbader "Kikriki"* 2 (1925): 5: 2–3.

Gotzmann, Andreas, Liedtke, Rainer, and Van Rahden, Till (eds.). *Juden, Bürger, Deutsche. Zur Geschichte von Vielfalt und Differenz 1800–1933.* Tübingen, 2001.

Graetz, Heinrich. *Tagebuch und Briefe,* ed. Reuven Michael. Tübingen, 1977.

Graetz, L. "Aus dem Leben des Prof. H. Graetz." *Ost und West* 4 (1904): 11: 755–764.

"Grandhotel Pupp, Evropa." http://www.cot.cz/data/cesky/01_07/7_reg_4.htm [Czech].

Grob, Josef. "Franzensbader Spaziergänge." *Jüdische Bäder- und Kurortezeitung* 1 (1929): 15: 1–2.

"Große Jugendkundgebung im Rahmen des Kenessio Gedaulo." *Die Kenessio Gedaulo* (1937): 3: 4.

"Eine große Seuda Schlischit." *Die Kenessio Gedaulo* (1937): 3:7.

Grunwald, Max (ed.). *Die Hygiene der Juden. Im Anschluß an die Internationale Hygiene-Ausstellung Dresden 1911.* Dresden, 1911.

Hahn, Karl Josef. *Kristallnacht in Karlsbad.* Prague, 1958.

"Hakenkreuz-Mord an Professor Lessing." *Prager Mittag,* 31 August 1933, 1.

Hanak, Werner (ed.). *Eden, Zion, Utopia. Zur Geschichte der Zukunft im Judentum. Ausstellungskatalog.* Vienna, 1999.

Hanel, Hermine. *Die Geschichte meiner Jugend.* Leipzig, 1930. Trans. in Wilma Iggers, *Women of Prague. Ethnic Diversity and Social Change from the Eighteenth Century to the Present.* Providence, 1995, 164–197.

Härtling, Peter. *Große, kleine Schwester.* Munich, 2002 [1998].

Hax, Iris. "'Gut getroffen, wie der Isaac schmunzelt, nicht wahr?' Zur Medien- und Rezeptionsgeschichte antisemitischer Bildpostkarten." In Helmut Gold and Georg Heuberger (eds.), *Abgestempelt. Judenfeindliche Postkarten. Auf der Grundlage der Sammlung Wolfgang Haney.* Heidelberg, 1999, 97–123.

Hecht, Dieter. "The Jewish World Relief Conference in Carlsbad, 1920 and 1924. A Struggle for European Jewish Self-Determination." *Judaica Bohemiae* 45 (2010): 1: 51–69.

Hellpach, Willy. *Nervenleben und Weltanschauung. Ihre Wechselbeziehungen im deutschen Leben von heute.* Wiesbaden, 1906.

Henisch, Heinz K. *Erster Tanz in Karlsbad. Jugenderinnerungen an das Böhmen der Zwischenkriegszeit.* Munich, 1996.

"Der Herbst ist wieder da." *Karlsbader "Kikriki"* 5 (1928): 9: 2.

"Hermann Leopoldi." Österreichisches Kabarettarchiv. Vienna, n.d. http://www.kabarettarchiv.at/Bio/Leopoldi.htm (accessed 15 August 2011).

"Herr Georg Schönerer und die jüdischen Ärzte." *Oesterreichische Wochenschrift* 6 (1889): 14: 249–250.

Herz, Max. *Sommertage in Marienbad, Franzensbad, Karlsbad und Prag. (Königswart, Elster und Kissingen). Praktischer und vollständiger Führer an der k. k. priv. Kaiser Franz Josef-Bahn.* Vienna, 1875.

Herzl, Theodor. *Briefe 1903–Juli 1904. Briefe und Tagebücher.* Vol. 7. Ed. Alex Bein, Hermann Greive, Moshe Schaerf, et al. Frankfurt/Main, 1996.

———. *Old New Land.* Trans. L. Levensohn. New York: M. Wiener, 1987 [1902].

————. *Zionistisches Tagebuch 1899–1904. Briefe und Tagebücher.* Vol. 3. Ed. Alex Bein, Hermann Greive, Moshe Schaerf, and Julius H. Schoeps. Frankfurt/Main, 1986.

Hesse, Hermann. "A Guest at the Spa." In *Autobiographical Writings.* New York, 1972 [1924], 72–169.

"Hilfe! Polizei! Der Weiß-Poldl will uns beißen!" *Karlsbader "Kikriki"* 3 (1926): 10: 1.

Hindus, Maurice. *We Shall Live Again.* New York, 1939.

Hirsch, Leo. "Der Dreitage-Jude. Kritik eines Übergangs." *Der Morgen* 10 (1934): 6: 295–298.

Hirschfeld, Magnus. *Women East and West. Impressions of a Sex Expert.* London, 1935.

Hödl, Klaus. "Galician Jewish Migration to Vienna." *Polin: Studies in Polish Jewry* (1999): 12: 147–163.

————. "Ostjüdische Armut und ihre Wahrnehmung. Die galizischen Juden um die Wende vom 19. zum 20. Jahrhundert." In Stefi Jersch-Wenzel (ed.), *Juden und Armut in Mittel- und Osteuropa.* Cologne, 2000, 309–332.

Hoffmann-Holter, Beatrix. *"Abreisendmachung." Jüdische Kriegsflüchtlinge in Wien 1914 bis 1923.* Vienna, 1995.

Holitscher, Arthur. "Karlsbad/Palästina (Sommer und Winter 1921)." In *Reisen.* Potsdam, 1928, 117–147.

————. "Karlsbad vor Palästina." *Die neue Rundschau* 32 (1921): 11: 1150–1165.

Höllerer, Walter. "Das verfilzte Ding Odradek." *Die Zeit,* 11 March 1966. http://www.zeit. de/1966/11/das-verfitzte-ding-odradek (retrieved 15 August 2011).

The Holy Scriptures According to the Masoretic Text. Philadelphia: Jewish Publication Society, 1917.

Hornemann, Andreas, and Laabs, Annegret. "'Bär aus Galizien.' Die Angst vor dem Fremden der 'Ostjuden.'" In Helmut Gold and Georg Heuberger (eds.), *Abgestempelt. Judenfeindliche Postkarten. Auf der Grundlage der Sammlung Wolfgang Haney.* Heidelberg, 1999, 176–186.

Howells, William Dean. *Their Silver Wedding Anniversary.* Charleston/SC, 2006 [1899].

Ibsen, Henrik. *An Enemy of the People.* Mineola/NY, 1999 [1882].

"In Memoriam Haarmann." *Karlsbader "Kikriki"* 2 (1925): 2: 1.

Jacobs, Joseph. *Jewish Statistics. Social, Vital and Anthropometric.* London, 1891.

Jacobs, Joseph, and Fishberg, Maurice. "Diabetes Mellitus." In *The Jewish Encyclopedia.* New York, 1901–1906.

Jahres-Bericht der Knaben und Mädchen-Bürgerschule in Karlsbad für das Schuljahr 1897–98. Carlsbad, 1898.

Jahres-Bericht des Carlsbader israelitischen Armen-Hospitals für das Jahr 1867, 1872, 1876, 1877, 1880–1882, 1884, 1885, 1892–1895, 1896, 1900, 1901. Prague, 1868–1902.

Jannidis, Fotis, and Lauer, Gerhard. "'Bei meinem alten Baruch ist der Pferdefuß rausgekommen.' Antisemitismus und Figurenzeichnung in Der Stechlin." In Konrad Ehlich (ed.), *Fontane und die Fremde, Fontane und Europa.* Würzburg, 2002, 103–119.

Jellinek, Adolf. *Der Mensch, als Spiegelbild der Natur betrachtet. Kanzel-Vortrag am Sabbat Nachamu (31. Juli) im israelitischen Tempel zu Carlsbad.* Leipzig, 1852.

———. "Rede zur Eröffnung des israelitischen Spitals im Curorte Gleichenberg gehalten am 23. Juni 1884." Vienna, 1884.

"Der Jude in den Kurorten." *Jüdische Bäder- und Kurortezeitung* 1 (1929): 9: 2–3.

"Die Juden in den Bädern." *Mitteilungen aus dem Verein zur Abwehr des Antisemitismus* 13 (1903): 31: 242–243.

"Die Juden in den Kurorten des Kaukasus." *Oesterreichische Wochenschrift* 33 (1916): 32: 534.

"Die Judenhetze in Böhmen." *Oesterreichische Wochenschrift* 14 (1897): 50: 1001–1002.

"Judenreine Sommerfrischen." *Die Welt* 3 (1899): 30: 9.

"Jüdische Ärzte." *Mitteilungen aus dem Verein zur Abwehr des Antisemitismus* 4 (1894): 338.

"Jüdische und antisemitische Ärzte." *Oesterreichische Wochenschrift* 4 (1887): 19: 298–299.

Judson, Pieter M. "'Every German Visitor Has a Völkisch Obligation He Must Fulfill.' Nationalist Tourism in the Austrian Empire 1880–1918." In Rudy Koshar (ed.), *Histories of Leisure*. Oxford, 2002, 147–168.

———. "Frontiers, Islands, Forests, Stones. Mapping the Geography of a German Identity in the Habsburg Monarchy, 1848–1900." In Patricia Yaeger (ed.), *The Geography of Identity*. Ann Arbor/MI, 1996, 382–407.

Julian, "Marienbader Saison." *Wiener Allgemeine Zeitung* (1881): 504: 1–2.

Jurecký, Ladislav. *Diabetesbehandlung ohne Insulin–in der Stadt und in Karlsbad*. Carlsbad, 1937.

Kafka, Franz. *Briefe. April 1914–1917*. Critical edition. Ed. Hans-Gerd Koch. Frankfurt/Main, 2005.

———. "The Cares of a Family Man." In *Franz Kafka. The Complete Stories*. Ed. Nahum N. Glatzer. New York, 1983 [1916/17], 427–429.

———. "The Departure." In *Franz Kafka: The Complete Stories*. Ed. Nahum N. Glatzer. New York, 1983 [1920/21], 449.

———. *Diaries 1910–1923*. New York, 1988.

———. *Franz Kafka. Letters to Felice*. Ed. E. Heller and Jürgen Born. Trans. J. Stern and E. Duckworth. New York: Penguin, 1978.

———. *Franz Kafka. Letters to Friends, Family and Editors*. Trans. Richard and Clara Winston. New York, 1977.

———. *Letter to His Father*. Bilingual ed. New York, 1966.

———. *Tagebücher*. Critical edition. Ed. Hans-Gerd Koch, Michael Müller, and Malcolm Pasley. Frankfurt/Main, 1990.

"Das Kaiser Franz Josefs-Regierungs-Jubiläums-Hospiz für arme Israeliten." In *Festschrift zur 74. Versammlung Deutscher Naturforscher und Aerzte*, ed. Stadt Karlsbad. Carlsbad, 1902, 482–483.

Kalender für Israeliten für das Jahr 5656 = 1895/96 zugleich Führer durch die israel. Cultusgemeinden in Oesterreich-Ungarn, ed. Oesterreichisch-Israelitische Union in Wien, Vienna, 1895.

Kanfer, Stefan. *A Summer World. The Attempt to Build a Jewish Eden in the Catskills, from the Days of the Ghetto to the Rise and Decline of the Borscht Belt.* New York, 1989.

Kaplan, Caren. *Questions of Travel: Postmodern Discourses of Displacement.* Durham/ NC, 1996.

Kaplan, Marion A. *The Making of the Jewish Middle Class. Women, Family, and Identity in Imperial Germany.* Oxford, 1991.

Karlovy Vary. Stadtführer. Prague, 1977.

"Karlsbad–antisemitisch." *Oesterreichische Wochenschrift* 14 (1897): 47: 941–942.

Karlsbad–Carlsbad–Karlovy Vary. Infocentrum města Karlovy Vary [ca. 2001].

Karlsbad. Klimatische Kurorte und Touristik in der ČSR. Ed. Verein ČSL. Karlsbader Kurgäste und Freunde Karlsbads. S.l., 1935.

Karlsbader Adress-Buch 1888. Carlsbad, 1888.

"Karlsbader Sprudelsalz." *Oesterreichische Wochenschrift* 14 (1897): 48: 961–962.

Kaschuba, Wolfgang. "Deutsche Bürgerlichkeit nach 1800—Kultur als symbolische Praxis." In Jürgen Kocka (ed.), *Bürgertum im 19. Jahrhundert.* 3 vols. Munich, 1988, vol. 3, pp. 9–44. (English translation: "German Bürgerlichkeit after 1800. Culture as a Symbolic Praxis." In Bo Strath [ed.], *Language and the Construction of Class Identities.* Göteborg, 1990, pp. 223–252).

Katz, Jakob. *Out of the Ghetto. The Social Background of Jewish Emancipation.* Cambridge/MA, 1973.

Katzenelson, Nissan. "Herzls letzte Tage in Franzensbad." *Selbstwehr* 4 (1910): 21: 2.

Kaulbach, Fritz August von. *Karlsbader Karikaturen und andere Zeichnungen*, ed. Franz Wolter. Munich, [1923].

Kessler, F. "Ueber die Disposition der jüdischen Rasse zu verschiedenen Krankheiten." *Die Neue Welt* 5 (1931): 192: 8.

Kieval, Hillel J. "Jews, Czechs and Germans in Bohemia before 1914." In Robert S. Wistrich (ed.), *Austrians and Jews in the Twentieth Century. From Franz Joseph to Waldheim.* New York, 1992, 19–37.

———. *Languages of Community: The Jewish Experience in the Czech Lands.* Berkeley/ CA, 2000.

King, Jeremy. *Budweisers into Germans. A Local History of Bohemian Politics, 1848–1948.* Princeton/NJ, 2002.

"King Edward Smiles on Maxine Elliot." *New York Times*, 22 August 1909.

Kisch, Egon Erwin. *Karl Marx in Karlsbad.* Berlin, 1953.

Kisch, Enoch Heinrich. *Blätter der Erinnerung an Marienbad und seine Umgebung.* Marienbad, 1866.

———. "Die böhmischen Kurorte in der Saison 1908." *Karlsbader Fremdenblatt* 29 (1908): 2: 1.

———. *Der Curort Marienbad in Böhmen in topographischer, historischer, physikalisch-chemischer Hinsicht und seine physiologischen und therapeutischen Wirkungen.* Vienna, 1870.

———. *Erlebtes und Erstrebtes. Erinnerungen*. Stuttgart, 1914.

——— (ed.). *Marienbad, Franzensbad, Teplitz-Schönau, Johannisbad, Liebwerda, Bilin, Giesshübl-Sauerbrunn, Krondorf, Neudorf*. Prague, 1902.

———. *Marienbad, seine Umgebung und seine Heilmittel*. Marienbad, 1874.

Klauber, Moritz. *Das Hospital für arme, kurbedürftige, in- und ausländische Israeliten zu Karlsbad, seine Gründung und Leistungen*. Carlsbad, 1851.

Klemm, Walter. *Jugend in Karlsbad*. Jena, 1936.

Klüger, Ruth. *Katastrophen. Über deutsche Literatur*. Göttingen, 1994.

Knoch, Habbo. "Das Grandhotel." In Alexa Geisthövel and Habbo Knoch (eds.), *Orte der Moderne. Erfahrungswelten des 19. und 20. Jahrhunderts*. Frankfurt/Main, 2005, 131–140.

König, Gudrun M. *Eine Kulturgeschichte des Spazierganges. Spuren einer bürgerlichen Praktik 1780–1850*. Vienna, 1996

Kohl, Christiane. *The Maiden and the Jew: The Story of a Fatal Friendship in Nazi Germany*. Hanover/NH, 2004.

Kohn, Oskar. "Franzensbader Brief." *Selbstwehr* 4 (1910): 35: 1.

Kohut, Adolph. "Julius Stettenheim gegen den Antisemitismus." *Im Deutschen Reich* 22 (1916): 11–12: 264–269.

Kokkelink, Günther, and Lemke-Kokkelink, Monika. *Baukunst in Norddeutschland. Architektur und Kunsthandwerk der Hannoverschen Schule 1850–1900*. Hanover, 1998.

Kolski, Christian. "Oscar Lassar als Gründer der "Deutschen Gesellschaft für Volksbäder."" In Nora Goldenbogen, Susanne Hahn, Caris-Petra Heidel, and Albrecht Scholz (eds.), *Hygiene und Judentum*. Dresden, 1995, 78–87.

Kongress-Führer. XII. Zionisten-Kongreß. Ed. Büro des XII. Zionisten-Kongresses. Berlin, [1921].

"Kongress-Spreu." *Selbstwehr* 17 (1923): 32–33: 2.

Kos, Wolfgang. "Zwischen Amüsement und Therapie. Der Kurort als soziales Ensemble." In Herbert Lachmayer, Sylvia Mattl-Wurm, and Christian Gargerle (eds.), *Das Bad. Eine Geschichte der Badekultur im 19. und 20. Jahrhundert*. Vienna, 1991, 220–236.

Kotowski, Elke-Vera. "Philosophie der Not–Theodor Lessing." In Michael Buckmiller, Dietrich Heimann, and Joachim Perels (eds.), *Judentum und politische Existenz. Siebzehn Porträts deutsch-jüdischer Intellektueller*. Hanover, 2000, 137–153.

Krauss, Wolfgang. "Die Hydrotherapie. Über das Wasser in der Medizin." In Herbert Lachmayer, Sylvia Mattl-Wurm, and Christian Gargerle (eds.), *Das Bad. Eine Geschichte der Badekultur im 19. und 20. Jahrhundert*. Vienna, 1991, 181–189.

———. "Die physikalische Medizin und die jüdischen Ärzte. Zur Entstehung eines medizinischen Spezialfachs Ende des 19. Jahrhunderts." Dissertation. Vienna, 1995.

Kressel, Getzel. "Solomon Rubin." In *Encyclopaedia Judaica*, ed. Michael Berenbaum and Fred Skolnik. 2nd ed. Vol. 17. Detroit, 2007, 514.

Kriechbaumer, Robert (ed.). *Der Geschmack der Vergänglichkeit. Jüdische Sommerfrische in Salzburg*. Vienna, 2002.

Křížek, Vladimir, and Švandrlik, Richard. *Marienbad, eine Plauderei über eine Stadt, die es im Laufe von knappen hundert Jahren schaffte, weltberühmt zu werden.* Prague, 1992.

Kudela, Jiri. "Die Emigration galizischer und osteuropäischer Juden nach Böhmen und Prag zwischen 1914–1916/17." *Studia Rosenthaliana* 12 (1989): 2: 119–134.

Kuhnert, Reinhold P. *Urbanität auf dem Lande. Badereisen nach Pyrmont im 18. Jahrhundert.* Göttingen, 1984.

Külz, Rudolf Eduard. *Klinische Erfahrungen über Diabetes Mellitus.* Jena, 1899.

Kundera, Milan. *The Unbearable Lightness of Being.* Trans. Michael H. Heim. New York, 1984.

Kurorte, Heilanstalten, Sommerfrischen in der Č.S.R. Aussig, 1934.

Lacan, Jacques. "The Mirror Stage as Formative of the Function of the *I* as Revealed in Psychonalaytic Experience" [1949]. In *Écrits: The First Complete Edition in English.* Trans. B. Fink. New York, 2007, 75–81.

Lachmann, S. "Die Mineralquellen Palästinas." *Palästina* 16 (1933): 7–9: 221–236.

Lamed, Meir. "Gesetz und Wirklichkeit. Zur Lage der Juden in Böhmen und Mähren in der Zeit des Vormärz." *Bulletin des Leo Baeck Instituts* 8 (1965): 32, 302–314.

———. "Marienbad." In *Encyclopaedia Judaica,* ed. Michael Berenbaum and Fred Skolnik. 2nd ed. Vol. 13. Detroit, 2007, 544.

Landau, Philippine. *Kindheitserinnerungen. Bilder aus einer rheinischen Kleinstadt des vorigen Jahrhunderts.* Dietenheim, 1956.

Landmann, Salcia. "Nachwort." In Sholem Aleichem, *Marienbad. Ein Roman in Briefen.* Munich, 1992, 221–244.

Lang, Sigmund. "Das Israelitenhospital." In *Festschrift zur 74. Versammlung Deutscher Naturforscher und Aerzte.* Carlsbad, 1902.

Langer, František. "My Brother Jiří." In Jiří Langer, *Nine Gates to the Chassidic Mysteries.* New York, 1961, vii–xxxii.

———. *Byli a bylo.* Prague, 1963, 1–28. Trans. in Wilma Iggers, *Die Juden in Böhmen und Mähren. Ein historisches Lesebuch.* Munich, 1986, 239–251.

Langer, Georg M. *Nine Gates.* Plymouth, 1988 [1937].

Lässig, Simone. *Jüdische Wege ins Bürgertum. Kulturelles Kapital und sozialer Aufstieg im 19. Jahrhundert.* Göttingen, 2004.

Lavsky, Hagit. *Before Catastrophe. The Distinctive Path of German Zionism.* Detroit, 1996.

———. "Chidat chotama schel 'Brit Shalom.' Al ha-pulmus ha-zioni bi-semana ule-ahar semana." *Ha-zionut* 19 (1995): 167–181.

Leiskau, Katja, and Geppert, Daniela. "'Alte Thaler, junge Weiber sind die besten Zeitvertreiber.' Sexismus und Voyeurismus." In Helmut Gold and Georg Heuberger (eds.), *Abgestempelt. Judenfeindliche Postkarten. Auf der Grundlage der Sammlung Wolfgang Haney.* Heidelberg, 1999, 205–214.

Leopoldi, Hermann, and Herz, Peter. *Karlsbad! Sprudel-Fox.* Vienna, 1931.

———. "Karlsbader Sprudelfox" [1931]. In Hermann Leopoldi, *In einem kleinen Café in Hernals.* Compact disc. Vienna, 1998.

Lesky, Erna. *Die Wiener Medizinische Schule*. Graz, 1965.

Lessing, Theodor. "Mein Kopf" [1933]. In Lessing, *Bildung ist Schönheit. Autobiographische Zeugnisse und Schriften zur Bildungsreform. Ausgewählte Schriften.* Vol. 1. Ed. Jörg Wollenberg, Ruth Schake, and Helmut Donat. Bremen, 1995, 69–71.

———. "Töchter- und Landerziehungsheim in Marienbad." [1933]. In Lessing, *Bildung ist Schönheit. Autobiographische Zeugnisse und Schriften zur Bildungsreform. Ausgewählte Schriften.* Vol. 1. Ed. Jörg Wollenberg, Ruth Schake, and Helmut Donat. Bremen, 1995, 165–168.

"Lessings stilles Begräbnis ein lauter Ruf an die Welt." *Prager Montagsblatt,* 4 September 1933, 1.

Lichtblau, Albert. "Die Chiffre Sommerfrische als Erinnerungstopos. Der retrospektiv-lebensgeschichtliche Blick." In Sabine Hödl and Eleonore Lappin (eds.), *Erinnerung als Gegenwart. Jüdische Gedenkkulturen.* Berlin, 2000, 89–128.

Lichtenstein, Ladislaus. "Das Judenbad zu Pistyan." In *Die jüdische Welt* 1 (1933): 3: 36–37.

"Lifnei ha-kongres." *Ha-aretz,* 12 September 1921, 2.

Linke, Eugen. *Kunstgeschichte. Baukunst und Bildnerei. Heimatkunde des Bezirkes Karlsbad.* Vol. 1. Carlsbad, 1937.

Löschner, Joseph von. *Carlsbad, Marienbad und Franzensbad und ihre Umgebung vom naturhistorischen, medicinisch-geschichtlichen und therapeutischen Standpunkte.* Vol. 1, in *Beiträge zur Balneologie. Aus den Curorten Böhmens.* Prague, 1963.

Lucca, S., and Lang, M. *Zur Orientierung in Marienbad. Ein Rathgeber und Wegweiser für Curgäste.* Marienbad, 1900.

Luft, Robert. "Nationale Utraquisten in Böhmen. Zur Problematik 'nationaler Zwischenstellungen' am Ende des 19. Jahrhunderts." In Maurice Godé, Jacques Le Rider, and Françoise Mayer (eds.), *Allemands, Juifs et Tchèques à Prague de 1890 à 1924.* Montpellier, 1996, 37–51.

Lukacs, John. *Budapest 1900. A Historical Portrait of a City and Its Culture.* London, 1988.

Lüthje, Hugo. "Die Behandlung des Diabetes mellitus in Kurorten." In *Balneologie und Balneotherapie,* ed. Stadtrat Karlsbad and Edgar Ganz. Jena, 1914, 36–57.

Mackaman, Douglas Peter. *Leisure Settings. Bourgeois Culture, Medicine, and the Spa in Modern France.* Chicago, 1998.

———. "The Tactics of Retreat. Spa Vacations and Bourgeois Identity in Nineteenth-Century France." In Shelley Baranowski and Ellen Furlough (eds.), *Being Elsewhere. Tourism, Consumer Culture and Identity in Modern Europe and North America.* Ann Arbor/MI, 2001, 35–62.

Macpherson, John. *The Baths and Wells of Europe.* London, 1873.

"Der Mädchenhandel in Karlsbad." *Karlsbader "Kikriki"* 3 (1926): 10: 2.

Makkabi Weltverband. Karlsbader Tagung. Berlin-Schöneberg, [1921].

Mann, Thomas. *The Magic Mountain.* Trans. H. T. Lowe-Porter. New York, 1979 [1924].

Mann, Thomas. *The Magic Mountain.* Trans. John E. Woods. New York, 1995 [1924].

Marienbad. Die Perle der böhmischen Weltbäder. Ed. Stadtrat Marienbad. Prague, 1926.

"Marienbad im Zeichen der Kenessio Gedaulo." *Marienbader Zeitung,* 13 August 1937, 3.

Marienbad und seine Heilmittel. Gedraengt skizziert für die Hygienische Ausstellung in Berlin. Marienbad, 1882.

Marienbad und Umgebung, mit Bad Königswart und Angaben für Automobilisten. Grieben Reiseführer. Vol. 42. Berlin, 1930.

"Marienbader Brief." *Jüdische Bäder- und Kurortezeitung* 1 (1929): 16: 1.

Das Marienbader Hospital für mittellose Curbrauchende aller Nationen im Jahre 1851. Eger, 1852.

Marx, Karl, and Engels, Friedrich. *Collected Works.* Vol. 45. London, 1991.

———. *Werke.* Vol. 33. Berlin, 1966.

Matheus, Michael (ed.). *Badeorte und Bäderreisen in Antike, Mittelalter und Neuzeit.* Stuttgart, 2001.

Mats, Hirsh. *Kurerter un turistik in poyln.* Warsaw, 1935.

Mattenklott, Gert. "Ostjudentum und Exotismus." In Thomas Koebner and Gerhard Pickerodt (eds.), *Die andere Welt. Studien zum Exotismus.* Frankfurt/Main, 1987, · 291–306.

Maurer, Trude. "From Everyday Life to a State of Emergency. Jews in Weimar and Nazi Germany." In Marion Kaplan (ed.), *Jewish Daily Life in Germany, 1618–1945.* Oxford, 2005, 271–374.

Mecklenburg, Norbert. "'Alle Portugiesen sind eigentlich Juden.' Zur Logik und Poetik der Präsentation von Fremden bei Fontane." In Konrad Ehlich (ed.), *Fontane und die Fremde, Fontane und Europa.* Würzburg, 2002, 88–102.

"Mein Freund, der Althändler Kohn." *Mitteilungen aus dem Verein zur Abwehr des Antisemitismus* 14 (1904): 23: 183–184.

Meisel, Wolf Alois. "Die Quellen des Heils." Rede, gehalten bei der Einweihung des israel. Bethauses und Hospitals in Marienbad in Böhmen am 9. Juli 1861. Prague, 1862.

———. "Wem gehört die Erde?" Rede, gehalten bei der Grundsteinlegung des israelit. Hospitals und Bethauses in Marienbad in Böhmen am 4. Juli 1860. Prague, 1860.

"Memories of the Czech Spas." *Phoenix: Journal of Czech and Slovak Jewish Family and Community History* 1 (1997): 284–286.

Mendes-Flohr, Paul R. (ed.). *A Land of Two Peoples. Martin Buber on Jews and Arabs.* New York, 1983.

Mendes-Flohr, Paul R., and Reinharz, Jehuda (eds.). *The Jew in the Modern World. A Documentary History.* New York, 1980.

Mentullus Mendl, Arthur. *Intimitäten aus einem Weltkurort. Was uns der Fremdenführer von Karlsbad verschweigt. Humor und Ernst in Poesie.* Carlsbad, 1932.

Mezan, Saul. "Morbus judaicus. Versuch einer jüdischen Sozialpolitik." In *Hygiene und Judentum. Eine Sammelschrift.* Dresden, 1930, 89–91.

Miškovský, Jaroslav. *Marianskolázeňské obrásky.* Prague, 1932.

"Der Mord an Professor Lessing." *Marienbader Zeitung* 60 (1933): 202: 1.

"Die Mordwaffe gefunden." *Marienbader Zeitung* 60 (1933): 198: 1.

Motzkin, Gabriel. "Forgetting Past Possibility." Unpublished ms. [2005.]

Münz, Sigmund. *King Edward VII at Marienbad: Political and Social Life at the Bohemian Spas.* London, 1934.

"Nach China!" *Die Welt* (1902): 19: 4.

Naimark-Goldberg, Natalie. "Health, Leisure, and Socialbility at the Turn of the Nineteenth Century. Jewish Women in German Spas." In *Leo Baeck Institute Yearbook* 55 (2010): 63–91.

Nash, Stanley. *In Search of Hebraism: Shai Hurwitz and His Polemics in the Hebrew Press.* Leiden, 1980.

"Nebbich, der Juwelier." *Karlsbader "Kikriki"* (1925): 2: 3.

Nekula, Marek. *Franz Kafkas Sprachen.* ". . . in einem Stockwerk des innern babylonischen Turmes. . . ." Tübingen, 2003.

Neuberger, N. *Österreichisches Biographisches Lexikon.* 7 vols. Vienna, 1922.

"Neue Verhaftungen in Marienbad." *Prager Mittag,* 2 September 1933, 1.

Nicolai, Bernd. "Lebensquell oder Kurschloss? Zum Spektrum der Kur- und Badearchitektur um 1900." In Rolf Bothe (ed.), *Kurstädte in Deutschland. Zur Geschichte einer Baugattung.* Berlin, 1984, 89–120.

Niel, Alfred. *Die großen k. u. k. Kurbäder und Gesundbrunnen.* Graz, 1984.

Noorden, Carl von. "Ueber Diabetes mellitus." *Berliner klinische Wochenschrift* 37 (1900): 1117–1118.

———. *Die Zuckerkankheit und ihre Behandlung.* Berlin, 1898.

Nordau, Max. *Degeneration.* London, 1898 [1895].

———. "Karlsbader Anblicke." In *Karlsbad im Munde seiner Gäste. Lob- und Danksprüche aus fünf Jahrhunderten,* ed. Stadtrat Karlsbad. Carlsbad, 1932, 177–178.

North-German Lloyd Guide through Central Europe and Italy. Berlin, 1896.

Oppenheimer, Hillel. *Mabat achora. Zichronot.* Jerusalem, 2004.

Osterloh, Jörg. *Nationalsozialistische Judenverfolgung im Reichsgau Sudetenland 1938–1945.* Munich, 2006.

"Ostjuden passt auf!" *Karlsbader "Kikriki"* 6 (1929): 10: 3.

"Die Ostjudenfrage." *Ost und West. Illustrierte Monatsschrift für das gesamte Judentum* 16 (1916): 2/3: 74–112.

Palmer, Francis H. E. *Austro-Hungarian Life in Town and Country.* London, 1903.

Pataky, Eduard. "Interview mit dem Munkaczer Wunderrabbi Spira." In *Jüdische Bäder- und Kurortezeitung* 1 (1929): 17: 1–2.

Pawel, Ernst. *The Labyrinth of Exile: A Life of Theodor Herzl.* New York, 1989.

Peretz, Jizchak Leib. *Briv un redes.* Ed. Nahmen Mayzil. New York, 1944.

Petrescu, Mihaela. *Vamps, Eintänzer, and Desperate Housewives: Social Dance in Weimar Literature and Film.* Microform ed. Ann Arbor, 2008.

"Pictures of Jewish Life in Europe." *Forverts–Forward 1923–1937.*

Pincus, Lily. *Verloren–gewonnen. Mein Weg von Berlin nach London.* Stuttgart, 1980.

Pirhofer, Gottfried, Reichert, Ramon, and Wurzacher, Martina. "Bäder für die Öffentlichkeit." In Herbert Lachmayer, Sylvia Mattl-Wurm, and Christian Gargerle (eds.), *Das Bad. Eine Geschichte der Badekultur im 19. und 20. Jahrhundert*. Vienna, 1991, 151–178.

Pollatschek, Arnold. "Zur Aetiologie des Diabetes mellitus." *Zeitschrift für klinische Medizin* 42 (1901): 478–482.

Porges, Max. "Marienbader Brief." *Zeitschrift für Balneologie, Klimatologie und Kurort-Hygiene* 8 (1915): 7/8: 44–46.

Průvodce po letních sídlech, lázeňských a léčebných místech. Informační kniha pro zdravé i nemocné. Prague, 1912.

Pustejovsky, Otfrid. "Politik und Badeleben." In *Große Welt reist ins Bad. Ausstellungskatalog*. Grafenegg, 1980, 18–23.

Rahden, Till van. *Jews and other Germans. Civil Society, Religious Diversity, and Urban Politics in Breslau, 1860–1925*. Trans. M. Brainard. Madison/WI, 2008.

Rand, Nathan. "Versammlung des Hilfskomitees für Kriegsflüchtlinge aus Galizien und der Bukowina in Marienbad." *Oesterreichische Wochenschrift* 34 (1917): 20: 334.

Rappaport, Samuel. "Aus dem religiösen Leben der Ostjuden. IV. Krankheit." *Der Jude* 5 (1920): 3: 147–156.

"Das Reich und die konfessionellen Bäder und Sommerfrischen." *Mitteilungen aus dem Verein zur Abwehr des Antisemitismus* 14 (1904): 28: 219–220.

Reichardt, Hans-Dieter. "Blaue Schlaf- und Speisewagen in Berlin." In *Die Reise nach Berlin, Ausstellungskatalog*. Berlin, 1987.

Richarz, Monika (ed.). *Jewish Life in Germany: Memoirs from Three Centuries*. Trans. S. P. Rosenfeld and S. Rosenfeld. Bloomington/IN, 1991.

———. *Jüdisches Leben in Deutschland*. Vol. 2: *Selbstzeugnisse zur Sozialgeschichte im Kaiserreich*. Stuttgart, 1979.

Riedl, Joachim (ed.). *Wien, Stadt der Juden. Die Welt der Tante Jolesch*. Vienna, 2004.

Riehl, Wilhelm Heinrich. *Land und Leute*. Stuttgart, 1894.

Ringer, Fritz. *The Decline of the German Mandarins. The German Academic Community 1890–1933*. Amherst/MA, 2001 [1969].

Robbe-Grillet, Alain. *Letztes Jahr in Marienbad. Drehbuch*. Munich, 1961 (Original: *L'Année dernière à Marienbad. Cine-roman*. Paris, 1961; English ed., *Last Year at Marienbad*. Trans. Richard Howard. New York, 1962.)

Robert, Marthe. *As Lonely as Franz Kafka*. New York, 1982.

Rompel, Josef. *Die wirtschaftliche und finanzielle Entwicklung von Wiesbaden als Fremdenstadt seit Beginn der preußischen Herrschaft von 1867 bis 1907*. Wiesbaden, 1910.

Rosenbach, Ottomar. "Zur Lehre vom Diabetes." *Deutsche medicinische Wochenschrift* 16 (1890): 30: 649–651.

Rosin, Heinrich. "Die Juden in der Medizin." Vortrag gehalten im Verein für Jüdische Geschichte und Literatur in Berlin. Berlin, 1926.

Rössler, Tile. " 'Hörst du Tile, Franz heißt die Kanaille!' " In Hans-Gerd Koch (ed.), *"Als Kafka mir entgegenkam . . ." Erinnerungen an Franz Kafka*. Berlin, 2005, 180–193.

Roth, Philip. *Shop Talk. A Writer and His Colleagues and Their Work*. New York, 2001.

Rozenblit, Marsha L. "For Fatherland and Jewish People. Jewish Women in Austria during the First World War." In Frans Coetzee and Marilyn Shevin-Coetzee (eds.), *Authority, Identity and the Social History of the Great War*. Oxford, 1995, 199–220.

———. *Reconstructing a National Identity. The Jews of Habsburg Austria during World War I*. Oxford, 2001.

Rozenblit, Zesi. *Mi-Berlin ad Genigar. Toldot chayim*. Tel Aviv, 1978.

Rubritus, J. A. (ed.). *Kurstadt Marienbad. Illustrierter Führer*. Marienbad, 1906.

Ruppin, Arthur. *Briefe, Tagebücher, Erinnerungen*, ed. Schlomo Krolik. Königstein/Taunus, 1985. (English ed., abridged, *Memoirs, Diaries, Letters*. London, 1972.)

"Sabbat-Vorabend. Orientalisches Intermezzo im westlichen Böhmen." In *Jüdische Bäder- und Kurortezeitung* 1 (1929): 7: 1.

Sacher-Masoch, Leopold von. *Venus in Furs*. London, 2008 [1870].

Sachs, Salomon. "Die gottgefälligen Opfer." Rede, abgehalten bei Gelegenheit der Einweihung des israelitischen Hospitals und des mit demselben verbundenen Bethauses in Karlsbad im Juli 1847 (Ab 5607). Prague, 1847.

Sallis-Freudenthal, Margarete. *Ich habe mein Land gefunden. Autobiographischer Rückblick*. Frankfurt/Main, 1977.

"Salvete medici!?!" *Karlsbader "Kikriki"* 5 (1928): 9: 1.

"Der Sammler Wolfgang Haney. Ein Gespräch." In Helmut Gold and Georg Heuberger (eds.), *Abgestempelt. Judenfeindliche Postkarten. Auf der Grundlage der Sammlung Wolfgang Haney*. Heidelberg, 1999, 157–159.

Sarasin, Philipp. *Reizbare Maschinen. Eine Geschichte des Körpers 1765–1914*. Frankfurt/Main, 2001.

Schachnowitz, S. "Von der Bedeutung der jüdischen Presse." *Die Kenessio Gedaulo* (1937): 3: 4.

Schäfer, Barbara. *Berliner Zionistenkreise. Eine vereinsgeschichtliche Studie*. Berlin, 2003.

Schäfer, Julia. *Vermessen–gezeichnet–verlacht. Judenbilder in populären Zeitschriften 1918–1933*. Frankfurt/Main, 2005.

Schlögel, Karl. *Berlin. Ostbahnhof Europas. Russen und Deutsche in ihrem Jahrhundert*. Berlin, 1998.

———. *Im Raume lesen wir die Zeit. Über Zivilisationsgeschichte und Geopolitik*. Munich, 2003.

Schlör, Joachim. *Das Ich der Stadt. Debatten über Judentum und Urbanität, 1822–1938*. Göttingen, 2005.

Schnitzler, Arthur. *Briefe 1875–1912*. Ed. Therese Nickl and Heinrich Schnitzler. Frankfurt/Main, 1981.

Scholem, Betty, and Scholem, Gershom. *Mutter und Sohn im Briefwechsel 1917–1946*. Ed. Itta Shedletzky. Munich, 1989.

Scholem, Gershom. *Lamentations of Youth. The Diaries of Gershom Scholem, 1913–1919*. Cambridge/MA, 2008.

———. *Von Berlin nach Jerusalem*. Rev. ed. Frankfurt/Main, 1994.

Scholem, Gershom, and Lamed, Meir. "Jellinek, Adolf." In *Encyclopaedia Judaica*, ed. Michael Berenbaum and Fred Skolnik. 2nd ed. Vol. 11. Detroit, 2007, 119–120.

Schönbach, Rudolf. "Aufstieg und Untergang der jüdischen Gemeinde von Karlsbad." In *Karlsbader Historische Schriften.* Vol. 1. Ed. Milan Augustin. Carlsbad, 2002, 157–166.

Schubert, Heinz. *Karlsbad. Ein Weltbad im Spiegel der Zeit.* Munich, 1980.

"Die SDP in Marienbad." *Selbstwehr* 31 (1937): 36: 2.

Sebestyén, György. "Die Kurpromenade oder die Erfindung der Kunstnatur." In *Große Welt reist ins Bad. Ausstellungskatalog.* Grafenegg, 1980, 36–42.

Seegen, Josef. *Der Diabetes mellitus auf Grundlage zahlreicher Beobachtungen.* Leipzig, 1870; Berlin, 1875 and 1893.

———. *Handbuch der allgemeinen und speziellen Heilquellenlehre.* Vienna, 1962.

Sennett, Richard. *The Fall of Public Man.* New York, 1977.

"Die sexuelle Ausbeutung in Karlsbad." *Karlsbader "Kikriki"* 4 (1927): 7: 3.

Shamir, Ziva (ed.). *Sadan. Mechkarim be-sifrut iwrit. Ijunim be-jetsirat Y. L. Gordon.* Vol. 3. Tel Aviv, 1998.

Shapiro, Chava. "Ha-ve'idot lifnej ha-kongres." *Ha-olam* 1921: 6–8.

———. "Mi-saviv la-kongres." *Ha-olam* 1921: 4–5.

Shneour, Zalman. "Me-pinat ha-kongres." *Ha-olam* 1921: 618–620.

Sholem Aleichem. "Briv fun sholem aleikhem 1879–1916." Ed. Abraham Lis. Tel Aviv, 1995.

———. "In di varembeder." In *Zumer-lebn.* New York, 1917, 73–118.

———. "Marienbad." In *Zumer-lebn.* New York, 1917, 119–292.

———. *Marienbad.* Trans. Aliza Shevrin. New York, 1982.

———. *Marienbad. Kein Roman sondern eine sehr verwickelte Geschichte, die zwischen Warschau und Marienbad spielt, in 45 Briefen, 14 Billetdoux und 47 Telegrammen.* Trans. Siegfried Schmitz. Vienna, 1921.

———. "To the Hot Springs." In *My First Love Affair and Other Stories.* Trans. Curt Leviant. Mineola/NY, 2002 [1959], 350–378.

Shumsky, Dimitry. "Introducing Intellectual and Political History to the History of Everyday Life. Multiethnic Cohabitation and Jewish Experience in Fin-de-Siècle Bohemia." *Bohemia* 46 (2005): 1: 39–67.

Simmel, Georg. "Excursus on the Stranger." In Simmel, *Sociology. Inquiries into the Construction of Social Forms*, ed. A. Blasi et al. Vol. 2. Lieden, 2009, 601–605.

———. *The Philosophy of Money.* New York, 2004.

———. "Über die Karikatur." *Der Tag*, No. 5, 27 February 1917.

Simmel, Georg, Frisby, David, and Featherstone, Mike. "The Sociology of Space." In *Simmel on Culture. Selected Writings.* London, 1997, 137–169.

Singer, Heinrich. *Allgemeine und spezielle Krankheitslehre der Juden.* Leipzig, 1904.

Singer, Isidor, and Haneman, Frederick T. "Rudolf Kolisch." In *The Jewish Encyclopedia.* New York, 1901–1906.

Singer, Israel Joshua. *The Brothers Ashkenazi.* Trans. Joseph Singer. New York, 1980 [1933].

————. *Yoshe Kalb.* Trans. Maurice Samuel. New York, 1988 [1933].

Singer, Miriam. "Hebräischstunden mit Kafka." In Hans-Gerd Koch (ed.), *"Als Kafka mir entgegenkam . . ." Erinnerungen an Franz Kafka.* Berlin, 2005, 151–154.

Sipöcz, L. "Skizzen über die Kurfrequenz von Karlsbad." Sonderabdruck a.d. Prager Med. Wochenschrift. Prague, 1895.

"Skandalia." *Karlsbader "Kikriki"* 5 (1928): 1: 3.

Slokar, Johann. *Die volkswirtschaftliche Bedeutung der Kurorte, in Österreichisches Bäderbuch. Offizielles Handbuch der Bäder, Kurorte und Heilanstalten Österreichs.* Ed. Karl Diem. Berlin, 1914, 159–162.

Soja, Edward W. *Thirdspace. Journeys to Los Angeles and Other Real-and-Imagined Places.* Cambridge/MA, 1996.

Sölch, Werner. *Orient-Express. Glanzzeit, Niedergang und Wiedergeburt eines Luxuszuges.* Düsseldorf, 1998.

Sommer, Hermann. *Zur Kur nach Ems. Ein Beitrag zur Geschichte der Badereise von 1830 bis 1914.* Stuttgart, 1999.

Spector, Scott. *Prague Territories. National Conflict and Cultural Innovation in Franz Kafka's Fin de Siècle.* Berkeley/CA, 2000.

Spicehandler, Ezra, et al. "Hebrew Literature, Modern." In *Encyclopaedia Judaica,* ed. Michael Berenbaum and Fred Skolnik. 2nd ed. Vol. 8. Detroit, 2007, 684–738.

Spitzer, Daniel. *Hereinspaziert ins alte Wien. Satirisches aus der Donaumonarchie.* Munich, 1970.

Stach, Reiner. *Kafka: The Decisive Years.* Trans. Shelly Frisch. New York, 2005.

Stark, H. "Krankenexpositur Karlsbad des Verbandes der Genossenschaftskrankenkassen und der allg. Arbeiter- Kranken- und Unterstützungskasse in Wien." In *Festschrift zur 74. Versammlung Deutscher Naturforscher und Aerzte,* ed. Stadt Karlsbad. Carlsbad, 1902, 553–555.

Statistical Yearbook of the Karlovarsky Region. "Tourism, Occupancy by Country, 16-3." Czech Statistical Office, Prague, 2010.

Statistisches Gemeindelexikon des Landes Böhmen. Auf Grund der Volkszählungsergebnisse vom 1. Dezember 1930. Prague, 1935.

Statuten der israelitischen Cultusgemeinde in Marienbad. Marienbad [1896]

Statuten des Israelitischen Frauen-Wohltätigkeits-Vereins in Karlsbad. Carlsbad [1897].

Statuten des israelitischen Hospitals in Marienbad. Prague, 1876.

Stein, Erwin (ed.). *Die sudentendeutschen Selbstverwaltungskörper.* Vol. 11: *Marienbad.* Berlin, 1932.

Steiner, Franz. "Als Kongreßgast in Marienbad." *Selbstwehr* 31 (1937): 36: 6.

Steiner, Josef. "Geschichte der Juden in Marienbad." In Hugon Gold (ed.), *Die Juden und Judengemeinden Böhmens in Vergangenheit und Gegenwart.* Brünn, 1934, 396–397.

Stenographisches Protokoll der Verhandlungen des XII. Zionistenkongresses in Karlsbad vom 1. bis 14. September 1921. Berlin, 1922.

Steward, Jill. "The Spa Towns of the Austro-Hungarian Empire and the Growth of Tourist Culture 1860–1914." In Peter Borsay, Gunther Hirschfelder, and Ruth-E.

Mohrmann (eds.), *New Directions in Urban History. Aspects of European Art, Health, Tourism and Leisure since the Enlightenment.* Münster/Westf., 2000, 87–125.

———. "Tourism in Late Imperial Austria. The Development of Tourist Cultures and Their Associated Images of Place." In Shelley Baranowski and Ellen Furlough (eds.), *Being Elsewhere. Tourism, Consumer Culture and Identity in Modern Europe and North America.* Ann Arbor/MI, 2001, 108–134.

Stiftsbrief und Statut des Karlsbader israelitischen Hospitals. Prague, 1868.

"Die Tage vor der Kenessio Gedaulo." *Die Kenessio Gedaulo* (1937): 1: 5.

"Die Tagung des Zentralrates der Jüd. Welthilfsorganisation in Marienbad." *Selbstwehr* 17 (1923): 32–33: 5.

Die Tätigkeit der zionistischen Organisation im Jahre 1921/1922. Berichte der Exekutive der zionistischen Organisation an die Tagung des Zentralrates (Jahreskonferenz). Carlsbad, 1922.

Teicher, Wilfried. "Der Anteil der jüdischen Ärzte an der Spezialisierung im ersten Drittel dieses Jahrhunderts in Preußen." In Nora Goldenbogen et al. (eds.), *Medizinische Wissenschaft und Judentum.* Dresden, 1996, 14–29.

"Theodor Herzls Krankheit, Tod und Begraebnis." *Ost und West* 4 (1904): 8: 626–630.

Thieberger, Friedrich. "Vorbemerkung." In "Ignaz Ziegler: Skizzen zu einer Autobiographie." *Bulletin des Leo Baeck Instituts* (1959): 8: 211–212.

Torberg, Friedrich. *Tante Jolesch or The Decline of the West in Anecdotes.* Riverside/CA, 2008.

Triendl-Zadoff, Mirjam. " 'Die Bügelfalte des Antisemitismus.' Karlsbad, in der Sprache der Ambivalenz." In Hanns Haas and Ewald Hiebl (eds.), *Politik vor Ort. Sinngebung in ländlichen und kleinstädtischen Lebenswelten. Jahrbuch für Geschichte des ländlichen Raumes* 4 (2007), 293–306.

———. "Herzl im Kurbad. Über Karlsbad und Tiberias, Projektionsräume der Diaspora und der zionistischen Utopie." In Sylvelyn Hähner-Rombach (ed.), "Ohne Wasser ist kein Heil. Medizinische und kulturelle Aspekte der Nutzung von Wasser, Medizin." *Gesellschaft und Geschichte*, Beiheft 25, Stuttgart, 2005: 119–136.

———. " 'L'schonnoh habbo! Nach dem schönen Marienbad . . .' On the Ambivalence of a Modern Sanctuary." *Bohemia* 46 (2005): 1: 87–101.

Die tschechoslowakische Republik. Teil 1. Karlsbad, ed. Stadtrat. Berlin, 1927.

Turner, Victor. *From Ritual to Theatre. The Human Seriousness of Play.* New York, 1982.

Twain, Mark. "Marienbad—A Health Factory." *Europe and Elsewhere.* New York, 1923 [1909], 113–128. http://tinyurl.com/3qtplne (accessed 15 August 2011).

"Ueber Rabbiner Dr. Ziegler in Karlsbad." *Selbstwehr* 4 (1910): 29: 4.

"Unterhaltungsabend in Karlsbad für die Weihnachtsbescherung unserer Soldaten im Felde und für die galizischen Flüchtlinge." *Oesterreichische Wochenschrift* 31 (1914): 49: 864.

Urry, John. *Consuming Places.* London, 1995.

Ussishkin, Menachem. *Devarim achronim.* Jerusalem, 1947.

"Das 'Vaterland' gegen die jüdischen Ärzte." *Oesterreichische Wochenschrift* 6 (1889): 28: 517–518.

Die Verfolgung und Ermordung der europäischen Juden durch das nationalsozialistische Deutschland 1933–1945. Vol. 2: *Deutsches Reich 1938–August 1939.* Ed. Susanne Heim. Munich, 2009.

"Vertreibung der Juden aus dem Kurort." *Marienbader Zeitung* 65 (1938): 265, 1.

Verwaltungs- und Geschäftsordnung für die Direction des Karlsbader israel. Hospitals. Prague, 1895.

Verzeichnis der judenfeindlichen Erholungsorte, Hotels und Pensionen nach ihrer geographischen Lage. Ed. Centralverein deutscher Staatsbürger jüdischen Glaubens e. V. S.l., 1926.

Vízdalová, Ivana. "Jiří Mordechai Langer und seine Tore zur Identität." In Armin A. Wallas (ed.), *Jüdische Identitäten in Mitteleuropa. Literarische Modelle der Identitätskonstruktion.* Tübingen, 2002, 111–118.

Volkov, Shulamit. *Germans, Jews, and Antisemites. Trials in Emancipation.* Cambridge, 2006.

———. "Juden als wissenschaftliche 'Mandarine' im Kaiserreich und in der Weimarer Republik." *Archiv für Sozialgeschichte* 37 (1997): 1–18.

———. "Soziale Ursachen des jüdischen Erfolgs in der Wissenschaft." In Volkov, *Jüdisches Leben und Antisemitismus im 19. und 20. Jahrhundert.* Munich, 1990, 146–165.

"Vom antisemitischen Karlsbad." *Oesterreichische Wochenschrift* 14 (1897): 52: 1041–1042.

Wachsman, Zevi Hirsch. "Bloy-vays, yidish un hebreyish. Tsveyter raysebriv fun tshekhoslovakye." *Der vidershtand. Nayes buletin* 8 (1947): 34: 1–4.

———. *Gute Nachbarschaft. Ein ernst-heiteres Reisebuch aus ČSR.* Vienna, 1937.

———. *In land fun maharal un masarik.* Warsaw, 1936.

———. "Nito keyn ayserner forhang arum tshekhoslovakye. Ershter raysebriv." *Der vidershtand. Nayes buletin* 8 (1947): 33: 1–2.

Wack-Herget, Gustav O. *Karlsbad. Wie es die wenigsten kennen.* Carlsbad, 1933.

Wagenbach, Klaus. *Franz Kafka. Eine Biographie seiner Jugend.* Bern, 1958.

Wagner, Benno. "Kafkas Krankheit. Rasterfahndung mit Briefen." In Tanja Nusser and Elisabeth Strowick (eds.), *Rasterfahndungen. Darstellungstechniken, Normierungstechniken, Wahrnehmungskonstitution.* Bielefeld, 2003, 119–137.

"Wahlahnungen." *Karlsbader "Kikriki"* 2 (1925): 9: 1.

"Was ist in Karlsbad los?" *Karlsbader "Kikriki"* 2 (1925): 6: 2.

"Was unsere Leser erfahren müssen." *Karlsbader "Kikriki"* 3 (1926): 3: 2.

Wasserman, Henry. "Peddling." In *Encyclopaedia Judaica*, ed. Michael Berenbaum and Fred Skolnik. 2nd ed. Vol. 15. Detroit, 2007, 708–711.

Weitz, Joseph. *Yomani ve-igrotai la-banim.* Bd. 1: *Banim ve-adama 1927–38.* Tel Aviv, 1965.

"Wer sind die Hintermänner? Der politische Mord an Professor Theodor Lessing." *Prager Tagblatt* 58 (1933): 204: 1.

Wertheimer, Jack. *Unwelcome Strangers. East European Jews in Imperial Germany*. New York, 1987.

Whiteside, Andrew G. *The Socialism of Fools. Georg Ritter von Schönerer and Austrian Pan-Germanism*. Berkeley/CA, 1975.

"Wie Karlsbad wählt." *Karlsbader "Kikriki"* 2 (1925): 10: 2.

"Wie Professor Theodor Lessing in 'Edelweiß' ermordet wurde." *Marienbader Zeitung* 60 (1933): 197: 1.

"Wiederaufstieg unserer Weltkurorte." *Marienbader Zeitung* 60 (1933): 2: 1.

"Wiener Werkstätte." *AEIOU*, http://goo.gl/kULhR (accessed 1 June 2012).

Wiesemann, Falk. "Hygiene des jüdischen Körpers. Der Pavillon 'Hygiene der Juden' auf der Düsseldorfer GeSoLei-Ausstellung 1926." In Hans Körner and Angela Stercken (eds.), *GeSoLei 1926–2002, Kunst, Sport und Körper*. Ostfildern, 2002, 200–208.

Wildt, Michael. "'Der muß hinaus! Der muß hinaus!' Antisemitismus in deutschen Nord- und Ostseebädern 1920–1935." *Mittelweg* 36 (2001): 4: 3–25.

Wilkowitsch, Armin. "Der chassidische Schriftsteller Chajim Bloch in Franzensbad." *Jüdische Bäder- und Kurortezeitung* 2 (1930): 14: 1.

———. "Das jüdische Karlsbad." *Jüdische Bäder- und Kurortezeitung* 1 (1929): 11: 4–5.

———. "Dr. Einpfennigs Erholungsreise." *Jüdische Bäder- und Kurortezeitung* 1 (1929): 4: 3.

———. "Franzensbad im Zeichen des Krieges." *Oesterreichische Wochenschrift* 32 (1915): 19: 355–356.

———. "Marienbader Brief." *Jüdische Bäder- und Kurortezeitung* 1 (1929): 18: 1–2.

———. "Mode und Religion im Kurort." *Jüdische Bäder- und Kurortezeitung* 1 (1929): 2: 2.

Winternitz, Wilhelm. "Vierzig Jahre Hydrotherapie." *Zeitschrift für diätetische und physikalische Therapie* 1 (1898): 1: 29.

"Wir rächen!" *Karlsbader "Kikriki"* 3 (1926): 1: 1.

"Wir wählten." *Karlsbader "Kikriki"* 2 (1925): 11: 1–2.

"Wissenswertes für den Kurgast." ed. Kur- und Verkehrsverein Karlsbad. Carlsbad [1937].

Wlaschek, Rudolf M. *Juden in Böhmen. Beiträge zur Geschichte des europäischen Judentums im 19. und 20. Jahrhundert*. Munich, 1997.

"Wo Juden unerwünscht sind! Verzeichnis judenfeindlicher Kurorte, Sommerfrischen und Gasstätten," Sonderbeilage zu Nr. 20 des "Israelitischen Familienblattes." Hamburg, 16 May 1929.

"Wohin im Sommer?" *Selbstwehr* 32 (1938): 22: 3.

Wolfe, Thomas, and Bernstein, Aline. *My Other Loneliness. Letters of Thomas Wolfe and Aline Bernstein*. Ed. Suzanne Stutman. Chapel Hill/NC, 2003.

Wollenberg, Jörg. "'Rückkehr unerwünscht'—Ada und Theodor Lessing als Bildungsreformer und Volkshochschulgründer in Haubinda, Hannover und Marienbad." In Elke-Vera Kotowski (ed.), *"Sinngebung des Sinnlosen." Zum Leben und Werk des Kulturkritikers Theodor Lessing (1872–1933)*. Hildesheim, 2006.

"Der Wunderrabbi von Sadagora in Karlsbad." *Selbstwehr* 3 (1909): 34: 2.

York-Steiner, Heinrich. "Theodor Herzl im Kreise seiner Familie und seiner Freunde." *Ost und West* 4 (1904): 8: 617–626.

Zadoff, Mirjam. "Außerhalb der Reichweite. Franz Kafka, Gershom Scholem und die Fluchträume einer nervösen Generation." In Ekkehard Haring, Mirek Nemec, and Benno Wagner (eds.), *Kafka in Frankenstein. Mitteleuropäische Nervenpolitik in der Periode des Ersten Weltkriegs*. Vienna, in press.

———. "Travelling Writers. The Creation of Eastern Jewish Hideaways in the West." *Leo Baeck Institute Yearbook* 56 (2011): 79–104.

Zatloukal, Franz. *Karlsbad und seine therapeutische Bedeutung. Ein praktisches Handbuch für Karlsbader Kurgäste*. Carlsbad, 1908.

Zibbell, Charles, Berman, Morton Mayer, and Skolnick Einhorn, Deborah. "Philanthropy." In *Encyclopaedia Judaica*, ed. Michael Berenbaum and Fred Skolnik. 2nd ed. Vol. 16. Detroit, 2007, 38–47.

Ziegler, Ignaz. *Dokumente zur Geschichte der Juden in Karlsbad (1791–1869)*. Carlsbad, 1913.

———. "Skizzen zu einer Autobiographie." *Bulletin des Leo Baeck Instituts* (1959): 8: 211–222.

———. "Zum 50jährigen Bestand der jüdischen Gemeinde in Karlsbad." *Oesterreichische Wochenschrift* 36 (1919): 41: 659–660.

Zilcosky, John. *Kafka's Travels. Exoticism, Colonialism and the Traffic of Writing*. New York, 2003.

Zimmermann, Hans-Dieter. " 'Distanzliebe.' Max Brod zwischen Deutschen und Tschechen." In Marek Nekula and Walter Koschmal (eds.), *Juden zwischen Deutschen und Tschechen. Sprachliche und kulturelle Identitäten in Böhmen 1800–1945*. Munich, 2006, 233–248.

"The Zionist Congress." *Palestine* 9 (1921): 25: 193–196.

"The Zionist Congress." *Palestine* 13 (1923): 1: 1–4.

"The Zionist Congress and Co-operation with the Arabs." *Palestine* 9 (1921): 25: 196–2006.

Der XII. Zionisten-Kongress. Karlsbad 1.–14. September 1921. Referate, Begrüssungen, Beschlüsse. Ed. Zentralbüro der Zionistischen Organisation. Berlin, 1922.

"Der Zionisten-Kongreß in Karlsbad." *Deutsche Tages-Zeitung*, no. 174, 3 August 1923: 2–3.

"Die zionistische Jahreskonferenz in Karlsbad." *Prager Presse*, 30 August 1922: 4.

Zizek, Slavoj. "Odradek as a Political Category." *Lacanian Ink* 24/25 (Winter/Spring 2005): 136–155.

Zörkendörfer, Karl. "Die öffentliche Gesundheitspflege." In Berliner Stadtrat and Erwin Stein (eds.), *Die sudentendeutschen Selbstverwaltungskörper*. Vol. 11: *Marienbad*. Berlin, 1932, 65–72.

"Zur Sexualgeschichte Karlsbads." *Karlsbader "Kikriki"* 4 (1927): 1: 2.

Zweig, Stefan. "Bei den Sorglosen" [1916]. In *Die Monotonisierung der Welt*. Frankfurt/
    Main, 1988, 40–46.

———. *Brennendes Geheimnis*. Frankfurt/Main, 1988 [1914].

———. *Briefe 1920–1931*. Ed. Knut Beck and Jeffrey B. Berlin. Frankfurt/Main, 2000.

———. *The World of Yesterday. An Autobiography*. Lincoln/NE, 1964.

Index

Acknowledgments

This book of past landscapes of the Bohemian spas was written in the midst of life in Munich. The Department of Jewish History and Culture at the University of Munich not only gave the project a scaffolding and framework but contributed in multifaceted ways to its form and content.

The financial support from a number of foundations—most particularly the German-Israeli Foundation for Scientific Research and Development, but also the Zeit Foundation Ebelin and Gerd Bucerius, the Robert Goldmann Scholarship Fund, and the Theodor Körner Fund for Science and Art—not only provided me with the opportunity to work in peace and quiet on the text but also allowed me to spend time in all the necessary archives and libraries. I wish to thank the staff members there—in Munich, New York City, the Czech Republic, and Israel—as well as László A. Magyar and Gabriel Kohner, who gave me valuable access to the memoirs of their relatives. I am also grateful to all those I interviewed and corresponded with, who conveyed to me their valuable recollections and personal impressions: Aharon Appelfeld, Judith Jägermann, Edith Kraus, Otto Meyer, Kurt Reichert, Mimi Ormond, and Ruth Shaingarten.

The present English translation was made possible by a generous grant from Geisteswissenschaften International—Translation Funding for Humanities and Social Sciences from Germany, a joint initiative of the Fritz Thyssen Foundation, the German Federal Foreign Office, the collecting society VG WORT, and the German Publishers & Booksellers Association. I owe special thanks to David B. Ruderman and Jerome Singerman for their support, and the decision to include the volume in the series Jewish Culture and Contexts at the University of Pennsylvania Press. In Bill Templer I found a thoughtful, exacting, and patient translator, whose many comments and remarks proved to be most helpful. I am grateful to him and to Lina Bosbach for an excellent index. In addition, the English version has also significantly profited from the attentive commentary by peer reviewers Michael Berkowitz and Marsha Rozenblit.

Academic teachers, colleagues, students, friends, and family members made a significant contribution to the genesis of this study with their constructive criticism, creative ideas, and substantial assistance in tracking material down, writing, and proofreading. I am grateful to all, and most especially to Michael Brenner and John Efron. Among the many others, I would like to mention Robert Alter, Peter Brod, Niels Eggerz, Saul Friedländer, Valerie Fuchs, Martin Geyer, Sander Gilman, Fabian Gottwald, Andreas Gotzmann, Stefan Haas, Katharina Hey, Michael Hubenstorf, Robert Jütte, Hans-Gerd Koch, Simone Lässig, Dan Laor, Tamar Lewinsky, Albert Lichtblau, Werner Lausecker, Gilad Margalit, Jonathan Meir, Andrea Pfeufer, Ada Rapoport-Albert, Itta Shedletzky, Friedrich Stadler, Benno Wagner, Yfaat Weiss, Evita Wiecki, and Efraim Zadoff.

I owe a debt of very special gratitude to my parents, Huberta and Richard Triendl, who accompanied the making of this book with patience, attention, and every kind of support and who enriched it by their critical reading of the text.

I wish to dedicate this book to my son, Amos Joel, who knows how to remind me on a daily basis of the diversity of present life and thus of the historical past, and to my husband, Noam Zadoff, whose questions, commentaries, ideas, and criticism have repeatedly helped to transform and change this text anew. Without our many fruitful discussions, I am certain the study would not have developed into its present form.